# Beyond the Nation

SEXUAL CULTURES

General Editors: José Esteban Muñoz and Ann Pellegrini

Times Square Red, Times Square Blue
Samuel R. Delany

Private Affairs: Critical Ventures in the Culture of Social Relations
Phillip Brian Harper

In Your Face: 9 Sexual Studies
Mandy Merck

Tropics of Desire: Interventions from Queer Latino America
José Quiroga

Murdering Masculinities:
Fantasies of Gender and Violence in the American Crime Novel
Greg Forter

Our Monica, Ourselves: The Clinton Affair and the National Interest
Edited by Lauren Berlant and Lisa Duggan

Black Gay Man: Essays
Robert Reid Pharr Foreword by Samuel R. Delany

Passing: Identity and Interpretation in Sexuality, Race, and Religion
Edited by María Carla Sánchez and Linda Schlossberg

The Explanation for Everything: Essays on Sexual Subjectivity
Paul Morrison

The Queerest Art: Essays on Lesbian and Gay Theater
Edited by Alisa Solomon and Framji Minwalla

Queer Globalizations: Citizenship and the Afterlife of Colonialism
Edited by Arnaldo Cruz Malavé and Martin F. Manalansan IV

Queer Latinidad: Identity Practices, Discursive Spaces
Juana María Rodríguez

Love the Sin: Sexual Regulation and the Limits of Religious Tolerance
Janet R. Jakobsen and Ann Pellegrini

*Boricua Pop: Puerto Ricans and the Latinization of American Culture*
Frances Négron-Muntaner

*Manning the Race: Reforming Black Men in the Jim Crow Era*
Marlon Ross

*In a Queer Time and Place: Transgender Bodies, Subcultural Lives*
Judith Halberstam

*Why I Hate Abercrombie and Fitch:*
*Essays on Race and Sexuality in the U.S.*
Dwight A. McBride

*God Hates Fags: The Rhetorics of Religious Violence*
Michael Cobb

*Once You Go Black: Choice, Desire, and the Black American Intellectual*
Robert Reid-Pharr

*The Latino Body:*
*Crisis Identities in American Literary and Cultural Memory*
Lázaro Lima

*Arranging Grief:*
*Sacred Time and the Body in Nineteenth-Century America*
Dana Luciano

*Cruising Utopia: The Then and There of Queer Futurity*
José Esteban Muñoz

*Another Country: Queer Anti-Urbanism*
Scott Herring

*Extravagant Abjection: Blackness, Power, and Sexuality in the*
*African American Literary Imagination*
Darieck Scott

*Relocations: Queer Suburban Imaginaries*
Karen Tongson

# Beyond the Nation

*Diasporic Filipino Literature and Queer Reading*

Martin Joseph Ponce

**NEW YORK UNIVERSITY PRESS**
*New York and London*

NEW YORK UNIVERSITY PRESS
New York and London
www.nyupress.org

References to Internet Web sites (URLs) were accurate at the time of writing.
Neither the author nor New York University Press is responsible for URLs that
may have expired or changed since the manuscript was prepared.

Library of Congress Cataloging-in-Publication Data

Ponce, Martin Joseph.
Beyond the nation : diasporic Filipino literature and queer reading /
Martin Joseph Ponce.
p. cm. — (Sexual cultures)
Includes bibliographical references and index.
ISBN 978-0-8147-6805-1 (cloth : acid-free paper)
ISBN 978-0-8147-6806-8 (pbk. : acid-free paper)
ISBN 978-0-8147-6807-5 (e-book)
ISBN 978-0-8147-6866-2 (e-book)
1. Philippine literature (English)—History and criticism. 2. Philippine literature—
History and criticism. 3. Homosexuality in literature. I. Title.
PR9550.P66   2011
810.9'89921073—dc22          2011015710

New York University Press books are printed on acid-free paper,
and their binding materials are chosen for strength and durability.
We strive to use environmentally responsible suppliers and materials
to the greatest extent possible in publishing our books.

Manufactured in the United States of America

c   10 9 8 7 6 5 4 3 2 1
p   10 9 8 7 6 5 4 3 2 1

THE
AMERICAN
LITERATURES
INITIATIVE

A book in the American Literatures Initiative (ALI), a collaborative
publishing project of NYU Press, Fordham University Press, Rutgers
University Press, Temple University Press, and the University of Virginia
Press. The Initiative is supported by The Andrew W. Mellon Foundation. For
more information, please visit www.americanliteratures.org.

*In loving memory of Minerva Nicolas Ponce
(1943–2002)*

# Contents

Introduction    1

1   The Romantic Didactics of Maximo Kalaw's Nationalism    29

2   The Queer Erotics of José Garcia Villa's Modernism    58

3   The Sexual Politics of Carlos Bulosan's Radicalism    89

4   The Cross-Cultural Musics of Jessica Hagedorn's Postmodernism    120

5   The Diasporic Poetics of Queer Martial Law Literature    153

6   The Transpacific Tactics of Contemporary Filipino American Literature    184

Epilogue    221

Acknowledgments    233

Notes    237

Index    279

About the Author    289

# Introduction

FROM THE VANTAGE point of the second millennium, the 1990s may be regarded as a period of unprecedented cultural and scholarly ferment by Filipinos in the United States. Ushered in by the publication of Jessica Hagedorn's National Book Award–nominated novel *Dogeaters* (1990), the decade came to a close with numerous critical and collaborative publications and events commemorating the centennial celebrations of Philippine independence from Spain in 1898. The years between saw a steady outpouring of literary production, and this "literary renaissance"[1] continues to thrive in the first decade of the twenty-first century, with a host of established and new Filipino writers not only seeing their work in print but also winning major awards.

This cultural explosion is marked by a relentless thematic and generic diversity. The range of issues taken up in the literature—transnational and international migration, generational conflict and continuity, gender and sexual nonconformity, assimilation and its inherent failures, labor under late capitalism and the contradictory pressures of upward mobility, racial misrecognition and differentiation, cross-color affiliation and aversion, racial hybridity, geographical dispersal and isolation, and historical reconstructions of the Philippine Revolution (1896–1898), the Philippine-American War (1899–1902), the Japanese occupation (1942–1945), and Ferdinand Marcos's martial law regime (1972–1986) in the Philippines—is matched by a broad array of literary forms—novels, short story collections, autobiographies, personal essays, poems, plays, and anthologies—used to evoke these themes. Even a cursory glance at this body of work makes evident that there is neither an ascendant set of issues with which contemporary Filipino literature has been engaged nor a particular form that writers have gravitated toward. And yet despite the tremendous growth of Filipino studies scholarship in the United States since the 1990s, this literary abundance has not been met with a corresponding critical recognition.[2]

1

*Beyond the Nation* provides what might be termed a queer diasporic history to this literary profusion by moving back in time and across the Pacific. The study traces the roots of anglophone Filipino literature to U.S. colonialism in the Philippines and examines how Filipino literature in the United States is shaped by the overlapping forces of colonialism, imperialism, and migration. Situated between the Philippine postcolonial and the U.S. ethnic, what I describe as diasporic Filipino literature exceeds the boundaries of either national frame in both its representational strategies and its performative articulations. Complicating approaches to reading "minority" literature that privilege, in this case, race and nation as the primary categories of analysis, *Beyond the Nation* theorizes and enacts a model of queer diasporic reading that tracks the ways that Filipino literature addresses multiple audiences at once and how those multivalent addresses are mediated through gender, sexuality, eroticism, and desire. This book seeks to elucidate how such complex articulations (expressions *and* linkages) contest, and sometimes capitulate to, the normative compulsions of "Benevolent Assimilation" in the Philippines, Filipino (cultural) nationalism, and assimilation in the United States, and how they proffer alternative relationalities and socialities that surpass or elude the nation as the default form of imagining community.

Diasporic Filipino literature does not lend itself to the construction of a "national" literary history whose consolidation would "[guarantee] a sense of cultural legitimacy," as Linda Hutcheon writes.[3] Since Filipino literature in the United States has remained a peripheral and marginalized literature in the U.S. academy and in the wider reading public, it may seem as though "a familiar bedrock narrative of development"—a "teleological" literary history that emphasizes "the importance of origins and the assumption of continuous, organic development" (5)—has "to be laid down *first*, before competing, correcting, or even counterdiscursive narratives can be articulated" (13, my emphasis). *Beyond the Nation* suggests instead that Filipino literature in the United States has long been "diasporic" and "queer"—a dispersed, coreless tradition whose relation to conventional political and social histories has invariably been oblique and ex-centric to the latter's normalizing dictates.[4] As such, this tradition's diachronic and synchronic contours can be mapped only through an episodic, nonteleological literary history "that does not inevitably betray the aleatory, accidental, contingent, random dimensions of literary creativity."[5] Such contingencies may indeed be surprising (if not entirely random), but my readings neither familiarize the foreign nor discipline the disruptive, pursuing instead interpretations that underscore rather than underplay the literature's peculiarities in ways that render inadequate cultural nationalist models of reading and that respect the "wild heterogeneity" of this literary archive.[6]

Spanning the twentieth century and moving into the twenty-first, the chapters examine how the intersecting sociopolitical issues of race, nation, gender, and sexuality are evoked through various formal practices at specific historical junctures. Chapter 1 explores the relations among imperial assimilation, independence politics, and the heterosexual erotics of Philippine nationalism in Maximo M. Kalaw's work. Chapter 2 analyzes the invention of anglophone Filipino modernism as a "queer" literary practice in José Garcia Villa's work. Chapter 3 focuses on the gendering and sexualizing of Filipino radicalism and transnational anti-imperialism in Carlos Bulosan's work. Chapter 4 examines how music as a gendered and sexualized social and artistic practice becomes a dense site for producing cross-cultural and diasporic affiliations in Jessica Hagedorn's work. Chapter 5 looks at the queer critiques of martial law and U.S. popular culture as staged in novels by Bino Realuyo, R. Zamora Linmark, and Noël Alumit. Chapter 6 discusses the transnational and cross-racial responses to racial misrecognition and "invisibility" in the work of M. Evelina Galang, Brian Ascalon Roley, Patrick Rosal, and Barbara Jane Reyes. And the epilogue returns to the politics of queer reading by meditating on a recent novel by Gina Apostol. While emphasizing these diverse aesthetic and political practices, I locate the literature within shifting yet shared historical contexts of U.S. colonialism and imperialism, migration, and assimilation and highlight how the politics of gender and sexuality inflect their multivalent modes of address.

As a poetic-theoretical entry point into this argument's terrain, let me turn first to a poem.

## Cutting a Figure

In 1949, José Garcia Villa published a poem in *Volume Two* (actually his fourth book of poetry, the second to appear in the United States) that gestures toward the kind of reading practice endeavored in this book:

Before , one , becomes , One ,
The , labor , is , prodigious!
The , labor , of , un-oneing ,

To , become , a , One!
The , precision , of , un-oneing ,
The , procedure , of , dissembling ,

Is , the , process , of , expiation ,
For , the , sin , of , Nothing.
*This , Absurdity , is — Unification.*[7]

As chapter 2 clarifies, poem "5" initially reads as one of Villa's meta-physical allegories of the self whereby the human ("one") and the divine ("One") are unified—but only after one has been divided from oneself, has become other to what one was. The process of "dissembling" as "ex-piation, / For , the , sin , of , Nothing" is absurd since to dissemble is not to deceive but to pursue the path toward godhood, which, paradoxically, is always part of oneself.

Villa's idiosyncratic "theology" aside, the lyric's formal experimental-ism and effrontery, abstraction, and philosophical play with logic and contradiction challenge what we might expect to find in "Filipino" litera-ture. There are no obvious signifiers marking racial or geographic differ-ence, no references to historical events or cultural traditions that might augment its "'ethnic' quotient."[8] As one example of Villa's infamous "comma poems," the poem's rampant (but regular) insertion of commas may recall the punctuational play of, say, e. e. cummings, but Villa's po-etics is neither derivative of Anglo-American modernism nor "a politi-cally radical act" performed at the formal level.[9]

Deliberately bracketing authorial intentionality, I exploit here Vil-la's tactic of abstraction and extrapolate the poem's central neologism as a flexible figure for framing, historicizing, and analyzing diasporic Filipino literature. The remainder of the introduction uses the con-cept-metaphor of "un-oneing" to chart the argument's itinerary and contentions, moving from considerations of framing, to the effects of U.S. colonialism on Filipino migration and racialization, to the limits of identity politics given the indeterminacy of the category "Filipino" itself, to the politics of English, to a formulation of queer diasporic reading that emerges out of these historical contexts and theoretical concerns.

## Filipino Exteriority

Though Filipino literature in the United States is typically regarded as a subspecies of Asian American literature, an examination of the inaugural survey of this body of work reveals the problems with this classification. Published in the landmark Asian American anthology *Aiiieeeee!* in 1974 and written by three writers of the "Flips" generation (Oscar Peñaranda, Serafin Syquia, and Sam Tagatac), "An Introduction to Filipino-American Literature" begins on an inauspicious note: "We were asked to write a literary background of Filipino-American works. . . . Here is our stand. We cannot write any literary background because there isn't any. No history. No published literature. No nothing."[10] If the Flips' pronouncements seem unlikely given the prior seventy years of Filipino migration to the United States, the subsequent statements create only more ambiguity: "No Filipino-American ('Flip'-born and/or raised in America) has ever published anything about the Filipino-American experience or any aspects of it. That is about two generations of an ethnic group wiped out; simply literary genocide. In those 'lost generations,' there are good, maybe great writers. We think that Filipinos in America can no longer afford to ignore these potentially great writers" (37–38). Were these previous writers barred from publication due to the biases of the literary marketplace? Was their "potential" never nurtured or actively suppressed so that they were denied the opportunity to pursue their literary ambitions? Or has their work simply been "ignored" and consigned to irretrievable oblivion?

It is practically impossible to answer these questions since there does not exist a comprehensive bibliography of Filipino literature in the United States.[11] What becomes clear from the rest of the essay is that the declaration of "no published literature" is more polemical than empirical. Rather than abandon the task of writing a "literary background" to their present, the authors go on to rehearse Philippine colonial history and anglophone Filipino literary history, mentioning such writers as José Garcia Villa, Juan C. Laya, Carlos Bulosan, Stevan Javellana, N. V. M. Gonzalez, Bienvenido Santos, Carlos Romulo, and Linda Ty-Casper. This historical outline, however, serves to distinguish what the Flips were looking for: literature published by U.S.-born and/or -raised Filipinos, not adult immigrants who, they allege, "wrote about the American experience through Philippine heads" (50). These demarcations enable the authors not only to differentiate themselves from previous immigrant writers but also to ally themselves with "Asian American" literature by denoting both as "ethnic" in relation to dominant U.S. culture.

Distinct from Philippine literature in English ("those writings of Filipinos in the Philippines about the Philippines" [37]), from Filipino immigrant literature, and from mainstream U.S. literature, "Filipino American" literature also turns out to be distinct from "Asian American" literature.[12] In the anthology's preface, the general editors announce that "Filipino America differs greatly from Chinese and Japanese America in its history, the continuity of culture between the Philippines and America, and the influence of western European and American culture on the Philippines. The difference is definable only in its own terms, and therefore must be discussed separately."[13] The introduction to the volume, subtitled "Fifty Years of Our Whole Voice," is thus not "whole" but split into two parts: "An Introduction to Chinese- and Japanese-American Literature" followed by "An Introduction to Filipino-American Literature." What the editors gloss over, of course, is precisely what subsequent scholars have sought to foreground. The "influence of western European and American culture on the Philippines" is hardly accidental but a consequence of Spanish and U.S. colonization of the Philippines and the continuing neocolonial relationship between the latter two countries.

Without detracting from the important Asian Americanist scholarship on Filipino American literature, this book "discusse[s] separately" the latter, building off the premise that "Filipinos and their practice of cultural production [should] no longer be subsumed under the rubric of 'Asian-American,'" as E. San Juan Jr. has argued.[14] The "interethnic" approach cannot account for what Oscar Campomanes calls "the irreducible specificity of the Filipino predicament in the United States and, corollarily, of the literary and cultural expressions that [they have] generated."[15] U.S. colonialism and imperialism constitute crucial contexts for apprehending what Kandice Chuh refers to as the "paradigmatic exteriority of 'Filipino America' from the dominant practices of Asian American studies."[16] Furthermore, by construing "ethnic" difference as simply one of several axes marking Asian American "heterogeneity," as Lisa Lowe refers to it, one is led away from perceiving the very basic point that the category "Filipino" (in this case) is itself heterogeneous.[17] Filipino identity is an intensely convoluted project whose genealogy is anything but a straightforward affair.

## Filipino In/Visibility

If generating a framework that "begins with the notion not of immigration but of imperialism" has become the point of departure for com-
prehending Filipino social life and cultural production in the United
States,[18] then it is necessary to consider the conduct and consequences
of U.S. imperialism in the Philippines. The conceptual-metaphoric language in Villa's poem "5" helps here. Many historians have noted that
one of the central debates between U.S. imperialists and anti-imperialists at the turn of the twentieth century revolved around whether the
United States would follow the lead of its European predecessors and
embark on the path of colonialism, or remain true to its supposed revolutionary ideals and republican political form.[19] The prodigious labor of
"un-oneing" that the United States undertook in becoming an overseas
empire (presaging the "One" superpower?) involved not only the massive deployment of the war machine (armed forces, supplies, budget appropriations) but also a concerted "pacification" effort that included both
genocidal killing and ecological ruination (reconcentration camps, death
zones, scorched-earth tactics, burned villages, indiscriminate shootings,
water-boarding torture tactics, howling wildernesses) as methods for
dealing with the treachery and incivility of guerrilla warfare,[20] as well as
extraordinary exercises in ideological "dissembling," pronounced most
fatefully in William McKinley's declaration of Benevolent Assimilation
(see chapter 1).

Clearly, the United States has never bothered to "expiate" its criminal acts of aggression against Filipinos because it sees no "sin" in its benevolent sacrifice to shoulder the "white man's burden" and remake the
Filipino "savage" into a self-governing subject—because it can counte-
nance "Nothing" that would absurdly contradict its mythos of freedom,
altruism, and uplift. As Stuart Creighton Miller argues, "the triumph
of American innocence" was poised to take over as soon as the war had
been declared over by Theodore Roosevelt's presidential fiat on July 4,
1902, despite military operations against Muslims in Mindanao persisting well into the twentieth century. "Amnesia over the horrors of the war
of conquest in the Philippines set in early, during the summer of 1902,"
writes Miller, while the "war of conquest and its atrocities and courts-
martial" have been all but lost to "America's collective memory."[21]

What the United States could not, and still cannot, repress or forget,
were and are the effects that overseas imperialism would have within its

"domestic" borders. In becoming an empire, the United States not only exposed the "procedure of dissembling" that has persistently contravened its national mythography but also made itself susceptible to another influx of brown hordes as racist anti-imperialists feared, "un-oneing" yet again its preferred racial stock and cultural lifeways. U.S. colonialism led to the government-sponsored *pensionado* program that sent Filipino students to study in U.S. universities for the purposes of nation-building, as well as to mass Filipino migration to Hawai'i, Alaska, and the mainland during the second and third decades of the twentieth century, peaking at between 120,000 and 150,000 individuals in 1930. After a lull during the period between the restrictive immigration policy that accompanied the Tydings-McDuffie Act of 1934 and the granting of independence in 1946, Filipino immigration would pick up again (about 65,000 people between 1946 and 1965). But it was not until the 1965 Immigration and Naturalization Act—which abolished national-origin criteria and introduced the family reunification and occupational preferences—that Filipino immigration increased exponentially. The 2007 U.S. Census reports about 4.3 million Filipinos in the country.[22] In the most basic terms, Filipino migration to the United States was and is a direct consequence of U.S. colonialism and neocolonialism: "Filipinos went to the United States because Americans went first to the Philippines."[23]

But if the war with and colonization of the Philippines needed to be repressed or retroactively dissolved into that "splendid little war" of 1898 against Spain to preserve the ideology of U.S. exceptionalism, then Filipinos themselves must be disappeared along with that history. In his touchstone essay "Filipinos in the United States and Their Literature of Exile," Campomanes traces the "sense of nonbeing that stalks many Filipinos in the United States" to "the immediate and long-term consequences of American colonialism": "The invisibility of the Philippines became a necessary historiographic phenomenon because the annexation of the Philippines proved to be constitutionally and culturally problematic for American political and civil society around the turn of the century and thereafter."[24] The turn to empire in recent Filipino studies evidently seeks to redress this institutionalized "invisibility" and to disrupt what Campomanes calls "the unbroken continuity of this historic amnesia concerning the Philippines" to maintain America's innocent self-conception.[25] Although there had been books published on the Philippine-American War and U.S. colonialism in the Philippines prior to the 1990s, the renewed interest in U.S. imperialism over the past two decades has redirected attention on the war and early colonialism and shown just how racially "visible" Filipinos were during that moment.[26]

Colonial amnesia was further abetted by the representational absence of this historical drama in U.S. literature of repute. Nick Joaquin notes that "the romance of the early American soldiers, teachers, and missionaries in the Philippines has been ignored by American literature" and that the "'Empire Days,' a theme worthy of a Kipling or a Maugham, have become merely an ironic footnote to history."[27] Miller speculates that this "literary lacuna is an unconscious means of forgetting an unpleasant history."[28] The implications of this lacuna for postcolonial literary studies cannot be overstated. Wondering why there is a "dearth of critical attention on the Philippine colonial experience as literary theme," Jaime An Lim offers an astonishing answer in his 1993 monograph *Literature and Politics*: "One likely explanation . . . is the fact that no significant Western writer has appropriated that theme in an important work. No colonial novelist, no Spanish, American, or even Japanese writer of international stature has dealt with the issue of Philippine colonial experience."[29] Lim's observation implies that critics of colonial literary discourse have been solely interested in those geopolitical areas first represented by renowned Western or colonial writers, and only subsequently by "native" or postcolonial writers. The usual procedure of approaching "postcolonial literature as a critique of Western tradition involving the rewriting of specific works (*The Tempest* and *Heart of Darkness*, for instance)"[30] thus proves problematic in this context since there exist no U.S. analogues to Shakespeare or Conrad. Without an equivalent to *The Tempest* or *Heart of Darkness*, how are we to determine what colonial images, literary strategies, and political effects Philippine literature is endeavoring to revise or remake if understood as "postcolonial"? What is more, like their counterparts in the Philippines, Filipinos in the United States have not been portrayed in U.S. literature of "stature" either. As Elaine H. Kim writes, "There had been Filipino characters in the writings of Peter B. Kyne, Rupert Hughes, William Saroyan, and John Fante, although they were never as grotesquely omnipresent in American culture as Chinese and Japanese caricatures had been."[31]

To the extent that identity politics typically operates by locating and contesting the material and ideological means through which a "minority" group is subordinated and denigrated,[32] one might posit that "invisibility" names the negativity that currently afflicts Filipinos in the United States. Although Filipinos were not (and have not been) depicted widely in canonical U.S. literature, they were, of course, represented in other forms of colonial discourse. Rather than arrive at a definitive crystallization of racial negativity, however, tracking some of these figurations leads only to further ambiguity. From a juridical standpoint, the status of the Philippines, Filipinos, and Filipinos in the United States during the U.S. colonial period was deeply vexed, shifting, and uncertain. Allan Punzalan Isaac has analyzed how legal decisions produced the indeterminacy of the Philippines and other overseas lands as "unincorporated territories" and, in so doing, created the ambiguous category of Filipinos as U.S. "nationals." Doubly negated for racial and cultural reasons as *"noncitizen nonaliens,"* Filipinos were allowed unrestricted entry "into" the United States prior to the 1934 Tydings-McDuffie Act for economic purposes through a process that Yen Le Espiritu terms "differential inclusion."[33] Dissenting Justice Fuller in the 1901 *Downes v. Bidwell* case described the colonized Filipino "national" as "a disembodied shade, in an intermediate state of ambiguous existence for an indefinite period."[34]

If the U.S. imperial project legalistically produced subjects positioned in a "twilight zone of indeterminacy,"[35] it simultaneously reembodied its new colonial subjects by shading in their racial contours, in part by drawing on preexisting racial stereotypes of African Americans and American Indians to characterize Filipinos as "uncivilized savages," "bestial rapists," "effeminate" Orientals, or infantilized inferiors, as Kristin Hoganson notes.[36] Nerissa Balce similarly has examined how "earlier representations of black and native subjects . . . merged and coalesced" to produce "the figure of the Filipino savage," and notes how often white soldiers referred to Filipinos as "niggers"—a racial slur that heightened the dissonance on the part of African American soldiers between patriotism and racism and led to some defections.[37] Complicating what he calls the export view of imperial racialization, Paul Kramer has argued that U.S. colonial administrators further differentiated the "Hispanicized" elite, with whom they could negotiate in colonial statecraft, from the "non-Christian tribes" and "moros" (Muslims) who would be brought into the national fold by force if necessary.[38] Whether derived or invented, such productions of racial difference sought to cast Filipinos as lacking the rational masculinity necessary for self-government and thus in need of colonial tutelage.

While cross-racializations of Filipinos regularly occurred throughout the twentieth century (see chapter 6), it is important to recognize that constructions of Filipino nationalism were no less contentious.

The social etymology of the term "Filipino" is instructive in this regard. Vicente Rafael points out that "Filipino," like the geographic area now known as the Philippines, has a curious history. When the Spanish colonizers arrived in the sixteenth century, they named the archipelago "las islas Filipinas" after Felipe II and "tendentiously misnamed the native inhabitants of las islas Filipinas indios." Up through the end of the nineteenth century, *filipino* (lower case) referred to the offspring of "Spanish parents born in Filipinas," subordinating them to the *peninsulares* (Spaniards born in the Iberian peninsula) while placing them on a higher rung than the *indio*, Chinese, and *mestizos*. As Rafael summarizes, "We could thus think of Filipino as that which initially referred to a liminal group, to individuals who were native neither to the place of their parents nor that of their birth. Indeed, it was not until the spread of nationalist consciousness in the last two decades of the nineteenth century that the term began to take on another meaning: those who would claim a fatal attachment to the *patria* regardless of their juridically defined identity."[39] The Spanish colonial origins of *filipino*/Filipino thus give rise to ambiguities around bloodline, nativity, geography, and class whose legacies persist to this day.

The ghostly metaphor by which Filipinos "were made to appear and disappear in the same moment" in the U.S. imperial imaginary,[40] the processes of cross-racialization during and after the Philippine-American War, and the *ilustrados'* transformation of the "liminal" *filipino* into the "national" *Filipino* as a political response to Spanish domination—all of these factors provide the historical grounds for reconsidering the "intractable instability" of Filipino identification.[41] The abundance of monikers—Filipino, Filipina, Filipino American, Filipina American, Filipino-American, Filipina-American, Filipino/American, Filipina/American, Filipino/a (American), Filipina/o (American), U.S. Filipino, Philippine (American), Pinoy, Pinay, Pin@y, Pilipino, Pilipina, Fil-Am—and the politics of nominalization that it has engendered may be understood as effects of and responses to these historical determinations.

Even the numerous explications of these terms, spellings, and punctuations have not coalesced into a single story, much less an agreed-upon usage. While the feminine "a" (Filipina, Pinay), for example, bespeaks the legacy of Spanish colonialism, the space, hyphen, or slash separating "Filipino" from "American" resonates with different connotations: the space signals a modified or ethnicized American, implying either a multiculturalist bid for inclusion in a pluralist United States or a semantic redundancy insofar as imperial assimilation sought to transform Filipinos into Americans; the hyphen, masking as an equal sign, conceals what San Juan calls a "relation of domination and subordination" between the two countries;[42] and the slash indicates "both the presence of Filipinos in the United States and the imperial presence of the United States in the Philippines," as Sarita See writes.[43] The use of the "*p*" or "*f*" also results from colonial history and migration, with some scholars using "Filipino" to describe the people and "Pilipino" to refer to the national language, others arguing that there is no "*f*" sound in the major Philippine languages, thereby rendering "*p*" more culturally authentic, with still others suggesting that the use of the phonetic "*p*" is insulting since it implies that Filipinos (especially recent immigrants) are incapable of enunciating the difference between the two sounds.[44]

Obviously, I am not about to adjudicate among this plethora of possibilities.[45] My point is that the archetypal script of identity politics—countering "invisibility" by critically visibilizing the figure of the Filipino in the historical archive and transvaluing its negative ascriptions—gets seriously compromised by these histories. Remembering U.S. colonialism in the Philippines does not yield a stable set of colonial categorizations ("disembodied shades" in the Philippines, colonial "nationals" in the United States) or stereotypes (even the epithets are borrowed from other racial slurs),[46] while the impossibility of designating Filipinos with a satisfactory name that is fully encompassing and "representative" of those to whom it purports to refer is an effect of multiple colonialisms, the politicization of "Filipino" at the end of the nineteenth century, and the manifold differences produced by migration, gender, generationality, class, and political disposition—to say nothing of the heterogeneities of ethnolinguistic and religious diversity in the archipelago. To point to the "liminality" and difference at the heart of "Filipino" is not, of course, to reinscribe those stupid stereotypes of Filipinos as being "without culture" or inhabiting a "damaged culture,"[47] let alone to imply that Filipinos are genetically disposed to disunity.

Rather, we can read the *effects* of this indeterminacy—having to negotiate with what Chuh describes as a "category that is always already eroding"[48]—in the innumerable efforts to locate secure origins, codify grand narratives of the nation, arrest the erosion of ethnicity: in short, to provide a more substantive answer to the question Nick Joaquin posed in the late 1980s than he himself famously gave: "What *is* the identity of the Filipino today?" he asks. "The identity of the Filipino today is of a person asking what *is* his identity."[49] Although Joaquin's essay is more serious and complex than his flippant response implies, we might still insert self-*questioning* as constitutive of Filipino identity. This practice of querying (which I indeed link to the process of *queering* below) gives rise to the "other" side of national grandiosity, what Joaquin himself had contentiously termed "a heritage of smallness," but which Campomanes has reappropriated as the basis for what he calls an "archipelagic poetics" enacted in diasporic Filipino literature.[50]

The literature discussed in this book hovers between the monumental pursuit of national identity and collectivity and the more modest investment in particularity, between the epic and the episodic, between the grandiose "One" and the proliferation of "one's." In the same year that Villa published *Volume Two*, Carlos Bulosan boasted in a letter to his friend Jose de los Reyes of "a secret dream" to write "a 1,500 page novel covering thirty-five years of Philippine history"—one book in "a series of four novels covering 100 years of Philippine history."[51] What we have, instead, is the "unmappable" mobilities of *America Is in the Heart* (1946) and the incomplete allegory of the Huk rebellion rendered in *The Cry and the Dedication* (ca. 1953).

Again, the point is not that Filipinos are inherently predisposed to fragmentation, or that there is a one-to-one correspondence between literary form and historical experience. Rather, the dynamics of destabilization/restabilization, disintegration/reintegration of identity and nation inform the politics of knowledge production more broadly. It seems to me that Filipino cultural studies in the United States has reached a kind of critical crossroads, poised between, on the one hand, the desire for a Filipino American identity that, while nonessentialist, is nonetheless grounded in a set of identifiable and unique cultural traits and practices, and, on the other, a more deconstructive approach to colonial and racial discourse that exhumes and examines the ways that the *figure* of the "Filipino" or "Filipina" emerges at specific historical moments through the production of hierarchical differences. If the former appears to appeal to a romanticized authenticity, the latter, under the sign of "Filipino American critique," counters this naïveté by focusing on the institutional and disciplinary forces that both elide and elicit the "Filipino" while remaining cautious about positing a "positive" (in both senses) cultural identity.[52] In a sense, both approaches are predicated on a politics of representation and recognition whose logic abides by the script of *U.S.* identity politics. Whereas the reconstructive effort assumes that

Filipinos have been oppressed and traumatized by centuries of colonial subjugation and must be restored to dignity and integrity,[53] the deconstructive perspective takes the Filipino *case* as an occasion to revise dominant disciplinary and methodological tenets in U.S. academic practice that render Filipinos "invisible" and "illegible" in the first place.

As I elaborate in the last section, my formulation of a queer diasporic reading practice negotiates this crux by engaging the politics of representation through the politics of address. While I sympathize with the desire to recover and recognize Filipino voices as part of an endeavor to reconstruct cultural identities, my approach complicates the notion that identity is locked in a Manichaean struggle between racism and self-representation and that the latter can simply be read off from the literature produced by Filipinos. Viewing literature as a formally complex medium engaged in multiple kinds of cultural and imaginary work, rather than as a transparent record of empirically verifiable experiences, my analyses discern the literature's *politics* by situating it within a diasporic frame and analyzing how its multivalent forms of address are routed through issues of gender and sexuality. To explain and qualify what I mean about "diaspora" constituted through transnational transactions between addresses and audiences, however, it is necessary to say a few words about English.

## The Politics of Language

Villa's poem "5" again offers an entrée into and example of this linguistic problematic. In her glowing review of Villa's earlier book *Have Come, Am Here* (1942), Babette Deutsch writes, "The fact that he is a native of the Philippines who comes to the English language as a stranger may have helped him to his unusual syntax."[54] Perhaps even more emphatically than in *Have Come, Am Here*, Villa in *Volume Two* reverses the charge of being a "stranger" to English and makes English itself strange by engaging in "the , labor , of , un-oneing" at the level of language. Violating their conventional usage in being deployed "*poetically*, that is to say, not in their prose function," as Villa explains in a prefatory note (5), the commas defamiliarize language, cutting up the lines into individual words (making each word "one"), while refashioning them to make "One" poem. The neologism "un-oneing" itself enacts "precisely" what it says, forcing the word "one" to become not-one by adding the negative prefix and the gerundial suffix.

We might read this "procedure" of estrangement not only as a response to being "foreign" to the United States, but more specifically in response to the United States as a colonial power and to English as the colonial language. Contextualized in this manner, the "sin" is in fact not "Nothing" but the introduction of English into the Philippine public school system, government, and commerce. Thus, by virtue of his colonial education, Villa does *not* "come to English" as a complete "stranger," but as a colonial subject schooled in Anglo-American and European literature. Rather than read "Villa's disruption of grammar and syntax" as "his own way of imposing mastery on English, the borrowed language,"[55] one might think of Villa's handling of English through the "catastrophic rather than grounded" properties of language advanced by Nathaniel Mackey. Emphasizing a view of language as a "subversive, unsettling force," an "engine of displacement," Mackey suggests that "none of us are at home in it and certainly no one owns it." He proposes that "language undoes any ostensible ground and that we have to part with notions of a sedentary relation to it. . . . One isn't born speaking one's so-called native language but has to be taught it. To remember this is to keep the weirdness of language in mind."[56] Villa's "unsettling" of English may be seen as practices of "displacement" that "dissemble" (act as if one is playing by the rules decreed by the colonial language) in order to disassemble such rules, to sunder both the poet's and the reader's "sedentary relation" to English. In short, language is a terrain of struggle ("no one owns it")—something that can be neither colonially instituted with absolute control nor reclaimed and "mastered" so that one might be "at home" in it.

In a 1940 essay, Villa reflects on the catastrophic effects of the colonial introduction of English. Rehearsing "The Rise of the Short Story in the Philippines," Villa attributes the perceived ineptitude of early efforts to the idea that the "young college students" who "were taught in English in the schools, nevertheless had not assimilated the language well enough and therefore were not at home with it. The fact was that, although they spoke English in the schools, it was still their native dialects that they spoke at home, so that English to them, thus far, was merely an academic or educational idiom." In Villa's assessment, U.S. colonial education resulted in a situation of linguistic "un-oneing" whereby the Philippine writers' English was "good enough for ordinary communicative purposes" but "when applied to creative work, proved inadequate, without distinction, without true artistic force—without that depth and force which those who possess a unity with language can invoke by the written word."[57]

By the time Villa offers this rather patronizing judgment, he has been living in the United States for ten years, where English is the "home" language, while the writers he is referring to live "at home" in the Philippines and therefore are not "at home" with English. And yet as his own work and reception attest, residing in the United States does not guarantee the poet's "unity" with English. Calling attention to the politics of language in a diasporic context, Villa's essay and poem anticipate Renato Constantino's famous polemic "The Miseducation of the Filipino" (1966), in which he criticizes the divisive effects of English in the Philippines:

> The first and perhaps the master stroke in the plan to use education as an instrument of colonial policy was the decision to use English as the medium of instruction. English became the wedge that separated the Filipinos from their past and later was to separate educated Filipinos from the masses of their countrymen. . . . With American textbooks, Filipinos started learning not only a new language but also a new way of life, alien to their traditions and yet a caricature of their model. This was the beginning of their miseducation, for they learned no longer as Filipinos but as colonials. . . . The lives of Philippine heroes were taught but their nationalist teachings were glossed over. Spain was the villain, America was the savior.[58]

According to Constantino, colonial education in English became the conduit through which U.S. administrators rewrote the deceit that led to the violent Philippine-American War and recast America as the liberators of hapless Filipinos held captive to centuries of Spanish tyranny.

While the impositionist view of English has become the standard interpretation in the postcolonial period, it is important to note that many Filipinos in the early decades of the twentieth century actively sought to cultivate the new language. To be sure, there were strong material incentives (such as English proficiency for the Philippine Civil Service),[59] but the eagerness to learn and wield English within Philippine literary culture was evidently keen. Edna Zapanta Manlapaz remarks that the "early generation of Filipinos appeared not to have entertained either skepticism or scruples about using a foreign language such as English as a medium for Philippine literature."[60] Recalling the 1920s, short-story writer Arturo Rotor says in an interview, "At that time, all of us, the nation, wanted to study English. . . . There was no division of opinion at that time."[61] Even the "proletarian" literary critic Salvador P. Lopez admits in an interview: "We accepted the fact that English had been imposed on our nation. . . . We did not question it until about the end of the 30s. Then there was the independence movement, which resulted in a resurgence of national self-esteem. People began to ask: 'Why English? What's wrong with our languages? Or one of our languages?'"[62]

Whatever the anglophone writers thought of Philippine languages during the first decades of U.S. colonialism, it is certainly the case that anglophone literature acquired its political power and cultural status in relation to Spanish and vernacular literatures. By the late 1920s, according to Resil Mojares, Spanish had "withered on the vine as the Spanish writers became writers without an audience," while the vernaculars "continued to have a vigorous existence as the medium of popular literature" but had "drifted down the cultural scale."[63] The effects of this linguistic discontinuity caused by rapid colonial succession were profound. Benedict Anderson describes the linguistic takeover of English by the American regime as a "collective lobotomy": "Up until 1900, the great bulk of the archipelago's written archive, including almost all the marvelous texts of its originary nationalist leaders, were in Spanish; but already by the 1940s, after a generation of American schooling, these had become inaccessible."[64]

If Spanish continued to decline from the late nineteenth century onward, the fate of the vernaculars has been less straightforward. The banning of English and the encouragement to develop Tagalog during the Japanese occupation of World War II "proved an unexpected and wholly fortuitous impetus for the resurgence of writing in the vernacular languages," according to Manlapaz. With the granting of independence in 1946 and the onset of U.S. neocolonialism, however, English resecured its eminent place in Philippine letters, buttressed by the experiences of writers who attended literature and creative writing programs in the United States and who returned to the Philippines armed with the formalist tenets of New Criticism.[65] The nationalist movements of the late 1960s and early 1970s foregrounded the language question once again and provoked renewed interest in and respect for vernacular literatures. Still, as Mojares has remarked, "Relegated to the backwaters, Philippine literature has never occupied a prominent place in the curricula of colleges and universities [in the Philippines]. Moreover, the teaching of

Philippine literature has been biased in favor of an English stream of writing and it is only over the past three decades that serious attention has been given to such vital constituents of the national tradition as our folk, popular, and so-called regional literatures."[66]

Clearly, then, the institutionalization of English under U.S. colonialism in the Philippines created and exacerbated ethnolinguistic, regional, and class divisions among the populace. Philippine literature in English, and its contested place, is a direct effect of this colonial history. Obviously, there would not exist over a century's worth of anglophone literature in the Philippines had Americans not recolonized the islands and its peoples and implemented English in the classroom.[67] The propagation of English-language instruction through the public school system, however sporadic or uneven, combined with the teaching of Anglo-American literary texts, virtually ensured the emergence of Philippine literature in English.[68] On the other hand, there was not, during the first half of the twentieth century, a default national language that Filipinos might have embraced to forge a national culture against the new invaders. As Andrew Gonzalez has shown, the elevation of Tagalog as the basis for the Philippine national language has long been subject to heated debate, with politicians and intellectuals from other ethnolinguistic regions vying for power and representation.[69] In sum, the anglophone Philippine writer's position has been and is a vexed predicament: English gets associated with class and intellectual elitism within the Philippines and thereby distances the author from the "masses," but it is also seen as a vehicle of connection with other anglophone publics;[70] viewed as a (dubious) asset in the global capitalist labor market, English has also been reclaimed by literary critics exploring variations of "Filipino English" distinct from "American English" or "British English."[71]

This multilingual background provides the context for my focus on the politics of address in diasporic Filipino literature, a focus that pivots on inferring and positing differently located audiences. My analysis of the invention, articulation, and transmission of voices that cross national boundaries and address U.S. and Philippine readerships seeks to account for the varied cultural and political work that various genres and formal gestures facilitate. When I suggest that writers positioned in the United States deploy diasporic modes of address, I mean this in a rhetorical sense (and sometimes in a quasi–book history sense when the publication site and venue matter). Nonetheless, these diasporic reachings are not *merely* imaginary: over 100 years of English-language use and instruction in the Philippines has created a sizable English-literate public, even if colonialism and neoliberal globalization have rendered English a highly fraught medium.

## Queer Diasporic Reading

By invoking this historical context, I am not implying that Filipino literature in the United States ought to be framed as an extension of Philippine literature in English, a diasporic appendage that would be the exact opposite of the Flips' conception of Filipino American literature as distinctly rooted in the United States.[72] Even as the diasporic framing I am proposing here enables one to include Filipino "immigrant" literature within the same history as "Filipino American" literature, I suggest that "the continuity of Filipino writing in English" across national contexts and "the fluid nature of the Filipino/Filipino American divide" may not be as seamless as some critics have suggested.[73] While the "linkage" between "Filipino/a" and "Filipino/a American" might be "inextricable,"[74] it is necessary to specify more rigorously what that connection consists of and the possible relations existing between the two. If, as I intimated above, framing Filipino literature in the United States as "ethnic" leads us to read it as primarily addressing a dominant U.S. audience (whether to educate that culture about marginalized experiences, to court its favor in seeking recognition, or to criticize it for its oppressive policies), then framing it as a tributary of Philippine literature in English leads us to read "Filipino American writers" inversely, as "articulat[ing] this same ancestral focus" as their Philippine-based counterparts.[75]

A glance at the reception of several authors examined in this book helps illuminate the limits of both approaches. While Villa is considered one of the seminal anglophone writers in the Philippines and was fairly well received by Anglo-American critics and reviewers when he published his most important work from the 1930s to the 1950s, he has virtually dropped off the U.S. literary radar, mainly because "critics of multi-ethnic American literature do not find Villa 'ethnic' enough to deserve serious attention," as San Juan puts it.[76] Conversely, Villa's contemporary Carlos Bulosan has become a canonical figure in Asian American literary studies precisely for his portrayals of Filipino working-class laborers in the United States during the 1930s and 1940s, but his relation to Philippine literary and social history has tended to get overlooked.

The reception of Jessica Hagedorn's well-known novel *Dogeaters* (1990) is also instructive in this regard. The reviewer in the *New York Times Book Review* criticizes Hagedorn's alleged failure to perform adequately the role of cultural mediator: "Filipino English will be an unfamiliar dialect [*sic*] to most readers. Conveying its nuances to an English-speaking readership is a task Ms. Hagedorn has set herself but one in which she has not quite succeeded. . . . Maybe because there is no equivalent, there is no colloquial way of talking about *merienda* in English . . . let alone *kundiman* and *halo-halo*. . . . The exoticisms become tiresome, more a nervous tic than a desire to make connections across the gulf of culture."[77] Mischaracterizing the "gulf" separating the United States from the Philippines—a gulf that *Dogeaters* undermines by alluding to the history of U.S. colonialism and popular culture in the Philippines—the reviewer presupposes that *of course* Hagedorn has "set herself" the task of speaking to a Western audience. Most revealing, the reviewer ignores the "English-speaking readership" in the Philippines (and around the globe) for whom "Filipino English" is hardly unfamiliar.

On the other hand, some Filipino readers have worried that the novel's less than "positive" representations of Manila's riotous denizens will reflect badly on the "race." Hagedorn recalls in an interview having an accusing finger pointed at her while giving a reading in Hawai'i: "I know, I know. I set the race back 400 years. . . . What is literature for? . . . You don't go to literature and say I need to feel good about my race, so let me read a novel."[78] Both the reviewer's perception of *Dogeaters* as botched cultural translation and the detractor's critique of the novel as regressive cultural representation presume that *Dogeaters* is oriented toward a Western audience and that its artistic and political implications (conducive or not to Western intelligibility or to Filipino positivity) must be discerned from that orientation (see chapter 4).

By arguing that diasporic Filipino literature articulates connections to and critiques of both U.S. and Philippine formations, I am calling for complex theorizations among the politics of authority (who is doing the writing), the politics of representation (who is being written *about*), and the politics of address (who is being written *to*). Though we customarily think of subjects as inhabiting multiple identities, it is perhaps less often acknowledged—especially when considering the thorny issue of "agency"—that those subjects are multiply *oriented* by virtue of the same forces, directing their representations and critiques of race, ethnicity, gender, and sexuality toward several audiences at once. In his book on *ilustrado* translation practices during the revolution against Spain, *The Promise of the Foreign*, Vicente Rafael observes that the "question of address—its formulation, conventionalization, disruption, and recuperation—animates the relationship between colonialism and nationalism in the Philippines and perhaps in many other parts of the world as well. 'Who speaks?' is always contingent on 'Who is spoken to?' Both in turn rest on the technical means with which they are asked and answered."[79] Rafael demonstrates that the ascribed social identity of the speaker (redeemer of the oppressed or subverter of the colonial hierarchy; fighter for Filipino freedom or murderer of Spaniards) shifts according to the composition of the audience and its conditions of reception. His book also shows that the "question of address" similarly underlies the political uses to which certain *forms* (novel, epic poem, periodical essay, letter) are put.

By reading such multivalent and multigeneric addresses as demonstrating what Brent Hayes Edwards terms "the practice of diaspora," this project seeks to deploy an "anti-abstractionist" model of diaspora that illuminates the connections, correspondences, and continuities as well as the dissensions, divergences, and disagreements structuring articulations of "Filipino."[80] Although invocations of diaspora "always can be re-articulated and abstracted into evocations of untroubled essentialism or inviolate roots" (12), such abstractionist uses both register and erase the palimpsestic etymology of "Filipino" sketched above.[81] By contrast, my approach takes into account its radical instability by analyzing the ways that the literary modes of address constituting Filipino diasporic discourse enact what Benito M. Vergara Jr. describes as a "repeated turning" between the Philippines and the United States,[82] turnings that are oriented toward multiple fronts and delivered with various, oftentimes competing, political and ethical objectives at stake.

Here, Stuart Hall's elaboration of "articulation" to analyze "societies structured in dominance" proves useful.[83] He reminds us that articulation can mean both "to utter, to speak forth" and to connect "two parts ... through a specific linkage," but that linkage "is not necessary, determined, absolute and essential for all time. . . . So the so-called 'unity' of a discourse is really the articulation of different, distinct elements which can be rearticulated in different ways because they have no necessary 'belongingness.'"[84] As Edwards points out, Hall's conception of articulation not only enables one to examine in a nondeterministic manner "the structural and the discursive" elements that combine to produce "relations of dominance and subordination" but also to view such combinations as "the ground of cultural resistance."[85] Thus, to riff off of Allan Isaac's and Sarita See's work, the practice of "articulating Filipino America" necessitates a critical "disarticulation of the [American] empire"—a simultaneous re-membering and refiguring of the dislocated social body made possible by remembering the fracturing ("un-oneing") and forgetting of U.S. imperial violence.[86]

Such acts of dis- and rearticulation, as I argue throughout this book, become legible through a queer diasporic framework that reads the multivalent modes of address embedded in the literature as articulating race, nation, and ethnicity to gender, sexuality, and eroticism. These braidings of "different, distinct elements" are not always articulated in the same way or for the same purposes and acquire their critical edge when historicized in particular contexts of enunciation and reception. My readings not only acknowledge the dangers and impossibilities of prioritizing one identity category of analysis over another (lessons that "intersectional" methodologies have been promulgating for some time now), but more specifically aim to unpack the ways that literary acts at a given conjuncture may seem "progressive" at one level (for example, Maximo Kalaw's critique of anti-Filipino racism and his persistent claims to nationalist independence during the first decades of U.S. colonial rule) but "conservative" at another (his recourse to reproductive heterosexuality as the affective and ideological means for securing nationalist feeling and imagining an independent future). Gender and sexuality are *constitutive* of Kalaw's articulation of anticolonial nationalism in *The Filipino Rebel*, as I suggest in chapter 1, but nonetheless expressed in a *contingent* manner: the "linkage" between reproductive heterosexuality and nationalism under the pressures of imperial assimilation and modernization is not foreordained, "absolute and essential for all time." And that contingency becomes starkly apparent when we note the very different ways that Villa, who begins his writing career around the same time that *The Filipino Rebel* is published, articulates (queer) eroticism and gender to race, nation, and metaphysical humanism (see chapter 2).

Another way to bring out the significance of the poetics of address and the politics of articulation is by thinking about the politics of (inter)disciplinarity. To invoke "diaspora" in the present Filipino context is necessarily to reference the current situation of international labor migration. Excepting the prosaic use of "diaspora" to designate Filipinos living anywhere outside of the Philippines, "the Filipino diaspora" has become synonymous with human export labor, a socioeconomic description referring to the some ten million Filipinos laboring in nearly 200 countries and remitting billions of dollars a year back to the Philippines. A number of social science scholars have examined how this "scattering" has been induced by radically uneven labor opportunities and incentives, national currencies, and global market needs; managed by state systems of brokerage and contract employment; and negotiated at individual levels by maintaining various material linkages (remittances, phone calls, texts, return visits, and so forth) with their families in the Philippines. This scholarship has also emphasized the ways that the institutions and discourses producing international labor are intrinsically gendered and sexualized—whether through the explosive national debates around Filipina femininity and motherhood in women's roles as domestic workers, care givers, or entertainers,[87] or through international metaphorologies that position the Philippine state vis-à-vis other nations through narratives of romance, hyperfeminization, prostitution, and infantilization (all of which are ideologically secured through developmental models of national formation).[88]

One of the ways that Filipino global workers have dealt with their subordinated status within the host country and negotiated their vexed relation to the homeland is through various writing practices—of which letter-writing is the most ubiquitous.[89] As the exemplary form that makes evident the transnational modes of address constituting Filipino diasporic discourse, the epistolary performs multiple roles: reconnecting dispersed workers along familial and affiliative lines, criticizing the receiving country's institutionalized and everyday practices of discrimination as well as the Philippines' "failures" at protecting its citizens abroad, providing comfort against the isolations endured while working abroad, and registering the contradictory meanings and expectations that accrue particularly around femininity and motherhood as female domestic laborers are caught between the need to care for their families through economic remittances and the criticisms leveled at them for allegedly neglecting to care emotionally for their own children. But it is equally important to emphasize that these letters represent epistolary *acts*, efforts to draw connections and deliver critiques across the sites of this social dispersal. When published in journals and magazines that cater to specific niches within the international labor market, these letters become part of *public* discourse—a discourse that is thoroughly gendered and sexualized.[90]

While the prominence and plight of overseas Filipino workers (OFWs) have made their way into creative literature,[91] [Ruth] Elynia S. Mabanglo's remarkable bilingual poetry collection *Invitation of the Imperialist/Anaya ng Imperyalista* (1998) is particularly pertinent here since several of the poems document the experiences of OFWs by drawing on the epistolary, that is, a form used by overseas workers themselves. The English part of the book opens with the manifesto-like "I Am a Filipino," evoking a version of "diaspora" ("I travelled overseas") that claims global unity in the face of "the bitter reality" of misrecognition and the "wounds" of the past: "I am a Filipino with children / Who will know their roots; / I am a Filipino with a soul / That will remain Filipino, / In whatever Country, in whatever Time, / In whatever Body."[92] The following title poem, "Invitation of the Imperialist," takes a more sinister turn as it details the gendered hierarchies that structure the male imperialist's relation to the female speaker/writer and that lead to subtle coercions and violent cannibalizations. The collection then offers a series of poems spoken through the voices of different OFWs: their economic and gendered reasons for working abroad (18, 60), the difficulties of being separated from family members (19, 31, 54), the costs of their attempts to assimilate into the receiving location (14), their humiliating interpellations and the insecurities afforded by paper IDs (14, 23–28), and the physical brutalities to which they are subject, including beatings (56–57), rape (15–17, 32), illegitimate children born of rape (49–50, 58), death (33–36), and execution (37–48).

Equally compelling are the poems' formal aspects, as the sequence moves from the poet assuming multiple voices by writing "As an OCW" (overseas contract worker) (14–18) about the "Land of Desire, Land of Despair" (19–36), to taking on individual voices ("A Conjectural Poem by Flor Contemplacion" [37–48]) issued from various locations via the epistolary form: "Pinay's Letter from Kuwait," from Japan, Singapore, Australia, Hong Kong, and Brunei (49–61). As Neferti Xina M. Tadiar points out, Mabanglo's use of the first-person in these lyric-missives "is not a matter of representing others or speaking in behalf of others. It is, rather, a practice of involving oneself in another. Mabanglo takes the substitutability of women, their exploitative exchangeability within a capitalist, sexist and racist socioeconomic order, and turns it into a means of partially experiencing the lives of the women for whom she feels."[93] Mabanglo's partial inhabiting of different Pinay voices further undercuts the de-individuating "substitutability" of women's labor and bodies. But it is the epistolary acts of address, sent from a range of geographic places and socioeconomic positions, that is particularly arresting. Although the letter-poems seem to pursue a politics of *self*-expression to counter the dehumanizations and isolations suffered by the speakers, their power rests on the *intersubjective* form of the epistolary, at times seeking understanding from those they have left behind (52–55), but more often casting their appeals to unspecified recipients. And it is through those acts of address and being addressed that, we might say, the contemporary Filipino diaspora gets articulated.

By calling concerted attention to the complex and contradictory ways that gender and sexuality are mobilized within diasporic contexts, the epistolary modes of address used by everyday workers and Mabanglo's poems provide a model for theorizing a queer diasporic approach to Filipino literature in the United States. Although my archive is limited to literary transactions taking place between the Philippines and the United States and does not purport to cover anglophone writing from around the globe,[94] I nonetheless use "diaspora" not to *name* a sociogeographical entity of dispersed Filipinos, but to *frame* the multiple modes of address utilized in Filipino literature within a transnational context of colonialism, imperialism, and migration.

At one level, then, this methodology places the literature within a diasporic frame and engages in queer readings that, on the one hand, expose the heteronormative logics underwriting conceptualizations and practices of U.S. colonialism, Philippine nationalism, and migration-assimilation narratives in the United States, and, on the other, seek out not so much "queer" identities as alternative relationalities, intimacies, and solidarities forged outside of state-sanctioned heterosexuality and its ideological enforcement through familial discipline. At another level, my readings focus intently on those textual moments when the writers employ the direct address to reach diverse audiences and to constitute multiple publics,[95] thereby construing these literary practices as performative acts rather than textually objectified facts. Those addresses, I am suggesting, invariably pivot on the politics of gender, sexuality, and eroticism.

Let me reiterate at this point that the reading practice delineated here is *not* restricted to identifying thematized representations of nonnormative sexuality, much less celebrating or condemning "global gays" or diasporic queers.[96] Although chapter 5 examines contemporary evocations of male same-sex desires within the contexts of martial law and migration, I employ "queer" throughout this study in its expansive theoretical sense that denotes not a positivist essential category of homosexual identity, but an unraveling of the normative lineup of biological sex, gender, and sexuality. As a politicized analytic, the term's critical force derives from its expulsion from and opposition to the normal, while as a literary approach it is distinct from "lesbian and gay readings that hunt the queer."[97] Kandice Chuh has suggested that the "history of the formation of 'Filipino' and 'Filipino American' identity formations, from a U.S. perspective, is also a history of sexuality";[98] however, my aim is not so much to trace a genealogy of Filipino sexuality through literature, but rather to elaborate on Sarita See's startling claim "that Filipinos are *structurally* queer to the United States."[99] See makes this point with regard to Nicky Paraiso's play *House/Boy* (2004), reading the "o solo homo" (106) performance as a critically queer allegory of colonial domesticity ("benevolent assimilation" as paternalist civilizing tutelage) and racial inassimilability ("foreign in a domestic sense") within "the 'house' of the American empire" (116). Echoing the liminal and unstable status of "Filipino" outlined above, See's insight enables us to perceive the sexual and erotic discourses that both constitute this categorical instability and seek to discipline its unruliness.

Influenced by scholars such as M. Jacqui Alexander, David L. Eng, Gayatri Gopinath, Martin F. Manalansan, and Jasbir K. Puar, who have pushed the boundaries of gender and sexuality studies into raced and classed transnational and imperial contexts,[100] this book is in conversation with the scholarship on "queer diasporas" that has interrogated the heteronormativities inherent in dominant notions of diaspora and anti- and postcolonial nationalisms, as well as the more recent homonormativities intrinsic to U.S. imperial claims to sexual exceptionalism and postcolonial claims to liberal modernity. But in its pursuit of queer diasporic *literary history*, this study also departs from this work in two significant ways. Rather than focus solely on contemporary texts and practices that, in a post-Stonewall sense, can be readily identified as sexually nonnormative, this project examines the constitutive roles of gender and sexuality from colonial to postcolonial periods and elucidates those roles by analyzing the poetics and politics of literary address.

Is this historically oriented queer diasporic reading practice anachronistic and culturally inapplicable? While there are a number of possible responses to this cautionary question, I emphasize here that although queer theory developed in the U.S. academy in the late 1980s and early

1990s out of poststructuralist critiques of gay and lesbian studies and antinormative political activism, the etymological provenance of the term "queer" as an adjective, according to the *Oxford English Dictionary*, is itself "uncertain," while its usage as a verb, deriving from Romance languages, is linked to the "Middle French *querir* to seek, to ask, request, to inquire" and the "Spanish *querer* to seek, to ask, inquire, to like, prefer."[101] In other words, as a style of scholarly pursuit, "queer" connotes both desire and inquiry, a mode of seeking knowledge that is itself driven by a practice of questioning unconsoled by fixed origins— a fitting analytic for exploring expressive forms produced by those not only rendered "structurally queer" by U.S. imperial racialization but also questioning and in quest of identity. This etymology resonates with Judith Butler's open-ended elaboration of "queer": "If the term 'queer' is to be a site of collective contestation, *the point of departure for a set of historical reflections and futural imaginings*, it will have to remain that which is, in the present, never fully owned, but always and only redeployed, twisted, queered from a prior usage and in the direction of urgent and expanding political purposes"[102]—and, I would add, literary purposes. In this respect, it is important to note that queer theoretical work has already been "redeployed" by several Filipino studies scholars in both the United States and the Philippines (see especially chapter 5).

Rather than attempt an exhaustive survey of Filipino literature in the United States, I have selected authors and texts that foreground the *politics* of queer diasporic reading. My analyses track the circulation of texts across various locations and the differing receptions and reactions that readers with different investments have recorded in print in order to unpack the ways that differing valuations of gender and sexuality get mapped onto differing geographies and temporalities in complex and sometimes contradictory ways. Challenging ahistorical assumptions that tether "traditional" patriarchy, sexual conservatism, and homophobia to the global south, and "modern" gender equality, homo-tolerance, and sexual progressivism to the global north, the following chapters provide historically contextualized readings that disrupt such colonialist, developmental notions.

Though *Beyond the Nation* is organized in roughly chronological order, it simultaneously argues against a developmental model of literary history *and* theory. By bringing to bear a queer diasporic framework to apprehend the cultural politics of Filipino literary production prior to the 1970s, I am suggesting that this literary history cannot be easily periodized through the colonial/postcolonial divide, the "waves" model of Filipino migration and U.S. immigration law (1900–1934, 1935–1964, 1965–present), or traditional categories of literary history.[103] At the same time, it would be historically inaccurate, politically problematic, and theoretically reductive to prioritize categories of colonialism, nationalism, and race when considering writers who come of age under U.S. colonialism in the first three chapters (on Kalaw, Villa, and Bulosan), and adopt a more robust analytic that includes gender, sexuality, eroticism, and desire when focusing on postindependence writers in the latter three chapters (on Hagedorn, Realuyo, Linmark, Alumit, Galang, Roley, Rosal, and Reyes). Although these issues do not intersect with each other in the same way across different historical contexts and political commitments, as I noted above, they are nonetheless present from the start and therefore demand flexible and dynamic reading strategies if we are to account for their interarticulations.

Far from simply controverting, then, the Flips' assertion that there is "no published literature" prior to the 1970s, this book aims to reframe the U.S.-centered assumptions that make such an assertion possible, trouble the customary focus on racial representation and ethnic identity, and reject the teleological, prescriptive notion that ethnic or postcolonial literature ought to consolidate a "positive" sense of cultural or national identity before accounting for "other" forms of difference. Offering neither the comforting idea that the U.S. civilizing mission has fulfilled its promise nor the consolatory notion that Filipinos have emerged out of "invisibility" into cultural visibility and particularity, the following pages endeavor instead to elucidate some of the ways that the literature is peculiar and queer, strange and estranging, by pursuing a critical practice of "un-oneing" against the normalizing coercions of imperialism, nationalism, and assimilation. But in order to see how and when such queer moments enter this literary archive, it is necessary to consider the immense pressures toward normativity that U.S. imperialism exerted on Filipinos in the early decades of U.S. colonialism, the topic of chapter 1.

# 1

# The Romantic Didactics
# of Maximo Kalaw's Nationalism

IN THE INTRODUCTION to the 1964 reissue of Maximo M. Kalaw's
*The Filipino Rebel*, Pio Pedrosa wonders why the author "turned to this
literary form [the novel] as the vehicle for the message he sought to
convey instead of using the essay or the treatise as was his wont."[1] Prior
to publishing his only novel around 1930,[2] Kalaw (1891–1955) had established himself as a staunch advocate of Philippine independence by
writing several books on "the Philippine question," including *The Case
for the Filipinos* (1916), *Self-Government in the Philippines* (1919), and *The
Development of Philippine Politics, 1872–1920* (1926), as well as numerous essays for U.S. academic and mainstream journals. In light of this
work, Pedrosa avers that the mix of fictional and historical characters in
*The Filipino Rebel* enables Kalaw to present "the clashes of ideas, the conflict of beliefs, and the quarrel of philosophies" during the early colonial
period and to draw portraits of "the opportunists and the principled, the
chauvinists and the dedicated, the fence-sitters and the true nationalists" (xiv). For Pedrosa, Kalaw's novel is little more than political theory
and debate personified: *The Filipino Rebel* "is Maximo M. Kalaw all over
again: political philosopher, essayist, teacher. Going through its argu-
mentation is . . . like sitting once more in the small cubicle adjoining his
Rizal Hall office as Dean of the College of Liberal Arts of the University
of the Philippines" (xi).

Kalaw's preface to the original edition tells a somewhat different
story. Acknowledging "the difficulties" involved in writing one of the
first Filipino novels in English, the author states that his pioneering endeavor was "induced" by his "studies of Philippine life, which revealed
to me a wealth of heroic deeds, romantic episodes and dramatic changes
which could be made the background of many novels" (xvii). While Pedrosa implies that the novel's heavy-handed use of "didactic discourse"
outweighs its "dramatic" elements (xiv), I focus here on its subtitle—*A*

*Romance of American Occupation in the Philippines.* By marking the text as a "romance," Kalaw intimates that the difference between his political writings and his novel lies in the centrality of the relationship between the revolutionary-cum-politician Juanito Lecaroz and the barrio woman–cum–diasporic nationalist Josefa. In counterpoint to what Nerissa Balce terms "*the erotics of the American Empire,* the discursive and material processes that created the sexual and racialized representations of the Filipina colonial subject in American popular culture,"[3] this chapter explores the erotics of Philippine nationalism, the ways that the novel's "message" is mediated through reproductive heterosexuality. *The Filipino Rebel's* engagement with the politics of independence—more than a decade after the passage of the Jones Law in 1916 and several years before the Tydings-McDuffie Act of 1934—seeks to recover what it deems the lost revolutionary spirit of 1899 by proffering the male offspring conceived by Juanito and Josefa in the "veritable Eden" of the guerrilla war as the nationalist promise of an independent future.[4]

My analysis approaches the gendered and sexualized underpinnings of Philippine nationalism that a number of scholars have opened up through the issue of genre and the politics of address.[5] Although *The Filipino Rebel* was published in the Philippines, Kalaw had spent considerable time studying and agitating for independence in the United States. Without constructing too rigid a binary linking genre and national audience, I would argue that Kalaw's political science texts are predominantly oriented toward a U.S. readership, while his novel attempts to address and constitute (however selectively by writing in English) what he names in the dedication "ANG BAGONG KATIPUNAN."[6] The particular pressures imposed by the competing demands of these different audiences give rise to shifting strategies: the former marshals sociological data and hard-hitting critique, while the latter moves toward the realm of affect. Whereas scholars such as Reynaldo Ileto, Vicente Rafael, and Sarita See have examined the political work of mourning and martyrdom as productive of nationalist (or anticolonial) affect,[7] I examine how "romantic" eroticism in *The Filipino Rebel* gets linked to nationalist feeling within the world of the novel and how it rhetorically seeks to inspire "a new nationalism," as the dedication reads, among "ang bagong katipunan."

My task in this chapter is twofold: to ground historically the argument that a focus on the politics of representation depends on an appeal to recognition by the imperial power and is therefore a fatal project, and to demonstrate the necessity of a queer diasporic reading practice given the heterosexual erotics and metaphorology of the family that suffuse dominant conceptions of Philippine nationalism. Maria Teresa Martinez-Sicat suggests in her analysis of *The Filipino Rebel* that the "representation of the Philippines in the international arena of nations as well as the address to an American public . . . may not altogether be without value. However, addressing foreign nations is only one recourse. Such an act is itself dependence; it is premised on independence granted by external forces, independence granted from without, in opposition to independence won by internal forces, independence gained from within."[8] Whereas the "external" address leads to further dependence on securing recognition from "an American public," the winning of independence "from within," I suggest, takes place on the terrain of the erotic. Kalaw's writings illustrate both points. His political science work, addressed to the United States, fails to bring about the guarantees of independence that he and his elite cohort strive to effect, while his reorientation to the homeland in *The Filipino Rebel* seeks to rouse nationalist affect by recurring to heterosexual eroticism and reproductive futurity.

## Addressing Annexation, Assimilation, and Independence

To gain a sense of where Kalaw's strategies enter, one might consider how the debates between U.S. colonialism and Philippine independence were constructed. Though the war and colonialism may have since been forgotten or repressed by mainstream U.S. history, the disputes regarding the Philippine question at the turn of the twentieth century were widespread and vigorous. Rather than rehearse these debates in detail, my concern here is to show how an examination of the politics of address can illuminate not only who has the authority to speak or "represent" the parties involved but also who is imagined legitimate enough to be addressed in the first place.

The justifications for war and annexation—the idea that overseas expansion is merely an extension of westward "manifest destiny" and a divinely ordained mission to civilize the savages; the allied concept that empire constitutes a natural progression in the United States' development as a world power; the notion that the Philippines represents a "stepping-stone" to China and its boundless markets; the proposal that war will reinvigorate a waning American manhood—have received critical attention by scholars. But the *forms* of those legitimations are equally significant. One of the loudest exponents of imperialism, Indiana senator Alfred J. Beveridge, for example, bellowed his position on the floor of the U.S. Senate on January 9, 1900:

> Mr. President, the times call for candor. The Philippines are ours forever, "territory belonging to the United States," as the Constitution calls them. And just beyond the Philippines are China's illimitable markets. We will not retreat from either. We will not repudiate our duty in the archipelago. We will not abandon our opportunity in the Orient. We will not renounce our part in the mission of our race, trustee under God, of the civilization of the world. And we will move forward to our work, not howling at regrets like slaves whipped to their burdens, but with gratitude for a task worthy of our strength and thanksgiving to Almighty God that He has marked us as His chosen people, henceforth to lead in the regeneration of the world.[9]

Beveridge effortlessly combines expanding capitalist markets and opportunities with Christian duty as justifications for imperialism, while perversely invoking the racialized figure of slaves "whipped to their burdens" to shame and cajole his colleagues into accepting their providentially ordained "mission" (recall that Rudyard Kipling's poem "The White Man's Burden" was published less than a year earlier in 1899).[10] The address to the president and the Senate enables Beveridge not only to cast Filipinos as "a barbarous race" who are "not capable of self-government," as he goes on to proclaim, but to constitute "we" as a "chosen people" without having to consider or consult Filipino perspectives (19). While this might seem obvious and inherent to the structure of colonial discourse, the point is that the "candor" with which Beveridge speaks acquires its urgency from *U.S.* anti-imperialists. Although Filipino views did make it into the pages of some U.S. magazines and periodicals with the assistance of the Anti-Imperialist League,[11] such views did not even warrant rebuttal since the only viewpoints that mattered were those held in the Senate itself.

The experiences of Felipe Agoncillo, one of political leader Emilio Aguinaldo's diplomatic emissaries, exemplify how the debates about imperialism actively shut out Filipino voices. A year before Beveridge's ringing oration, Aguinaldo sent Agoncillo to Washington, D.C., "to represent the Philippine Republic and begin negotiations with the American government."[12] Such negotiations in August 1898 sought recognition for the recently declared Philippine Republic and tried to intervene in the conversations leading up to the signing of the Treaty of Paris between Spain and the United States on December 10, 1898, and the treaty's ratification by the Senate on February 6, 1899. Stuart Creighton Miller describes Agoncillo's reception in Washington and Paris: "McKinley handled the situation in his usual style. He received Agoncillo and spent an hour talking to him, but refused to give him any assurances about the future of the Philippines since that was still being negotiated in Paris. Agoncillo then went to France in an attempt to testify before the Peace Commission. There he was completely cold-shouldered, and he 'returned to the Philippines with considerable bitterness toward the American government'" (46).

Spurred by "the ardent desire to let the American people know the whole truth," Apolinario Mabini, architect of the Philippine Republic's constitution and prominent member of Aguinaldo's cabinet, puts it more bluntly: Agoncillo was given "instructions to lay before President McKinley the grievances of the Filipinos and to ask for the recognition of the independence of the Philippines, in fulfilment of the promises made by the Americans generals . . . [but] was not received by the President, nor heard by the American Commission in Paris."[13] While Agoncillo's voice would probably not have made much difference in the treaty talks (since Spain and the United States had already decided that they were the only two powers with the authority to negotiate) or with the Senate vote, the point is that the strategy of attempting to address the U.S. government was based on a politics of recognition that enabled the power-holding entity not merely to decline the validity of the "grievances" but to deny their very hearing.

Whereas Beveridge's speech and Agoncillo's rejection indicate how U.S. imperial discourse excluded Filipino perspectives by ensuring that Americans would only be talking and listening to each other, one might think that Mark Twain's famous essay "To the Person Sitting in Darkness" (1901) would attempt to speak to Filipinos. Despite its title and anti-imperialist thrust, however, it, too, remains addressed to other Americans. Framed as a broad critique of bungled and violent attempts by various European powers to bring the "Blessings of Civilization" to distant lands and peoples (the Boxer Uprising, the Boer War, Russian aggression against Japan and in Manchuria), the satire turns to U.S. involvement in Cuba and then to "the Philippine temptation."[14] Twain's rhetorical approach shifts here, not simply voicing what "the Person Sitting in Darkness" must think of these imperialists' exploits but also articulating what Americans should say to that person. On the one hand, Twain speculates, "The Person Sitting in Darkness is almost sure to say: 'There is something curious about this—curious and unaccountable. There must be two Americas: one that sets the captive free, and one that takes a once-captive's new freedom away from him, and picks a quarrel with him with nothing to found it on; then kills him to get his land'" (170). On the other hand, Twain ironically inhabits what he refers to as "the Master's" position. Given this split, hypocritical image of "two Americas," Twain writes, "We must arrange his opinions for him" (170). He then rehearses the events from Dewey's defeat of the Spanish fleet in Manila Bay in May 1898 through the Treaty of Paris and up to the essay's present when the brutality of the war, theretofore filtered through the War Department's censors, had finally reached the public.

Twain's rendering of these events and its expression of sympathy for the Filipino cause—arguing that "the Filipino nation" ought to have been returned to its "rightful owners" upon Dewey's victory (171); that the U.S. military and government deceived the Filipinos by first aiding their war against Spain and then wresting "the Archipelago" from those "patriots struggling for independence" (172); and that this deception undermined the sovereignty of "a just and intelligent and well-ordered republic" (174)—are still directed toward Americans. Indeed, Twain frames these attempts to "arrange" the "opinions" of the person sitting in darkness with the phrase "Let us say to him" (171). However, he proceeds not to address a "you" but to continue to refer to "them" over there: "We knew that they were fighting for their independence, and that they had been at it for two years. We knew they supposed that we also were fighting in their worthy cause—just as we had helped the Cubans fight for Cuban independence—and we allowed them to go on thinking so. *Until Manila was ours and we could get along without them*" (171). In short, Twain's rhetorical modes of address either ventriloquize and thereby silence the Filipino voice ("The Person Sitting in Darkness is almost sure to say . . .") or venture and ultimately fail to *address* the person sitting in darkness. Though perceptive of U.S. deceit and hypocrisy, Twain leaves the titular person still shrouded in darkness, unseen, unheard, and unrecognized.

One of the most important documents to set the tone and terms of the Philippine debate was President William McKinley's Benevolent

Assimilation Proclamation, delivered on December 21, 1898. The document sought to claim "the authority of the United States" and guide U.S. colonial policy in the Philippines following "the surrender of the Spanish forces" and the signing of the Treaty of Paris only eleven days earlier.[15] McKinley infamously heralded the "benevolence" of U.S. control by stating, "It will be the duty of the commander of the forces of occupation to announce and proclaim in the most public manner that we come, not as invaders or conquerors, but as friends, to protect the natives in their homes, in their employments, and in their personal and religious rights." Such friendliness, "support and protection," however, would be extended only to those "who, either by active aid or by honest submission, co-operate with the Government of the United States to give effect to these beneficent purposes." "All others," McKinley ominously warned, "will be brought within the lawful rule we have assumed, with firmness if need be, but without severity, so far as possible." After promising to protect "private rights and property" and pursue "the repression of crime," McKinley closes by articulating the meaning of "benevolent assimilation":

> Finally, it should be the earnest wish and paramount aim of the military administration to win the confidence, respect, and affection of the inhabitants of the Philippines by assuring them in every possible way that full measure of individual rights and liberties which is the heritage of free peoples, and by proving to them that the mission of the United States is one of BENEVOLENT AS- SIMILATION substituting the mild sway of justice and right for arbitrary rule.

Many historians have noted the fundamental discrepancy between rhetoric and reality that this proclamation prophesied, documenting the ways that U.S. colonial policy and practice was overtly or insidiously less than "benevolent."[16] But what did "assimilation" mean at this moment? Paul Kramer writes that the term "held more than a hint of malice: the very fact that it required the adjective 'benevolent' to soften it suggested more or less directly that there were kinds of assimilation that were not."[17] Kramer's gloss implies that "assimilation" was something that the United States would do *to* Filipinos. That is, the U.S. government and its many civic, educational, political, and economic projects would assimilate the Filipino—if not to itself (Filipinos would not be given access to

U.S. citizenship until after independence was granted in 1946) then at least to its cultural, capitalist values.[18]

In contemporary discourse, assimilation typically means the opposite, a process that the "foreigner," immigrant, or marginalized outcast undertakes or undergoes if he or she is to become a participating member in society and be granted the rights and responsibilities of national citizenship. In this sense, assimilation is conservative in that the receiving society seeks to remain unchanged by the presence of newcomers and outsiders. McKinley's proclamation, by contrast, placed the United States in the active role of assimilating foreign Filipinos, and it should hardly be shocking therefore that the United States did not remain impervious to this campaign.[19] Indeed, by leaving its borders open to Filipinos as U.S. "nationals" until 1934 (while closing them to other Asian laborers racially ineligible for citizenship), it made possible the conditions that the racist anti-imperialists feared most: an *invasion* of *unassimilable* dark hordes.[20]

The politics of assimilation put Filipinos in a vexed position. Since the primary rationalization for annexation was that Filipinos were incapable of self-government, the diligent pupils of colonial "tutelage" would have to demonstrate that capacity by measuring up to whatever criteria the imperial power decided to lay down. Again, the conservative and normative character of this policy cannot be overstated. Any signs of nonassimilation—social dissent or disorder, disease, religious "superstition," or personality "flaws"—could be seized upon as evidence that the time had not yet arrived for independence.[21]

As rhetorically persuasive and fervent as they are, the positions that Filipinos articulated in U.S. magazines and periodicals during the first two decades of colonial rule nonetheless reflect this political and moral conservatism. While much has been written about U.S. anti-imperialism during this period, much less consideration has been given to the Filipino voices that spoke out against imperial aggression and duplicity.[22] Despite the passage of the Treaty of Paris, a number of Filipino intellectual elites continued to issue statements trying to persuade the United States to cease fighting and, once the war was declared over in 1902, to grant independence. Broadly speaking, their arguments adopted two tactics: contesting and correcting what they considered slanderous falsehoods about Filipinos disseminated by the U.S. press, and using the United States' own revolutionary history and political values to expose the fundamental contradiction between republican democracy and overseas imperialism. To focus on just one example that combines both strategies, a year and a half into the war, Galicano Apacible, on behalf of the Central Filipino Committee in Toronto, issued a pamphlet titled *To the American People* in June 1900, whose anguished appeal is audible right from the start:

> God Almighty knows how unjust is the war which the Imperial arms have provoked and are maintaining against our unfortunate country! If the honest American patriots could understand the sad truth of this declaration, we are sure they would, without the least delay, stop this unspeakable horror. And, that they may have a just understanding of it, we entreat them to hear our voice, to meditate on our exhortations and to weigh our statements against the misrepresentations under which Imperialism seeks to conceal its designs. Turn not away from our prayer, Americans, but listen, and give judgment according to reason and conscience.[23]

The pamphlet seeks to rectify those "misrepresentations" first by asserting the good character of Filipinos. "We, the Filipinos," it proclaims, "are a civilized, progressive and peace-loving people," presenting as evidence the availability of university education in the islands; the achievements of "artists, scientists, magistrates, generals and dignitaries of the church"; the establishment of civic order once Manila was freed from Spanish control; and the general "path of progress" on which Filipinos had embarked, which was "disturbed" and "destroyed" by "the Imperialists." The address proceeds to dismantle the "specious arguments" propounded by the imperialists: "that we are incapable of self-government," that the "deep divisions among us" and "the withdrawal of American troops would create anarchy and misgovernment in our country," that "the Philippine Republic had never been recognized by the whole country," that "the existence of these mountain races [that is, indigenous peoples] makes the Philippine Independence impossible," that the "different dialects" spoken in the country prevent the possibility of "national unity," that "the majority of the Filipinos are in favor of the American sovereignty," that Filipinos "were the aggressors in the present war," that the country's mines and lands are exploitable, that "the higher interests of Christianity demand the retention of the islands," and that "God trusted in their [the imperialists'] hands the government of the future destinies of the Filipinos."

Countering each of these points with reference to past accomplishments in self-governance, cross-ethnolinguistic communication and negotiation, restraint in the face of American contempt and harassment, and disbelief at the hypocrisy of invoking Christian providence when $20 million exchanged hands and "quick-firing guns" are "mutilating the unfortunate Filipinos," the pamphlet also appeals to the United States' supposed traditions of democracy and freedom:

> Can it be possible, sons of America, that you will allow us to become subjects or slaves? Should this happen, how will you reconcile it with the wise and noble principles set forth in your Declaration of Independence: "That all men are created equal; that they are endowed by their Creator with certain inalienable rights; that among these are life, liberty, and the pursuit of happiness; that to secure these rights governments are instituted among men, deriving their just powers from the consent of the governed." Will you transform these beautiful and honorable sentiments into specious deceits, fraudulent promises, and high-sounding but hollow words? No! You cannot belie your whole history. You cannot tolerate the violation which Imperialism is so evidently working against your most venerable and fundamental principles.

Appalled that "the McKinley government could possibly be guilty of such a direct departure from the principles of just government as to endeavor by force of arms, by the slaughter of unoffending and friendly people, to filch from us the sacred right of liberty," Apacible anticipates the argument that would continually be used to stall Philippine independence: "If we did not fight under the circumstances . . . we should be giving proof of our utter unfitness for self government." It is this practice of restraint—broken only by mistreatment, harassment, and gunshots— that Apacible attempts to convey to the Cincinnati Single Tax Club in hopes "that you will put it very clearly before your countrymen that the Filipinos do not regard the American people as their enemies."

The Filipino political elite did not desist in speaking truth to power after the war was declared over in 1902. Following the establishment in 1907 of the Philippine Assembly and the post of resident commissioner (politicians who "were elected by the U.S. colonial government in the Philippines,"[24] represented Philippine interests in the U.S. House of Representatives, but were denied voting rights), and the formation in 1916 of the bicameral House of Representatives and Senate, no fewer than nine missions were sent to Washington, D.C. As Bernardita Churchill has thoroughly documented, these missions were primarily for the purpose of securing independence, though they also took up other issues such as trade policies and immigration, and ultimately assisted in passing the Tydings-McDuffie Act in 1934, which provided for independence in ten years.[25] Though Churchill views these envoys as ultimately efficacious, the allegedly altruistic act of promising independence was motivated equally, if not more, by the aim to "end the Philippine invasion of the United States," as Kramer describes it—that is, to bring to a halt the "brown hordes" that were infiltrating the West Coast shores.[26]

## Displaying Evidence, Extending Deferral

Maximo Kalaw's political treatises and essays form part of the discourse that addressed the U.S. colonial government in an effort to obtain independence. A political scientist who lived in the United States during the second and third decades of the twentieth century, Kalaw worked as an aide to then resident commissioner Manuel Quezon while the latter issued the bilingual monthly *The Filipino People*, earned a law degree from Georgetown University and an honorary Ph.D. from the University of Michigan, returned to the Philippines, published several political science books and one novel, and eventually became dean of Liberal Arts at the University of the Philippines.[27] By situating his political writings and novel within the broader context of imperial assimilation, one can appreciate the pressures surrounding the politics of Filipino representation during this period, the dogged insistence on pushing the issue of Philippine independence for consideration, and the marked shift in linguistic register and mode of address that Kalaw employs in *The Filipino Rebel*.

To read through Kalaw's nonfiction texts—from the treatise *The Case for the Filipinos* (1916) to "The New Constitution of the Philippine Commonwealth" (1935), which followed on the heels of the Tydings-McDuffie Act and the ratification of the Philippine Constitution in 1935—is an exercise in wonderment at the sheer perseverance with which he pursues Philippine independence. One of Kalaw's abiding tactics is to probe into the meaning of the phrase "a stable government" contained in the preamble to the 1916 Jones Law: "it is, as it has always been, the purpose of the people of the United States to withdraw their sovereignty over the Philippine Islands and to recognize their independence as soon as a stable government can be established therein."[28] Kalaw compares the situation in the Philippines to international points of reference, noting first that Cuba was granted independence in 1902 (albeit with the neocolonial provisions attached in the Platt Amendment) after holding general elections and establishing "a government capable of maintaining order and fulfilling international obligations."[29] He argues that this same policy applied to the Philippines and was "converted into law" through the passage of the Jones Bill. But even though "there is now a stable government in the Philippines," independence has not been forthcoming (20).

In the years after the Great War (Filipino politicians thought it imprudent to press their case during the war) and the formation of the League of Nations in 1920, Kalaw expanded his sites of comparison to include newly recognized nations. In 1925, he acknowledges "the nationalistic current which is sweeping practically every subject people on earth" and that the "nationalist movements" in Asia and Africa are "demand[ing] self-determination" (21). He challenges the United States to demonstrate "which side she inclines her might, whether on the side of the reactionaries bent on the return of the old order, or whether she still believes in her vaunted principles of self-determination and the consent of the governed" (23). Appealing to this international context, Kalaw writes in a 1923 essay, "At this time when the United States champions the cause of mutual understanding among peoples, of common councils, of round-table conferences to discuss and decide frankly and openly their mutual problems and differences, it does seem strange that she cannot pursue and act upon those very same principles in the Philippines."[30] Rehearsing Felipe Agoncillo's rejection as diplomatic envoy in 1899, the independence delegations, writes Kalaw, receive "not even a frank conference, a round-table discussion, but [only] evasive answers" (629).

The palpable exasperation evident in Kalaw's essays of the early 1930s results from such evasiveness. In "Why the Filipinos Expect Independence" (1932), Kalaw runs through the numerous assurances given by U.S. statesmen—from McKinley to Taft to Roosevelt to Wilson to Governor-General Harrison—that the Philippines would eventually become independent. He then traces the possible meanings of "stable government" with reference to the League of Nations' admissions criteria, arguing that "any impartial observer will compare the condition of the Philippines favorably with those of the countries

which were in 1921 declared by the League of Nations to be the pos-
sessors of stable governments."[31] Based on his analysis of McKinley's
and Secretary of War Elihu Root's statements, "stable government"
means the ability "to maintain order and insure peace and tranquillity
and the security of citizens," "to observe its international obligations,"
to hold "peaceful" elections, and "to protect the people from the arbitrary actions of the government" (313)—all of which, Kalaw asserts,
the Philippine government fulfills as revealed even in the highly biased
Wood-Forbes fact-finding mission.[32]

In "International Aspects of Philippine Independence" (1933), Kalaw extends his points of reference to East Asia, aligning Filipino sentiments with China's "struggle for independence," while implying an
association between U.S. retentionism, Euro-American intervention in
China, and Japanese imperialism: "If America condemns Japan's acts
as imperialistic [following the invasion of Manchuria in 1931], that
should make her the more inclined to redeem her own pledge to the
Filipinos. . . . After all, is not the record of European nations and the
United States in securing territories and concessions in Asia one of the
moral excuses Japan has in pursuing aggressive policies in Manchuria
and China proper?"[33] Kalaw criticizes the notion that the Philippines
ought to be retained because of Japanese imperial aggression. "If the
criterion of ability to repel invasion were applied to all nations desiring
to maintain their independence," he reasons, "not more than five or six
of them could qualify today" (20). More specifically, he notes that "no
American military strategist has ever claimed that the United States
would be able to protect the Philippines against a Japanese invasion"
(18). In a prescient prediction of what would come to pass in eight
years, Kalaw writes, "In case of a war with America, Japan could easily take the Philippines. The only spot in the Philippine Islands which
might resist is Corregidor, the small fort at the bay of Manila. The ef-
fectiveness of even that resistance is being doubted now." As we know,
Corregidor fell to the Japanese in 1942. "In case of a war with Japan,
therefore, the Filipino people would be the first victims, although they
would be in fact a mere third party alien to the question at issue. It
is true that America probably would, through her superior resources,
succeed in taking the Islands back, but only after the expenditure of a
great fortune and the loss of valuable lives" (19). Corregidor was recap-
tured in 1945 and the islands "liberated" the same year. The Filipino
death toll was approximately 500,000 to 1,000,000 people.

The numerous guarantees by U.S. politicians that the Philippines would not remain forever under U.S. sovereignty, the presence of a stable government, the nationalist impulses spreading across the (de)colonized world, the favorable comparisons of the Philippines to Cuba and countries recognized by the League of Nations, the unfavorable comparisons of the United States to Japanese and European imperial powers—none of these arguments could command any real weight. Kalaw's unremitting attempts to demonstrate that the period of tutelage was over mattered little in the end since, as he concluded in 1932, "the fact is that the phrase 'capacity for self-government' is as broad and elastic as the purposes of the person using it at the moment require."[34] This elasticity, Kalaw argues, is not only "unfair and unwarranted" but practically inapplicable to any existing nation in the world. The endless and arbitrary criteria "range from the establishment of an ideal democracy and the building of more hospitals to the formation of a government that will stand up against the most powerful foreign aggression and prevent all economic penetration. We submit that no nation on earth can qualify under each and every one of these conditions. They seem to us mere words to tease us along" (315).

The frustration found in these essays is moderated by a seemingly inexhaustible effort to reason clearly and cogently with the profoundly duplicitous Americans and to convey those arguments in measured prose. This temperance is not only a rhetorical function of political science but also an effect of the transnational politics of representation. In the preface to his 1916 treatise *The Case for the Filipinos*, Kalaw registers the competing obligations that different audiences exert on the Filipino writer forced to engage in this representational terrain. Whereas the retentionist focuses on "American achievements in the Islands," the proponent of independence "enumerates in detail the unmistakable signs of capacity manifested by the Filipinos during American occupation, and then urges the granting of independence without any further delay."[35] Within this dichotomous struggle, not only is U.S. colonialism treated in stark binaries as either benevolent or baleful, but "the case for the Filipinos" themselves becomes one-dimensional. Since the retentionists often depict Filipinos "in the darkest colors, if not, indeed, flagrantly misrepresenting them, ridiculing their characteristics, exploiting their supposed ignorance, and exaggerating, if not entirely creating new, native vices and shortcomings" (xi), the "advocate of independence" is forced to counter these portrayals and display Filipino character and "capacity" in the best light possible. In the final chapter of the book, Kalaw elaborates on this problematic:

> What effect has this campaign on the Filipino body politic? Humiliated by such tactics, hurt in their most sensitive feeling of national pride, they have naturally assumed an attitude of self-defense. They have become guarded in all their manifestations as to their own shortcomings and habitually refer only to what is creditable in their civilization. Every spirit of self-criticism has been buried. Reformers have ceased to write of conditions that should be improved, undesirable habits that should be changed, antiquated ideas that should be modernized, and superstitions that should be wiped out. (240–241)

Adopting this "tactic" of "self-defense" and the logic of modernization and progress on which it rests, Kalaw's own political science books seek to impart what is most "creditable" to Filipinos. While *The Case for the Filipinos* focuses mostly on U.S. imperialism, from Dewey's incursion into Manila Bay to the debates around the Jones Bill and the Clarke Amendment, it nonetheless devotes two of its eleven chapters to "the protest of the Filipinos" (the attempt to prevent the ratification of the Treaty of Paris) and "the voice of the Filipino people" (basically a collection of statements made by Manuel Quezon).[36] Carrying the diplomatic story forward from the Jones Law to the end of the Great War, *Self-Government in the Philippines* (1919) aims to "place before the public a record of what the Filipino people have done since the establishment of Philippine autonomy, and the reasons which impel them as a people to demand their separation from the United States."[37] Containing chapters on the organization of the new government, the budget system, economic development, local and provincial governance, and metropolitan treatment of the "non-Christian tribes," the treatise seeks to prove that a "stable government" has been established and that the Philippines should therefore be granted independence as stipulated by the Jones Law.

*The Filipino Rebel*, as we will see, provides a more complex depiction of Philippine political life during the first three decades of U.S. colonial rule. Though the novel by no means abandons its critique of U.S. colonialism, it also performs the sort of "self-criticism" of Philippine politics that the unidirectional address to a U.S. audience in the earlier essays had largely foreclosed. Though it is true that *The Case for the Filipinos* reflexively addresses both audiences ("This book, however, is not intended solely for Americans"), Kalaw implicitly concedes that the majority of the book engages with "the attitude of the American people" toward Filipinos. *The Filipino Rebel*, on the other hand, focuses specifically on "the drama of their [Filipinos'] national future as it is staged" in the Philippines.[38]

## Eroticizing Nationalism

*The Filipino Rebel* opens with Dewey's defeat of the Spanish fleet in Manila Bay on May 1, 1898, and narrativizes Filipino political history up through the late 1920s by tracing the decisions and actions of its three main characters, Don Pedro Ricafort, Juanito Lecaroz, and Josefa. Don Pedro is depicted as the principled idealist "more inclined to scholarly pursuits than to warfare," whose power lies in his considerable wealth and in his moral authority (3). Though he initially sides with the Spanish against the Americans, believing in reform rather than separation, he is soon convinced of Aguinaldo's cause, is drafted into the Filipino army, and, as "the personification of loyalty itself," is entrusted with preserving the revolutionary papers from confiscation (81). An opponent of guerrilla warfare, Don Pedro embodies the upright man of honor who "preferred to be shot" than bow to "a bloodless surrender" at Tirad Pass (82). As the pillar of loyalty, Don Pedro refuses to divulge the location of Aguinaldo, is transported to Manila, and rejects the oath of allegiance recognizing U.S. sovereignty over the Philippines. Along with Apolinario Mabini, he is exiled to Guam for a year, again refuses to sign the oath when he returns, and is exiled a second time. He travels first to Hong Kong, where he "unofficially joined the Revolutionary committee" (87–88); next to the United States, where he means "to tell her the truth about the Philippines" (89); then to Europe; and finally back to Hong Kong. We are told that his life in exile is funded by his real estate in Manila: "Thanks to the public improvements made immediately after the American occupation—a fact which he would not admit—his lots and houses in Manila increased in value and their rents were more than sufficient to finance his indefinite stay abroad" (88).

When Don Pedro is permitted to return to the Philippines after thirty years of exile to mourn the death of his daughter Leonor, he becomes the voice of critique—both of U.S. colonial tutelage and of Philippine political opportunism. Surveying life in the provinces, for example, he learns that a sugar mill installed with U.S. capital yields little to the land-owner, that there is "very little visible material progress" on the farm it-self (163), that the people who work there are "badly in debt" (164), that the smattering of English taught in the public school is practically use-less and quickly forgotten, and that the pupils are not being instructed in their own vernacular. Kalaw even stages a debate between Don Pedro and Governor-General Henry Stimson. The former argues that the plan "to prepare us for independence" has been a "failure" and that "the spirit of sacrifice" has "been lessened rather than strengthened by the patron-age, the pork barrel, and other political favors that you have placed in the hands of our leaders" (169). He concludes that Filipinos would have been far better off without U.S. colonial tutelage: "Then we would be able to direct our intellectual and social development as best suits our national genius and needs instead of simply following American mod-els and ideas" (173). And to demonstrate his unyielding opposition to American sovereignty, Don Pedro declines the governor-general's offer to remain in the Philippines even without taking the oath.

On the other hand, a banquet held to honor an independence mission being sent to the United States provides Don Pedro the platform to act as the moral conscience of Philippine politics and to enact the sort of "self-criticism" that Kalaw had claimed was missing from the indepen-dence debates. Addressing a distinguished audience of politicians, Don Pedro goes on for some five pages, inveighing against the "petty wran-glings" and internecine fighting among them and indicting the eco-nomic dependence of the Philippines on the U.S. market (192). He con-demns the independence missions as mere "Lip service! Propagandist nationalism! Not spiritual nationalism! Not economic nationalism! Not intellectual nationalism!" (194). When charged by a representative that "it is easier to preach than to practice" (196), Don Pedro is defended by his godson Juanito, who discloses to the amazed audience that the ex-iled figure had anonymously spent one-third of his "fortune" on various causes: campaigning for the Clarke Amendment, providing for Filipino lecturers in the United States, preventing the Americans from buying Moro signatures alleging that they were against independence, seek-ing to get European leaders interested in Philippine affairs, and work-ing with the Anti-Imperialist League in the United States. Exercising a version of what Benedict Anderson has termed "long-distance national-ism,"[39] Don Pedro retains his moral authority—his capacity to keep alive "the spirit of the revolution"—by inhabiting "the sanctuary of his exile" and dispensing his wealth behind the scenes (197). Indeed, in response to the postrevolutionary Aguinaldo's claim that "your absence from the Philippines has made you a mere theorist and philosopher," Don Pedro asserts, "There may be some truth in that, General. But right now, I prefer to be a theorist and idealist, rather than dip my hands in the mire of present politics" (185).

In contrast to Don Pedro's idealistic, inflexible nationalism practiced from afar, Juanito represents the figure who gets mired in the machinations of the domestic political scene. What is noteworthy is how his transition from "the spirit of the revolution" of 1899 into the compromised world of Philippine politics is rendered through his erotic attachment with and subsequent abandonment of Josefa (197). Don Pedro's nationalism is largely disembodied and abstract. In his impassioned speech, he censures the politicians for failing to "renounc[e] our political privileges, our pork barrels, and our posts as executives and legislators." If "we did not win our immediate freedom," he goes on, "we would, at least, have triumphed over our greatest enemy—ourselves. The spirit would have conquered over matter" (195). Whereas Don Pedro's austere "didactic discourse" and shaming exhortations allegorize at the political level the novel's "spiritual" nationalism, the romance of Juanito and Josefa operates on the dramatic, affective level by constituting and appealing to an "eroticized nationalism."[40]

Filipino nationalism as it emerged at the end of the nineteenth century is implicated in heteronormative presumptions. Whereas scholars have examined the integral roles that gender and the "romance" played in propelling and legitimizing U.S. imperial intervention in the Philippines,[41] it is equally crucial to recognize how gender and eroticism were constitutive of early justifications for the revolution and imaginings of the nation. As Vicente Rafael writes, "the revolution was conceived in the writings of both Spaniards and Filipinos in the most intimate of terms: as a family romance gone awry":

> To the Spaniards, Filipinos were ungrateful children whose demands for separation meant only one thing: the murder of all Spaniards. The Filipinos . . . thought of themselves as once loyal sons and daughters who were no longer able to bear the neglect, the insults, and the violence of the father and so were forced to rise and kill him. By so doing, they, or at least the sons, could in turn seek to father a new nation. In giving up their desire for Mother Spain, they also conjured a new mother, *Inang Bayan* or Mother Philippines, of

which they were both its sons and its fathers. And they did so only by repudiating, to the point of killing, those who had long claimed primacy over the country's paternity.[42]

By narrating the separation from Spain as a resu't of a "mother's" neglect and abuse of her "son," the *ilustrado* rendering of revolution constructed an elaborate metaphorics of the family w¹ ,reby the Filipino (male) patriot's once-affectionate regard for Mˑ ᵤer Spain is transferred to *Filipinas*—a feminized entity that fˑ ₋s at once as motherland and as female lover. Usurping the ⌐ ᵤ of the old Spanish "father," the sons of Mother Philippir⌐⌐ ₋₂⁴ ᵤmultaneously become the new fathers of the reconstruⲅ ᵥith the onset of U.S. colonialism, Rafael proceeds to sⱱ ᵤghly charged metaphors of family, love, betrayal, ingratitude, ᵣₑₘ.enge" are replaced with such "evolutionary" tropes as "'tutelage,' ᵢ ᵤturity,' 'race,' and 'development'" (368). While Kalaw's political treatises reflect this tropological transition, *The Filipino Rebel* recurs to the family-romance narrative as a means of reinvigorating "a new nationalism."

A youthful twenty years old at the start of the novel, the "attractive" Juanito is the orphaned son of "a wealthy Filipino girl" and a father of Spanish descent (5). While in Aguinaldo's army, Juanito and a few fighters flee the punishing reconcentration system and General Bell's announcement to create a "howling wilderness" in the province and head toward Mount Makiling (47). On the way, they are shot at by American soldiers, Juanito jumps into a nipa hut where a family is eating breakfast, and the daughter Josefa attempts to protect Juanito from the Americans by embracing him as her "esposo" (50). Juanito is nonetheless identified as a revolutionary; the two of them are arrested, escape their captors, and return to Josefa's house—only to find it burned to the ground, her mother killed by the "shock" of her daughter's capture, and her father shot by the Americans (58).

Fatefully brought together by improbable chance and family tragedy, Juanito and Josefa engage in a brief love affair during "the halcyon days of the revolution" (97). In a chapter suggestively titled "Love in a 'Howling Wilderness,'" Kalaw writes:

> The misfortune that befell Josefa's family, and Josefa's own plight had a strange effect on Juanito. On the one hand, it did not take him long to be convinced that he loved her and that he gloried in

being near her. His enthusiasm to continue the fight was increased because of her presence and his desire to avenge her wrongs. Still he could not but feel guilty for being indirectly the cause of such a misfortune. He was in love; yet during those days of grief, how could he dare press his case or show his affection to one so burdened with sorrow? (59)

Here, erotic attraction becomes the impetus for nationalist vengeance, even while it is the accidental encounter between Juanito and Josefa that had embroiled the family in the turmoil of war. Death mediates both patriotic and erotic fervor, inciting the former while checking the latter.

But it is when Juanito reveals his love that the eros of nationalism and romance become indistinguishable:

Josefa, please do not evade me any more. I love you. In the midst of our country's sufferings, in the midst of my hardships and privations for our ideal, you have come into my life. You have come to stay. You have come as the very symbol of our beloved land, young, beautiful, and deserving of a better fate. Let me care for you, just as I care—as you care—for our dear Filipinas! (61)

In Juanito's mind, Josefa simultaneously serves as consolation for the "privations" of freedom and independence, as the embodiment of the "ideal" for which the revolutionaries are fighting, and as the twinned object and subject of nationalist "care."

The identification of the beloved female with the "beloved land" is a familiar trope of male nationalist thought, and Kalaw's initial descriptions of Josefa certainly support that conflation.[43] When Juanito wonders whether Josefa's embrace of him as her husband had indicated anything but a guileless ruse to save him from his pursuers, Josefa's "pretty face and expressive brown eyes" assure him that "there was nothing of the flirt and the wanton in her behaviour, and he felt satisfied it was a spontaneous desire to save him." Her barrio background, untainted by shameless urbanity, makes her "an innocent but intelligent country girl . . . unmarred by any artificial devices" (51). Josefa's provincial lack of artifice is reinforced when the two of them head farther into "the virgin forests of Mount Makiling" (67). Juanito's elation in this new environment stems from the same source as does his attraction to Josefa: "What a feeling of mixed pride and ecstasy the sight of those forests gave him! What a change from the cultivated lands of Corrales!" (67). Kalaw uses the term "virgin" no fewer than three times on the same page. The link between the virgin forest and the unsullied maiden is made plain as Juanito looks "at the girl beside him, fresh and young, modest and demure, unspoiled by the conventionalities of the city, brave and courageous, fearless in the face of danger" (68). In these early scenes, Josefa is portrayed as a kind of pastoral figure whose local knowledge enables the small group of guerrilla fighters to survive on edible vines, whose "rich though unschooled voice" lifts their morale as she sings "those native airs which she knew so well" (63), and whose "tender care" nurses Juanito and "infuse[s] life in him" when he falls ill with malaria (68).

Given the close association of Josefa with "our dear Filipinas," it is not surprising that Juanito's downfall is dramatized by his rejection of Josefa as he embarks on what the novel calls "political materialism." Persuaded to surrender to the Americans, Juanito takes "the oath of allegiance without a moment's hesitation" (75), studies and practices law, and eventually becomes an aspiring politician on the national stage. By the time he decides to run for the Philippine Assembly in 1907, Juanito believes that "he must ally himself with a wealthy and influential family to insure his political supremacy" and rationalizes that "he was not married to [Josefa] legally" anyway (80). The blissful effulgence of cross-class love that had blossomed in the crumbling social structures during the war gets de-romanticized and reconfigured into a neofeudal means of securing political alliances among "prominent" families once the colonial government is institutionalized.

Juanito eventually marries Don Pedro's daughter Leonor, "an entirely different type from Josefa," who had "been brought up a spoiled child" in a French convent in Hong Kong (100). Juanito reckons that "Leonor was the girl—for him" since she is "wealthy, and the daughter of the famous Don Pedro whose prestige in Philippine politics was ever on the ascendant" (100, 101). While using the Ricaforts' wealth in campaigning for the assembly and later for the senate, Juanito gets mired deeper in corruptive political practices of buying votes and exchanging favors. He is eventually brought to defeat by Don Pedro himself, who decides that his godson's collusion with a U.S. corporation is the final straw. Leonor, meanwhile, acts as the conduit through which the two male politicos are "reconciled" (160). Her death not only effects the reunion of her husband and her father but also clears the way for a revaluation of Josefa.

Though abandoned by Juanito, Josefa does not remain the passive female who must be rescued by a more heroic male savior. When Juanito and his fellow guerrilla fighters surrender to the Americans, Josefa immediately recognizes that their class differences, which seemed incidental during wartime, will adversely affect their relationship during peacetime: "We have been so happy here in the midst of our hardships that I am afraid of what will happen to our love once we enter the peaceful life" (74–75). Juanito's subsequent actions confirm Josefa's well-founded anxieties.

Josefa's initiative first takes the form of remaking herself into someone "worthy" of her beloved's new station (97). She moves from the barrio to Manila, attends the American Mrs. Jones's class, devotes herself to studying English, and seeks to learn "the ways of high governmental society" from Doña Maria (95). In four years, Josefa transforms herself from "the rustic country maiden of the revolution" into "a refined and well-educated city girl, speaking both Spanish and English fairly well" (96). At the same time, given Josefa's identification with the feminized pastoral homeland, we are assured that "she did not adopt the free ways of the American girl" (96). Despite her efforts at self-transformation, her class and regional background remain liabilities to one who treads the path of political materialism. When she later learns of Juanito's marriage to Leonor, Josefa extends her practices of self-cultivation to traveling to the United States. "There," Josefa thinks, "she would attain success and distinction so that she could return to the Philippines a woman of whom even Juanito, in his own selfish political ambitions, would have to sit up and take notice" (109).

Josefa eventually makes good on her vow and becomes a truer representative of "Filipino patriotism" abroad than Juanito could ever be at home (178). What the Philippine political system, established and evolved by the U.S. colonial administration, had offered the aspiring male politician Juanito—upward mobility and social prestige—so would "America" itself offer the ambitious Filipina patriot. Indeed, Josefa takes advantage of her class position and resolves "to show you and your people that the people in the barrio can, if given the opportunity, progress," as she asserts to Mrs. Jones in Manila (110). Positioning herself as a cultural ambassador, Josefa states, "I will also make it my task to tell your people what I know of my people" (111).

Oddly, however, we do not actually witness her life in the United States. That Kalaw eclipses Josefa's experiences in the United States may be symptomatic of the broader lack of Filipina representation during this period. The small number of Filipina migrants resulted from gendered ideologies and economic realities that encouraged young adult men to work and/or study abroad, while confining daughters' and wives' roles to the domestic sphere to preserve transnational familial ties.[44] Those women who did migrate took up a range of occupations, from household and janitorial work, to teachers and entrepreneurs.[45] In this respect, the sparse details that Don Pedro gives about Josefa are rather remarkable: "She is coming partly on behalf of the Woman Suffrage Association of America, to see if our women could be more active in their campaign for suffrage. For the last ten years, Miss Liwanag has been doing public-speaking work for our cause. . . . She has addressed more American audiences than Quezon or any other Filipino" (200–201). As though reprising the role that Clemencia Lopez had performed at the turn of the century,[46] Josefa locates herself as "a happy median" between Don Pedro's rigid nationalism and Juanito's complicit compromises and fulfills her self-appointed task: "It is only a question of telling them the facts," she informs the two men. "In all my travels in America, I have always met with the finest considerations. I have always felt myself safe. My appeals have produced often the most unexpected response" (203).

On the one hand, Josefa's optimistic picture of America starkly contrasts with the one Don Pedro paints of male workers in the United States. In his "nationalism" harangue, he reminds the political elites that "out there in the 'land of the free' our laborers were insulted and mobbed by infuriated thousands, their clubhouse bombed, and one of them actually killed!" (194–195). On the other hand, Josefa's sponsorship by a U.S. women's organization to push for Filipina suffrage suggests a more dynamic and politically complicated interchange, whereby a transnational and interracial women's agenda potentially comes into conflict with Filipino men's nationalist agendas (demanding independence without granting women the right to vote).[47] Clemencia Lopez had memorably stated in her address to the New England Woman Suffrage Association in 1902: "I believe that we are both striving for much the same object— you for the right to take part in national life; we for the right to have a national life to take part in."[48] Some twenty-five years later, Josefa combines both of these causes through multivalent modes of address, lobbying for Philippine independence while in the United States and for the Filipina vote while in the Philippines. As Mina Roces and Denise Cruz suggest, for Filipino women to take part in "national life" during the 1920s, however, would mean reconfiguring the image of "the Filipino woman" itself, expanding her designated place beyond the home, the club, and educational institutions and into public politics proper.[49]

Ultimately, however, we are given not firsthand accounts of Josefa's political work, but rather mediated reports of her U.S. successes transmitted through Philippine newspapers. After his defeat by Don Pedro, Juanito comes across the article "Filipino Woman Defines Patriotism," which describes Juana Liwanag (Josefa's pseudonym) at a Filipino convention in San Francisco declaring: "We have a past hallowed by the heroism and sacrifices of men who fought and died not for money, not for greed, not for social station, but for the triumph of an ideal, for the victory of a principle, for our liberty and independence" (178). Clearly, by having Juanito read this stirring oration, Kalaw is leveling a critique against politicians like him who have traded "liberty and independence" for "greed and materialism" (179). Indeed, although Juanito is unaware at this point that Juana Liwanag is Josefa, the exhortation nonetheless recalls her memory and his deserted ideals: "Josefa! The revolution! The lost Republic! These were what haunted the poor hunter as he roamed in the forests and the plains of Luzon in search of forgetfulness and solitude!" (179).

Though Don Pedro and Josefa, from their locations outside the nation, act as admonishments of Juanito's moral decline, none of the three positions is fully endorsed in the end. All of them are shown to be complicit with and somehow dependent on U.S. colonialism: Don Pedro's livelihood is funded by the skyrocketing real estate market of Manila; Juanito's political dealings are a result of the U.S. administration's "Filipinization" project of controlled appeasement; and Josefa's return as "conquering heroine" (205) is made possible by her belief in the ideology of "self-reliance" (109) and the optimistic notion that Americans are a "just and liberty-loving people" who "mean well towards us" (203). Her strategy of "telling them the facts" echoes the earlier addresses of Filipino intellectuals to end the Philippine-American War and resonates with the ongoing attempts of people like Kalaw himself to describe the implementation of a stable government and civic life—both of which, as we have seen, were patently ineffective. At the same time, Josefa does not merely speak but acts. Even as she symbolizes the barrio girl who can progress into a respectable and respected spokeswoman for her country, she also functions as a mechanism of castigation for Juanito's abandonment of her and his patriotic ideals. When he intuits that Juana Liwanag is Josefa, he thinks to himself,

"What an irony! He was a political failure; while she, the woman he had cast away, was a conquering heroine!" (205).

Though pragmatic insofar as it recognizes that the movement for independence is necessarily circumscribed by the conditions enforced by U.S. colonialism, the novel nonetheless remains idealistic insofar as it projects a future heralded not by a specific, individual character, but by an unnamed figure whose lack of particularity renders him as a kind of stand-in for a phantom (albeit male) collectivity. The novel's political "message"—its advocacy of independence—literally hinges on sex. In a letter reproaching Juanito for "forgetting" her, Josefa had earlier informed him of "our boy, your boy conceived in the revolution, in those heroic days when you fought for your country's freedom" (98). Juanito not only betrays woman and nation by reneging on a promise uttered "in the name of their country's freedom" (97); he is also unpersuaded to rejoin Josefa at the news of his son.

But it is the double meaning of "*conceived* in the revolution"—as intellectual creation and biological procreation—that is crucial to the figuration of Josefa and Juanito's child, the figure in whom the novel entrusts the nation's future. While Don Pedro and Josefa, in their speeches to Philippine and American audiences, respectively, recall and attempt to reinstill the lost "spirit of the revolution," the child, the product of love and war, literally embodies that spirit and brings it into the novel's present—but only by being de-particularized, rendered "anonymous." The novel closes with these lines:

> There is another hero that lives on, an anonymous hero. We have not even given him a name. We have not followed him; and we have lost track of him. But he lives on. He may have joined the rank of the common worker, the sinew of every nation, to help with his honest toil in the permanent upbuilding of his country. He may be a genius obscurely working in the laboratory, waiting for an opportunity to present his contribution to his country and to mankind. Perhaps, if you are generous enough, we may see him in this story as a national leader who, with his intelligence, his imagination, his patriotism, and his power of command, will at the appointed time lead his country to victory.
>
> We do know that in whatever line he has bent his energies, he will use them to clean the blot that his father has left behind, to the

supreme joy and everlasting happiness of his noble and sacrificing
mother—
    The son of Josefa. (211)

It is this figure of "the child"—nameless, untracked, and therefore potentially anywhere and everywhere—who, as Lee Edelman puts it, embodies "the telos of the social order and come[s] to be seen as the one
for whom that order is held in perpetual trust."[50] *The Filipino Rebel's*
gesture toward futurity is all the more pressing and poignant since Kalaw's dream of independence seemed to hover on an ever-receding horizon thanks to the colonial administration's de facto policy of indefinite
deferral.

By keeping open the male child's occupation—common worker, genius scientist, national leader—Kalaw envisions a future collectivity
whose class distinctions dissolve into the shared "contribution[s]" made
toward the "upbuilding of [the] country." And yet for all this progeny's
anonymity, the child remains beholden to the particularities of his pro-
genitors, born to redeem his father's moral "blots" and his mother's self-
less "sacrifices." In this regard, Kalaw proffers within the constraints of
U.S. colonialism "a new nationalism" whose gendered underpinnings
consign the female patriot to the symbolic role of long-suffering "mother"
awaiting redemption and renewal by her dutiful son: Josefa quite literally embodies the position of "Mother Philippines" and thereby reveals
the constitutive function of reproductive heterosexuality to the novel's
politics of independence.

To be sure, Kalaw implicitly interrogates the politics of kinship, class,
and marriage when he makes the child the offspring of two unmarried
orphans, neither of whom can claim familial privilege or status. That
Don Pedro's well-off, spoiled daughter Leonor is depicted as the wrong
choice for Juanito demonstrates not merely an idealization of the unspoiled barrio woman but, more important, the belief in individual merit
and progress, as opposed to fixed status stemming from class pedigree.
In fact, Kalaw had argued in one of his political essays that the Philippines had not had a feudal system based on blood lineage "for more than
two hundred years." According to him, "the centuries of Spanish domination completely effaced from the Christian population all blood and
family distinctions."[51] While recent historians would no doubt dispute
Kalaw's claim by pointing to the handful of extremely wealthy dynas-
tic families in the Philippines that make possible what Mina Roces calls

"kinship politics,"[52] Kalaw's rhetorical point appeals to the evolutionary advancement toward independence and democratic rule, exemplified by the *Propagandistas* who became "national leaders" "not for their princely blood, for they had none, but for their unquestioned ability."[53] "Without belittling what America has done for the Philippines," Kalaw argues, "it must be recognized that the progress towards democracy in the Philippines has been due mainly to the materials that America found there" (416). The orphaning of Josefa and Juanito thus dramatizes the moral and political stakes of individual "progress" beholden not to bloodline but to nation.

The novel's adamant belief in national redemption is premised on the promise of Juanito and Josefa's unnamed and unspecified bastard son. But this technically illegitimate child, whom Josefa passes off as her nephew to everyone except Juanito, is born "legitimately" from Josefa's point of view. In a letter from Josefa to Juanito, we are given assurances, again, of Josefa's sexual morality, that she is no "wanton" vixen but had "considered herself as his legal wife; for had he not assured her that that was the fact during the halcyon days of the revolution? Did he not ask Nanoy, the faithful assistant, to officiate as the priest, out there in God's woods while the stars were gazing at them, when he swore, in the name of their country's freedom, to take her as his real wife? Were not her scruples vanquished only when she was assured that when a priest was available they would be married according to form?" (97). Though the "halcyon days of the revolution" enable a momentary cross-class heterosexual romance, they do not entail a complete break with traditional marriage norms. As for what was "conceived" and brought forth under those unusual circumstances of "love in a howling wilderness," the potentially ubiquitous child evokes a decidedly secular order of hope, a political futurity whose fulfillment lies on and beyond the horizon of independence.

## Sexual Normativity and the Politics of Address

A few years after *The Filipino Rebel* was published, the Philippines was given a definite timeline for independence through the Tydings-McDuffie Act in 1934. Whether the monovalent modes of address used by Filipino "insurgents," politicians, or Kalaw during and after the imperial war made a serious impact on U.S. colonial policy is debatable given the length of time it took to pass the act. My point in discussing that early history is not to suggest that those intellectual and political leaders pursued misguided strategies or that those strategies were, in the end, opportunistic methods for maintaining what power they held under the U.S. colonial administration. Rather, I mean to draw out a basic history lesson that bears repeating. As Kalaw himself came to realize and articulate by the early 1930s (if not well before), the logic of U.S. colonial rule was predicated on a temporality of indefinite deferral such that the criteria for "fitness" for self-government could be manipulated in whatever ways the colonial government saw fit. No matter how much evidence was presented before Congress "proving" the Filipinos' capacity for self-rule, the colonial rulers held the power to recognize or not recognize those appeals. "While the hegemon was, in theory, compelled to cede some power when its criteria were absorbed and realized," writes Paul Kramer, "under the politics of recognition it would, by definition, never cede the authority to evaluate, to interpret or change standards, or to adjust the relationship between those standards and the granting or withholding of power."[54] Moreover, the evidentiary grounds of those presentations had to appeal to the "standards" that the U.S. government had already set up, thereby ensuring an intrinsically normative character to the arguments presented by the aggrieved. Never mind that what many of the nonelite classes who rebelled against Spain and the United States desired was something other than the formation of a modern nation-state cast in the mold of post-Enlightenment Europe.[55] Those manifestations of social dissatisfaction could not only be dismissed as sporadic "uprisings" instigated by superstitious religious "fanatics," but more devastatingly be regarded as further proof of the instability of the Philippines itself and therefore justify the need for continued colonial control.

Such historical reminders force us to think differently about the politics of representation, recognition, and address, particularly if "invisibility" is cited as the primary signifier of racial oppression that afflicts Filipinos in the United States, for it faces and makes demands upon the dominant culture to be *seen*. Delivering power over to those presumed already to possess it, this logic assumes that only the dominant culture has the privilege to dispense or withhold recognition—thus precluding or overlooking the possibility of Filipinos and others in nonprivileged positions of holding the reins of recognition.

To the extent that *The Filipino Rebel*'s "homeland" mode of address links reproductive heterosexuality and national futurity, it is also important to note that the close association between family and nation persists well beyond the colonial era. As Rhacel Salazar Parreñas points out, such imaginings have become institutionalized and written into Philippine law. The 1986 Philippine Constitution "unequivocally declared the 'Filipino family' as the foundation of the nation" and called on the state to "strengthen its solidarity and actively promote its total development."[56] The 1987 Family Code stipulates that "the Filipino family is founded on the absolute marriage and mutual respect of a man and woman and follows the script of cohabitation, women's maternity, men's authority, and familism, including filial piety" (36). Naturalizing hetero- and gender-normative ideologies, one judge and framer of these documents declared, "We must have strong marriages and strong families in order to have a strong nation" (35).

Though *The Filipino Rebel* participates in and reinflects this discourse of nation-as-family (a reconfigured nationalist family given Juanito's desertion of Josefa and their bastard son), it is not as though Kalaw's out-of-print novel holds a prestigious place in anglophone Filipino literary history. I have nonetheless analyzed it here to give some sense of how the other writers in this book engage differently with the politics of eroticism and nationalism. Implicitly and explicitly refusing the logic of assimilation, these writers also remain ambivalent about the equation between the family and the nation. As I explore in the next chapter, José Garcia Villa's modernist poetics emerges precisely as a rejection of the sexual norms operative in Philippine literary culture as well as the assimilative and ambassadorial expectations of U.S. social and literary culture.

# 2

# The Queer Erotics
# of José Garcia Villa's Modernism

ANGLOPHONE FILIPINO MODERNISM begins with a scandal. In the spring of 1929, a series of poems called "Man-Songs" appeared in the *Philippines Herald Magazine* under the name O. Sevilla. The pseudonym apparently did little to screen the poet's identity since, shortly after the third installment, José Garcia Villa was brought to court and fined 50 pesos for allegedly "polluting public morals."[1] Dean Jorge Bocobo of the University of the Philippines followed suit, deemed the poems "indecent and obscene," and suspended Villa, a sophomore in the College of Law, for a year.[2] In the midst of a subscription campaign, the *Herald* apologized in its subsequent Sunday issue for "offend[ing] the sensibilities of the readers" by printing "reading matter of ultra-modernistic tendencies."[3]

While these offensive poems led to Villa's suspension from the University of the Philippines, a rather different literary text enabled his departure from the Philippines itself. In August of the same year, Villa's story "Mir-i-nisa" was selected as the monthly winner of the first *Philippines Free Press* short story contest (which recompensed Villa his 50 pesos). Praised for its portrayal of "emotions . . . both human and elemental," the story went on to win the grand prize of 1,000 pesos—which its author promptly used to set sail for the United States.[4]

Villa's own estimation of "Man-Songs" and "Mir-i-nisa" was exactly the opposite of the judgments accorded them. In a letter solicited by the College of Law, he ardently defended "Man-Songs," as I explore below, while he later denounced "Mir-i-nisa" (tellingly not included in his only fiction collection published in 1933), calling it "absolute trash" merely "written to win the P1000 prize." "Without the money," Villa told interviewers years later, "I could not have come to the States; my parents wouldn't pay."[5]

These disparate evaluations arise from radically distinct conceptions of sexuality and the erotic. The folktale "Mir-i-nisa," set in a distant pre-colonial era, endorses normative sexual conventions by narrating a familiar story of two men competing for a beautiful woman. The honest suitor Tasmi wins Mir-i-nisa's hand, and we learn at the end that this "moral" is being passed down from mother to son, who is himself about to undertake a similar test. Heteropatriarchal pedagogy and generational transmission merge seamlessly in this "elemental" fantasy.[6]

"Man-Songs" could hardly be more different in its play with gender ambiguity and in its overt descriptions of nude bodies and sex. The opening lines of the final lyric "Testament," a sort of *ars poetica*, gesture toward what might be called Villa's queer modernism: "I have not yet sung as I want to sing. My songs are queer songs but when I grow older they will be queerer still."[7] In a formal sense, Villa's poems of the 1940s and 1950s did become more queer. Announcing his arrival with characteristic bravado in his first U.S. book of poems, *Have Come, Am Here* (1942), Villa went on to foreground a new poetic innovation in each of his three main collections: *Have Come, Am Here* introduced what he called "reverse consonance," a kind of inverted end-rhyme; *Volume Two* (1949) brought forth his infamous "comma poems" in which each word is followed by a comma; and *Selected Poems and New* (1958) presented a handful of his poetic "adaptations" of existing prose.[8]

Tracking Villa's "queer" experiments across a range of texts in his corpus, I contend that the literary practices through which he became "the inventor of modernist writing in English in the Philippines"[9] are elaborated not only through formal innovation but also through an equally experimental logic of love that de-privileges heterosexual coupling, procreative sexuality, and normative masculinity, while prioritizing an ethic of receptivity and intersubjectivity—a disposition akin to what Eric Keenaghan has theorized as a "queer ethic of vulnerability."[10] As the *Herald*'s ambiguously euphemistic reference to the "ultra-modernistic tendencies" of "Man-Songs" implies, Villa's "modernism," his revolt against tradition, takes place on both artistic and sociosexual terrains.

Philippine poet and anthologist Gémino Abad has written that, in "having rejected the Romantic and Victorian molds in poetry," Villa "was also the first to break the taboo on explicit sex, passion, and homosexuality in our fiction and poetry."[11] Abad's "our" reminds us that Villa's modernist "break" initially occurs in the Philippines, prior to his departure to the United States. The eroticism of "Man-Songs," published around the same time as Maximo Kalaw's *The Filipino Rebel*, is thoroughly distinct from the nationalist reproductive heterosexuality expounded in Kalaw's novel. Accounting for this earlier period in Villa's literary career thus necessitates a queer diasporic and cross-generic approach that an exclusive focus on his more well known poetry published in the United States renders impossible. But it also forces us to be wary of teleological readings that mark the Philippines as the site of repression and the United States as the place of liberation.[12] However much Villa may have resented what he perceived as the Philippines' aesthetic and sexual conservatism, his U.S.-produced poems may be read as "queerer still" only to the extent that the sexualized embodiment depicted in a poem like "Man-Songs" is transmuted into formal experimentality and metaphysical eroticism.

Villa was the first Filipino writer to garner acclaim from prominent Anglo-American poets and critics (including Marianne Moore, Edith Sitwell, Mark Van Doren, and e. e. cummings), but his experimental metaphysicality has led many critics in both the Philippines and the United States to view his work with skepticism.[13] While some U.S. commentators saw his formal inventions (especially the comma poems) as mere gimmicks or nuisances, Filipino detractors have faulted Villa for refusing to produce and promote a socially engaged literature that would address issues of class disparity, racism, and U.S. colonialism. Though Villa may no longer be "the most neglected twentieth-century writer on the planet," as E. San Juan Jr. described him in the 1990s,[14] the prevailing perception of him as an apolitical aesthete has nonetheless impeded approaches that exceed the colonialism/nationalism, aestheticism/proletarianism binaries.

My analysis intervenes in this critical deadlock by reconceiving the terrain of the "political" to include the erotic and the sexual—even, and *especially*, if Villa does not thematize "homosexuality in a politically self-conscious way," as J. Neil C. Garcia has written of Villa's autobiographical stories.[15] Though I agree that we should view Villa as "a socially conscious writer," my emphasis here aims less at constructing a Villa who "confronted the social stigma attending the nature of his desire, and wrote out this desire and celebrated it,"[16] than in examining the relations among artistic practice, form, and eroticism in a diasporic, colonial context. Extending San Juan's characterization of Villa "as a poet protesting commodified and reifying capitalist social relations" structured by colonial and imperial modernization,[17] my discussion suggests that Villa's valuing of art over the "attainment of a high [governmental] post or wealth" delivers an implicit critique of the colonial project of "Benevolent Assimilation" (CV 133). Declining a career as a doctor or lawyer (much less civil servant or politician) expected by his father and his family's well-to-do class position in Manila, Villa dedicated himself to art in an obsessive, even neoromantic fashion.

While some critics have interpreted that pursuit as a capitulation to U.S. colonial values at the cultural level, my analysis of several texts in Villa's *oeuvre*—"Man-Songs," the autobiographical stories in *Footnote to Youth: Tales of the Philippines and Others* (1933), poem "3" in *Volume Two* (1949)—provides a more complex account of the interplay among aesthetic theory, queer erotics, and formal innovation in Villa's work. Closing with a consideration of Villa's roles as critic and anthologist of Philippine literature in English, I further suggest that whereas Kalaw calls for a new nationalism embodied in the figure of the child, Villa challenges idealizations of reproductive heterosexuality and seeks to construct, even bequeath, a literary tradition whose peculiar domain is located in the tension between the national and the universal.

## A Queer Testament

"Man-Songs" has taken on a legendary aura but has not been analyzed in detail.[18] These poems retain interest because they reflexively figure Villa's poetics through embodied sexual and erotic metaphors, while also indexing the ways that Villa's reputation has waxed and waned according to the vicissitudes of colonial and neocolonial history. In 1929, when Villa was castigated by the university administration, he was also lauded by fellow students as a "hero" for his insistence on artistic autonomy. One editorial asserts that Villa's name "shall go down in history as that of a student who refused to be cowed by a Name, a Position. It is the name of a student who came to a death-struggle against a dean—and won gloriously."[19] The hyperbolic language notwithstanding, by the late 1960s and the resurgence of nationalist sentiment, Villa became "an easy target for charges of irrelevance, neocolonialism, and elitism."[20]

Although early editorials constructed Villa as a solitary, persecuted artist, "Man-Songs" itself is instigated by and thematizes intertextual and intersubjective relations. The first installment of the serial poem, dedicated "To Mona Vita and her woman-songs," is cast as a response to

Mona Vita's (Loreto Paras's) "Songs of Serenity," which appeared in the *Philippines Herald Magazine* the week before and is itself dedicated "To J. V. and his man-songs."[21] The third set of poems is similarly dedicated "To Mina Lys and her songs of desire," this time referring to Paz Latorena's pseudonym.[22] Both of these prominent women writers produced well-received stories (which Villa himself praised in his essays) and also wrote numerous "poems in prose" during the late 1920s for the *Herald*.

"Man-Songs," in other words, did not burst onto the Manila literary scene without precedent but is placed in a dialogic relationship with the "woman-songs" and "songs of desire" of Paras and Latorena, respectively. Paras's "Songs of Serenity" closes with this stanza:

> I shall give you the gift of serenity
> Like a cool kiss on your brow;
> You will learn the ways of soft-eyed songs,
> You will know the secret haunts of lost swans.[23]

In return, "Song I" of Villa's "Man-Songs" opens:

> You who have written songs for me,
> Listening to my man-songs,
> Have grown flower-soft
> With your love-hunger,
> Do you want my breasts?
> My breasts are desireless
> And yet man-hard:
> They could sow little male flames
> In you.[24]

Clearly, Mona Vita's "gift of serenity" did little to "cool" O. Sevilla's "man-songs." Right from the start, Villa plays with gender and body parts; the putatively male speaker's "breasts" are at once "desireless / And yet man-hard," able to "sow little male flames / In you."

Although the intertextual dialogue between "woman-songs" and "man-songs" seems to imply a heterosexual poetic exchange, Villa's "Man-Songs" becomes most "queer" when read as a nonlinear *series*. The ambiguity of what constitutes a "man-song"—some are sung by a man, while others are about or addressed to men—is enacted in the way the lyric voice oscillates between genders or is undecidable. The clever pseudonym "O. Sevilla" thus claims attribution (through the phonetic rhyming of names) for the poem's experimentalism, while simultaneously concealing José Villa's identity from possible recrimination.[25] But the "O." also leaves undefined the poet's gender identity, opening up possibilities for a more fluid poetic persona.

This shuttling between genders is constitutive of the ways that Villa stages artistic inspiration and reciprocity. In "Song to Artists," the feminine speaker acts as the erotic muse who calls upon the artist to "appreciate" her beauty and hear her song:

I shall be naked. I shall stand still. I shall lie.
I shall call on you to behold my nakedness.
You will understand: you are an artist.
I shall point to you my beautiful parts, my full parts:
I shall sing to you as I point.
I shall be rejoiceful,
I shall be a woman who has called, a woman who is not afraid.

Though the female speaker's "desire" to have her "nakedness . . . appreciated" appears to position her as the passive object of the artist's gaze, she is not silent; she casts out her voice in hopes that an artist can "[catch] the meaning of my song."[26] In doing so, the artist, one assumes, will respond in kind with a work of art that evokes her beauty. The antiquated "shall" thus posits a future in which the woman's call will be heeded, at the same time that it asserts the prerogative of sounding that call and rejoicing unafraid in her beautiful nakedness.

As though responding to this call, the speaker of "Song of the Waiting Lover" addresses and recognizes the source of his song: "You have come to me scattering songs from your woman-bosom. / I have picked up your songs with the gentleness of a bird yearning for a mate."[27] In metaphorizing poetic creativity as a transmission of "song" from "woman-bosom" to poet, "Song of the Waiting Lover" presages the more sexualized "Song of Ripeness," the notorious poem singled out for "offend[ing] the sensibilities" of the *Philippines Herald*'s readers. Likening coconuts to breasts ("The coconuts have ripened, / They are like nipples to the tree"), the poem represents the speaker as an immature "child" who will pick up the fruits and "suck their milk" once they have "grow[n] heavy and full." Whereas "Song of the Waiting Lover" figures inspiration as the conveying of "songs" through the airwaves, as it were, this poem imagines the acquisition of creativity through the transfer of bodily fluid: "I shall suck out of coconuts little white songs."[28]

Villa explicitly connects erotic and poetic energy in "Song of a Swift Nude" by reconfiguring the act of "sucking" in "Song of Ripeness" as a submission to sexual penetration. Here the two senses of fluidity (gender and sexual liquid) come together to figure poetic creativity:[29]

> I am naked,
> I am beautiful,
> I am swift:
>> There was a man clung to me and he was big
>> and tall and his arms were as wrought iron.
>> The muscles of his body rippled as he sowed
>> his song into me and I quivered bravely.
>> He was weak when his song was ended and I
>> became strong with it.
>> I arose and I danced:
>> I was become swift and I ran away from him.[30]

Depicting a male as the source of music, "Song of a Swift Nude" figures sexual intercourse as the conduit for the transference of song. "Song," here, is both a metaphor for seminal fluid ("he sowed / his song into me") and the product of that insemination—the poem itself. The shift from present to past tense, marked by the indented lines, clarifies this circular temporality. The beautiful swift nude can only sing of and celebrate itself once it has received the man's song. Moreover, the power relations implied by the speaker's "feminized," penetrated position and the man's "wrought iron" muscles are reversed: the latter has become "weak" and spent after ejaculation, while the former has become "strong with it." And yet the paradoxical description "quivered bravely" also connotes orgasmic shuddering, the body losing—even sacrificing—control at the very moment that semen/song is sown into that body. Thus, even as Villa inverts gendered categories of strength/weakness, penetration/reception, he also points to the fear and vulnerability that being penetrated—possessed by song—involves and the consequent bravery entailed if the speaker is to go on to sing its song.

The concluding poem of "Man-Songs," "Testament," reflects on the poet's achievements and shortcomings while projecting a future when his ambition to create "stranger songs" will be matched with the competence to do so. It begins:

> I have not yet sung as I want to sing. My songs are queer songs but when I grow older they will be queerer still. I shall write stranger songs. It is that I am filled with many quaint thoughts and I myself cannot understand them. I am confused and helpless. I cannot understand my own unorthodoxy.
> I write songs to put the house of my mind in order.[31]

In this counterintuitive testimony, the poet seeks to come to terms with his confusion and "unorthodoxy" not by producing more familiar poems but by formally ordering poems that create queerness.

Such a literary practice, however, is not without its risks. While Villa would garner plenty of disparaging commentary for his formal iconoclasm,[32] the last stanza of "Testament" registers the threat that a queer poetics poses to the poet's subjectivity: "A song is a knot untied. I have many knots to untie. As I untie them I become a poet whose hands are trembling." As with the swift nude's brave quivering, involuntary shuddering arises at the very moment that song is born. If to be penetrated by song is to be open to the power of song, then to untie a knot signals the reverse: an opening up that releases song, a surrendering of the control that knottedness attempts to preserve. The poet's trembling hands, moreover, not only figure this anxious abdication of psychic, emotional, and bodily control, but also resonate with religious overtones: the fear and trembling that attend the presence of the divine—resonances that the religious language of Villa's later poetry evokes more explicitly.

Given the graphic nature of "Man-Songs," it is not surprising that Villa was reprimanded by the court and Dean Bocobo. Villa's response in his letter of defense to the University of the Philippines, however, is less obvious. He moves from legitimizing representations of nude bodies and sex, to reconceptualizing what constitutes "beauty" and emphasizing the spiritual realm behind those depictions: "Artists find beauty even in physical ugliness, in grotesqueness, in what is dark—it is the beauty behind, the beauty transcendental. This the ordinary mind, the untutored, cannot see" (*CV* 301). If the Philippines were less "backward in the arts," argues Villa, its readers would be more adept at deciphering the beauty beneath the nude body: "Why is it that the public sees only the superfice? If the physicalities involved in my poems are offensive to them, why can't they go deeper? I am sure they will find something beautiful behind. Unearth, unearth" (302). Villa goes on to chastise those "prudes" who "see only the body": "you touch it with Pharisai fear, so you cannot reach the soul. But you must reach for the soul—always" (302). This injunction to "unearth" and "reach for the soul" not only exhorts a "fettered" reading public to see through the "screen of conventional morality" (302). It also explicates Villa's poetics. To "unearth" is to disinter and bring to light what lies buried beneath the "superfice," to illuminate what Virginia Woolf memorably called "the dark places of psychology."[33] But it also means to spiritualize, to make not-of-this-earth, a practice of divinization that his short stories and his later poetry repeatedly enact.[34]

## Serial Eroticism and Migration

Insofar as the prospect of writing "queerer" songs at least partly motivates Villa's migration to the United States, the autobiographical stories in *Footnote to Youth*—"Wings and Blue Flame: A Trilogy" (which includes "Untitled Story," "White Interlude," and "Walk at Midnight: A Farewell"), "Song I Did Not Hear," and "Young Writer in a New Country"—record the process whereby he is able "to put the house of [his] mind in order." These interconnected stories trace an unnamed narrator's migration from the Philippines to the United States, his first year as a student at the University of New Mexico, and his arrival in New York. Intensely focused on interiority and metaphysicality, these stories are organized around a dialectic of "spiritual decentralisation" and "later integration," as he writes in his first essay composed after moving to New Mexico, enacting a dynamic that weaves together the dislocations of migration and erotic loss, while bringing forth a portrait of the artist narrative that enters to rescue, as it were, this "dissociated" self. The "spiritual precipitate" that emerges is indeed a new self—given birth through the very practice of autobiographical writing (*CV* 52).

The innovative form of these stories—a trilogy (or tetralogy, to include "Song I Did Not Hear") structured by numbered paragraphs—combined with the candid representation of homoeroticism, constitutes his queer modernist practice at this juncture. Formally and erotically queering what he had disparaged as the ubiquitous "Love Story" in Philippine literature in English (*CV* 37), Villa invents a serial form that reconstructs narrative continuity out of the experiential discontinuities caused by displacement and unrequited love. Seriality enables Villa to cross national divides and disrupt linear assimilationary time, returning to past memories in the Philippines (and even imagining birth itself) while projecting fantastical experiences of living in New York even before he moved there. In this regard, the numbers do not so much record "the mechanical aftermath of loss,"[35] or mimetically reflect the "breakdown of realistic continuity" produced by "Villa's shock of initiation into industrial society";[36] the "open form" of seriality refuses "the 'mechanic' imposition of an external organization"[37]—including the rigid conventions of immigration and heterosexuality. Rather, the digressive drifts and compulsive repetitions instance what Judith Halberstam describes as a mode of "queer temporality" that develops "in opposition to the institutions of family, heterosexuality, and reproduction."[38]

The numbered paragraphs not only queer time and enable narrative flexibility but also give shape and intensity to the homoerotic affect. Villa's definition of literature, proffered while in the midst of publishing the trilogy in *Clay*,[39] is particularly suggestive: "great literature is predicated on a far higher, nobler concept [than entertainment]: the concept of sublimation, of transfiguration. Great art is the spiritual sublimation of the unassimilable reality: it has to do with spiritual experience, with internal crucifixions, with visions transcendent. True literature is the notation of the incommunicability of the soul" (*CV* 59). However much this "sublimation" theory of literature resonates with connotations of the closet, Villa does speak that love through a peculiar mix of frank declaratives and elaborate metaphorologies. Unlike some of the U.S. male homosexual fiction of the period,[40] the narrator's suffering does not arise from an intolerant society's homophobic persecution but from the unrequited love he bears for his friend Jack at the University of New Mexico. Whereas the *New Republic* claims that "reality" in these stories is "bursting forth" out of control "in spite of the author's effort to mold it into conventional forms,"[41] I view the numbers as channeling "into controlled flow," and even helping to produce, that "pure, searing emotion" that most reviewers find so troubling by imbuing the stories with a kind of measured "rhythm"—perhaps, even, a "pulse."[42] One might further read the stories' "lyricism" as a fusing of the serial form with the autobiographical "I," approximating and moving toward the lyric form itself. Although the paragraphs are not represented as individual or distinct prose poems, they nevertheless anticipate the seriality of Villa's later numbered lyrics.

The stories' associational structure defies plot summary, but the pattern of loss and substitution remains constant, a kind of serial monogamy that mirrors the narrative's form. The trilogy opens with the narrator in "Untitled Story" being separated from the homeland and his beloved:

1

Father did not understand my love for Vi, so Father sent me to America to study away from her. I could not do anything and I left. (73)

Once enrolled at the University of New Mexico, the narrator first substitutes Vi with David:

14

One day a boy knocked at my room. He was young and he said he was alone and wanted to befriend me. He became dear to me.

15

The boy's name was David. He was poor and he wore slovenly clothes but his eyes were soft. He was like a young flower. (75–76)

When David's poverty renders him unable to pay for school, the narrator writes one isolated sentence: "I died in myself" (76). He eventually replaces David with Georgia, and then, after an unexplained "quarrel" with her (79), forms an attachment with Aurora, who substitutes for Vi and assuages the narrator's anger against his father (89).

It is unfortunate that "Untitled Story" has been anthologized on its own, since it gives a false impression of formal closure and heterosexual resolution.[43] The second story, "White Interlude," breaks through the temporary peace of Aurora's "song of serenity" by combining the serial form of the trilogy with queer erotics (87). The narrator's love for and loss of *David* undoes the previous story's happy ending:

1

After David left, because he had no money for school, I was very alone. I thought of him much as if he were part of me and his going away left me unwhole. I cried at night wanting to be whole again but knowing it would never be. (93)

With the loss of homeland and Vi giving way to the loss of David, "White Interlude" and the subsequent stories become increasingly homoerotic as the female characters drop out almost entirely and the narrator's love for Jack attempts to compensate for David's departure. Worried about the impending summer break and the departure of his college friends, the narrator reflects:

86

I did not want to miss Jack now. I wanted to ask Jack if he would miss me but I could not ask it. In the night I cried because I could not tell Jack I liked him. (111)

Though the narrator does not elaborate on what prevents him from divulging his feelings, his silence seems to stem more from Jack's lack of reciprocation than from any shame or fear about revealing homoerotic desires.

The narrator discovers that his love for Jack will never be returned when the latter "crush[es]" a letter from his previous friend Morgan, whom he now calls a "son of a bitch" for writing to him (113). The narrator's attempts to retrieve the letter prove in vain, and he recognizes that "I would never be lost to Jack for Jack never could lose anything" (114). He nevertheless resolves to uphold his earlier decision to remain love's protector ("I am like a great mother wing nourishing loves and never deserting them" [95]):

23

And now I learned to like Jack a lot.—Now I have a friend and I will keep him. I will love him. I will be good to him. God, let him love me even as I love him. . . . (122)

His prayer does not come true, and the figuration of love as introjection of the beloved leads the narrator to expel Jack. In the climactic scene of the trilogy, the narrator heads out onto the desert mesa at midnight and experiences a kind of spiritual purgation: "And I knew that when I lay on the ground, with the sky wet with stars above me, I was taking Jack out of me and giving him to the earth and to the sky, and the white flowers in my hands were my gifts of forgiveness" (130). Witnessed by his faithful companion Johnny (who quietly and unreciprocally loves him), the narrator resists the suicidal seductions of the divine ("stronger God ran His fingers through my hair") and refuses reunification with God in death (130).

Though this scene of expulsion and forgiveness seems to round out the trilogy, "Song I Did Not Hear" again disrupts narrative closure by carrying the serial form beyond the bounds of the trilogy proper. Unable to "unlove Jack" (256), the narrator reinterprets his experience so that "it was not Jack that died by God's hands but myself. God took pity on me and gave me a new life, free of the hurt of the past, but my new life carried too the spark of love for Jack" (257–258). Answering the narrator's death when David departed ("I died in myself"), this "new life" is not exactly a transcendence of "unwholeness." Rather, the narrator manages to accommodate the love-object without experiencing that incorporation as either an irritant that needs to be removed or a loss that needs to be regained.

The narrator's resolve to remain love's custodian despite the pain it causes is intimately tied to his artistic vocation. Villa's portrait of the artist positions love and art in opposition to his "moneymaker" father, who is tellingly described as "not a lover" (78, 105). Reflecting on his father's decision to send him away from Vi to study in the United States, the narrator states:

39

I was very angry I became a poet. In fancy my anger became a gorgeous purple flower. I made love to it with my long fingers. Then when I had won it and it shone like a resplendent gem in my hands I offered it to my father.

40

My father could not understand the meaning of the gorgeous purple flower. When I gave it to him he threw it on the floor. Then I said, "My father is not a lover." (80–81)[44]

In this imaginary generational conflict, the narrator's powers of "fancy" not only enable him to convert emotional crises into literary metaphors but also to reconstitute himself as an artist. Becoming a lover-artist entails rejecting both the father's stony prohibition against love and art, and his insistence on imperial education.

The oblique retrospective narrative "Young Writer in a New Country" dramatizes the narrator's love, loss, and "new life" as the birth of the artist, simultaneously rendering a queer critique of both the father and of biological reproduction (thus, of father*hood*). The piece adopts a queer temporality from forced exile, to loneliness in "the new country," to homoerotic companionship, to literary production, to rebirth:

> Little by little calm comes to my mind. Little by little comes my white birth—a white cool birth in a new land.
>
> It was then that my stories were born—of the homeland and the new land. Some of you may have read them—they were cool, afire with coolth.
>
> I, father of tales. Fathering tales I became rooted to the new land. I became lover to the desert. Three tales had healed me. (301–302)

Recasting the language of reproduction to figure literary creativity, Villa at once authorizes himself as an artist by usurping the position of "father" and lays claim to the United States, imagining that his stories, fathered in the "new land," might sponsor their progenitor for citizenship in the "Republic of Humane Letters," as San Juan ironically terms it.[45]

Does this therapeutic literary self-genesis depend on erasing racial and colonial difference? That Villa's stories construct a social world devoid of other Filipinos appears to imply as much.[46] Furthermore, it might be tempting to read the narrator's love for Jack—the most "Nordic" character (his father is Swedish) as well as the least effeminate (David, the young flower with the soft eyes, recites poetry [76]; Johnny sings arias from *Tannhäuser* in the streets [103]; Joe, who also insists on his soft eyes, writes a love letter of reproach to the narrator [260])—as energized by his position as the feminized "foreigner" (99) of color who seeks to secure the recognition of masculine whiteness and, failing that, attempts to reinvent himself in the image of his love-object. A contemporary perspective might look on this desire with deep reservations, presuming that it indicates a sense of racial self-loathing and a misplaced yearning to become "white."[47]

As politically seductive as these interpretations may be, "Young Writer in a New Country" turns out to be a critique of Depression-era "America" delivered along the axes of gender and class, if not race. First of all, Villa does not portray the narrator as the unloved feminized foreigner forever fated to chase after whiteness. Not only does Johnny love the narrator, but Joe Lieberman at the end of "Song I Did Not Hear" writes a letter rebuking the narrator for preferring Jack over himself:

> I saw light and beauty in you—I laid myself at your feet waiting for your door to open. I knocked many times. I knocked with prayer and madness and love. But now . . . I am tired. God, I am tired. I waited for your hand to stretch a little beauty to me, a little softness, a little warmth—it never came, it never came. If you could feed honey to swine . . . you could have fed me too. I *too* am low. But now I have run away from you. I have run away from *you*. . . . (260)

Alluding to Matthew 7:6, Joe implies that Jack is a swine who tramples underfoot and tears to pieces what is holy—Morgan's letter and the narrator's love, "light and beauty." Although the narrator had earlier vowed to "come to you, to you who have lost me" (113), he does not "hear" Joe's "song" until Joe has left school. This passage also echoes the narrator's previous description of Jack: "The house of Jack's life was walled thickly and nobody could break into him. . . . When people knocked at the gate of his life he did not understand" (255–256).

Jack's impenetrable masculinity contrasts with the portrayal of David, the figure to whom Villa returns to produce his critique of America. Employing the direct address in "Young Writer," Villa writes: "Do you see America getting clearer in my mind? Do you see myself getting articulate, getting voice?" (301). He implicitly answers his questions by pointing to "David who was poor, who wore slovenly clothes, whose eyes were soft. Of nights, walking on the streets, reciting poetry" (302). Asking "the country America: Why don't you make more Davids?" the narrator asserts, "But I know: Davids die poor. Even in my country Davids are not many. Civilization does not want Davids: You got no speed, David. You must be left behind" (302). Villa gets his voice, so to speak, by casting the impoverished, honest David as the abjected figure callously "left behind" by imperial "civilization" and modernization.

This critique encompasses the imperial metropolis as well. Retracing his journey from the Philippines to New Mexico to New York City, the narrator refuses the urban center as the endpoint of his migration and wants to return to "the peace of the *desert*" (303). As though articulated from this middle or "third" space, the final lines of "Young Writer" stage a multivalent ambiguity that renders the ending remarkably inconclusive—neither wholly triumphant nor utterly disillusioned:

Will the native land forgive? Between your peace and the peace of a
strange faraway desert—Between your two peaces—
O tell softly, softly. Forgive softly. (303–304)

Facing a U.S. audience, his yearning for "the peace of the *desert*" constitutes
a refusal of the modern city and whatever possibilities it might have afforded
for elaborating a queer sexuality.[48] Facing a Philippine audience, the narrator
could be asking the "native land" to forgive his abrupt departure, or asking
forgiveness for "telling" the kinds of "queer" stories that he has published.
But it is also possible that the final two injunctions arrive as if from elsewhere and are turned inward on himself, telling him to forgive those who
would stipulate a more "respectable" literary practice. Rejecting that man-
date, Villa conjures an in-between, imaginative space where he can leave
aside the burdens of representation demanded by either the native land or
the new country and pursue the writing of queer stories and "queer songs."

## Beyond the Controversy

The reactions on both sides of the Pacific indicate that Villa did not receive the kind of forgiveness or forbearance that "Young Writer" called
for. Among the more benign U.S. reviewers, Horace Gregory (the only
one to remark on U.S. imperialism in the Philippines) lamented Villa's
failure to perform the roles of immigrant interpreter of America or cultural ambassador of "important truths about his people": "his writing
springs from deeply seated emotional convictions, convictions I think
that will force him to write until the day of his death."[49] More derisive is
the reviewer from the *Washington Post* who makes overt the queer eroticism latent in Gregory's allusion to "emotional convictions," warning
readers of the "kaleidoscopic nightmare of highly colored adjectives denoting equatorial love in its various aspects: Filial, maternal, idolatrous,
and that David-and-Jonathan type which exists curiously indiscriminate
between boy and boy, boy and girl."[50]

In a re-created conversation between himself and Villa, Philippine
critic Carlos Quirino attributes this erotic indiscriminateness directly to
Villa's presumed sexuality:

"What do I think of your trilogy?" I replied to his question. "Well,
frankly speaking—I—I thought sex was the motivating factor . . . "

"No—no! I tell you—it isn't that . . ."

Perhaps Villa himself does not know how his trilogy ("Wings and Blue Flame") would strike other people. It is really an autobiography; a narrative of his life in New Mexico. . . . Although I'm no rabid Freudian, any modern psychologist could readily perceive the sex motivations that propelled his impulses and emotions. Like a delicate seismograph, Villa merely registered on writing what he felt—perhaps without knowing why. . . .

As his slight physique testifies, Villa is distinctly non-athletic. An occasional game of tennis is his only form of physical recreation.[51]

While Quirino's psychologism reads the texts as reflective of Villa's sexual "impulses" and dubious masculinity, I have been arguing that "the motivating factor" of the stories is not Villa's own sexuality, or even sex at all, but "love"—"love in the great sense," as he puts it in a 1936 essay: "By 'love' here is meant the struggle of the soul through loneliness and despair for unity and godship" (CV 134). Villa's evasion of sexual terminology bespeaks his insistence on the spiritual dimensions of experience.

While the autobiographical stories of *Footnote to Youth* depict the experiential basis of Villa's queer, erotic poetics (the reconstitution of the "artist self" as the outcome of lost homolove), his critical essays from the late 1920s through World War II provide the theory behind that literary practice, elaborating on the clustering of love, longing, and metaphysicality that becomes prominent in his poetry of the 1940s and 1950s. Abandoning fiction writing altogether, Villa foiled Edward O'Brien's conjecture in the introduction to *Footnote to Youth* that the Filipino immigrant "might well give us a new reading of the American scene in novels of contemporary life."[52] As a supporter of Villa's stories during the years leading up to the book's publication, O'Brien should have seen that Villa's work was moving in the opposite direction, away from documenting local "scenes" and toward evoking metaphysical and interior dramas, invisible to the casual observer, but compelling to the perceptive artist.

Though Villa emphasizes the need for formal innovation as we might expect ("I believe that experimentation is necessary for the revitalization of art" [CV 170]), his first essay, published in 1927, specifically targets the ubiquity of "The Love Story—not A Love Story": "The new writers who spring up like mushrooms simply cannot do without the love element," he wryly notes (CV 37). Urging Philippine writers to "unfetter themselves" from the reading public's "demands" for "ready-made, for-mularized stories," he nonetheless qualifies his critique in the following year's essay: "Of course we cannot totally discard the Love Story. . . . But an overdose of it is to be feared" lest "it becomes a sickly sentimentality, a fatuity" (*CV* 41). To avoid such sentimentalism, Villa recurs, in part, to the body/soul distinction first broached in his letter of defense. A few years after arriving in the United States, Villa reiterates his claim that the short story "is concerned with the revealment of the inner man": "Only insofar as it aids spiritual progress, only insofar as it unfolds char-acter, is external actual valuable" (*CV* 78).

Villa's emphases on interiority and spiritual reality would not go un-challenged by other Philippine critics and writers. In 1936, one of his contemporaries, Amador Daguio, takes Villa to task for promoting a "disembodied" poetics that "manifest[s] the spirit of man and woman by robbing them of the body" and thereby fails to "[reveal] the distinct race, the distinct country."[53] Though others disagreed with Villa, none was more systematic than Salvador P. Lopez during the late 1930s. In what has become known as "the Villa-Lopez controversy," Lopez advocated a "proletarian" stance toward literature and vilified Villa's alleged "aesthet-icism." Although this debate is well known in Philippine literary history, what has gone unnoticed is the extent to which Lopez's class critique of Villa is routed through gender and sexuality. To Lopez, Villa's "experi-ments in unintelligibility" are reprehensible not only because they fail to fulfill "the fundamental object of literature which is *communication*,"[54] but also because they are the weak effusions of a "degenerate" mind.

Throughout his denunciations, Lopez links masculinity with vigor-ous vitality and femininity with ailing anemia. In his discussion of Villa's first book of poems, *Many Voices*, Lopez writes: "There is something effete and bloodless in the lines of Villa, something that smells of the study and the parlor. . . . Here is no incisive phrasing, no robust energy as of a clear stream rushing swiftly through the woodlands" (143). In another essay, Lopez takes a thinly veiled stab at Villa by describing "a decadent aesthete who stubbornly confuses painting with literature and refuses to place words in the employ of man and his civilization" (157). Lopez's attack ul-timately rests on a rise-and-fall notion of history that views "decadence," and its connotations of effeminacy and aberrant sexuality, as a symptom of cultural decline. Referring to "the revival of a dogma once favored by Oscar Wilde and the coterie of aesthetes who agreed with him," Lopez as-serts, "the dogma of Art for Art's sake is the mark of a decadent generation, advanced and defended most stoutly by those who have irretrievably lost something of the vitality of nature through vicious self-indulgence or by those who have been tainted in the blood by some inherent vice" (162, 167).[55] Lopez makes clear that such a "tainted," masturbatory literature is deficient next to "clean, wholesome and vigorous" proletarian literature (199), what he calls a "red-blooded literature" (206–207).

Lopez was not the first to criticize Villa for "self-indulgence." Manuel Burgos Jr. published a parody of "Man-Songs" just three weeks after Villa's poem appeared:

> I am a Genius,
> I am a Poet,
> I am a Cad.
> I have many unsung songs to sing. And in the name of freedom, of liberty, of art I can be a libertine, I can sing songs of lust, deride virtue, laugh at innocence.
> Conventions to me are less than useless—clothes are indecent—virtue is a mere hypocrisy—innocence is deceit.
> . . . . . . . . . . . . . . . . . . . . .
> I can, therefore, express my thoughts stripped of all sense of propriety, of modesty, of decency.
> In the name of art, protected by the shield of the Poet, I can afford to be obscene, impure, indecent, lewd—with impunity.
> I commune with Shakespeare, with Chaucer, with Spencer [sic], with Whitman, with Anderson, and with the sainted Milton. Consequently, I can afford to be pornographic. I can teach sadism to the woman and the child.
> . . . . . . . . . . . . . . . . . . . . .
> I am physically unfit for certain physiological functions. I am epicene. I am a follower of Onan.
> What of it? I can say in songs that will never die what normal men would act—what I would do if I myself were normal.
> And the greater my impotence, the louder my songs, the lustier, the filthier. For I sing the song of Genesis, of Procreation, of Life, of Immortality.
> I am an Artist,
> I am Immortal,
> I am a God.
> I do not sin. I never err.[56]

Leveling the same criticisms of "Man-Songs" as the court and Dean Bo-cobo (lewd, indecent, obscene), Burgos's satire also reads the poem as reflective of Villa's epicene depravity (an abnormal and impotent liber-tine). Although Lopez's jabs are not quite as vicious, they nonetheless seek to skewer Villa's supposed heteromasculine shortcomings.

In "The Best Filipino Short Stories of 1937," Villa refutes Lopez's class critique. Describing how Lopez had accused him of squandering his stature as "the white hope of Philippine literature" by staying "aloof" from "social disorder" and "economic uncertainty and death" (*CV* 178), Villa defends himself by sharply separating art and politics: "Although I am a Left literally (which is to say, I have digressed from the conven-tional Right path of writing, and believe in experimentation) and (here is where Mr. Lopez is wrong, this fact he never presaged) although I *am* inclined to the Left politically and economically, still *I do not mix my politics and economics with my art*. It is for not mixing these together that Mr. Lopez assails me and has seen my literary perdition" (*CV* 178). Villa argues against the idea that "the economic readjustment of society [is] the function of literature" and emphasizes instead "the revolution of the internal personality of man. No matter how many economic issues and strikes a writer may involve in his work—such a work will always be overshadowed by one which portrays a single but true revolution of the human spirit" (*CV* 179).

Throughout his essays, Villa recurs to a wide range of European, British, and U.S. writers and philosophers—including Blake, Emerson, Goethe, Henry James, Lewisohn, Mann, Pascal, Rilke, Schopenhauer, and Thoreau, among others—to elaborate on his pursuit of the meta-physical and to insist on the moral dimensions of literature, contrary to Lopez's caricature of him as a frivolous "florist, scissors in hand, gather-ing lovely blossoms."[57] As Villa writes in a 1938 essay, "If a man is an artist he cannot approach things other than with love, and his work will therefore always be moral" (*CV* 198). And he extends this amorous dis-position to the effects of literature in a 1936 essay: "for great art, though pursued for esthetic reasons, always has a moral effect" (*CV* 135).

While some have read Villa's appropriation of Western sources as "colo-nialist,"[58] I interpret his citations as a transcultural practice of selective sifting for ideas that support his artistic views. In fact, Villa's metaphysical poetics is eccentric to some strands of Anglo-American poetry (one thinks, for exam-ple, of Pound's imagism or Williams's dictum "No ideas but in things"). In a 1955 biographical statement, Villa responds to the allegation that his poetry is "'abstract,' contrary to the general feeling for detail and particularity that characterizes most contemporary poetry," by saying: "The reason for it must be that I am not at all interested in description or outward appearance, nor in the contemporary scene, but in *essence*."[59] In refusing to be aligned with a particular "scene," it is as though Villa wants to be understood not according to categories of "outward appearance" but *as* "essence," an "Identity," as he calls it, that can only be accessed and evoked through experimental poetic techniques and that cannot be subsumed within the identitarian categories of "race" or nation—or sexuality for that matter.

In a Guggenheim application, Villa explains that his poetic interest in "essence" is motivated by "the search for the metaphysical meaning of man's life in the universe":

> It is my aim as artist to strive for the development and unification of the human personality—to arrive at the essential "I" . . . the "I" more than the individual, surpassing him and yet him—the very force and dignity of man. To reach that point where Man and God are in kinetic and heroic balance. The arrival at this Identity, and the working for it, I consider of primal importance: for only upon the Moral Man can the structure of a Good Humanity subsist.[60]

Again, in its adamant engagement with "Moral Man," Villa's lofty ambition is not aestheticist. Moreover, his pursuit of the "unification of the human personality" does not simply refer to economically induced alienation or a wishful Romantic organicism, but alludes to the psychological and social dissonance that U.S. colonialism created in the Philippines, as well as the "dissociations" of migration and unrequited love. One might read Villa's "essential 'I'" as that which is unseen, inaccessible to the gaze of a racializing regime and its optic techniques of surveillance.

A number of poems in *Have Come, Am Here* and *Volume Two* depict the relation between human and divine through scenes of embattled struggle and logics of inversion and reversal (divinizing the human, humanizing the divine). Though some have read Villa as a religious poet,[61] his "Theology , / Of , rose , and , // Tiger," as he puts it in one poem, is evidently not an orthodox Christianity.[62] Christian symbols and myths perform a similar kind of work in Villa's poems that the Western literary-aesthetic tradition had in his critical essays—as a repository of ideas and imagery to be improvised on rather than dogmatic tenets to be adhered to. In a 1936 essay, Villa writes that "the spirituality of great art is not theological, not the spirituality of religion—but is *metaphysical*. By metaphysics, I would have it mean: the consciousness of *being*, the knowledge of *becoming*: the path, the progress towards the godhead" (*CV* 135). In a 1950 letter to Philippine critic Cornelio Faigao, Villa further describes his unorthodox theology: God "is a name for the Fire in me. It exists Within me and not outside of me. 'God' is the Pure and the Good and the Noble that I create out of my energies and faculties; when I die, this I 'God' dies with me—i.e., his *actual* existence dies with my life—although the works he has instigated me to do may remain as Evidences of my God's having lived."[63] Again, Villa's "works" are posed as implicit substitutes for biological progeny, a view of literary posterity that I return to obliquely at the end of this chapter.

Poem "3" in *Volume Two* offers one evocation of this internal divine "Fire" by dramatizing the speaker's queer erotic relation to Christ, the iconographic (perhaps iconoclastic) "point where Man and God are in kinetic and heroic balance." Allegorizing the politics of recognition, Villa replaces the colonial gaze, as well as the gaze of the "native land," with that of the divine and pursues a metaphysical order altogether at odds with the social order he so deplored.[64] This is poem "3":

Much , beauty , is , less , than , the , face , of ,
My , dark , hero. His , under , is , pure ,
Lightning. His , under , is , the , socket ,

Of , the , sun. Not , Christ , the , Fox , not ,
Christ , the , Lord , His , beauty , is , too ,
Sly , too , meek. But , Christ , Oppositor ,

Christ , Foeman: The , true , dark , Hero.
He , with , the , three-eyèd , thunders , he ,
With , the , rigorous , terrors: , this ,

Man's , under , is , pure , lightning. This ,
Man's , under , is , the , socket , of , the ,
Sun. After , pure , eyes , have , peeled ,

Off , skin , who , can , gaze , unburned? Who ,
Can , stand , unbowed? Well , be , perceived ,
And , well , perceive. Receive , be , received.[65]

The poem's thematic complexity depends on its formal technique. According to Villa's "A Note on the Commas," "the commas are an integral and essential part of the medium: regulating the poem's verbal density and time movement: enabling each word to attain a fuller tonal value, and the line movement to become more measured." This emphasis on deceleration is consistent with Villa's dissatisfaction with the speed-up of modern life heralded in his sympathy for "the slowness of David." The "density" that the commas create on the page force the reader to slow down and consider the word's "tonal" resonance ("tone" implying both aurality and attitude). Though he says that the commas are used "*poetically*, that is to say, not in their prose function," the punctuation nevertheless regulates meaning in addition to time and sound.[66]

The disruption of linguistic instrumentalism and the rejection of racialized embodiment inform one another in poem "3." The inverted syntax of the first sentence mimes the queer erotics structuring the relationship between the speaker and Christ. These two elements come together when the transformation of the word "under" from preposition to noun figures an androgynous Christ: Christ's "under" is both a "socket" (the hollowed-out space where the sun rests) and the "pure lightning" that blazes from it. The resonances with "three-eyèd , thunders" and "pure , eyes" further figure the "under" as an eye-socket. The last phrases combine these meanings through the visual ("perceive") and sexual imagery of penetration ("Receive , be , received"). However, unlike the physicality of "Man-Songs," eroticism in this poem moves into the metaphysical as the focus on visuality gives way to the visionary. The question, "After , pure , eyes , have , peeled , / Off , skin , who , can , gaze , unburned?" implies that the "true , dark , Hero" has become the radiant Christ of the Transfiguration. It is not clear whether the skin has been peeled off the viewer's eyes (the proverbial shedding of scales), or whether it is the dark hero's skin that has been peeled off. In either case, the "dark hero" removing skin to reveal the divine within the human resonates with suggestive racial connotations.

This process of transfiguration extends to human beings in the last two lines. The "violation" of the comma's usual "prose function" renders ambiguous these phrases—direct addresses similar to those that close "Young Writer in a New Country" ("O tell softly, softly. Forgive softly"). The first "Well" could be read as an adverb modifying "perceived," meaning: "be perceived well." It could also be read as an interjection: "Well! Be perceived," or even "so then" or "in any case" be perceived. Its grammatical usage matters in identifying the speaker and the addressee, and in ascertaining the tone of that address. It might be the speaker addressing his dark hero, or the transfigured Christ speaking to the persona, or even the speaker addressing himself, closing the poem in a quiet murmur of self-consolation.

But it could also be the speaker addressing the reader directly. In this scenario, notice that "be , perceived" comes *before* "And , well , perceive." The poet does not say, "Perceive well and you shall be well perceived." Rather, it is Christ Oppositor's pure eyes that have peeled off the reader's skin, revealing the essential "I" within the human. This transfiguration comes through in the enjambed lines that begin the fourth stanza. Read straight across without the article of the previous lines, we get: "Man's , under , is , pure , lightning"; "Man's , under , is , the , socket , of , the , / Sun." What lies "under-neath" the surface of human beings (that is, their skin) is the same androgynous divinity that has been identified in Christ.

More often than not, Villa himself was not and has not been perceived by his readers in this light. His detractors have not been willing to receive him since he neglected or refused to engage in an aesthetic emphasizing class critique, Filipino nationalism, or ethnic pride. That the kind of recognition Villa sought was far from guaranteed may also shed light on the serial form of his poetry books. Like the numbering of paragraphs in the autobiographical stories, the numbering of lyrics is not geared toward teleological linearity, but rather makes possible a poetics of emergence and becoming ("the progress towards the godhead") through repetition and rehearsal. The yearning for "reintegration" with the divine turns out to be a process whose finality can never be achieved (save in death). The numerical ordering of the "Divine Poems" in *Volume Two*—"*The Divine Poems should be read in sequence as they form a progression,*" as Villa instructs at the beginning of the book—could thus be seen as the poet's attempt to guide the reader through a similar process of becoming. It might even serve an analogous function at the level of the book as the commas at the level of the poem: to regulate "the time movement" from poem to poem, while maintaining a sort of momentum that the isolation of each lyric threatens to curtail.

In this sense, the projected audience of Villa's poetry, unlike the transnational addresses to Filipino writers articulated in his critical essays, or the direct address to "America" in "Young Writer," is not nation-based. The next poem in *Volume Two* is addressed to God: "No!

*I , will , not , speak , softly. / — I , am , Thy , Lover , Lord!"*[67] It is as though the *mis*recognitions of his work and the nonreciprocity thematized in the autobiographical stories lead Villa to invent an alternative mode of address oriented toward an entity that recognizes the poet's aesthetic vocation and reciprocates his erotic longings. Consequently, the knowledge that his poems attempt to illuminate is meant to be universal, what he calls in his rebuttal to Lopez the "true revolution of the human spirit." While Carlos Bulosan, as we will see in the following chapter, invests, like Lopez, in the Marxist meaning of class revolution, Villa spins "revolution" to valorize a mode of subjectivity-in-process that revolves around "the internal personality of man." What is striking about Villa's reenchanted "humanism" in poem "3"—the perception that human beings are, in essence, divine—is that it does not rely on a lower order of subhumanity to secure itself as ontologically human (the enduring racial logic of colonialism). In relation to the divine, we are all relegated to a lower position. The poem suggests that the divine gaze guarantees human "dignity" precisely because its "pure" form of recognition is situated beyond the fallibility of human perception. Received in this light, we might then concede that our own otherness-to-ourselves—our own interior queerness perhaps—frees us to perceive, well, each other.

## The Critical Doveglion

Despite his efforts to extricate his work from national literary traditions, Villa was and continues to be located within national frames. U.S. reviewers invariably cited Anglo-American poets that he "must have" read (Blake, Dickinson, Stevens, cummings, and so forth), while more recent scholars have routinely accepted the corollary premise that Villa sought "access to the modernist canon"[68] and "elected to class himself, not with native writers, but with the literary avant garde in England and the U.S."[69] While understandable, this impulse to place Villa within an Anglo-American modernist tradition overlooks his critical and editorial work. His essays of the 1920s and 1930s and the four Doveglion anthologies of Philippine poetry in English that he assembled and published between 1962 and 1993 make evident that he did not abandon the Philippine literary scene when he left Manila in 1930 and try to insert himself into an Anglo-American one.[70]

The cultural work he performed as critic and anthologist enacts at the level of *criticism* what "Man-Songs," the autobiographical stories, and much of his later poetry thematize at the level of content by engaging in an ethics of reciprocity and a politics of recognition. Virtually no one in the United States was reading, much less writing essays about, Philippine literature in English prior to the 1970s. While Villa did not always follow his own counsel about approaching literature with "love" (in 1933, he began a "Criminal Record" in "contradistinction to the Roll of Honor" to commemorate "the most miserable examples of creative writing to come to my notice during the past year" [*CV* 94]), he did give praise when he thought it was due. The year after he started his Criminal Record, he writes that "although I am by nature a very unpatriotic man," "the Philippine short story makes me feel proud of the country. In rereading the stories that I have chosen for this year's Roll of Honor, a pride upsurged in me, a delight and satisfaction with the country that could produce such stories" (*CV* 99).

Villa's admission that he is "unpatriotic" points to another reason that his editorial endeavors are significant, for even while his literary practices strive to move beyond the nation as the primary evaluative frame of reference, the essays and anthologies repeatedly recur to the Philippines as a qualifying marker: "the best Filipino short stories," *A Doveglion Book of Philippine Poetry*. As early as 1935, he voiced his universalist aspirations: "in all my work, *I do NOT write about the Filipino, I write about MAN*. I am not interested in the Filipino as a separate brand of humanity—I am interested in him as a *human being*, as a *man*" (*CV* 110). Filipinos did, of course, comprise "a separate brand of humanity" in U.S. colonial and racial discourses of the first half of the twentieth century. And while Villa himself did not address these sociopolitical concerns in his own writings, his status as Filipino certainly inflected his reception.

In his criticism, he was equally adamant about dispensing with the nation as a criteria for judgment: "The inference is right that I have no chauvinistic interest in the Philippine short story. . . . I have never pleaded for the *Filipino* short story as pathetic American 'critics' plead for the 'the Great American Novel.' . . . American or Filipino, Scandinavian or Swiss, the nation is merely adjectival to true art: the noun is art and ever the universal humanity that it contains" (*CV* 168). This tension between the universal and the national is inherent to Villa's literary project: the "best Filipino short stories" of the 1930s and the anthologized Doveglion poems are supposed to transcend both their specific temporal moments and their national boundaries on the basis of their literary value.

Contrary to the commonplace that he was reclusive and *onanistic*, then, Villa remained deeply committed to reading, recognizing, and directing the course of Philippine literature in English. His efforts to construct a tradition of anglophone Philippine literature suited to his aesthetic views formalize a context in which his own work could be situated, made meaningful, and acquire a broader historical value. Far from escaping into a nonexistent universality,[71] Villa strove throughout his long career as writer and editor to ground his work within a Filipino literary culture (if not social reality) that, though influenced by him, could not possibly be circumscribed by his own proclamations.[72]

The late prose poem „A Composition,, (1953) might be read as allegorizing this tension between Villa's self-elaborating, divine-seeking, interiority-driven lyrics and his impulse to anthologize others' work. The second section of the piece reads:

> I was born on the island of Manila, in the city of Luzon. My country is the Country of Doveglion.
> The Country of Doveglion is a strange country: Boundaries it has none—and yet boundaries it has:
> Subhumans cannot live there.
> Only the *Earth Angels*, the true humans, may live there. These perceive my rigors, my perils and fervors, my hazards and possibles, my graces, my invincibles, and claim my citizenship: them I greet.[73]

Rearranging geographical names and their referents, Villa discovers his own "strange country" named after one of his pseudonyms (a contraction of "dove, eagle, lion") and lays claim to yet another "third" space that points to the limits of Villa's "I." Even as the speaker grandly deigns to "greet" the "*Earth Angels*" whom he so generously admits into his country, his "I" is nevertheless dependent on those who "perceive" him. Analogous to poem "3," the perception by the "true humans" enables the speaker to "fundamentalize and situate the I" (135), to "claim my citizenship"—not the other way around. Read next to his editorial work (the elitist rhetoric of "subhumans" notwithstanding), the poem implies that Villa's essays and anthologies enact the work of situating his "I" and his lyrics—in a space that is both imaginative and national.

Why should Villa have to invent this fanciful place? I suggested above that his autobiographical stories confound the archetypal trajectories of immigration-assimilation and exile-return. The narrator's yearning for the desert prefigures his "discovery" of Doveglion, and both spaces refuse being conscripted into nationalist projects. But if we return to the event that seems to have precipitated his departure from Manila—his suspension from the University of the Philippines for writing the "obscene" poem "Man-Songs"—we could also read the impossibility of assimilation and the consequent creation of the "Country of Doveglion" as a critique of the erotic and sexual norms operative *in the United States.* In the letter defending "Man-Songs," Villa compares the eroticism of "Man-Songs" to a host of passages from Sherwood Anderson's book of prose poems *A New Testament* (1927) and short-story cycle *Winesburg, Ohio* (1919), and yet the American author has "not been branded offensive or obscene" (*CV* 303). But if Villa surmised that migrating to and publishing in the United States would yield a more welcome reception, he was sorely mistaken.

The shift in Villa's poetics from the embodied erotics of "Man-Songs" and the homoeroticism of the autobiographical stories to the agonistic, yet socially acceptable, metaphysical desire of the poet for Christ and God constitutes both a concession to and a critique of those sexual norms. Villa's literal and literary trajectory (from Manila to New York, from fiction to poetry) implicitly interrogates what anthropologist Martin F. Manalansan identifies, with respect to contemporary diasporic Filipino gay men, as the reductive yet powerful "teleological narrative of the movement from tradition to modernity."[74] Emphasizing Villa's metaphysics and his conception of an internal, individualized God also complicates Luis Francia's allegorical reading: "Villa's God, with whom he wrestles, argues, talks, and plays, could be reasonably interpreted as the idea of America, a kind of promised land where the poet could find liberation from an oppressive society and a domineering father, to replace—though never completely—Old World/Old Testament contexts with New World/New Testament ones."[75] However "oppressive" Villa might have regarded the Philippines and his father, "America" did not turn out to be a "promised land" of sexual "liberation," judging by his writings. Whatever rigors, perils, fervors, hazards, and graces that the speaker of „A Composition„ pursues, suffers, and experiences, Villa would not or could not write about them in an explicit way, but rather mediated them through these alternative symbologies and ontologies.

His final poetic tour de force, "The Anchored Angel" (1953), carries Christian iconography and poetic opacity to new heights. Unabashedly obscure in its use of archaic images, neologisms, ungrammatical structures, and jagged line schemes, the poem elaborates again on the vertical connections that link the "*Earth Angels*" and God, with "the , swift , red , Christ" acting as intermediary.[76] Describing a kind of second creation, it begins: "And , lay , he , down , the , golden , father , / (Genesis' , fist , all , gentle , now)" (152). This seventh day of rest gives way to Christ, "The , red-thighed , distancer , swift , saint, / Who , made , the , flower , principle" and who links heaven and earth:

> Light's , latticer , the , angel , in , the , spiderweb:
> By , whose , espials , from , the , silk , sky ,
> From , his , spiritual , ropes ,
> With , fatherest , fingers , lets , down ,
> Manfathers , the , gold , declension , of , the , soul. (152)

This scene appears to portray Christ or "the , angel , in , the , spiderweb" unwinding "Manfathers" that descend from on high. The play on "declension" implies both linguistic inflection and "unclenching"—a release from the divine "soul." The poem goes on to celebrate "he , / Who , builds , his , staircase , fire— / And , lays , his , bones , in , ascending , / Fever" (152–153). After what seems to be a "Deadlock" battle in the sky, the "I" of the poem winds up with his "prince": "So , soon , a , homecoming , love , / Nativity , climbs , him , by , the , Word's , three , kings" (153). The speaker claims his "birthright" (once "lanced" and now "Lightstruck") and "Lie[s] , down , sweet , by , the , betrayer , tree," figuring Christ as "First-lover-and-last-lover" (153). Despite the semantic difficulty produced by the poem's verbal audacity, the eroticism of his earlier work remains. "The Anchored Angel" ends:

> —Anchored , Entire , Angel:
> Through , whose , huge , discalced , arable , love ,
> Bloodblazes , oh , Christ's , gentle , egg: His , terrific ,
> sperm. (153)

If the anchored angel is the "I" transformed by his ascension into the sky, the speaker depicts himself as a member of a religious sect ("discalced" referring to orders that walk unshod or wear sandals) whose "love" is fertilized ("arable") by another androgynous or hermaphroditic Christ with his "gentle , egg" and "terrific , / sperm." In short, the poet-as-angel's creative power derives and "Bloodblazes" forth from his coupling with Christ in this unearthly, metaphysical space.

We might extend Villa's metaphor of "Manfathers" to his role as editor and anthologist, as self-appointed "father" of modernist anglophone Filipino literature. Deeply political acts, Villa's tradition-making practices are also contingent on the transnational circulation of texts and modes of address. His critical essays and anthologies evaluated and collected literature written and produced almost exclusively in the Philippines, and he published those judgments and collections *back* in the Philippines. The effects of these addresses were thus largely felt in the anglophone Philippine literary world—*not* in the United States. While Villa's critical essays and anthologies "worked to give direction to, and preserve, and form the groundwork of, a valid Philippine literature in English," as he put it in a 1936 essay (*CV* 167), his editorial work did not operate in the reverse direction of delivering anglophone Philippine literature to U.S. readers. With the exceptions of the slim war-time anthology *Chorus for America: Six Philippine Poets* (1942) edited by Carlos Bulosan, and the "critique and anthology" *New Writing from the Philippines* (1966) by Leonard Casper, Philippine literature in English would have to wait until 1993 when Rutgers University Press published *Brown River, White Ocean: An Anthology of Twentieth-Century Philippine Literature in English* edited by Luis Francia (himself a student of Villa's studio workshops) to receive serious recognition by the U.S. publishing establishment. Nearly a century of anglophone Philippine writing would go by before U.S. audiences could gain relatively easy access to the literature produced in a language for which their own imperial predecessors were responsible.

In the same year that *Footnote to Youth* (1933) appeared and six years before Villa's first volume of poetry was published, Philippine critic Leopoldo Yabes echoed the *Philippines Herald Magazine*'s euphemistic description of "Man-Songs" in his ambivalent assessment of Villa's poetry:

> Much as I should like to praise his poems, I cannot convince myself to do so. In fact, I am of the belief that his poetry leans toward the base side of life, and that instead of keeping literature on a high plane, it tends to make it cheap. It is too ultra-modernistic to be

appreciated by any one except perhaps by a mind of a similar texture and technique as Villa's. As an excuse, Villa perhaps would say with Rizal's famous character, Filosof Tasio [in the novel *Noli Me Tangere* (1887)], that he is not writing for this generation but for future ages, for generations which will be educated enough to be able to understand him and the beauty of his poetry. Time may yet prove he is right. Who knows?[77]

Some seventeen years later, Carlos Bulosan would offer similar sentiments about Villa's future reception in a letter to his friend Jose de los Reyes: "When we speak of literature as a continuous tradition, a growing cultural movement, Villa is out of place and time. Perhaps the years to come will relegate him to his own cultural country and literary time, but it will not be in the Philippines or in our time. So it comes to the old maxim: that culture belongs to the world and to all time. Perhaps this is his greatness."[78]

Progressive developments of wisdom and backhanded compliments aside, the current moment is certainly ripe for reinterpreting Villa's "ultra-modernistic" work as various attempts to invent "his own cultural country and literary time" precisely due to the constraints imposed by his own "place and time." By relocating his literary experiments and editorial practices within the contexts of colonialism, nationalism, and race, as well as eroticism, interiority, and metaphysicality, this chapter has sought to demonstrate that Villa was neither an apologist for U.S. imperialism nor an advocate of Filipino nationalism but a complex figure whose queer "works," created out of the intimacy with his personal "God," "remain as Evidences" of the fraught diasporic terrain that his literary endeavors were forced to navigate. By tracing how his queer modernist practices shifted over the course of his career, I hope to have laid the groundwork for reassessments of Villa's work that will take seriously his "unorthodox" relation to national traditions and political ideologies and read his writings in ways that are queerer still.

# 3

# The Sexual Politics of
# Carlos Bulosan's Radicalism

AT AROUND THE time that José Garcia Villa published his last major poem "The Anchored Angel," his compatriot Carlos Bulosan was engaged in writing an equally ambitious work. Composed during the early 1950s and posthumously published as *The Cry and the Dedication* in 1995, nearly forty years after the author's death in 1956, Bulosan's novel could not be more dissimilar from Villa's poem.[1] Whereas "The Anchored Angel" weaves idiosyncratic metaphors and distressed images into a dense web of religious and erotic evocations, *The Cry and the Dedication* is an expansive narrative rooted in social history and organized into a form of almost "geometric simplicity."[2] Taking place in the central Luzon region of the Philippines in the wake of U.S. "liberation" of the Philippines from Japanese occupation (1942–1945) and the granting of Philippine independence on July 4, 1946, the novel rejects the Cold War notion that the United States "saved" the Filipinos once again (echoing the exceptionalist ideology at the turn of the twentieth century that the United States "rescued" Filipinos from Spanish tyranny) and defies sentiments of prostration or gratitude toward the former colonial power.

Indeed, the novel offers a literary representation of what critics take as the Hukbalahap rebellion (abbreviated from *Hukbo ng Bayan Laban sa Hapon*, the People's Anti-Japanese Army). Perhaps the most significant peasant revolt in the Philippines during the twentieth century, the Huk movement emerged out of the agrarian unrest during the 1930s in central Luzon and was formally constituted in 1942 to oppose Japanese occupation. Following the war and after a temporary disbanding (owing in large part to the demand by U.S. and Philippine military forces to disarm), the group re-formed as the HMB (abbreviated from *Hukbong Mapagpalaya ng Bayan*, the People's Liberation Army) and assumed a staunch position against the collusion between U.S. neocolonialism and the Philippine government's "mailed fist" policy of anti-Communist/antiradical repression.[3]

Although Bulosan uses Huk code names, *The Cry and the Dedication* is not a "documentary transcript" of the movement, as editor E. San Juan Jr., points out.[4] Rather, the fictional narrative tracks a group of seven members of the "underground" (the novel never uses "Huk" or "Hukbalahap") who are charged to meet up with Felix Rivas in Manila. A Filipino expatriate who has returned from the United States, Felix is to deliver a large sum of money to the underground's political cause and provide information on how to procure additional arms and medicine. En route to the concluding rendezvous in Manila, each of the characters is assigned to return to his or her provincial hometown so that Hassim, the leader of the guerrilla unit, can collect intelligence from the people regarding the social conditions in those areas and can disseminate their political message. While Old Bio, Legaspi, Dabu, Mameng (the sole female member), and Dante fulfill their respective "homecomings," Dante's death at the hands of his brother (a corrupt, landowning priest) brings the narrative to an uncertain close. Dante knew Felix Rivas when both men lived in the United States and therefore was designated to identify Felix since the "enemy" might subvert the plot with an impersonator. The novel's final pages portray the group headed toward Linda Bie's hometown, the penultimate destination before Manila, where Hassim grew up and where, presumably, Felix Rivas continues to await them.[5]

Engaging the Huk rebellion from the viewpoint of a sympathetic Filipino radical living in the United States, Bulosan's novel departs in some ways from his previous work as well as from diasporic Filipino literature more generally.[6] Although the autobiographical *America Is in the Heart* (1946) remains Bulosan's most well known text, *The Cry and the Dedication* has garnered some critical attention, especially since its setting and serial homecoming plot seem to enact a kind of symbolic return to the homeland, which Bulosan himself was unable to fulfill during his lifetime. This "return to the source" has typically been understood in teleological terms, whereby the trajectory of Bulosan's literary career neatly maps a narrative of political maturation (disillusionment with American ideals provoking a recuperation of Philippine revolutionary traditions) onto a sequential narrative of diaspora (migration to the imperial center followed by return to the homeland).[7] As San Juan argues, "Bulosan's novel thus critiques the utopian humanism of *America* [*Is in the Heart*] and rewrites it in the allegory of revolutionary praxis."[8]

This linear understanding of Bulosan's literary and political development risks perceiving his previous work as outdated and naive, over-
simplifying his engagement with U.S. imperialism as an unambivalent
critique, and underestimating the continuities—and conundrums—that
exist across his literary production. This chapter situates *The Cry and the
Dedication* in the context of some of Bulosan's earlier work (particularly,
*America Is in the Heart*) and in conversation with Huk leader Luis Taruc's autobiography, *Born of the People* (1953).[9] But rather than reinscribe
a developmental story of increasing "revolutionary" consciousness, I
tease out some of the tensions and contradictions that arise as Bulosan
seeks to insert a diasporic voice—a voice from afar, transmitted from
within the space of the imperial power itself—into the debates around
"national liberation" and political radicalism.

Lauded for exposing peasant exploitation in the Philippines and racial and class oppression in the United States, Bulosan has usually been
regarded as José Garcia Villa's antithesis: the Marxist materialist committed to social justice versus the modernist formalist committed to
aesthetic innovation. Without denying their obvious differences, my
discussion of *America Is in the Heart* elucidates how Bulosan's efforts to
claim literary authority depend, not unlike Villa's, on autobiographical
experience and autodidacticism, and how his critique of U.S. racial exclusion and class domination is intimately linked to gender and sexual
oppression. Bringing this context to bear on *The Cry and the Dedication*,
I explore how Bulosan invents new strategies of authorization by having his alter egos, the returned expatriates Dante and Felix Rivas, make
substitutions to compensate for Bulosan's lack of direct experience with
the guerrilla movement in the Philippines. Ultimately, I suggest that Bulosan's critique of Filipino marginalization in the United States and his
diasporic articulation of solidarity with anti-imperialist radicalism in the
Philippines hinge on revising each social formation's sexual norms (antimiscegenation and married heterosexual monogamy, respectively).

By offering a queer diasporic reading of Bulosan's work that emphasizes his self-authorizing endeavors, this chapter not only illuminates
how his multivalent modes of address are articulated through sex, gender, and sexuality but also gives some sense of the formal complexity of
his writing. Though not invested in the sort of artistic experimentation
that Villa pursued, Bulosan's literary production is also not as transpar-
ently documentative as it may seem. Examining the way his writing is
in dialogue with Philippine literature in English, my analysis also seeks

to reconsider Bulosan's place not simply within Asian American studies (in which context he was "resurrected" in the 1970s) but also within
diasporic Filipino literary history.[10] I conclude by bringing these threads
together—authority, sexuality, literary productivity, and diasporic dialogue—in order to ask, rather impudently, what it might entail to think
of Bulosan less as the quintessential "representative" of Filipino American radicalism than as a "queer" anomaly whose literary legacy calls for
reevaluation.

## Authenticity, Sexuality, Literacy

*America Is in the Heart* portrays the protagonist-narrator Allos's life as
a rural peasant in the Philippines just after the Great War and his experiences as a migrant worker and labor activist on the U.S. West Coast
during the Great Depression up through the eve of World War II. Unlike Villa's metaphysical, erotic, autobiographical stories, Bulosan's autobiographical text draws on the experiences of the predominantly male
Filipino working class and attempts to "give a literate voice to the voice-
less one hundred thousand Filipinos in the United States, Hawai'i, and
Alaska," as he puts it in a late essay.[11] However hubristic and impossible
a task, Bulosan nonetheless seeks to authorize such a project through a
dialectical process of identification, on the one hand, and escape, on the
other. While the former abides by a familiar logic of authenticity based
on lived experience as a Philippine peasant and a working-class Filipino
in the United States, the latter shows his alter ego Allos breaking free
from those same social constituencies, eventually extricating himself
from the condition of "voicelessness" through reading and writing and
thereby accessing a mode of authority based on literacy.[12]
　　These narratives converge in ideological terms around the politics of
sexuality, whereby "degraded" modes of sex—prostitution, nonmonoga-
mous and extramarital sex, and homosexual advances—enter to figure
the debased forms of social life that Filipino migrant workers endure
during the Depression years in the United States and which Allos de-
plores and ultimately detaches himself from in order to become a morally trustworthy narrator. Unraveling the ways that race and sexuality
diverge in the text complicates the critical tradition's assumption, and
even celebration, of Bulosan's fiction of authenticity.[13] According to that
logic, Bulosan's reputed identity as a peasant/working-class Filipino

guarantees the authenticity of his "collective" representation.[14] As I argue here, however, Bulosan's authority rests not only on racial and class identification but also on sexual disidentification. Sex in *America Is in the Heart* indexes what Allan Punzalan Isaac refers to as "the abject condition of Filipino masculinity in America,"[15] even as it provokes Allos's desire to free himself from that condition.

Bulosan thematizes this dialectic in Part 2 of *America Is in the Heart*. Just after Allos flees from a fight involving two Filipino men, Poco and Pete, over Pete's wife, a white woman named Myra, he reflects:

> There were times when I found myself inextricably involved, not because I was drawn to this life by its swiftness and violence, but because I was a part and a product of the world in which it was born. I was swept by its tragic whirlpool, violently and inevitably; and it was only when I had become immune to violence and pain that I was able to project myself out of it. It was only then that I was able to integrate my experiences so that I could really find out what had happened to me in those tragic years.[16]

Displaying his authentic credentials by asserting that he "was a part" of this social world, Allos simultaneously has to distance himself from the "barbarous" maelstrom that he had been "swept" into in order to comprehend and write about those "tragic years" (152).

It is telling that this meditation on what might be viewed as a kind of ethnographic poetics whereby "insider" knowledge is mediated by "outsider" observation and reflection takes place in the wake of sexualized violence, since the "tragic whirlpool" from which Allos repeatedly strives to escape is so often marked by conflicts that erupt over sexuality.[17] Melinda Luisa María de Jesús notes that "despite Allos' expressed desire for human contact, Bulosan is determined that Allos remain celibate or asexual."[18] This preservation of Allos's sexual "purity" represents one important axis along which Allos's "un-oneing" from other Filipino men takes place. As he asserts, "I tried hard to remain aloof from the destruction and decay around me. I wanted to remain pure within myself" (174).

Bulosan's construction of a nonsexual first-person narrator reads as a response to the stereotypes of the "hypersexual" Filipino male that circulated during this period. While helping his brother Macario work as a house servant, for example, Allos overhears a conversation between a wealthy movie director, his wife, and several acquaintances. The husband declares, "You can hire these natives for almost nothing. . . . They are only too glad to work for white folks." A woman's qualification, though, shows how the naturalizing of colonial and class hierarchies is confounded and threatened by sexual preconceptions: "I won't have a Filipino in my house, when my daughter is around." One man asks whether it is "true that they are sex-crazy," especially when it comes to "white women." Another affirms that "they are all sex-starved" (141). Here the Filipino comes across as a mindless bundle of urges and appetites, ravenous for low-paying domestic work and white daughters alike.

Allos's attempt to "remain pure" in light of these stereotypes of Filipinos as "hot little rabbits," as one Californian called them,[19] entails that he guard against both hetero- and homosexual temptation. Regarding the latter, Allos rebuffs the touch and offer of food presented by "a young Mexican whose voice sounded like a girl's" (128). At another point, Allos flees from "an old man" in a homeless shelter who starts "caressing my legs" (155). Although these characters disappear as quickly as they enter the narrative and are denied any subjectivity (coded simply as working class, sexually deviant, and sometimes racially other), Allos's flights from homosexual entreaties are paralleled by his refusal to participate willingly in heterosexual encounters as well. Not long after his arrival in Seattle, Allos enters a "Manila dance hall" but merely watches as his compatriot Marcelo gets ripped off by the blond dancer and then is struck with a lead pipe by one of her admirers (105–106).

Even when Allos does have sex with a woman, Bulosan portrays the narrator as an involuntary participant. Soon after he flees from the homeless shelter, Allos joins a crew of Filipino migrant laborers, and several of them effectively force him to have sex with "a naked Mexican woman" in the bunkhouse: "The men pinned me down on the cot, face upward, while Benigno hurriedly fumbled for my belt. The woman bent over me, running her hands over my warming face" (159). Afterward, Allos again rushes away from the scene of sex: "I plunged through the wall of sheets and started running between the cots to the door. Benigno and the other men laughed, shouting my name. I could still hear their voices when I entered my tent, trembling with a nameless shame" (160). While de Jesús and Kandice Chuh read the homosocial "violence" inflicted on Allos as a critique of heteronormativity (the forced ritualism of the act denaturalizing heterosex),[20] it is the language of "shame" that becomes paramount in Bulosan's later revision of sexual ethics, as I suggest below.

Allos's depiction of the pull and repulsion of sex is further figured through metaphors of disease and death. Following another episode of homosocial conflict over a woman, Allos narrates: "I almost died within myself. I died many deaths in these surroundings, where man was indistinguishable from beast. It was only when I had died a hundred times that I acquired a certain degree of immunity to sickening scenes such as took place this night" (135). By striving to "remain aloof" from these scenes, Allos gains a kind of moral authority, even as it enables him to challenge stereotypes of Filipino hypersexuality, portraying the ways that U.S. racism and classism precipitate the "degeneration" of Filipino male sexuality: "I knew that our decadence was imposed by a society alien to our character and inclination, alien to our heritage and history" (135).

Recruited through technologies of colonial capitalism and imperial interpellation, Filipino laborers during this period were simultaneously racialized and sexualized as aberrant others, as these moments imply. Roderick A. Ferguson's materialist queer of color analytic is useful here:

> As U.S. capital had to constantly look outside local and national boundaries for labor, it often violated ideals of racial homogeneity held by local communities and the United States at large. As it violated those ideals, capital also inspired worries that such violations would lead to the disruption of gender and sexual proprieties. If racialization has been the "site of a contradiction between the promise of political emancipation and the conditions of economic exploitation," then much of that contradiction has pivoted on the racialization of working populations as deviant in terms of gender and sexuality.[21]

In *America Is in the Heart*, Bulosan not only registers how the anxieties and contradictions produced by capital's need for racialized labor are displaced onto sexual deviancy (partly justifying political disenfranchisement) but also how racial-sexual discourse thereby becomes the terrain on which social critique is made salient.

Given the metaphors of disease and death that Bulosan invokes to characterize this sexually "decadent" Filipino working-class culture (152), it is fitting that Allos's efforts to escape culminate in a two-year period of convalescence in a county hospital when he is on the brink of death. This respite from labor, hunger, violence, and incessant movement grants Allos the opportunity to read voraciously and eventually become "literate." Allos foreshadows this period of his life soon after he arrives in the United States:

> As time went by I became as ruthless as the worst of them, and I became afraid that I would never feel like a human being again. Yet no matter what bestiality encompassed my life, I felt sure that somewhere, sometime, I would break free. This faith kept me from completely succumbing to the degradation into which many of my countrymen had fallen. It finally paved my way out of our small, harsh life, painfully but cleanly, into a world of strange intellectual adventures and self-fulfillment. (109)

These two trajectories—Allos's extrication from the Filipino underclass and his literary and intellectual formation—intersect in an extended scene of reading and writing in Parts 3 and 4 of *America Is in the Heart*.

Again, it bears emphasizing that Allos's literacy narrative (his extensive reading and poetry writing in the hospital and his continued search for literary models afterward) is heavily gendered. A number of scholars have noted how white women in Bulosan's work are either idealized as embodiments of a "feminized America" or sexualized such that they disrupt "brotherly unity."[22] White American female characters who support Allos's/Bulosan's "intellectual possibilities" include Mary Strandon in the Philippines (70), and Judith (173), Dora Travers (224), Harriet Monroe (227), and the Odell sisters in the United States. Alice Odell, states Allos, assists in "directing my education . . . and I read everything she sent me" (232). Her sister Eileen also lends Allos books and temporarily satisfies his "insatiable hunger for knowledge and human affection" (236). These "angelic" mentors stand in stark contrast to the Mexican women and male queers who embody dangerous sexualities and imperil Allos's moral purity.

It is thus not surprising that Allos's relationship with the Odell sisters is desexualized. To be sure, this is partly a result of antimiscegenation law and sentiment pervasive among white working-class men during this economically depressed period.[23] Allos wonders about his relationship with Eileen, "Could I walk with her in the street without being ashamed because of my race?" (234). The feelings of shame and fear serve as the departure points for one of the more famous lines of *America Is in the Heart*: "I came to know afterward that in many ways it was a crime to be a Filipino in California" (121). This alleged "crime" is not simply about race, however, but specifically involves heterosexual, interracial liaisons: "I came to know that the public streets were not free to my people: we were stopped each time these vigilant patrolmen saw us driving a car. We were suspect each time we were seen with a white woman" (121). Whereas heterosex and homosexual propositions mark the "bestiality" of Filipino working-class life, here antimiscegenationism thwarts the public display of interracial heterosexuality, resulting in a "narrowing of our life into an island, into a filthy segment of American society" (121).

At the same time, Allos's relationship with Eileen Odell is curtailed by the function of gender in Bulosan's revolutionary imagination. Although women may serve as caregivers in the hospital and assist in the acquisition of literacy skills, they do not figure as active subjects of revolution. They are either left behind (as with Allos's mother and sisters in the Philippines) or "disappeared" from the text.[24] Women may provide Allos with reading material, but they do not (or rarely) speak or write their own ideas. Even Eileen "talked but little when she came to see me. When she left, leaving some books, I imagined I read the words she would have spoken. And so from week to week, Eileen came and sat quietly near me, leaving just as quietly" (235). Most pointedly, though, white American women like Eileen represent the future *objects* of revolutionary transformation and thus remain unattainable in the present. For Bulosan, "America" will have fulfilled its promise of equality only when interracial relationships between a Filipino man and a "respectable" white woman are legally possible *and* socially acceptable. In this regard, Bulosan's narrative parallels Villa's autobiographical stories in that both frame the (im)possibilities of assimilation in eroticized terms. The posing and ultimate failure of socially sanctioned, mutually reciprocal, interracial relationships in both cases (whether hetero- or homoerotic) denote not so much a romanticized desire for "America" but a critique of its racial and sexual exclusions.

To the extent that white American women serve as Allos's intellectual mentors, and white American men violently oppose social and sexual assimilation (graphically depicted in the "lynching" scene where José, Millar, and Allos are brutalized by vigilantes [207–209]), it is noteworthy that the books comprising Allos's political and literary education are drawn from a wide range of international sources. As recounted in *America Is in the Heart*, Allos's reading list extends well beyond U.S. traditions and includes literature from Russia, France, Germany, Spain,

Cuba, Ireland, China, Korea, and Japan. He also recalls reading political and historical nonfiction books, "the poetry of the proletarians in the United States" (251), fairy tales, and various left-wing magazines of the 1930s such as *New Masses, Partisan Review, New Republic, Left Front, Dynamo,* and *Anvil.* Much as Villa in his critical essays of the 1930s quotes heavily from selected Euro-American sources to authorize his aesthetic views, so does Bulosan display his "intellectual adventures," as though assuring readers that, despite his lowly background, he has become quite well-read.

Here, his literary endeavors are gendered in another sense. Referring at one point to Rilke, Kafka, Toller, Lorca, and Heine, Bulosan writes: "These writers collectively represented to me a heroism of the spirit, so immeasurably had they suffered the narrowness of the world in which they lived, so gloriously had they succeeded in inspiring a universal brotherhood among men" (237–238). Echoing his own escape from the "narrowness" of Filipino social life, this passage anticipates a later one where his reading pursuits "creat[e] a spiritual kinship with other men who had pondered over the miseries of their countries" (246). In this respect, Bulosan's articulacy is sponsored not by a social collectivity named "Filipino" but by a "spiritual kinship" forged with writers throughout the world, beyond the "filthy segment of American society" allotted to working-class Filipinos. Not coincidentally, that international formation is also gendered: it both inspires "a universal brotherhood among men" and constitutes a brotherhood of writers. Indeed, Bulosan names only one female writer, Laura Clarendorn (even that is a pseudonym), and says that "what attracted me to the book was its Filipino protagonist" (238), a male labor organizer among Pacific Northwest workers.[25]

Although one might expect Bulosan to engage most intensely with U.S. and Philippine literary traditions in his search for models, he cites only one Philippine writer—Manuel Arguilla—throughout this episode of the narrative (246). As I argue elsewhere, in *America Is in the Heart,* Bulosan borrows from and revises the pastoralism found in Arguilla's early short stories in *How My Brother Leon Brought Home a Wife* (1940) and the proletarianism propounded in critic Salvador P. Lopez's essays in *Literature and Society* (1940), the same intellectual who criticized Villa's poetics.[26] In the following section, I explore the ways that *The Cry and the Dedication* similarly weaves pastoral and radical modes into its textual fabric, in part by appropriating and complicating ideas advanced in Luis Taruc's autobiography, *Born of the People.* The terms of that diasporic dialogue on the politics of "national liberation" and class radicalism are inscribed through Bulosan's articulations and reimaginings of sex and sexuality.

## Pastoralism, Radicalism, Anti-imperialism

Whereas *America Is in the Heart* bases Allos's legitimacy on a logic of experiential authenticity and literacy acquisition, those methods of self-authorization do not operate as easily in *The Cry and the Dedication*. The former is rendered impossible, strictly speaking, since Bulosan cannot claim firsthand knowledge of the events he describes in the novel.[27] The latter is confounded by the fact that the books Bulosan records himself reading during this period (ca. 1936–1938) have little to do with Philippine peasant exploitation, radicalism, national liberation, or anti-imperialism, the themes pursued in *The Cry and the Dedication*. To deal with these conundrums, Bulosan distributes his persona to two characters, attributing to Dante and Felix Rivas traits shared with his previous autobiographical narrator, Allos. Those attributes are allocated precisely along lines of literary education and production (Dante) and labor organizing and subjection to racial-sexual violence (Felix).

Dante, who spent fifteen years in the United States and became a writer, not only serves as Bulosan's returning proxy but also implicitly theorizes the author's diasporic literary strategy of threading pastoral and radical discursive modes into *The Cry and the Dedication*.[28] The pastoral functions as the technique through which Bulosan endeavors to reconnect his fictive persona Dante with the homeland. Initially, Dante claims that the very act of writing about his childhood in the short-story collection *Tales of My People* links him, and impels him to return, to his birthplace: "I found happiness and a feeling of closeness to the Philippines and the people when I wrote it. I can say with frankness that it was the beginning of my realization that I should come back to the land of my nativity" (194).

Dante also returns to fulfill a promise he had pledged to an old storyteller named Apo Lacay. This scene of intergenerational male transmission substitutes for the informal education that Allos had received through the succor of white American women. In *The Cry and the Dedication*, Bulosan inserts a fable of how Dante's stories are derived from, and interwoven with, the tales he had heard from Apo Lacay as a child.

When Dante bids the old man farewell before "leav[ing] our country," (198), he states, "if my retelling your stories will give me a little wisdom of the heart, then I shall have come home again" (199). Apo Lacay responds, "You mean it will be your book as well as mine? Your words as well as my words there in that faraway land?" Dante assures him, "Your book as well as mine" (199). This mode of self-authentication via generational storytelling is further buttressed by the folkloric ideology that frames this pastoral portrait. Describing the valley and mountain where Apo Lacay used to reside, Dante speaks of the peasants' "primitive" lifeways: "The passing of time and the intensification of settlers in this valley helped preserve a common folklore that was related from mouth to mouth and from one generation to another, so that now it is no longer possible to distinguish which tale is indigenous to the tribe living there and which is borrowed from other tribes" (196). The unmediated interchange between Apo Lacay and Dante echoes the oral transmission and intermingling of folklore among the peasants and settlers and thereby confirms the "validity" of Dante's stories (196).

Moreover, the process of "passing on" that occurs between the two figures adopts the same trajectory of death and continuity that Bulosan had deployed in *America Is in the Heart*.[29] As with Allos's succession of the deceased Filipino writers Estevan, Pascual, and Florencio in that text, Dante positions himself in *The Cry and the Dedication* as Apo Lacay's literary heir when he discovers that the old man "was already dead": "And in that land, writing many years later, I didn't exactly remember which were the words of the old man of the mountain and which were mine. But they were his tales as well as mine" (199). Apo Lacay's legacy persists through Dante's publication of *The Tales of My People*, ensuring that the tales "will not be forgotten" (199).

Although this pastoral tableau allegorizes Bulosan's strategy of imaginatively rerooting himself in Philippine folk culture and disseminating folktales abroad, Dante also makes reference to a history of colonial violence. During his final visit with Apo Lacay, Dante sees the old man lost in reverie, "listening to the lost cries and agonies of men and women and children in the midst of abject poverty and ruthless tyranny. For that was the time of his childhood, in the era of great distress and calamity in the land, when the fury of an invading race impaled their hearts on the tragic cross of slavery and ignorance" (199). Though not literal in its rendering of Spanish colonialism (Apo Lacay was obviously not alive when the Spanish arrived in the sixteenth century), the brief interpolation of

foreign domination into Dante's recollection demonstrates how Bulosan mediates the pastoral with a radical, anti-imperial mode of writing.
Analogous to the way that Estevan's death in *America Is in the Heart* signals the shortcomings (for Bulosan) of Arguilla's lyrical fiction, so does
Apo Lacay's death spell the end of the pastoral—both the "enchanting"
life of the unmolested peasantry and the literary mode that idealizes that
social world (196).

Enacting this mix of pastoral and radical modes, chapters 7 and 8
illustrate their intersections and divergences. At this point, the seven-
member group splits up; Hassim and Old Bio enter the first rendezvous
(Old Bio's hometown), while the others wait for them in the hills. To
ease the monotony, Linda Bie plays "a lively dance tune" on his flute,
and Legaspi and Mameng dance together (111). While providing "music to make people dance," Linda Bie feels nostalgic for a childhood that
the "rugged life he lived in the underground" has driven him away from
(111). Much as Dante's pastoral fiction-writing transports him back to
his own carefree childhood days, music enables Linda Bie to recapture
"some lost threads of his life" (111).

This musical interlude carries into the present the pastoralism of
Dante's recollection by connecting Philippine peasant culture with folk
music. The peasant Legaspi calls for a folk dance: he "whistled a folksong
that was popular in the northern part of the island," "trying his best to give
Linda Bie an idea of what he wanted his flute to play for Dante and Mameng" (112). Linda Bie picks up the tune, titled "The Lady Dayang-Dayang,"
which, according to Legaspi, was "originally" an "Igorot folksong" but "is
Ilocano now" (112). Legaspi authenticates his folk knowledge by singing
the words to Linda Bie's accompaniment. Whereas Dante's pastoral story
occurs through intergenerational male transmission, this fleeting moment
of collective recreation takes place on the more familiar ground of hetero-
sociality, as Mameng dances first with Legaspi and then with Dante. Interestingly, though, when Dabu espies Hassim and Old Bio returning up the
hill (the others had worried that the gunshots reported their comrades'
deaths), the group's merry-making takes on renewed zeal: "Legaspi and
Dante could not resist the contagion of Dabu's happiness. They kicked the
knapsacks away and held each other, Legaspi taking the part of a woman"
(114). Given the heterosexual banter that occurs throughout the novel,
this moment of male-male dancing is striking for the lack of amusement it
elicits. The only narrative commentary is that "Linda Bie played on, trying
hard not to sob; his heart was aching so" (114).

The meaning of this lyrical scene depends not only on its gender inscriptions but also on the temporality of Bulosan's revolutionary imagination. The possibility of "happiness" is framed as the recovery of Linda Bie's (romanticized) past as well as the projection of a (utopian) future when such happiness might be "know[n] again" (113). Jeffrey Arellano Cabusao argues that "this strange moment of distancing within the text—of breaking into song and dance amidst tragedy—. . . reveals the promise of what is to come, but also suggests that this promise cannot come to fruition in the current society."[30] It is important to note, though, that the events of this chapter take place simultaneously with Hassim's and Old Bio's rendezvous in the latter's hometown. That is, this lyrical "song and dance" is both continuous and discontinuous—politically and narratively—with the chapter that precedes it. Rather than view this moment as merely a utopian anticipation of a joyful life that can only be known on the other side of revolutionary transformation, one can read it as the dialectical counterpoint *in the present* to the radical political program propagated by Hassim and Old Bio in chapter 7 and elaborated in all of the characters' homecomings.

In outlining that program, Bulosan draws principally on Taruc's *Born of the People* and reiterates a number of sociopolitical themes in Taruc's autobiography. Both texts render the exploitative peasant working conditions—absentee landlordism, the unequal sharing of the crop harvests, and the mirage of legal reforms meant to redress the peasants' grievances—as the most important components of widespread radicalization.[31] In the face of these state-endorsed oppressions, Bulosan and Taruc call for organizational unity that would draw together the numerous guerrilla units (some of which were recruited by the U.S. military to fight not the Japanese but the Huks) and form the basis of a radical political party when the Japanese are deposed.[32] Following the war, however, the Roxas administration refused to seat several senators, including Taruc as a representative of Pampanga, so that the Bell Trade Act could be approved by a two-thirds majority vote in Congress.[33] For Taruc, these flagrant "betrayals of the people" led the Huks to abandon legal channels of reform and to fight more directly against "imperialist-feudal rule" (*Born*, 263).

Although both texts diagnose the conditions precipitating revolutionary impulses and actions in similar ways, they begin to diverge in their respective engagements with U.S. imperialism. Taruc's critique of U.S. imperialism is unambiguous and takes shape through the idea of historical repetition:

What happened in 1945 was almost a duplication of what had happened in 1898. The American army, on both occasions, landed to
find a revolutionary movement fighting against the common enemy.
On both occasions they took steps to crush it, and on both occasions
they found allies in the exploiting classes of Filipinos. . . . Within
three years after the end of the war, the operation of American imperialism had resulted in converting the Hukbalahap guerrilla struggle
into a national liberation movement. (*Born*, 274–275)

During both the Philippine-American War and World War II, as Taruc
sees it, the United States suppressed revolutionary forces fighting for independence (the Philippine Revolutionary/Republican Army and the
Huks) and took over the reins of colonial control from its predecessors
(Spain and Japan) with the help of the Filipino "exploiting classes."

Although Bulosan's *The Cry and the Dedication* links the underground's struggle with the past through Old Bio, who had fought "during the revolution against Spain" (*Cry*, 5), the novel's critique of U.S.
imperialism is not quite as resounding as Taruc's. According to Hassim,
Dante had produced a book "tracing our history from the revolutionary viewpoint, from Chief Lapu-Lapu and his pagan men who killed
Magellan and most of his mercenary soldiers and drove the others to
their boats thence to Spain, to the formation of the underground in
Mt. Arayat, where Alipato took the military leadership in this our latest struggle against tyranny" (*Cry*, 5). This "revolutionary" history skips
over U.S. colonization, jumping from the sixteenth century right into
the underground resistance (Alipato was Taruc's nickname) against this
"latest" tyranny, the recently ousted Japanese and the current repressive
administration.

In the introduction to the poetry anthology *Chorus for America: Six
Philippine Poets* (1942), Bulosan does something similar. Writing in the
midst of World War II, Bulosan asserts: "These are poets whose ideas
are relevant to the revolutionary tradition which is the very foundation
of Philippine history."[34] To make this "revolutionary tradition" of Philippine literature meaningful for a U.S. wartime context—that is, to direct the "chorus" of Filipino voices "*for* America"—Bulosan has to ex-
cise mention of U.S. colonialism from that history. He leaps in the first
paragraph from "the death knell of Spanish sovereignty" at the end of
the nineteenth century straight into "recent years" to begin the second
paragraph (xi). Though we might attribute this elision to the Popular

Front program of uniting against fascism, the immediate postwar period warrants no such explanations.

I suggest that Bulosan's less than emphatic critique of U.S. imperialism has to do not only with his positioning within the United States but also with a subtle but important difference between Taruc's anti-imperialist *nationalism* and Bulosan's anti-imperialist *transnationalism*. It is true that Bulosan draws the kind of historical parallel that Taruc had made. When Legaspi returns home and spreads the word about the underground's political ideology, he explains to his father:

> The Katipunan had the same program against Spain. But there is a great difference between that revolution and the one we are setting in motion. For one thing, you fought against foreign tyranny and their native underlings; it was a fight for independence, which was successful until the Americans came to our country under the guise of liberators. Now the present revolution is different: we are fighting colonialism under the aegis of American imperialism and their native partners in plunder. (*Cry*, 160)

Perhaps the most forthright statement of anti-U.S. imperialism in Bulosan's published fiction,[35] this exposition posits virtually no difference between 1898 and 1945; both are struggles against "foreign tyranny" and "native" collaborators.

When Legaspi does elaborate on "the difference between the two revolutions" (160), he also complicates the notion that "liberation" is bound by national borders, that it emerges only from within. Invoking a worldwide fraternity of workers—mirroring Allos's international brotherhood of writers—Legaspi tells his father: "You fought against an oppressive government, but we are fighting against a system of exploitation. . . . This system recognizes no national boundaries, racial classifications, and religious beliefs, for its main thesis is the economic slavery of the working class everywhere in the world. You are brother to the peasant in China, the coal miner in England, the factory worker in the United States, the farmer in Russia" (160).

This international brotherhood of workers seems to echo ideas found in the closing chapter of *Born of the People*. Defending himself against charges of demagoguery and Russian manipulation, Taruc declares:

> The tenant-farmer of Central Luzon is the same as the tenant-farmer of Indo-China, or of India, or of the state of Mississippi, the same

as the peasant of old tzarist Russia, or of old China. All have been exploited in the same way. It is not surprising, then, that they should all arrive at the same answer for ending their exploitation. . . .

The peasants in the barrios below me are Filipinos, but they are brothers in toil to the Chinese peasant and to the American factory worker. No struggle by any of us is isolated. (*Born*, 280–281)

Despite the thematic and ideological similarities between *The Cry and the Dedication* and *Born of the People*, Bulosan's novel interrogates Taruc's resolute political agenda of "national liberation." For Taruc, the rhetorical appeal to global sites of economic exploitation, and the Communist "solution" to those problems, works by analogy and conflation ("is the same as"). This theorization would effectively preempt Bulosan's attempt to interject a transnational voice from abroad. While *The Cry and the Dedication* seems to endorse Hassim's call for "a strictly coordinated national organization" (98), the question of the "national" and its complex relations to anti-imperial liberation and class revolution gets complicated by the guerrilla members' messages to the peasants. "There are no longer national and geographical boundaries," Hassim proclaims at one point to a grieving father and son who have lost family members to the constabulary. "There is no longer 'my country' or 'my countrymen,' because these barriers have been scaled. There is only 'my fellow workers' now" (211). By insisting that the struggle transcends national borders, Bulosan (via Legaspi and Hassim) opens up a space where he can assert the uses of his two returned expatriates.

One way to approach this tension between the national and the international is to examine the text's multivalent modes of address. Tim Libretti suggests that "rather than returning with the torch of enlightenment to the Philippines," Bulosan "symbolically returns to the cultural-national space of the Philippines to import the enlightenment of a militant history and culture of resistance to U.S. imperialism from the Philippines to Filipinos in the U.S. to provide a model and agenda for their self-liberation from internal colonialism."[36] Although this interpretation accords with the position that views the homeland as the "source" of any ethnic-nationalist politics in the United States, the circumstances that gave rise to the Huk rebellion—oppressive land-tenancy conditions, the Japanese occupation and the collaboration of elites, the imposition of U.S. imperialist policies, and unmitigated anti-Communist repression—are hardly "the same as" those facing Filipinos in the United States.

On the one hand, the pastoral fable of Dante listening to, absorbing, and disseminating abroad Apo Lacay's stories, as discussed above, allegorizes Bulosan's role as transnational mediator, representing one instance in which he endeavors "to translate the desires and aspirations of the whole Filipino people in the Philippines"[37] for audiences in a "faraway land." Constituting a reflexive figuration of Bulosan's diasporic poetics, it also signals that the novel is oriented—in one sense—toward a non-Philippine reading public. That Bulosan himself initially wrote the fable as a separate essay titled "How My Stories Were Written"[38] confirms the autobiographical connection with Dante and supports the notion that the novel addresses a U.S. readership.

On the other hand, though, the return of Dante and Felix—modeled after Bulosan (or at least Allos)—implies that Bulosan was not only "writing for Filipinos in the U.S."[39] but also *to* Filipinos in the Philippines. An unpublished poem titled "Letter to Taruc" (1952) provides evidence that Bulosan sought to conduct a literary dialogue with the Huk leader. Deploying a diasporic mode of address through a combination of the epistolary and the lyric, the poem demonstrates that he not only aimed to *retrieve* a Philippine radical tradition and "import" it to the United States but also to *articulate* a transnational connection of solidarity. Written in the Firland Sanitarium in Seattle, "Letter to Taruc" opens:

> At night when the fir trees are still
> And all around me the silence of dying men dominates,
> I long to hear news of you. Hourly
> One fearsome thought oppresses me:
> In those dark forests of our beloved Luzon,
> Where the legions of Bonifacio in another age
> Gave life to our revolutionary heritage,
> Blood compacting blood so that we should have liberty—
> Are you alive? Are you free, my brother?

Linking again the current radical movement to the "revolutionary heritage" forged against Spain (Andres Bonifacio formed the Katipunan, the secret society that opposed Spanish control at the end of the nineteenth century),[40] the poet worries over Taruc's fate, having been "three years" since he has heard news of the Huk leader. The poem closes with a variation on the refrain: "Where are you, my brother? Where are you, my comrade? / Across the years I shout your glorious name."[41] Claiming fraternal commonality with "my comrade," Bulosan casts his voice across time *and* space, attempting to reach his "brother" who hides in "our beloved Luzon," "our dear Philippines."

While *The Cry and the Dedication* offers a similar gesture of solidarity with the beleaguered Huks, the introduction of Dante and Felix Rivas into the narrative literalizes and renders complex this transnational act of cohesion. Certainly, Taruc's *Born of the People* makes no mention of Filipino emigrants, much less calls on them for assistance or to return "home." Bulosan's novel thus seems to ask: what role, if any, can and should exilic Filipinos play in the efforts toward "national liberation" during this period of conservative retrenchment and anti-Communism in both the Philippines and the United States (and in the interplay between the two governments)? The question can be posed not only to Filipinos in the United States (enjoining them to attend and possibly contribute to the peasant struggles there, as well as draw on that revolutionary tradition for the purposes of political struggle in the United States), as Libretti argues, but also to the Philippine radical movement itself.

Philippine writer and critic Luis Teodoro Jr. suggests "that Bulosan saw himself in [Felix] Rivas' shoes, as the expatriate returning in triumph, bearing aid for his people."[42] Felix, according to Teodoro, is "depicted in almost mythic proportions, as a liberator whose experiences in the United States have qualified him to bringing into a country weighed down by its own corruption a rejuvenating dose of awareness" (11). Teodoro indicts the "fantasy, perhaps shared by many immigrants and exiles, of returning to the homeland as liberator" (12–13) largely on the basis of his interpretation of the gender and sexual issues raised by the novel, that is, Mameng's seemingly inexplicable duty to have sex with Felix in order to identify him as the rightful assistant, and the sexual union between Dante and Mameng that supposedly prepares her for this final rendezvous. It is to these issues that I turn in the next section.

## Sex, Shame, Futurity

Whereas Dante represents Bulosan's intellectual-writer alter ego, Felix evokes his activist-organizer side. Dante reports that Felix spent two years in a hospital recovering from tuberculosis, where "some well-meaning Americans including two women . . . gave him books to read . . . on trade unions and race relations in the United States" (*Cry*, 40). Released from the hospital, Felix organizes farm workers in San Diego in 1939 and later winds up in another hospital after being "beaten by vigilantes in San Jose, not far from Stockton, where he had gone to organize the fruit pickers" (40). The momentous revelation materializes when Dante discloses to the guerrilla unit: "They crushed his testicles." The men respond with shock and outrage, "so unthinkable was it to them" (41). All of these occurrences befall Allos in *America Is in the Heart*: he spends two years in the Los Angeles county hospital where he is befriended by Alice and Eileen Odell, who provide him with emotional sustenance and access to reading materials (*America*, 226–254). Prior to this scene, Allos had been viciously beaten by anti-union vigilantes not far from San Jose: "The man called Lester grabbed my testicles with his left hand and smashed them with his right fist" (208).

This bodily affliction indicates that Felix does not return to the Philippines with a superiority complex for having lived in the United States, bursting with confidence or wealth. Similarly, Dante returns bitterly disillusioned by his experiences during "the despairing years of the depression and the heartbreaking years after" (*Cry*, 37). More to the point, the emasculated Felix's return offers a critical supplement to Philippine radicalism. Serving as crucial reminders of the Filipino exilic experience, the background sketches of Dante and Felix act as the diasporic pedagogical counterpoint to the underground's dissemination of political ideology by emphasizing the importance of gender and sex to Philippine radical thought and practice. In other words, while the homegrown members of the guerrilla unit educate the peasants in their respective hometowns of Central Luzon about the organization's radical program, Dante instructs the underground itself about the "tragedies" he and Felix experienced and witnessed while living, working, organizing, and writing in the United States.

By focusing on Felix's "vital disfigurements" as the particular sign and symbol of oppression inflicted upon the labor organizer (26), Bulosan alludes to the history of sexualized violence visited upon Filipino men during the two decades leading up to World War II. These sadistic acts resulted from racialized economic competition during the Depression, anti-unionism and strike-breaking, class antagonisms articulated through racial and gender hierarchies (reassertions of white masculinity through patriarchal prerogatives to white women), and ideologies of racial purity (institutionalized in antimiscegenation laws).[43] To the extent that white women—particularly those of the "respectable" classes—were largely inaccessible to Filipino men on legal and "informal" grounds, it seems sensible to interpret the sexual act between Dante and the Filipina guerrilla fighter Mameng, as well as the anticipated union between Felix and Mameng, as the novel's means of redressing the expatriate Filipino men's sexual marginalization. As Viet Thanh Nguyen argues, "If [Felix] Rivas's manhood has been taken away from him in the United States, there is the possibility that it might be restored in the Philippines, thanks to the revolution."[44]

The carnal knowledge, so to speak, that Dante carries with him across the Pacific acts as the experiential surrogate for the exploitation that the peasants in Taruc's account suffered during the 1930s and 1940s (coinciding with the years that Dante and Felix spent in the United States). Bulosan could have stayed within the parameters of class critique laid out by Taruc (who does not engage with the politics of sexuality in *Born of the People*) since Filipino migrants in the United States, like other Asians during the first half of the twentieth century, were ineligible to own land and were therefore subject to seasonal migratory labor, with its miserable working conditions and scant financial rewards. Instead, Bulosan brings to the table the articulation of racial difference, class hierarchy, and sexual violence when addressing the possibilities and politics of transnational radicalism.

Determining why this sexual knowledge is significant and how it is supposed to affect the underground's political agenda is a complex affair. One might begin by considering the conceit that Felix's identity is to be verified through his damaged body. When the underground members learn that Felix's "right ball is this size [of a fist] but soft as cotton" and the "left is gone," leaving "only a wrinkled bag," Old Bio asks "about the other thing . . . by drawing a phallic symbol in the air" (*Cry*, 42). Dante responds, "It is there, all right. But I don't know if it still works. That is for someone to find out" (42). This turns out to be why Mameng has been assigned to join their mission. Hassim had earlier "resented the idea of bringing a woman with him" (21) and even now wonders why the Central Committee had not sent "the more attractive and experienced" Luming since there supposedly "would be no pain and remorse for her" (43). It is thus misleading to assert, as both the novel and critics claim, that Dante "is the only one who can identify Felix" (25). According to the bizarre logic of verification, unless Dante himself were to have sex with Felix, even *he* would not be able to identify his old acquaintance from the United States.

At one level, the authentication of Felix's disfigurement through sex "proves" his authenticity, not simply in confirming his genuine identity but in authorizing his assistance through past pain. His "wrinkled bag" becomes the corporeal emblem by which he displays his radical credentials, assuring the underground that his suffering in the United States results from his political organizing and furthers his radicalization, even as his functional phallus ensures that identification take place through heterosex. At another level, though, this seemingly arbitrary means of recognizing the "real" Felix serves as a pretext for Bulosan to pursue a revaluation of sexual practice that contests the sanctities of female virginity, sex within marriage, and monogamy.

In her feminist analysis of the Huk movement, Vina A. Lanzona analyzes the politics of gender and sex in Huk ideology, official statements, and daily life, since "theirs was the first major political and military organization in the country to include and actively recruit women."[45] She suggests that the Huks "rejected the Catholicism, monogamy, and sexual conventionality of mainstream Philippine society" (185), in part by presiding over "special marriages" that joined Huk members to each other and to "the struggle," and by issuing in 1950 "The Revolutionary Solution to the Sex Problem" to address the tensions that surfaced around extramarital liaisons between already-married male Huk members and their (theretofore single) "forest" wives. At the same time, Lanzona suggests that the male leadership's recourse to biological notions of sexuality such as in-born instincts and physical "necessities," lack of attention to female perspectives and needs, and submersion of the "personal" to the "political" reinforced the subordination of women within the organization. As much as the Huk's views toward gender relations, sex, reproduction, and family life challenged the feudal, Catholic, and capitalist norms of patriarchy and wealth accumulation, "most of its members," argues Lanzona, "acted according to highly conventional notions about gender and sexuality" (248).[46]

Bulosan's novel takes up similar issues but does not pursue them in the same way: none of the cadres is married, gets pregnant, has children, or forms "abnormal sexual relationships" as the Huks referred to adulterous liaisons. The Cry and the Dedication's diasporic reimagining of sexual morality takes place through Mameng's story and the reflections that her presence and role inspire. Worrying that she might be a virgin and perceiving her "initiation" into sex as a "death sentence," no less a figure than the unit leader Hassim is forced to question his traditional ideas (44). He imagines that "some defilement of human character was inevitable" for Mameng to carry out her task, and seeks "a way of consecrating it," of "mak[ing] it less degrading and painful" (45). And yet he wonders whether Mameng's charge represents "a challenge to his convictions": "Did he still carry with him the hypocrisies of the world they were trying to destroy? Was he still heir to the schizophrenic attitudes toward the life of that world?" (44–45).

Although Mameng initially asks Hassim to "prepare" her for her encounter with Felix, he "can't" because he, too, has been emasculated— not by vigilante Americans or by the Japanese, but by "our own people," as Dante later informs Mameng (116). It then befalls Dante to have sex with Mameng. But before they engage in intercourse, Mameng recounts to Dante how she had nearly had sex with a boy named Fedilio when she was sixteen. When she and her young beloved undress in a twilit banana grove, Fedilio halts their proceedings: "It is all wrong because we are not married." Mameng tells Dante that she felt the need "to cleanse myself of the shame," and Fedilio's suggestion that they "just look at each other" accomplishes that objective: "So we stood naked in the clear moonlight looking at each other, each turning around twice for the other to see; and in that act I felt cleansed and purified. I can still see the dancing shadows on his body and the deep hollows sloping down where the young flesh tautly receded into his underbelly and the mass of enticing darkness there where life stirred and raised its proud head in the moonlight" (57).

The lyrical and even "consecrating" scene of sexual union between Mameng and Dante challenges the "shame" that both Mameng and Hassim ascribe to sex outside of marriage (45). In one sense, the evocative description represents a familiar masculinist and nationalist poetics in which the female figure is identified with the landscape and heterosexual intercourse solidifies the male patriot's love for his country. Bulosan recurs to a kind of anticipatory pathetic fallacy as the two of them look at "a rise on the hillside below," which becomes "a woman in repose, undinal and containing the orgiastic truth of life," while "the fecundity of it all" reflects "a phallic truth" (54). In another sense, though, Mameng and Dante's approach to and enactment of sex achieve "the vanquishment of shame" and "the birth of dignity": The "shame would be given another name," asserts the narrator. "It would become truth and beauty" (54).

The association between sex and shame in Bulosan's work does not explicitly derive from religious injunction, as one might expect, but appears as a wholly naturalized and embedded social norm. Bulosan's focus on transvaluing nonmarital sex and the inviolability of female virginity arises in part from his investment in progressive temporality. The sex scene between Mameng and Dante contrasts with an early moment in *America Is in the Heart* where Allos describes a "primitive custom" in which his brother Leon determines whether his new bride "were virginal" (*America*, 6). When no black smoke issues from the hut, ostensibly implicating Leon's wife, the villagers rush the house; drag the woman out; tie her to a guava tree; spit in her face; tear off her clothes; call her "obscene names"; throw stones and sticks at Leon, who tries to guard her with his body; and whip Leon's father, who tries to protect them both (7–8). The retrospective, politicized narrator enters to denounce the "ritual," calling it a "cruel custom, because the women could no longer marry when they were returned to their parents [failing the virgin test], and would be looked upon with abhorrence and would be ostracized." Slyly attributing the residual custom to "the hill people," who carried it "down to the peasants in the valley" through intermarriage (reading it as a result of cultural contamination), the narrator argues for its extirpation: "But it was a fast-dying custom, in line with other backward customs in the Philippines, yielding to the new ways of the younger generation that were shaping out sharply from the growing industrialism" (7).

This reliance on historical progressivism, combined with Bulosan's use of Dante in *The Cry and the Dedication* as the agent for revising heterosexual morality in the Philippines, brings us to the politics of queer diasporic reading. First of all, we should not assume that Bulosan's critique of the alliance between sex and shame derives from "cultural difference." The scholarship in the United States on shame and sexuality amply attests to the pervasiveness of these associations in so-called modern, first world contexts.[47] And yet we cannot ignore the fact that Bulosan links the choice of Dante as Mameng's "initiator" to his expatriate experience: *"Because it was Dante who had seen other lands and years*, it was through him that the expression of the resolution would be realized, then to be poured warmly upon Mameng, who was the denuded landscape on a prudish island. It would be through him that the sweet currents of experience would be siphoned into the very depths of her" (54–55, my emphasis). It is this language of sexual penetration and ejaculation used to describe the transporting of working-class "experience" back to the homeland that critic Luis Teodoro finds problematic (13).

Without denying the heteromasculine imagery, it is important to note that Dante's "rejuvenating dose of awareness" is not based on felicitous and unfettered sexual experiences gained during his U.S. sojourn. After they have sex, Dante and Mameng share stories that link them through parallel sexual oppressions. Dante tells Mameng that his previous sexual relationships in the United States had either been with prostitutes (experienced more as a "business arrangement" than with "real feeling") or with married women (one woman's husband was "impotent") (60, 61). Though he may not have had his testicles smashed, Dante indicates that his sexual encounters have been unfulfilling. Mameng's past is more horrific. Explaining to Dante how she got the "ugly disfigurements" on her body, Mameng recalls that Japanese soldiers had "dragged [her] into one of their houses of pleasure" and that to escape being raped she "scarred" herself: "When they came and stripped me and saw the bleeding sores, they thought I had been infected by a horrible disease. They did not even touch me with their rifles" (57). After a priest nurses her back to health, she joins the underground. Thus, sex for Mameng is integral, not extraneous, to her radicalism, and she reclaims her sexuality not only from the shame of being unmarried to Fedilio but also from the violence of militarized near-rape. As Caroline S. Hau puts it, Mameng "invests the performance of her duty as a revolutionary with the erotic and emotional charge largely missing in her male counterparts' present experience."[48] In this regard, Mameng and Dante's sexual encounter enables them both to "vanquish" the shame associated with their past sexual experiences.

If Dante and Mameng facilitate this ethical revision of heterosex, then Felix and Mameng foreground issues around the politics of reproduction, family, and futurity. Dante dies toward the end of the novel, shot by his brother Bernardo Bustamante, a landowning priest who colludes with repressive forces. Analogous to Dante's succession of the deceased storyteller Apo Lacay, Felix Rivas remains on the horizon of the novel, Dante's successor who will bring aid to the underground. Although it is possible to read the anticipated union of Mameng and Felix as a process of healing the "wounded" Filipino male body, as Viet Nguyen suggests, that sexual act would necessarily be nonprocreative. Felix's sterility is the first inference that Old Bio draws from Dante's story: "There is nothing left?" he asks of Felix's genitals. "He was thinking what a great waste that such a man could not bring forth children into the world. For that was always his first thought of men: their primal obligation to mankind" (42). He later demands of Dabu: "How many children have you given to the world?" (49), a question he aggressively poses to various characters throughout the novel.

Bulosan's imagining of revolutionary temporality in millenarian terms (death to the old world and rebirth of the new) gives rise, at times, to figurations of futurity through reproductive sexuality, much as the anonymous son at the end of Maximo Kalaw's *The Filipino Rebel* embodies the hope for independence (see chapter 1). The closing poem of Bulosan's second book of poetry, *The Voice of Bataan* (1943), a slim volume of wartime monologues cast in the voices of diverse soldiers, illustrates this theme. In "Epilogue: Unknown Soldier," the speaker addresses his son and projects a "a new world / where new seeds / and new fruits / will nourish you into maturity" and for which the anonymous soldier sacrifices himself: "I die for a bright future."[49]

Not surprisingly, generational futurity often entails a conventional view of the family. In *The Cry and the Dedication*, Hassim ponders the wayfarer's return to his "closely knitted lovely family. . . . Your children had been waiting for you to give them assurance that they could live in the world and not be afraid. And your wife had been waiting for you because she wanted to tell you that the seed of your fertile manhood had grown big inside her again, making her a living part of you always" (76). Here, children become the products and promises of heterosexual, masculine duty fulfilled, while women become waiting wives and mothering machines forever tied to their husbands. Hassim directly links political and reproductive futurity in an internal apostrophe to Mameng: "Oh, Mameng! We can't easily give a better world. We will make one, but it belongs to the children after us. We have seen the future, and it is good. So we will prepare that world for the children of the future" (72).

In tense relation to these investments in conventional family structures and procreative sexuality are instances in which marriage and fatherhood *impede* the male radical activist's work. In Part 1 of *America Is in the Heart*, Allos and his cousin are forced to flee from his village to avoid two sisters who demand to marry them after they danced at a social gathering (78–79). In short order, Allos has to escape the fishing village where he attended high school classes when his landlady thinks that he is the father of an orphaned baby (85–86). Soon after this episode, Allos returns to his hometown of Binalonan to bid farewell to his brother Luciano, whose family life Allos rejects as a model for his own: "His wife had just given birth to another baby. I knew that he would have a child every year. I knew that in ten years he would be so burdened with responsibilities that he would want to lie down and die. I was glad that I was free from the life he was living" (89).

The evasion of marriage and paternity not only makes possible Allos's departure for the United States but also enables him to persist in his labor activism once there. In a scene that echoes his pitying view of Luciano's misery, Allos encounters José, a former union organizer who is now married and has a little boy: "I named him after you. I hope he will grow up to carry on the tradition!" Though Allos agrees, he proceeds to reflect: "I knew that he hated to be tied down. José knew that it was the end, that the happy yet violent days in the labor movement were over" (257). Whereas in Lanzona's account of female Huks it is often the women who were "torn between their revolutionary duties and their family lives,"[50] here it is a male radical who is "tied down" by fatherhood. The idea of progeny as bearers of the future who will both "carry on the tradition" and benefit from it conflicts with the reality that raising children entails being burdened by family life. Rather than "settle" for this reproductive life narrative, Allos pledges to "vindicate" and "succeed" those who cannot or will not continue "the fight" (257).

In light of these examples, we might understand the projected, extramarital, nonprocreative sexual union of Mameng and Felix Rivas to allegorize in ambiguous ways the connection between the homegrown female peasant/guerrilla fighter and the returned expatriate/labor organizer. Arriving not as an exultant "liberator," Felix is to provide material aid, specifically, "five million dollars" and "the possibility of having a shipload of ammunition and medicines from the United States" (*Cry*, 101).[51] Most important, he does not come bearing the seed of the diasporic returnee. Mameng will thus become something other than the lone female guerrilla "who would inundate with all her fertility the sterility of the world they were remaking" (59). Sex between the two will not yield children who could suture the national and the diasporic, or who might act as the inheritors and agents of revolutionary futurity. What sort of relationship follows from Mameng and Felix's encounter is impossible to say given the state of the text as we have it. In a sense, this uncertainty is fitting since the fate of the Huk rebellion when Bulosan wrote his novel in the early 1950s, while declining, was still unknown.

When placed within a diasporic frame, Bulosan's radicalism generates a multivalent sexual critique. With respect to the United States, he dramatizes the physical violence and psychological effects that antimiscegenationism and the stereotype of hypersexuality inflict on male working-class Filipinos. Class exploitation and racial subordination are made possible and driven by the management and containment of Filipino male sexuality. With respect to the Philippines, the new world that revolution might bring into being, according to Bulosan, must also bring about a transformation of sexual ethics, interrogating the "old verities" of female virginity, marriage, and procreation cherished by Hassim and Old Bio. In this regard, and in a way somewhat similar to Villa's work, neither the United States nor the Philippines serves as the site of (hetero)sexual liberation. Whereas the politics of interraciality and class hierarchy obstruct its fulfillment in the United States, traditional mores and prohibitions do so in the Philippines. If we take Bulosan's work at its most utopian, we might say that his overlapping critiques of racism, classism, and imperialism demand a revision of sexual normativity that implicates the entire social order, while leaving the place of sexuality within this "new world" an open question.

## Toward a "Queer" Bulosan?

The politics of gender and sexuality in Philippine Communism and radicalism have remained significant issues long after *The Cry and the Dedication* was written and the Huk rebellion dwindled in the mid-1950s, as texts like Patricio N. Abinales's monograph *Love, Sex, and the Filipino Communist* (2004), Ninotchka Rosca's novel *State of War* (1988), and Jessica Hagedorn's *Dogeaters* (1990), which I discuss in the next chapter, make evident.[52] Rather than trace these lines here, however, I close by considering the themes of futurity and sexuality as they relate to the archive, collaboration, and Bulosan's posthumous reception.

In a letter to his compatriot Jose de los Reyes, dated February 4, 1948, Bulosan remarks on how prolific he has been, two years after the publication of *America Is in the Heart*. He is "edit[ing]" an anthology of Philippine poetry," "looking for a publisher" for "a collection of Philippine short stories," working on a "novel," preparing "two volumes" of stories, collecting his "poems into a little volume," and considering a "long one-act play." Summarizing his industriousness, Bulosan writes: "I will have seven manuscripts for my agent. That is not bad, eh? . . . Perhaps someday your children will be looking at a big shelf of my own books, fifty of them, and wondering what kind of a guy I was to write so furiously and angrily in so brief a time." He then imagines what de los Reyes's children might think of him:

> "Look," they would probably say, "Just look at this crazy peasant who thought he could lick the world! Now he is dead. Did he love many women? Did he hate many men? He must have been a queer like Whitman and Hart Crane. Understand he never married. Let's read his letters; perhaps he revealed himself there."
> It would be fun to hear them talk about me.[53]

Bulosan's literary fecundity gives rise to a meditation on the future reception of his work, surmising that his friend's children would infer that the "kind" of guy who would "write so furiously" is not "an angry man," as he publicly proclaims in his essay "I Am Not a Laughing Man" (1946),[54] but rather "a queer like Whitman and Hart Crane."

Although Bulosan alludes to the two U.S. poets elsewhere in his work, he says nothing about their sexuality (let alone compares theirs to his) but rather emphasizes their roles as American writers. In *America Is in the Heart*, he refers to Whitman's "passionate dream of an America of equality for all races" (251) and to Crane's *The Bridge* as "the symbol of his faith in America" (245).[55] A previous letter written to de los Reyes sheds some light on Bulosan's recourse to "queer": "I have married my work, my dream, my hope for the future. No woman can take the place of my work; and all the women I have known realized it, and so in time they all went away."[56] Falling outside the normative trajectory of marriage and reproduction, Bulosan posits his "work" as his spouse and as his surrogate progeny. We might then think of his literary production as a substitute for biological reproduction (the nonprocreative sex between Mameng and Felix Rivas; the irreconcilable obligations of marriage, parenthood, and political activism)—rendering ironic the fact that *The Cry and the Dedication* would not be published in the United States until 1995, one major document of his "hope for the future" nearly lost.

*The Cry and the Dedication* is not the only belated text in Bulosan's corpus. In the same year that Bulosan told de los Reyes that he was married to his work, he was also corresponding with Philippine scholar Leopoldo Y. Yabes about assembling "an anthology of the best Filipino short stories" to be published in the United States. Bulosan poses the idea to Yabes, asking him to choose stories "from all the best known native writers"; he would then shape the "selections to fit the currents of American thought and temperament [and] to assure its wide circulation without sacrificing the integrity of Filipino writers."[57] Upon receiving Yabes's draft a few months later, Bulosan writes, "I am amazed. You really have it complete. . . . If possible I would like to represent each writer with one story. I found out that Filipinos write singing English, so beautiful, so like a melody."[58]

This transnational collaboration did not come to fruition in the manner proposed. Yabes describes the circuitous history of the anthology that would eventually become *Philippine Short Stories 1925–1940*, published by the University of the Philippines Press in 1975. Yabes had originally compiled an anthology of stories in 1940, but the outbreak of the war prevented its publication. In 1946, he reassembled the volume at the behest of Bulosan, who thought that "the heroic record of the Filipino soldiers in the defense of Bataan and Corregidor" would interest "the English-speaking world" in the anthology. "Besides," writes Yabes, "Bulosan also wanted to be of help to his fellow writers in the Philippines by introducing them to the English-reading public abroad. Only a handful of them had had the distinction of being published in America." However, Bulosan was unable to secure a publisher for the manuscript, "possibly on account of the cool reception the reading public showed towards a war novel by a Filipino which was published in 1947."[59] As it is, Yabes's *Philippine Short Stories 1925–1940* remains in print in the Philippines but off the radar of most readers in the United States.

This aborted collaboration is noteworthy for two reasons. As I mentioned in the previous chapter, despite the impact of U.S. colonialism on literary education and production in the Philippines from the dawn of the twentieth century onward, Philippine literature in English would not become readily available in the United States until Luis Francia's anthology *Brown River, White Ocean* in 1993, and most Americans to this day do not know that an anglophone literary tradition there even exists (see also chapter 6). Would the volume put together by Yabes and marketed by Bulosan have changed the course of anglophone Filipino literary history in the United States? Possibly, but perhaps not, given the vicissitudes of public taste and consciousness.

But I do think it might have changed the course of Bulosan's reception *in the Philippines*. In the same letter to Yabes that discusses the anthology, Bulosan writes:

> I was really surprised to know that several writers in the Philippines have contrary feelings for me. I have nothing but affection and pride

for writers in our native land. When I say something that seems to indict them, I do it only because there is a better way of using their talents. There is no need for Filipino writers to feel that I am inferior to them, or that their books are better than mine; neither should they feel that they are educated because they went to colleges, nor should they think that I am ignorant because I lack formal education.[60]

Similarly, in the letter Bulosan writes after receiving the manuscript, he states, "There is so much hate and distrust among men and among Filipino writers. . . . I feel that we must appreciate each other's work and personality."[61]

By referencing this transpacific collaboration, I am not implying that the "contrary feelings" and "distrust" separating Philippine writers from Bulosan would have magically dissipated if the anthology had been published, nor am I suggesting that his homosocial correspondence with Yabes replaces heterosexual marriage. But by publishing their work in the United States and "introducing them to the English-reading public abroad," Bulosan would have demonstrated in concrete terms the "affection" he had for Philippine writers and possibly have allayed some of the resentment they felt toward him for his criticism of their alleged lack of political engagement.[62] And although the anthology would not exactly have accorded with Bulosan's views about the politics of literature in the way that Villa's Doveglion anthologies had (Yabes draws heavily on Villa's "best of" series for his selections), it would at least have generated a more visible transnational and comparative context in which to situate Bulosan's work. This chapter's discussion suggests, however, that such a diasporic framing would not have rendered him more "Filipino," much less more *American* "like Whitman and Crane," but perhaps more "queer" to the extent that his sexual critiques of U.S. racial and class hierarchies *and* Philippine radical and social formations would have been thrown in bolder relief.

# 4

# The Cross-Cultural Musics
# of Jessica Hagedorn's Postmodernism

IN HER "PARTLY AUTOBIOGRAPHICAL" second novel *The Gangster of Love*,[1] Jessica Hagedorn "honor[s] the memory of [her] 'real-life' band,"[2] The Gangster Choir, which she founded in 1975 and for which she served as singer and lyricist until the group disbanded in 1984. Part immigrant bildungsroman, part *künstlerroman*, *The Gangster of Love* reads analogously to José Garcia Villa's autobiographical stories and critical essays as well as Carlos Bulosan's *America Is in the Heart* and autobiographical essays—as a portrait of the artist that describes migration from Manila to San Francisco and later New York City as coterminous with the author's alter ego, Rocky Rivera, coming into being as a writer. But in Rocky's/Hagedorn's case, writing is enabled by and coincident with her engagements with music.

Staging the interrelation of writing and music as a cross-cultural practice, Hagedorn not only memorializes The Gangster Choir but also inventories her eclectic musical and poetic influences, including R&B and 1970s funk, early spoken word and Black Arts poetry, French symbolism and surrealism, Filipino *kundimans* (Tagalog ballads), and a range of African American musicians, from Curtis Mayfield to Martha and the Vandellas. "I stayed in my bedroom listening to Aretha Franklin and Sly Stone on KSOL," narrates Rocky early on, "while tapping out minimalist poems on the secondhand Underwood my mother had bought me for my birthday. The poems imitated my male favorites of the moment: Antonin Artaud, Mallarmé, Gil Scott-Heron, and LeRoi Jones."[3] A page later, Rocky heads "down to City Lights Books for *The Selected Poems of Federico García Lorca*, then over to Tower Records for The Original Last Poets and Nikki Giovanni's 'Ego Tripping,' then to Flax's for another blank journal bound in black" (17). Whereas her brother Voltaire is "determined to save up enough for airfare back to the Philippines," Rocky's investment in (European and African American) poetry and (black) music/spoken word provides her with cultural resources that keep her "content to hole up in my room, writing and dreaming to the funky music on the radio" (17).[4]

This spirited interest in music extends across Hagedorn's corpus. Her first group of published poems, included in Kenneth Rexroth's edited *Four Young Women: Poems* (1973), features texts entitled "Autobiography Part Two: Rock and Roll" and "Filipino Boogie."[5] Her debut book *Dangerous Music* (1975) contains such poems as "The Great Young Drummer," "Latin Music in New York," "Canto Negro," and "Solea."[6] Hagedorn's second book, *Pet Food and Tropical Apparitions* (1981), includes the poems "Motown/Smokey Robinson," "The Woman Who Thought She Was More Than a Samba," and "I Went All the Way Out Here Looking for You, Bob Marley."[7] And the title of *The Gangster of Love* is itself taken from a 1957 song by rhythm-and-blues singer Johnny "Guitar" Watson.

As this brief sketch indicates, Hagedorn references a wide array of musics throughout her work. She describes her band The Gangster Choir in terms that further proliferate genres, while evoking its boundary-crossing ambitions: "Pop music, rock music, funkadelic, punkadelic, psychedelic, jazz fusion, acid house, gangsta rap, Bali-ghali, bhangra-jangra, hip-swaying, knee-bending, nitty-gritty, soul music—call it what you will. The Gangster Choir defied categories. The band's surreal name embraced contradiction and ambiguity, a bit of glorification and romantic identification with the rebel/outlaw/outsider."[8] Its half-ironic tone notwithstanding, Hagedorn's description suggests that the types of music she was drawn to, and certainly draws upon, imply a project aimed toward excavating dissident, "outsider" expressive traditions that dwell *within* the cultures of the former colonizers. These musical practices figure the defiance—the rejection and transgression—of dominant cultural forms organized around nation and race, and Hagedorn seems keen on searching out the underside of the colonizing cultures, those resistant expressive practices that have been marginalized (or appropriated) in the name of national culture. In effect, Hagedorn forges her complex poetics out of the manifold forms invented in the wake of Spanish and U.S. colonization of the Philippines, as well as the "multiculturality" of the United States.[9]

This chapter tracks the ways that Hagedorn's queer, cross-cultural, diasporic critiques of U.S. assimilation, Filipino American cultural nationalism, and Philippine nationalism take place most insistently through music. My focus on music provides a way to recover some of her literary production eclipsed by the critical tradition's fixation on her first novel *Dogeaters* (1990) and thereby reframe the scholarly attention given to the politics of Hollywood film and the operations of visuality in that novel. Hagedorn's early work, in one sense, was part of the "exuberant Pinoy arts movement in San Francisco"[10] of the 1970s that produced such poets as Virginia Cerenio, Jaime Jacinto, Al Robles, Luis Syquia, and Cyn Zarco, as well as the three authors who wrote "An Introduction to Filipino-American Literature" for the *Aiiieeeee!* anthology, Oscar Peñaranda, Serafin Syquia, and Sam Tagatac.[11] Three of Hagedorn's poems appeared in the important multimedia anthology *Liwanag: Literary and Graphic Expressions by Filipinos in America* (1975).[12]

At the same time, Hagedorn's fictionalized treatment of this moment in *The Gangster of Love* exhibits some ambivalence toward the movement's fleeting cultural nationalism. Reminding us of the role that Bulosan's legacy played for the West Coast artists,[13] Hagedorn depicts an argument between Rocky and the Carabao Kid, a "Pinoy poet from Watsonville" who is "totally obsessed with the Philippines," though he has "never been there," and is especially obsessed with "the essence of a true F(P)ilipino" (199). The Carabao Kid asks Rocky whether she "enjoyed reading *America Is in the Heart*": "'Bulosan's a bore,' I said. 'A noble martyr. An overrated, sentimental writer. A mediocre poet.'" She goes on to declaim to the "stunned" Kid that the "outcome's too goddam predictable. Suffering, heartache, yearning. Pain with a capital *P*—and more pain! I'm sick of humility. I'm sick of being grateful. America in the heart? Bullshit. You say Pinoys love to party? I say we love to suffer" (207). While in the previous chapter I interpreted the "suffering" endured by working-class Filipinos in Bulosan's narrative as a critique of America's social and sexual hierarchies, Rocky reads it as a "predictable" willingness to bear the slings and arrows of racism and class exploitation in return for a nominal sense of national inclusion. Whatever the validity of that interpretation, Rocky's repudiation of *America Is in the Heart* and the memorial service that the Filipino American community holds for the Carabao Kid after he dies of an aneurysm (206) may be read as Hagedorn's elegy to this historical moment, one that pays homage to its influence on her poetics even as it distances her own work from that cultural nationalist approach.

By the time Hagedorn writes *The Gangster of Love*, the "essentialism" and authenticity ascribed to ethnic identity have been seriously questioned, and Hagedorn is well aware of this, as her ironizing of the unpronounceable "F(P)ilipino" implies. In the introduction to the first edition of her anthology *Danger and Beauty* (1993), Hagedorn writes, "It is 1992 in New York City. Identity has been discussed, refuted, celebrated, collapsed, reconstructed, and deconstructed."[14] By situating Hagedorn's work within the context of 1970s identity politics and emphasizing her critical reflections on that moment, I do not mean to construct a teleological narrative that moves from essentialism to deconstruction. In fact, Hagedorn's opening remarks send her right back to San Francisco, 1973: "I am reminded of previous forays into that same jungle within. Who are we? People of color? Artists of color? Gay or straight? Political or careerist? Decadent or boring? Or just plain artists?" (ix). This re-collection—a historical paralleling and circling back between New York City, 1992, and San Francisco, 1973—not only argues against theoretical and aesthetic progress but also signals Hagedorn's self-conscious appreciation of her exposure "to Filipino American writers and artists who were cropping up in the Bay Area," as she says in an interview: "and that was like coming home."[15] Nonetheless, when viewed broadly, Hagedorn's corpus complicates artistic and political incarnations of cultural nationalism that are rooted in the United States and subordinate the significance of gender and sexual difference.

Here we might recall that Hagedorn's work was not only published in Filipino American venues such as *Liwanag* but also in the multiracial anthologies *Third World Women* (1972) and *Time to Greez! Incantations from the Third World* (1975), as well as the journal *Yardbird Reader*.[16] As a writer and performance artist, Hagedorn has also collaborated with her "satin sisters" Thulani Davis and Ntozake Shange,[17] and with Laurie Carlos and Robbie McCauley in the group Thought Music.[18] As she describes the energetic Bay Area arts scene of the 1970s, "Rock 'n' roll, R&B, the funk mystique of Oakland, the abstract seduction of jazz, and the glorious rants and changes of *loup garous*, gypsies, sympathetic cowboys, and water buffalo shamans.... They are my teachers and peers, kindred spirits, borders be damned."[19] Such multiracial affiliations and cross-media experiments are most visible (or audible) in The Gangster Choir. Hagedorn writes that the band "drew an astonishing group of musicians that came and went over the years" and that they spent much of their time "grappling with complex combinations of spoken word, music, rhythms, and the very notion of improvisation and 'performance.'"[20]

The following discussion takes these collaborative ventures and hybrid aesthetic practices as points of departure for examining several musical sites in Hagedorn's literary production: the references to John Coltrane in the story "The Blossoming of Bongbong," to Spanish/Andalusian flamenco and Thelonious Monk in the poem "Solea," to Jimi Hendrix and black popular music in *The Gangster of Love*, and to the Filipino *kundiman* in *Dogeaters*. In keeping with this study's queer diasporic framework, I elucidate the ways that music serves as the expressive, figural, and erotic terrain on which Hagedorn's cross-cultural and transnational acts of address take place. Operating as both a marker of cultural specificity and as a model for aesthetic hybridity, music serves as a kind of nodal point where cultural meanings associated with race, nation, gender, and sexuality converge and compete with one another, on the one hand, and where formal possibilities and artistic lineages are constructed and reinvented, on the other.

At one level, such multifaceted orientations enable us to see how music as an embodied practice of playing and listening moves the protagonists of "The Blossoming of Bongbong" and *The Gangster of Love* away from heterosexual and middle-class conventions of assimilation and toward alternative conceptions of subjectivity and sociality. Bongbong's and Rocky's uses of African American music raise the issue of the politics of appropriation. My analysis of *The Gangster of Love* confronts this question and explores how Hagedorn's poetics enacts what she describes as "the more positive side of appropriation: you take from many different sources, not to steal, but to pay homage to it, to say these are your influences, to add your own thing."[21] Whereas these narratives explore the limits and possibilities of U.S. socialities, "Solea" and *Dogeaters* take up music in a diasporic register, compelling us to consider the musics' formal structures, cultural meanings, and erotic connotations in transnational frames. The conjunctures between music and literature, I argue, reveal Hagedorn's remarkable reconfiguration of diasporic cultural politics, one that eschews straightforward cultural and anti-imperial nationalisms in pursuit of a cross-cultural, queer, improvisatory expressive practice.

## "Stay Crazy Under Pressure"

"The Blossoming of Bongbong" links queerness with avant garde jazz to produce a counterassimilationist immigration narrative.[22] The story begins with Bongbong leaving the Philippines "for the very reason that his sanity was at stake." Although he tells his painter friend Frisquito that the Philippines "is full of contradiction" and that he has "to leave before I go crazy," we are also told that Bongbong "had been in America for less than two years and was going mad."[23] The story's opening suggests that the protagonist's attempt to escape and resolve the unspecified contradictions of the homeland by migrating to the United States is thwarted. Living in the United States only amplifies his madness.

Bongbong's nonassimilation delivers a critique of the bourgeois demands of normative heterosexuality and utilitarian careerism. Coming off as sexually ambiguous, Bongbong is greeted in San Francisco by his brother-in-law Pochoy Guevara and his sister Carmen, who "feared he was homosexual, especially since he was such good friends with Frisquito" (41). Carmen's staidness, what Bongbong calls her "inhumanity" in his letters to Frisquito, renders Bongbong's queerness all the more conspicuous, as he fails "to find a job," refuses to attend college "and go into computer programming" like Pochoy (41–42), and rejects Carmen's "sacred temple" of reproduction (the nursery) when he is forced to move out to make room for her baby (51).

On the other hand, Bongbong's relationships with Charmaine, who is from Nicaragua, and her lover Colelia, whose background is "all mixed up" (45), only mark him as more queer. Charmaine first misrecognizes Bongbong as "Chicano" (the "offended" Bongbong thinks to himself, "No, I'm Ethiopian, or Moroccan, or Nepalese, what the fuck do you care" [44]), then later asks him whether he is "gay": "At first he didn't understand the term. English sometimes escaped him, and certain colloquialisms, like 'gay,' never made sense. He finally shook his head and mumbled no. Charmaine told him she didn't really mind. Then she asked him to go down on her" (45). In Bongbong's universe, a term like "gay" (linguistic competency aside) would not make sense. If it did, it might hold the key to his madness, and therefore his salvation. At the height of his relationship with Charmaine, we are given a blunt description of Bongbong's queerness and a hint at provisional hope: "He never fucked her. Sometimes he went down on her, which she liked even better. She had replaced books and television in his life. He thought he was saved" (46). Shortly, however, Charmaine's ravenous sexual appetite and her desire to be "the center of attention" direct Bongbong away from her—and the world in general (48–49). Diagnosing him as a "paranoid schizophrenic," Colelia links his "unnaturalness," again, to sexuality: "He doesn't like women basically. That's the root of his problem. . . . I mean, the guy doesn't even jack off! How unnatural can he be?" (52). Eventually, the two women move out.

If Bongbong is distinctly unsuited for computer programming and heterosexual pairing, the story suggests that perhaps music can "save" him. Whereas Carmen and Pochoy enjoy Johnny Mathis (42) and Charmaine "loved Sly Stone and Willie Colon" (46), Bongbong becomes attached to John Coltrane, particularly his 1965 recording *Meditations*, which "a friend of Charmaine's named Ra" gives him (50). He writes to Frisquito in the Philippines, "Every morning I plan on waking up to this man's music. It keeps my face from disintegrating" (50). Bongbong buys a soprano saxophone from a pawnshop and studies under Ra, "who taught him circular breathing. He never did understand chords and scales, but he could hear what Ra was trying to teach him and he surprised everyone in the house with the eerie sounds he was making out of his new instrument" (51).[24] Though Charmaine thinks that "Bongbong had at last found his 'thing,'" it turns out that "Bongbong's music only increased his natural visionary powers. He confessed to Ra that he could actually see the notes in the air, much as he could see the wind" (51–52). Bongbong's "visionary powers" compensate for his inability to read music or understand music theory; the "eerie sounds" he produces out of the saxophone seem to evoke his "natural" strangeness, not ameliorate his madness or transmute it into something coherent.

Bongbong's craziness reaches its climax in the conclusion of the narrative. He does not, however, disintegrate into nothing, pieces of his face crumbling to the pavement. He loses himself. After Charmaine and Colelia leave the apartment and Ra stops visiting him, Bongbong persists in playing the saxophone and discovers that "the powers of levitation were within him, so while he practiced the saxophone he would also practice levitating" (54). In his final letter to Frisquito, Bongbong writes, "The power of flight has been in me all along. All I needed was to want it bad enough" (55). The letter is signed "Love" with no comma or signature: "He didn't sign his name or his initial, because he had finally forgotten who he was" (55). The word "finally" implies that forgetting himself was Bongbong's goal "all along."

Working toward this telos of self-forgetting, the narrative endows listening to Coltrane's *Meditations*, practicing saxophone and levitation, and realizing the "power of flight" with climactic, even spiritual, significance. Hagedorn's reference to *Meditations* is apt since Coltrane's music during this late period of his career has often been understood in spiritual (though not religiously orthodox) terms. James Hall describes Coltrane's "quest for the ecstatic, a search that would rarely be confined to accepted or conventional musical practice."[25] Biographer Lewis Porter similarly writes that the opening track on *Meditations*, "The Father and the Son and the Holy Ghost," "suggests the religious ecstasy that the piece intends to convey, here taken to exquisitely painful limits."[26] Referring to Coltrane and other practitioners of "free jazz" as "God-seekers," Amiri Baraka writes in "The Changing Same (R&B and New Black Music)," "The titles of Trane's tunes, 'A Love Supreme,' 'Meditations,' 'Ascension,' imply a strong religious will, conscious of the religious evolution the pure mind seeks. The music is a way into God."[27] And *Meditations* is typically seen as "the most important *spiritual* follow-up to *A Love Supreme*," Coltrane's highly popular record released earlier in 1965.[28]

While Baraka places the music within a black historical context, several commentators note that Coltrane's "path" toward the transcendental was not "sectarian" but "dramatically cross-cultural."[29] Crucial to such cross-culturality was Coltrane's increasing interest in African and Indian musics and Eastern religions. De Sayles Grey speculates that "Coltrane's intense interest in the roots of African spirituality, as well as his growing fascination with the spirituality of India and the Far East, contributed to this spiritual culmination."[30] Describing Coltrane's encounters with Indian classical sitarist Ravi Shankar in the 1960s, Madhav Chari suggests that Coltrane's "work was influenced by the 'spirit,' 'energy,' or 'essence' of Indian music," and he goes on to quote Coltrane himself: "I'd like to point out to people the divine in a musical language that transcends words. I want to speak to their souls."[31]

Bongbong's ecstatic experience may thus be read as the effect of Coltrane's musical soul-speaking on one attuned listener. Though Kimberly W. Benston's analysis of the "Coltrane Poem" considers the musician's impact on Black Arts poetry, his notion that these poems operate according to a dynamic of "orphic-elegiac struggle"—the dual pursuit of *gnosis* as "concealed knowledge essential to salvation" and *askesis* as "a revisionary movement of self-discovery by way of self-purgation"—is pertinent here.[32] Hagedorn's evocation of Coltrane may not be elegiac, but her portrayal of Bongbong's relation to Coltrane implicitly partakes of this orphic trajectory, of seeking "salvation" not through conventional values of education, professionalization, and reproduction but through ascetic practices. Coltrane's music provides the aural-philosophic lift that enables Bongbong's ethereal "self-discovery."

In the liner notes to *Meditations*, Nat Hentoff quotes Coltrane as saying that his goal "is to uplift people, as much as I can. To inspire them to realize more and more of their capacities for living meaningful lives." While "uplift" reverberates with special significance in African American history, Bongbong's levitation literalizes this effect. If there is an "orphic" descent that presupposes this ascent, we might postulate that it is Bongbong's frustrated encounters with U.S. immigration (racial and sexual misrecognition and the obligations toward social propriety and productivity). Furthermore, his signature as "Love" resonates with Hall's claim that Coltrane's "cultural criticism" centered around the "injunction to 'love'" (115).

Hagedorn's references to the spiritual tropes of love, meditation, and ascension are especially significant when read within the context of the mythic sexuality and masculine prowess attributed to the black jazzman.[33] Bongbong's embrace of Coltrane is precisely *not* an attempt to stabilize his ambiguous racial identity by "passing" as black, or to quell rumors of his queerness by assuming the heteromasculinity associated with "blackness"—or even to resolve the contradictions he had tried to leave behind in the Philippines by reconciling himself to life in the United States. If Bongbong takes "flight" out of himself, then music serves as his wings.

## "How We Appropriated You"

Hagedorn has said of Bongbong that "he's a version of me, but more naive and more spiritual."[34] More than twenty years later, she would publish a female version of herself in *The Gangster of Love* that similarly narrates immigration as counterassimilation. Rejecting the normative trajectory of de-ethnicization, upward mobility, and nuclear familyhood, Rocky pursues music and writing, engages in a variety of nontraditional relationships (including a tumultuous, queer relationship with the female photographer Keiko), and eventually returns to the Philippines as an ambivalent mourner of the past.[35] Rocky's formation of the multiracial band The Gangster of Love not only takes her away from the domestic space epitomized by her mother, Milagros, but also raises the issue of appropriating "black" music.

Critics who have written about Asian Americans taking up expressive practices construed as not their own—especially jazz and hip-hop—have remarked on how tropes of authenticity, and charges of inauthenticity, saturate the way those artists are perceived, received, and discussed.[36] Although recent "Afro-Asian" scholarship has sought to debunk what Vijay Prashad calls myths of cultural purity by documenting the long history of connections (and conflicts) between the groups,[37] such relations are politically charged sites that exceed easy interpretations of antiracist and anti-imperialist solidarity, or interracial animosity and distrust. Moreover, while some critics have commented on how Asian American men in jazz and hip-hop confront and seek to revise stereotypes of Asian male effeminacy and black hypersexuality, very little has been said about Asian American women who "appropriate" black expressive practices. In both performance and scholarship, women are either relegated to music video eye candy or removed from the framework of appropriation in the Afro-Asian cultural genealogy. In short, men of color appropriate from each other; women of color collaborate with each other.

If the verbs hit a gendered nerve (aggressive taking versus supportive nurturing), that is the point. Rocky's position (and, by extension, Hagedorn's) as the Filipina lyricist, singer, front-person, and bandleader of the multiracial, generically undefined The Gangster of Love forces us to contend with the raced, gendered, and sexualized politics of popular music. After a dismal show in Detroit where the band is "heckled mercilessly" (125), Rocky reflects, "I thought I could do everything myself: write songs, perform, hire and fire musicians, pay the rent with my part-time jobs" (126). The paragraph following this admission begins: "On one of my visits back to San Francisco, my mother asks me why I try so hard to be a man" (127). The implication is that for Rocky to "do everything," she has to act like a "man."

Although Rocky's pursuit of music is ideologically and geographically distanced from her mother's domesticity (Milagros, too, is hardly the conventional maternal figure, having ditched her adulterous husband in the Philippines and started up her one-woman catering service, Lumpia X-Press, in San Francisco), Hagedorn does not represent The Gangster of Love as a utopian form of sociality. To be sure, the band's composition (Filipina Rocky, Chinese American guitarist Elvis Chang, and African American drummer Sly) bespeaks Hagedorn's interest in portraying a multiracial social landscape. Nonetheless, the sexually charged relationships among the band members, and their disagreements over what Hagedorn describes as "the political contradictions inherent in making art and making commerce,"[38] ultimately reveal that The Gangster of Love will not serve as some paragon of harmonious multiculturality.

The band's eventual decline is prefigured by a scene in which "Sly and Elvis keep buggin'" Rocky about the direction the group should take:

> They want session types to back me up, flashy women in spandex with booming gospel voices, big hair, and plenty of attitude. "Enough of this arty shit. It doesn't work."
> "I'm a poet," I remind them.
> "People want something they can dance to," Sly says.
> We trudge from one dead-end gig to another, bickering and demoralized, and still no record deal in sight. (146)

Here, "arty shit" is posed against the inclusion of backup singers whose description packages the women in much the same way that the men want to package the music. The women performers, commodified into "types" through their clothing, vocal, and hair styles, are for show, not art.

The vexed relation between art and commerce becomes most acute when Hagedorn addresses the politics of appropriation, imitation, and authenticity. Well before this argument, the novel self-consciously registers the history of expropriating black cultural production for economic gain. When the group is scheduled to perform with the satirically named White No More, Sly reproves Rocky's compliments:

> "Fuck 'em," Sly said. His tone became whiny and self-righteous. "You're too kind to those white boys, Rocky. They're fuckin' copycats. They steal shit. *Our* shit. And they get press coverage, record deals, and we don't."
> "Enough," I shot back, glaring at him. "We do the same thing, don't we? We cop from Jimi, from Sly Stone, from George Clinton, from Miles, and Betty Davis—"
> At the mention of Miles's ex-wife, Sly's eyes bugged out. "Okay, okay, I hear you. Nothing's original. But please . . . Betty Davis?" (73)

The chapter that follows this acknowledgment is titled "Our Music Lesson #1, Or How We Appropriated You: An Imaginary Short Starring Elvis Chang, Rocky Rivera, and Jimi Hendrix" (75). Despite Sly's concession that "Nothing's original," the novel segues into what would promise to be a more forthright explanation of how The Gangster of Love (and implicitly Hagedorn) appropriates black music.

Before turning to that music lesson, it is worth looking at one instance where the gendered and raced politics of imitation and appropriation become explosively apparent. In the chapter "Nostalgia for the Mud," Rocky narrates the band's dissolution: "I packed all our tapes in boxes, copies of the one record we made in another. Sealed the boxes, pushed it all into the back of a closet. Fifteen years or so worth of shit. Over" (247). But this narrative thread does not fade out in a murmur. In an intense tableau taking place in the oneiric "Zamboanga or Zimbabwe of my [Rocky's] imagination," The Gangster of Love play their final gig as opener for Sister Mercy's No-Bullshit Satin Soul Revue, who prove true to their name: "They immediately expose us as fakes" (243). In this nightmarish scenario, Hagedorn implies that The Gangster of Love cannot compete with "the real thing" (243), not coincidentally coded "black": "Sister Mercy is a living legend and authentic survivor of the chitlin circuit, magnificent, gritty, temperamental priestess-bitch and godmother to James Brown. . . . Sister Mercy dismisses my band as postmodern, postcolonial punks. Monkey see, monkey do. We F(P)ilipinos can imitate, but this audience prefers the real thing" (241, 243). Alluding to one of the bestial slurs used to describe Filipinos during the Philippine-American War, Hagedorn reminds us that even cross-color imitation can be dismissed as "postmodern, postcolonial" play—disrespectful, superficial, disingenuous. While the crowd boos and throws rotting bananas at the band, Sister Mercy "disapproves of the covers I've chosen to deconstruct and desecrate" (246). Mayhem breaks out on stage, Sister Mercy brandishes an Uzi, "government troops are forced to intervene. We are tried without a jury, condemned to exile as second-rate, Western imperialist, so-called artists before being shoved into a Philippine Airlines jumbo jet. We are flown out of Zamboanga in the middle of the night, back to the safety of Motown memory" (246). Surely this is one of the strangest self-flagellating dreams in Hagedorn's work. It is not as if the Zamboangan/Zimbabwean mob is screaming for local Filipino or African music (they clamor for "Madonna and Sting. Their brand of blond exotic, without gravity" [245]). So why should The Gangster of Love—comprised of members of Filipino, Chinese, and African descent, performing Motown classics (246)—be denounced as "second-rate, Western imperialist, so-called artists"?

Though The Gangster of Love is not a typical R&B or blues band but a poetry and music ensemble, it is nonetheless striking that this hallucinatory scene accuses the band of playing derivative imitations. The novel alludes to the notion that Filipinos are natural-born imitators earlier on when, at a wedding reception for Rocky's cousin Peachy, the narrator remarks of the hired band, "Rudy and the Romantics are absolutely amazing, segueing expertly from one musical genre to another" (205). Hagedorn reinforces this point in the essay "Music for Gangsters," referring to Filipinos as "hybrid and resilient masters of eerie mimicry and witty appropriation" who can "segue smoothly from perfect covers of Prince's naughty 'Kiss' to Debbie Boone's super-schmaltzy 'You Light Up My Life.'"[39] However skillful Filipinos may be as musical mimics, the nightmare in *The Gangster of Love* registers a sort of racialized inferiority complex whereby mimicry compares poorly to black originality. Sister Mercy thus operates as the stalwart figure of Hagedorn's misgivings, she who guards the gates of "the real thing" and exposes all others as poseurs.

The "music lesson" with Jimi Hendrix offers a partial response to this impasse. Challenging the impermeability of racial categories, the conversation between Rocky, Elvis, and Hendrix "*as he looked in 1970, the year he died*" takes place in an empty nightclub with "Voodoo Chile" playing in the background (75). The preface to the dialogue remarks on Rocky's "*questionable*" ethnic identity, paralleling Bongbong's racial uncertainty: "*She could be Mayan, Malay, Pinay, or Gypsy. Her hair is cut very short; she wears heavy eye make-up and has a wary, tough look about her*" (75). Referencing the "rebel/outlaw/outsider" theme that saturates Hagedorn's work, the term "gypsy" here connotes a sense of nomadic wandering and persecution, while Hendrix's "Voodoo Chile" is less an anthropological approach to religiosity than an assertion of "outsider" status.[40] The lyrics of the song—the fifteen-minute blues version, not the five-minute rock rendition "Voodoo Child (Slight Return)" that closes the album *Electric Ladyland* (1968)—make explicit the connection between voodoo child and gypsy: "The night I was born, / I swear the moon turned a fire red / Well my poor mother cried out 'Lord, the gypsy was right!' / And I seen her fell down right dead."[41]

Hendrix's allure for Hagedorn may lie in the way that his "outlaw" positionality attempted to break down racial boundaries in music, challenging what Jeremy Wells refers to as "sonic essentialism."[42] The contradictory meanings that Hendrix generated from the clashes among his racial appearance, his on-stage wildman antics, the sounds he produced out of his electric guitar and in the studio, and the styles of music he composed and performed have made him a deeply contested figure in popular culture. By most accounts, Hendrix's final album, *Band of Gypsys* (1970), recorded live with African American musicians Billy Cox (bass) and Buddy Miles (drums), represents at least a partial concession to the cultural nationalist detractors who thought that he not only reinforced stereotypes of the hypersexual black male for predominantly white audiences but also took the path of "white" rock instead of continuing the "black" tradition of the blues. Hagedorn seems alive to these debates, and her vignette places Hendrix in a continuum of black music while positioning him as a vanguard artist as well. "If you listen carefully," Rocky says, "the 'Voodoo Chile' melody is exactly the same as 'Catfish Blues,'" a traditional blues that Hendrix covered and was released on the album *Blues* in 1994 (76). Elvis similarly asserts, "You were in sync with the times, but ahead of it too. Before you, there was no one. Maybe Chuck Berry. Maybe Little Richard" (75). At the same time, a number of critics have also emphasized "the hybridity that so influenced his artistic vision," as Wells puts it (60).[43] In Hendrix, Hagedorn seems to find a "fellow eclecticist,"[44] one who "defied categories" based on racially circumscribed art forms.

The "lesson" that this minidrama imparts, then, is that appropriation is part praise, part dialogue and address ("How We Appropriated *You*"), and part grappling with the dead. The novel proper begins with a chapter titled after Hendrix's famous song "Purple Haze": "Jimi Hendrix died the year the ship that brought us from Manila docked in San Francisco" (5). Hendrix is only the most audible ghost in the book, which, as Hagedorn says, "is haunted by the musical spirits of Jimi Hendrix, Sly Stone, and Miles Davis."[45] In fact, Hendrix is resurrected not once but twice. Miming the reprise structure of "Voodoo Chile" and "Voodoo Child (Slight Return)" on *Electric Ladyland*, Hagedorn has Hendrix return a second time: "Our Music Lesson #2, Or How We Appropriated You" (233). Although much of the first version is repeated verbatim, in the second one Hagedorn makes explicit the coincidence between Rocky's arrival and Hendrix's death in 1970: "Everybody I love is dead or dying" (236).

The two dramatic shorts represent Hagedorn's way of bringing Hendrix back from the dead, endowing him with a voice in the debates waged over his iconicity, giving him "proper credit" when the band covers "Voodoo Chile" (236), praising him as a musical innovator, while contesting the rigid logic that equates bodily appearance with racialized musical forms and thereby excludes racialized others from participation. On the other hand, Rocky slyly interrogates Hendrix's own racial identity: "Has anyone ever asked you if you were Pilipino? You look like you might have some of that blood" (236). This insinuation of Filipino "blood" into Hendrix's heritage is counterpoised with an earlier scene in which Rocky's mother questions whether the father of her as-yet unborn baby is "black" (165). Exasperated by Milagros's "irrelevant, offensive question," Rocky retorts, "Goddammit, Ma. So fuckin' what. We're *all* black"—a response that Milagros deems "preposterous" (165). In a sense, racism, or at least what Paul Gilroy terms "raciology,"[46] underlies both scenarios—the collisions of black musical authenticity and artistic/racial hybridity in the figure of Hendrix, and the antiblack prejudice that polices the norms of respectable Filipina heterosexuality.

Undermining these racialist tenets in favor of mixed musics and respectful exchange, the shorts also theorize cross-cultural "dialogue" in gendered and sexualized terms. Rocky's "*tough look*" alludes to the necessity to act like a "man" in the rock music business—a charge that Hendrix also levels at her: "Why you try so hard to be a man?" "You sound just like my mother," Rocky responds, to which Hendrix replies, "Fuck me, then. Save my soul" (77). Rebuffing Hendrix's proposition, Rocky launches into a dream that could be interpreted as a sexualized allegory of appropriation. A "young girl" who is "maybe Japanese or Chinese" tries to pass a note to Hendrix through a security guard who, in turn, tells her: "Suck my dick first" (77). Rocky recalls that in her dream, "We're all in line behind the poor little lost yellow girl, trying to get in backstage, to the inner sanctum, so we can pay our respects to the pope. King Kong was the keeper of the flame, and I did not want to be that poor little yellow girl. She sucked King Kong's dick to get to you—" (77–78). Although the Asian girl is not herself a musician, one might still read this dream as a critical commentary on what it takes to gain access to the guitar-god: sexual favors as the price of admission. Is this what it *means* to pay homage to your idols? Hendrix's sorry excuse is to take refuge in the inevitable: "Have you any idea how much pussy was thrown at me?" (78).

Whereas this disturbing scene of sexploitation ends "Music Lesson #1," the reprise takes a less troubling turn, closing with Hendrix and Rocky singing "Voodoo Chile" together and then engaging in "*a long, meaningful kiss*" (237). It is as if the self-defining lyrics "'Cause I'm a voodoo chile / voodoo chile" render the two parallel, if not identical, to one another (236). Here appropriation is not predicated on forced fellatio, but enabled, and perhaps given sanction, by a kiss. In sum, one might consider Hagedorn's dialogues with Hendrix as de-mythified tributes to a kindred spirit who also worked to cross racial categories guarded on both sides of the color line.

## "Fractured Lyricisms"

Similar to the way that the protagonist of "The Blossoming of Bongbong" comes to terms with his "madness" through music, and to the way that *The Gangster of Love* insists on musical hybridity as a critical response to appropriation, the poem "Solea" makes recourse to music to address themes of alienation and cultural borrowing. The structure of the poem alternates between objective descriptions of a racially and sexually violent social world, and lyric addresses to an absent "you." Here, however, the allusions to *solea*, a type of flamenco song and dance that formed in southern Spain, and to Thelonious Monk, a jazz pianist and composer who has inspired numerous literary tributes much like Coltrane, traverse both national and racial borders. Rather than a mimetic representation of a musical scene, a formal transposition of song into poetry, or a simple celebration of musicians, "Solea" draws on flamenco and Monk to evoke a complex affective mood and to effect a formal breaking of the lyric voice. Neither consolation for the speaker's isolation nor a narcissistic echo of her psychic and emotional state, music in "Solea" becomes a frame for articulating a gendered and raced poetic subjectivity under duress.

Despite its title, nothing in the content of the poem refers to flamenco—no heel-pounding dancers or whipping skirts; no furiously strummed guitars or exclamatory cries. Even its setting is contemporary New York City, not the sun-baked landscape of Andalusia studded with olive groves and fig trees. Rather than follow directly in line with, say, Federico García Lorca's *Poema del cante jondo* (1921/1931) or *Romancero gitano* (1928), or with the myriad U.S. poets who have taken up Lorca in diverse ways,[47] Hagedorn's "Solea" sets the mood of the poem by playing on the Andalusian version of *soledad*, meaning "solitude" or "loneliness." Alone, the speaker begins:

> there are rapists
> out there

some of them don't like asian women
they stab them
and run off to lake tahoe
in search of more pussy
in casino parking lots[48]

"Out there" functions as a sort of refrain, intensifying the speaker's solitude and demarcating her internal thoughts from the misogynist, racist,
imperialist, murderous, external world: "there are sad men / out there
/ some of them / don't like me / they like to talk / about corpses and
dirt / and how life used to be / so good / when they were young / in the
war"; "there are killers / out there / some of them / smile at me" (62).
    Woven in between these dangerous threats are stanzas of personal in-
timacy that invoke not only the solitary mood of the *solea* but also the
music of Monk:

thelonious monk
reminds me of you
and i forget
about this place
it's nice

but then
i have to put in
an appearance
at family dinners
and listen to other voices
my blood
in the warm gravy
and the kiss i reserve
only for little children

i can't play
those records
all the time
thelonious monk
is only joyful
in a hurting kind
of way (61)

Given Hagedorn's interest in jazz, one might expect a more direct reference to Miles Davis's 1959 recording *Sketches of Spain*, which closes with a twelve-minute "Solea"—or even to the track "Flamenco Sketches" on Davis's *Kind of Blue*, released the same year. While the poem may implicitly resonate with Davis's music, perhaps he is not alluded to by name because of the way his trumpet performance has been understood to capture so well the voice of the flamenco singer. In the liner notes to *Sketches of Spain*, Nat Hentoff gushes, "It is a measure of Miles' stature as a musician and a human being that he can so absorb the language of another culture that he can express through it a universal emotion with an authenticity that is neither strained nor condescending." As we have seen, Hagedorn is much more cautious about such practices of cross-cultural absorption. It is as if Hagedorn sidesteps Miles in favor of Monk precisely because the connection—between trumpet and voice, between Davis and flamenco—would be *too* direct, too "obvious."

The lack of flamenco details in the poem suggests that the *solea* of "Solea" gets filtered into *Dangerous Music* via its mediations through black expressive culture. Many scholars and writers have drawn parallels between flamenco and the blues. In the liner notes to *Sketches of Spain*, Hentoff quotes Gilbert Chase, who describes the *solea* as "a song of longing or lament, like the Afro-American blues." María Frías has documented some of the musical and literary connections between the two forms and the analogous social conditions (displacement and persecution) out of which they emerge, and cites guitarist Paco Peña: "Flamenco is similar to the blues. It has a tinge of sadness, an element of fight and rebellion. It is pain and suffering with explosions of great happiness."[49] In a 1954 essay, Ralph Ellison links "Cante Flamenco, or *cante hondo*" (deep song) to black music through its "feeling": "In our own culture the closest music to it in feeling is the Negro blues, early jazz, and the slave songs." He goes on to interpret flamenco in much the same way he understands the blues, remarking on "the note of unillusioned affirmation of humanity which it embodies. . . . In its more worldly phases flamenco voice resembles the blues voice, which mocks the despair stated explicitly in the lyric."[50] Two years later, Langston Hughes would echo Ellison's sentiments in his second autobiography, *I Wonder as I Wander* (1956), upon witnessing La Niña de los Peines, Pastora Pavón, in Madrid:

> Shortly, without any introduction or fanfare, she herself sat up very straight in her chair and, after a series of quavering little cries, began

> to half-speak, half-sing a *solea*—to moan, intone and cry in a Gypsy
> Spanish I did not understand, a kind of raw heartbreak rising to a
> crescendo that made half the audience cry aloud with her after the
> rise and fall of each phrase. . . . I found the strange, high, wild crying
> of her flamenco in some ways much like the primitive Negro blues
> of the deep South. The words and music were filled with heartbreak,
> yet vibrant with resistance to defeat, and hard with the will to savor
> life in spite of its vicissitudes.[51]

While Hagedorn's poem, by juxtaposing the *solea* with the music of Thelonious Monk (who, of course, composed a number of blues tunes, including the standard "Blue Monk"), implicitly connects flamenco with
the blues or jazz, it seems more skeptical toward the emphasis on transcendence. Not unlike the way she eschews a sketch of the flamenco
singer or dancer, Hagedorn also leaves aside "Monk's personal eccentricities," such as "dancing in performance, donning an array of traffic-stop-
ping hats, and so on," that Sascha Feinstein identifies in many a "Monk
poem." What attracts Hagedorn rather is "Monk's musicality, which
combined a brilliant sense of time with textured, dissonant harmon-
ics."[52] In the first stanza that references Monk, Hagedorn seems to be
following in the wake of commentators like Ellison and Hughes. Monk's
music has salutary effects on the speaker: it "reminds me of you / and i
forget / about this place / it's nice." Analogous to the way that Bongbong
forgets himself through Coltrane's *Meditations*, Monk's music transports
the speaker out of "this place" stalked by racists, rapists, and killers.

But the prosaic "it's nice" signals that Monk will not ultimately serve
as the means for overcoming the pain of solitude. The combination of
joy and pain—"thelonious monk / is only joyful / in a hurting kind /
of way"—echoes the "heartbreak" that Hughes discerns in Pavón's singing. That such emotional mixing should be evoked through flamenco
and Monk is apposite, for Monk's playing often merges melodious runs
with peculiar harmonies and unusual rhythmic stresses. It is this "insis-
tent dissonance" and "rhythmic disjunction"—what one critic calls the
"angularity" of Monk's style[53]—sounded unexpectedly within the context of a seductively sweet lyricism, that "hurts," that cuts into you, that
rends the fabric of any easy joy one might weave out of Monk's music.

That breaking of moods is formally reflected in the unusual syntax of
the following stanza:

i like to kiss you
like i do
little children
it tastes good
but i have to leave
the room sometimes
is deep
wanting to be crazy
and painting my toenails
gold
and seeing universes
in my colors (62)

The phrase "the room sometimes" seems to perform double duty. It makes sense with the line above it and some (metaphorical) sense with the line below it, but no sense when read in tandem with the succeeding four lines. The subjects of "is deep" and "wanting to be crazy" are missing. It would seem that the speaker has to leave the room sometimes because kissing you "tastes" *too* "good." Like the joy that hurts when listening to Monk, the kiss cannot be tolerated and drives the speaker out of the room, where she can "be crazy" and see universes in the colors of her painted toenails.

The closing stanzas of the poem comment more explicitly on the speaker's "craziness," induced, it would seem, by both the presence and absence of "you."

new york
reminds me of you
so do the locks
on my door
and the way i look
sometimes
when i feel
schizophrenic

there is real beauty
in my eyes
when i lose my mind

> i understand you better
> this way
> and it doesn't hurt
> so much
> anymore (63)

The language of visuality again leads to ambiguities. "the way i look / sometimes" could refer to the speaker's "schizophrenic" physical appearance—in disarray, disheveled, out of sorts. But "look" might also refer to the act of looking, as in "the way i *see* sometimes." Thus, the beauty in the speaker's eyes could refer to the appearance *of* her eyes (insisting that her eyes are *really* beautiful when she loses her mind). But it could also refer to the beauty that she sees *with* her eyes (the beauty she beholds when she loses her mind). Craziness, schizophrenia, losing her mind—these become the psychological mechanisms through which the speaker can see "you," "understand you better," and alleviate some of the pain produced by both your absence and memory.

To link this split psychology back to the poem's formal aspects, "Solea" does not so much record the rambling thoughts of a wounded agoraphobe (all those evildoers "out there," I'd rather paint my toenails) as use flamenco and Monk to connote this complex mood and to figure formally a breaking of the lyric voice, a breaking that Hughes's description "half-speak, half-sing" intimates. The subject's multiplicity and splitting implied by "schizophrenia"—"*wanting* to be crazy" to keep from going crazy—is enacted in the syntactically disjointed middle stanza. The line "is deep" breaks the narrative *and* poetic line at exactly the moment when the speaker has to leave the room. Something similar happens in the earlier stanza where Monk's music had provided temporary solace. When the speaker has "to put in / an appearance / at family dinners / and listen to other voices," the voice drifts away from family dinner chitchat and imagines "my blood / in the warm gravy." The incoherency of the subject is mimed by and results in a fragmented voice—a breaking that is figured, to use Hagedorn's memorable phrase, in the "fractured lyricisms of jazz," of Monk.[54]

And the fractured voice of flamenco. This breaking—of the subject, heart, syntax, voice—accords with Nathaniel Mackey's explication in his essay "Cante Moro" of Lorca's notion of *duende*, that elusive force in flamenco. "One of the things that marks the arrival of *duende* in flamenco singing," Mackey writes, "is a sound of trouble in the voice. The voice becomes troubled. Its eloquence becomes eloquence of another order, a broken, problematic, self-problematizing eloquence."[55] In "Solea," the speaker's troubled, broken voice registers an "eloquence of another order," an order (of "beauty" one might add) that Hagedorn gives the name "craziness"—an order, too, that is not synonymous with transcendence.

Furthermore, insofar as this recourse to flamenco invokes a diasporic context, Hagedorn does not simply reinvest in Spanish culture. Flamenco's origins, as many have pointed out, are uncertain and impure.[56] In a piece called "Los Gabrieles" that appears to be autobiographical, Hagedorn remarks on the impossibility of digging up or putting down roots in Spain. "Lured by the somnambulant invocations of Lorca," she reproduces a conversation in Andalusia with an "Irish expatriate" who exhorts before they part ways: "You must come back to Spain. . . . You must investigate your roots!" to which Hagedorn says to herself: *"Roots? I want to laugh and say: 'I was born in the Philippines, I'm a quintessential bastard, my roots are dubious.'"*[57]

Neither a typical "Monk poem" nor a search for origins in Spain, "Solea" summons the affective and formal force of Monk and flamenco to intimate what remains inarticulable in the poem's verbal composition—a dissonant and fractured lyricism that takes an "angular" approach to both the racially and sexually threatening social world and the precarious intimacy promised by, and premised on, the lyric address. Whatever hope the speaker holds out in understanding "you" better is compromised or "problematized" by her loss of mind. In "Solea," as in "The Blossoming of Bongbong," going crazy becomes a survival strategy, a reframing of (self-)perception that Monk's joyful-painful music and the *duende* of flamenco help to bring about and "sound." And it is this contradictory mix of affect (solace and suffering, love and lament) that Hagedorn reaches after in her use of the *kundiman* at the end of *Dogeaters.*

## "A Love [Song] to My Motherland"?

This musical context provides an alternative frame for examining the gendered and sexualized politics of cultural imperialism, martial law nationalism, antiauthoritarian resistance, and diasporic address in *Dogeaters.* Many critics have followed E. San Juan Jr.'s description of the novel as a "cinematext" that "render[s] in a unique postmodernist idiom a century of U.S.-Philippine encounters."[58] While bringing to bear feminist and queer perspectives, most scholars still accept San Juan's presumptions that *Dogeaters* is postmodernist and obsessed with, even written as, cinema.[59] The debate has consequently revolved around whether Hagedorn's representations of Hollywood film simply register—if not reproduce—the soporific effects of U.S. cultural imperialism (the colonizing of the Filipino imagination), or whether the novel depicts "the capacity of oppressed peoples to transform the possibilities of their oppression," as Rachel Lee puts it.[60]

Superimposing the late 1950s and the early 1980s, *Dogeaters* evokes a sprawling, class-stratified Manila out of whose teeming mass of humanity Hagedorn builds a multileveled political allegory: the ideological/imaginative and military/material impact of U.S. imperialism on the Philippines; the violent state repressions imposed by martial law; and the various modes of resistance to empire and dictatorship ranging from political demonstrations to guerrilla tactics—all the while underscoring how gender and sexuality are integral to those competing forces. To the extent that the New People's Army represents the most serious threat to martial law in the novel, it is noteworthy that Hagedorn has the radicalized ex-beauty queen Daisy Avila and the mixed-race ex-queer hustler Joey Sands constitute part of a guerrilla unit that coalesces in the mountains. In this remote location, we glimpse an alternative sociality that cuts across class, color, and gender lines and substitutes for familial bonds: "Except for her [Daisy's] cousin Clarita, her comrades are her only family, now."[61] Bereft of parents, lovers, and children, Daisy and Joey turn to each other and to their "comrades" for support and solidarity. Intersecting their respective narratives in this moment of promise and danger, Hagedorn keeps open the possibility of a radical collective posed against the state's imaging as the First Couple (see chapter 5).

This guerrilla formation, however, does not constitute the definitive site of political critique because Hagedorn desists from narrating its subsequent activities. Noting her use of the future tense at this point, Allan Punzalan Isaac writes that Hagedorn draws "away from the temptation of narrative and nationalist closure" and "chooses instead to maintain an asymptotic relationship with a definitive 'national' telos to suggest one as yet unimagined."[62] Rachel Lee similarly suggests that *Dogeaters* thwarts the desire for "an affirmative ending" and "refrain[s] from positing a harmonious collectivism."[63] In considering this open-endedness, it is worth pointing out that Hagedorn does not close with the 1986

"People Power" revolution, an "affirmative" popular uprising in which hundreds of thousands of demonstrators flooded Epifanio de los Santos Avenue and forced the Marcoses to flee Malacañang Palace with the aid of an American military escort. Instead, the last three chapters following the political allegory of Daisy and Joey consist of Rio narrating the fates of her family members ("Luna Moth"), her cousin Pucha calling into question Rio's memory and narrative reliability ("Pucha Gonzaga"), and a reference to the Tagalog love song known as the "Kundiman."

In its allusion to a musical genre, the "Kundiman" ending might be understood as a coda to the novel. It opens out onto another horizon, an expansive vista that steps not only beyond the plot/character summaries and revisions of the "Luna Moth" and "Pucha Gonzaga" chapters but also away from the modes of print, film, and gossip used up to that point. Furthermore, in contrast to the novel's epigraph from French travel writer Jean Mallat's *The Philippines* (1846), "Kundiman" seems to sound an emphatically nationalist note—only to swerve dramatically again once the chapter begins: *"Our Mother, who art in heaven. Hallowed be thy name. Thy kingdom come, thy will be done. Thy will not be done. Hallowed by thy name, thy kingdom never came"* (250). The crux of this coda lies in determining how its formal framing as *kundiman* relates to the pious and sacrilegious mix of the Catholic prayers. Ultimately, I will argue that the novel's final pages transpose film with music, print with prayer, representation with direct address, thereby shifting the expressive terrain from spectacle and visuality to sound and aurality. The issue raised here is not so much whether the postcolonial Filipino can be seen—represented outside the exoticizing mechanisms of the imperial gaze—but whether she can be heard through the strains of "native" music.

While Pucha's interrogatory voice questions Rio's memory and calls attention to the novel's historiographic reflexivity, as critics have noted, it also positions her as the *recipient* of Rio's postmigration narrative: "You like to mix things up on purpose, *di ba? Esta loca, prima. Que ba*— this is cousin Pucha you're talking to" (248). In the first chapter, "Love Letters," Rio reproduces one of Pucha's grammatically challenged missives, the close of which reads: "Write to me why dont you I always do the writeing its not fair. I miss you LOVE always, PUCHA" (7). The "Pucha Gonzaga" chapter implies that Rio's part of the narration, at least, is cast in the form of a letter to her cousin, in effect, responding to Pucha's request to write back.

To recognize that *Dogeaters* is self-consciously situated in a dialogic relationship with the Philippines undermines the idea that the novel is addressed to and consumed by a Western audience that consequently converts it into a commodified spectacle.[64] The "Kundiman" ending, drawing on the music's form, national meanings, and mode of address, further challenges this presumption. In an interview, Hagedorn explains why she turns to the *kundiman*:

> There's a lot of brutality in *Dogeaters*, and I think that especially with the suffering that the character Daisy goes through and the loss of the senator and all the other people who die or are tortured, and just the daily suffering of the poor there, which is enormous, the Philippines is still a beautiful country and I wanted somehow to convey that. So I decided originally that the Kundiman section was going to be the grandmother's prayer. I mean, actually, that was one of the titles I thought of, *The Grandmother Prays for Her Country*. But I thought, "No, I want to even lift it above a specific character's voice, and maybe it's my voice that speaks at the end. But how do I convey this sort of longing in this prayer, and the rage? There's a lot of rage in the prayer." So I decided on the Kundiman because it's music in a ballad form. It's very melancholy music. It's a love song often sung, it seems to me, in a way or played in a way as if the love will never be satisfied.[65]

Here, the "melancholy" *kundiman* serves as a formal vehicle that can lift the voice above a particular character's utterance, counteract the pain and brutality that *Dogeaters* depicts in quantity, and interact with the prayer to convey longing and rage.

Echoing the notion that Rio writes back to Pucha, Hagedorn has described *Dogeaters* as "a love letter to my motherland."[66] But in the "Kundiman" chapter, that letter has been transformed into a song and a prayer. How does the diasporic writer address the homeland, a homeland that is both brutal and beautiful? What is left, the novel seems to cry out, when the spectacular illusions of Hollywood cinema, the hallucinatory antics and evasions of the First Lady, the very real disappearances, rapes, murders, and decapitations make for an impossible postcolonial condition? What voice could possibly be summoned to address an unredressible order? Improvising on José Rizal's dedication "To My Motherland" in his novel *Noli Me Tangere* (1887),[67] Hagedorn's "Kundiman" apostrophizes the "motherland" so as to embrace her and her contradictions: "*I would curse you but I choose to love you instead*" (250).[68]

In this ambivalent address to the motherland, Hagedorn manipulates the gendered conventions of the *kundiman*. Prototypically performed by a male suitor who courts a young woman in serenade fashion, the *kundiman* has been called "the Philippines' signature love song, generally expressing the forlorn lament of a faithful lover pining for his beloved."[69] The longing evoked in the music connotes subordination of the lover to the beloved. According to one description, "the beautiful girl . . . always stood on a high pedestal" while "the young man" places himself at her feet, "the perpetual slave and the eternally suffering one."[70] "Through the song," another description runs, the man "expresses his utmost abnegation to her wishes."[71] Composer and musicologist Antonio Molina speaks of one *kundiman* as "a song of miserable surrender and of meek submission."[72]

The *kundiman* singer's position of self-subordination has been linked to nationalist sentiment during the latter half of the nineteenth century when the form came into prominence. By many accounts, the *kundiman* "serv[ed] as a vehicle for veiled patriotic expressions and love of country at a time when Philippine independence was being suppressed."[73] In this doubling of love song and patriotic song, the female beloved figures "the very soul of the beloved motherland,"[74] while the suitor becomes the patriot willing to sacrifice himself for the cause of national liberation. The two composers in the first half of the twentieth century who sought to "elevate" the folk *kundiman* to the status of art-song, Francisco Santiago and Nicanor Abelardo, were also driven by nationalist impulses. Santiago's biographer writes that the composer was "propelled by the feeling of Filipino nationalism in his compositions,"[75] while Abelardo himself commented on the "nationalism of our music" in 1932: "How about our *kundimans, awits* and *kumintangs*? Let us dig them up and from them fashion a music truly Filipino."[76]

In light of this history, one wonders whether Hagedorn, too, is injecting a "truly Filipino" nationalist note into her book. It is important to point out, first of all, that the "nationalism" of the *kundiman* is not intrinsically liberatory or revolutionary. In *Dogeaters*, Daisy Avila wins the beauty pageant in part based on her singing of the popular *kundiman* "Dahil Sa Iyo" (Because of You) (102). Performed by the daughter of the opposition senator Domingo Avila, the song allows the dictatorship the charade of an alibi via the reinscription of traditional gender roles: "You see? This is a free country," asserts the president (102). Furthermore, the television talent contest *Maid in the Philippines* that Baby Alacran watches makes evident that the *kundiman* has fully entered the world of commercialized popular culture: "Someone else starts to sing, someone named Naty, a ballad of unrequited love in Tagalog" (157). Even Baby Alacran, who seeks refuge in these shows, "finds the TV images suddenly depressing" and "vulgar" in the wake of Avila's assassination (157).

These mutating contexts and political ambiguities render Hagedorn's improvisations on the musical form all the more striking. Although the courtship/patriotic relationship summoned by the *kundiman* helps to make sense of the direct address, as well as the addressee's gender as female, the chapter itself embodies neither the stanzaic form nor the lyrical content of the traditional *kundiman*. According to Ramón Santos, early composers of formal *kundimans* pursued "an art form wherein poetry and music did not merely compliment [*sic*] each other but became one formal unity."[77] Analogous to the way that Hagedorn's "Solea" does not purport to enact *cante jondo*, so does her "Kundiman" break the "formal unity" between poetry and musical accompaniment by displaying the text as paragraphs that stretch across the page, not as stanzas or strophes. Moreover, Hagedorn's speaker/singer does not assume a posture of humble submission, nor does the beloved addressee sit high upon a pedestal, gleaming, secure, and untouchable. It is not the lover but the motherland, *"Dolores dolorosa,"* that is *"suffering"* with *"insane endurance,"* having *"been defiled, belittled, and diminished"* (250).

These changes result from Hagedorn's improvisations on the Catholic prayers as the content of the song. The religious imagery used to evoke *"Our Mother"* as wounded national symbol harks back to the *pasyon*, the folk resource of anticolonial resistance that was coterminous with the emergence of the *kundiman*. According to Reynaldo Ileto, though the *pasyon* was meant to effect sympathy with Christ, it also evoked compassion for the anguished mother who has been separated from her son, "making the pasyon just as much an epic of Mother Mary's loss."[78] Discussing the familial allegory constructed by the Katipunan, the secret society founded by Andres Bonifacio in 1892 that revolted against Spain in 1896, Ileto notes that the suffering and solicitous "Mother Philippines" replaces "Mother Spain" who has reneged on her maternal duties to her "orphaned" children (the colonized) (85). In order to pursue *kalayaan* (freedom/liberty) and free Mother Philippines from her colonial pain, the Katipunan initiates experienced "compassion or pity for Mother Country" (98).

Hagedorn's reworkings of the *kundiman* and the Catholic prayers draw on the political and affective dimensions of the love song and the *pasyon*. When fused, however, both are transformed. While the *kundiman* conveys an erotic-nationalist expression of love for the beloved/ homeland, the addressee turns out to be a suffering motherland that resembles more the dolorous Mother Mary/*Inang Bayan* of the *pasyon* than the aloof woman of the Tagalog ballad. And whereas in the *pasyon* it is Mother Mary who sorrowfully addresses her departing son as he embarks on his "untraditional mission,"[79] in Hagedorn's "Kundiman" the mode of address is reversed. This reversal returns us to the question of the coda's voice.

Leaving open the gender identity of the speaker/singer/prayer of the "Kundiman," Hagedorn challenges the adamant heterosexualism of the traditional *kundiman*, flirting with and overlaying several forms of love—familial (child-mother), queer (female-female), and national (suitor-beloved). Lifted above a specific character's speech and rendered mostly in italics,[80] the voice of Hagedorn's "Kundiman" swings between the plural "our" of the prayer and the singular "I." Not coincidentally, the latter emerges when attempting to apprehend traces of the homeland:

> *I listen for snatches of melody, the piercing high-pitched wail of your song of terror.*
> *Here, clues to your ghostly presence in the lingering trail of your deadly perfume.* (250)

This swinging between the collective and individual first-person reflects the position of the diasporic writer who declines to speak on behalf of the nation, and who, from abroad, must listen for and seek out fragments of the homeland. At the same time, it renders the eros that suffuses Hagedorn's "Kundiman" irreducible to the lover-beloved dynamic of the *kundiman* and forges a kind of fractured collectivity constituted by the invocation to "*Our Mother.*" Even as the prayer calls on the mother to "*dazzle us with your pity*" (250) and show compassion to her supplicants as the "ideal Filipino mother" of the *pasyon* ought to,[81] it also enjoins its collective speakers to be moved by the mother's wounds and take pity on her: "*let the scars tattooed on your face be a reminder of your perennial sorrow*" (250).

It is important to note as well that the early *kundiman*'s nationalist affect arises from its lyrical structure and content, not its origins, which have been traced to the transcultural contact between indigenous and Spanish music.[82] Hagedorn herself remarks in the interview cited above: "When I finally went to Spain, I found out the Gypsies play it there and the Spanish have claimed it. But actually maybe the Arabs brought it, the Moors. And so maybe that's how it came to the Philippines. Who knows?"[83] Hagedorn's use of the *kundiman* does not lead us to a pure, autochthonous musical tradition that could be recovered to oppose and supplant colonial impositions. The music's uncertain roots take us elsewhere.

In much the same way that "Solea" accesses flamenco and Monk's music as strategies for figuring the fracturing of poetic voice and subjectivity, the use of music in the "Kundiman" chapter might also be understood as a "cultivation of another voice," to quote Mackey again: "A different medium is a different voice, an alternate vocality."[84] The idea of *duende* that Mackey extrapolates from Lorca as "a taking over of one's voice by another voice" echoes Hagedorn's statement that music can "lift [the prayer] above a specific character's voice."[85] Music enters here as a kind of formal support or scaffolding, a taking on of "another voice" in order to "sound" what cannot be expressed in the prayer alone: "the love [that] will never be satisfied"—"a kind of longing," as Mackey puts it following Lorca, "that has no remedy."[86]

Is this inconsolable lament, this unsatisfiable love, a capitulation to resignation and despair? San Juan dismisses the ending by claiming that the "prayer of exorcism concluding *Dogeaters* can only be a stylized gesture of protest."[87] Jacqueline Doyle, by contrast, holds that the conclusion "opens a hybrid, heterogeneous space for resistance to multiple levels of colonial authority."[88] I suggest that the "Kundiman" chapter calls into question the very desire for a straightforward "protest" literature of "resistance" whose efficacy could be rooted in an oppositional form of cultural politics. The final invocation gestures toward this refusal: "*Ave Maria, mother of revenge. The Lord was never with you. Blessed art thou among women, and blessed are the fruits of thy womb: guavas, mangos, santol, mangosteen, durian. Now and forever, world without end. Now and forever*" (251). In this last paragraph, Hagedorn reworks the "Hail Mary" rather than the "Our Father" and literalizes the "*fruits of thy womb*" into tropical fruits—not "Jesus," as in the original prayer. Unlike Maximo Kalaw's anonymous male child as the deliverer of independence (see chapter 1), Hagedorn refrains from figuring the motherland as the reproductive origin of a nationalist savior and redeemer of her wounds.

In its pursuit of an "alternate vocality" attuned to *"ghostly presence[s],"* Hagedorn's affective mix of the *kundiman's* eroticism, the *pasyon's* suffering, and the prayers' rage simultaneously bespeaks "a spiritual discontent," to cite Mackey in another context, a "kind of reaching . . . that refus[es] to be satisfied with mere material achievement."[89] Moving beyond whatever tenuous relation the previous chapters bore toward historical reality, the "Kundiman" chapter reaches toward another, perhaps metaphysical, reality—not as a transcendence of the material world but through the affect of longing that structures the *kundiman*. This alternative might be divined in one theory of the term's etymology. *Kundiman* is thought to be a "contraction of *kung hindi man,"*[90] words that begin early *kundimans* and which translate as "if it were not so," and "should it not be so."[91] The subjunctive mood imbues the music with its oft-noted plaintive character. Thus, *kundiman* itself contains intimations of alterity, a state of affairs that might be otherwise. Hagedorn's prayer as *kundiman* expresses a "love [that] will never be satisfied" precisely because the motherland is in no condition to reciprocate. This love does not merely register the idea that for the diasporic writer, the urge "to be one again with the mother," as Stuart Hall has written, "can neither be fulfilled nor requited" and therefore constitutes "the infinitely renewable source of desire, memory, myth."[92] The "Kundiman" chapter erupts specifically out of the Philippines' *post*colonial predicament: it is a lyric of longing whose fulfillment—the motherland's reconstruction, the end of her torment—would spell the end of that longing, and hence, that song.

Whereas the *kundiman* and the *pasyon* developed in response to Spanish and U.S. colonialisms, Hagedorn's remixing of the two forms reveals that political independence from colonial rule in 1946 has not liberated the motherland. The novel itself makes clear that both U.S. neocolonialism and martial law remained profoundly oppressive and repressive forces for the vast majority of Filipinos. Like the *kundiman* itself, whose sole reason for being is to convince the beloved to relent and accept the lover's regard, the "Kundiman" chapter only exists because the homeland still suffers. These final pages, to be sure, are no rescue mission. If they are compelled to evoke an alterity through an alternate vocality, if the "Kundiman" summons song to unleash a queer keening for kin,[93] it is because there can be no unmediated message sent by her distant daughter proffering solutions. As Rocky Rivera confesses toward the end of *The Gangster of Love*: "So much pain, I had to sing" (247). And perhaps the "Kundiman" ending represents something similar, an impossible attempt for a novel to "sing" not only the author's pain but the motherland's as well.

Neither wholly nostalgic nor condemnatory, *Dogeaters* may be read as analogous to what Kwame Anthony Appiah describes as the "second phase" of African postcolonial novels that emerged in the late 1960s—those that turned away from the earlier "realist legitimations of nationalism" and toward acts of "delegitimation: they reject not only the Western *imperium* but also the nationalist project of the postcolonial national bourgeoisie" and base this shift "in an appeal to a certain simple respect for human suffering, a fundamental revolt against the endless misery of the last thirty years."[94] In its diasporic critique of U.S. neocolonialism and martial law authoritarianism, *Dogeaters* engages in this sort of delegitimation, even as it gestures toward and calls forth nonnationalist socialities.

Appiah's question—"Is the Post- in Postmodernism the Post- in Postcolonial?"—resonates rather differently, however, in the Philippine context. While most Philippine critics have responded favorably to *Dogeaters'* diasporic reaching, Caroline Hau has written a more ambivalent critique of the novel. In "*Dogeaters*, Postmodernism and the 'Worlding' of the Philippines," published in the anthology *Philippine Postcolonial Studies* (1993/2004), Hau focuses on the novel's "production, distribution, exchange and consumption" and notes that it "was written by a Filipino-American through the grants and endowments of American institutions, published in the States, read by Americans and reviewed by American critics and writers."[95] Hau's position is not "nativist" insofar as it converses with postmodernist and postcolonialist theorists (Fredric Jameson, Linda Hutcheon, Gayatri Spivak). But it does imply that *Dogeaters'* "postmodernist" techniques, such as its self-reflexive textuality or "simulacrum" aesthetic (121) and its "spatialization of temporality" (125), contribute to the novel's specific process of "worlding." Reworking Spivak's notion that "the worlding of the world generates the force to make the 'native' see himself as the 'other,'" Hau suggests that Hagedorn's positioning "in the metropolis" "generates an *accretion of othering*"—that is, the "'worlding' of the Philippines extends not only to the Othering of the West" as inscribed within colonial discourse proper "but also to an Othering of the Other of the West" that inflicts an "epistemic violence" on those other others (127, 128).

I reference Hau's critique not only to highlight the endemic competing investments that mark Filipino diasporic discourse but also to make a point about the politics of "postmodernism." As mentioned, the critical tradition has typically inferred that *Dogeaters*' representations of Hollywood films and other forms of mass consumption, its nonrealist form, and its presumed address to Western audiences make it a "postmodernist" text. It is important to recall in this regard the critiques of postmodernism delivered by scholars such as Barbara Christian and Nancy Hartsock in the 1980s. In her classic "The Race for Theory," Christian finds it suspicious that the totalizing "New Philosophy" of postmodernist thought "proclaim[ing] that reality does not exist, that everything is relative, and that every text is silent about something" emerged at precisely the moment "when the literature of peoples of color, black women, Latin Americans, and Africans began to move to 'the center.'"[96] Against this historical coincidence, she reminds us of an alternative genealogy of the politicization of literature rooted in the "black arts movement of the 1960s" and "the feminist literary movement of the 1970s" (70).

My attempt to recover some of Hagedorn's work from the 1970s and use that work to reframe an analysis of *Dogeaters* similarly seeks to counter this forgetting. Hau suggests that "Hagedorn's writing about the Philippines for the American audience . . . is a product of exteriority, of implied distantiation" that results in "nostalgia" and an inevitable "Orientalism" (117). Without dismissing that charge, I am stressing the need to historicize the diasporic writer's positionality in relation not only to the homeland but also to the complex social worlds she inhabits and negotiates in "exteriority." To situate *Dogeaters* within the context of Hagedorn's other work and recognize her multivalent modes of address is to place her creative output within a broader field of cultural production that includes her collaborations with other artists of color in the United States. To overlook that history is to see *Dogeaters* as simply another martial law novel,[97] or to invoke overgeneralizing pronouncements about "postmodernism" drawn from critics who evidently had very different archives and histories in mind when formulating their theories. Ironically, the very circulation of *Dogeaters* as "canonical" text contributes to its decontextualization, making it available for "theoretical" consumption and appropriation.

The "collective endeavors," as Christian calls them (69), of diasporic Filipino criticism, as I am arguing throughout this book, are invariably fraught with tension and conflict. By reminding us of *Dogeaters'* material conditions of possibility and its conflicting receptions, Hau's critique represents a vital part of that diasporic discourse. Rather than close on a note of discord, let me return to the politics of identity and culture with which I began this chapter. Having traversed the cross-cultural, queer, diasporic terrains of Hagedorn's work, we might hear Voltaire's response to Rocky's "unbearable questions"—"What's Filipino? What's authentic? What's in the blood?"—resonate anew: "We're blessed with macabre humor and dancing feet—a floating nation of rhythm and blues."[98] The metaphor not only denotes the diasporic movement of Filipinos and the incommensurability of nation/culture and state/territory produced by global migration ("floating nation"); it also recurs to and plays on a musical genre whose individual terms suggest that the rhythms by which the "nation" floats are structured by contradictory affects ("macabre humor," the "blues"). What Hagedorn's work shows or makes audible is that what is Filipino has less to do with what is authentic or in the blood than in what keeps us afloat, the rhythm and (the) blues that move us.

# 5

# The Diasporic Poetics of Queer
# Martial Law Literature

WITH ITS ABUNDANCE of sexually nonnormative characters, Jessica Hagedorn's corpus presages and participates in the proliferation of queer diasporic Filipino cultural production over the past two decades. Far from marginal, the sheer wealth of this work—novels, poetry, stories, essays, drama, performance art, visual art, documentaries, and independent feature films—implies that it is part and parcel of contemporary diasporic Filipino expressive culture.[1] To be sure, these texts take up issues of homophobia in Filipino culture, racism in U.S. queer culture, and racism and homophobia in dominant U.S. culture, the main targets of critique often identified in queer of color studies.[2] But it is nevertheless the case that queer diasporic Filipino literature has entered the field of Filipino American cultural production without a whole lot of politicized fanfare.

This chapter analyzes a select group of texts—Bino Realuyo's *The Umbrella Country* (1998), R. Zamora Linmark's *Rolling the R's* (1995), and Noël Alumit's *Letters to Montgomery Clift* (2002)—that re-view the 1970s and 1980s by locating the emergence of queer male sexualities and genders in the martial law period of Ferdinand Marcos, and by highlighting the impact of U.S. popular culture on erotic fantasies. Traversing across issues of youth sexuality, cross-age sex, and gender transitivity, these novels link martial law to exilic departures and desires and thus implicate the United States—not simply as Cold War supporter of Marcos's efforts to stanch the spread of Communism but also as the supposed site of freedom from political *and* sexual persecution.

Focusing on queer reconstructions of this historical period unfortunately sidelines women's literature. I have been unable to locate full-length literature that offers queer Filipina takes on martial law.[3] Chea Villanueva's serial epistolary novellas "Girlfriends" and "The China-girls: A Butch and Femme Epistolary" feature the Filipina/o protagonist

Pearly Does who tells her "true love" Wilnona toward the end of the first installment: "I'm going to the Philippines to join the revolutionaries."[4] Although the bawdy multiracial narrative (enthusiastically described on the title page of "Girlfriends" as "A story about love, suspense, and sex between women!") is not deeply invested in history, it is still odd that Pearly announces her intention in a letter dated September 8, 1986— some six months after the "People Power" revolution toppled the Marcos government. More important, the continuation of the story in "The Chinagirls" opens on January 1, 1988, with Pearly being jailed for "writin' them things for overthrowin' the government," and then getting deported back to the United States.[5] The narrative immediately plunges back into the boisterous romp of "sex between women"—including that between Pearly and a sixteen-year-old Chinese girl named Jadine whom Pearly married in Manila while disguised as a "Filipino gentleman" to save her from being sold as a mail-order bride by her own mother, who happens to be a frontwoman in New York's Chinatown mafia. Except for this brief, eclipsed reference to Pearly as a lesbian revolutionary and transgendered husband in the Philippines, Villanueva's novellas are more concerned with queer life in Philadelphia and New York City during the late 1980s.

Though there exists some literary production by and about Filipina/o "lesbians" or "tomboys"[6] in both the Philippines and the United States, it has not flourished to the extent that male-authored literature has. As Jhoanna Lynn Cruz notes in a 2005 editorial, "The silence surrounding the lesbian in Philippine literary history is appalling. Anglo-European lesbian critics can at least complain about the negative images of lesbians in the works of both male and female writers; they can have a party decoding the works of Virginia Woolf or Emily Dickinson, but I have not found a lesbian tradition of writing in the Philippines."[7] Silence and invisibility seem to be the predominant tropes in the critical and creative lesbian/tomboy texts currently available.

The bracketing of queer Filipina literature notwithstanding, the focus on queer martial law texts provides a historically grounded way to continue this book's consideration of diasporic cultural politics through the lens of gender and sexuality. Here I hope to further the growing scholarship in Filipino queer studies (discussed below) and, more obliquely, in studies of the antimartial law movement in the United States[8] by turning to diasporic literary texts that stage the encounters among sexuality, martial law, migration, and U.S. popular culture in ways that render queerness central to remembrances of this fraught historical period, while also eschewing simple equations between queerness and political resistance. In a sense, Realuyo's, Linmark's, and Alumit's books take up the relations among desire, dictatorship, and diaspora in the wake of Jessica Hagedorn's *Dogeaters* (1990). That novel alludes to the explosion in international sex tourism (such as shower dancing [141–143] and the trafficking in minors [73–75]); the disappearance, detainment, and torture of political dissenters (65, 97), grimly dramatized in Daisy Avila's brutal interrogation and gang-rape (211–216); and the impoverishment of the general populace owing to government corruption and to the structural adjustment programs instigated in 1980 under the auspices of the International Monetary Fund (IMF) and World Bank. These export-oriented reforms led to two major demographic shifts: internal migration from provincial regions to Metro Manila, and international labor migration on a global scale.[9]

The story of Joey Sands illustrates these sociosexual conditions. The offspring of a Filipina prostitute and an African American GI stationed at Subic Bay, Joey embodies the bastardizing consequences of sex work that proliferated around the U.S. military bases in the Philippines during the neocolonial period. His street-life poverty reads as one symptom of this dire economic situation, while his hustling reflects the sexual permissiveness that resulted from Mayor Lim's deregulation policies.[10] Joey's ambition to use his sexual allure as a means of escaping Manila— boasting that he would gladly accept either a sugar daddy or mommy (44)—is further indicative of the large-scale flight from the country from the 1960s onward. Refusing to play native informant to the German film director Rainer's tourist, Joey responds: "Waterfalls and volcanoes? You're crazy. Let's go somewhere fun. Let's go to Las Vegas" (146). Whisked away not to Vegas but to the mountains where the political rebels reside, Joey is proffered two polarized life courses: catering to white Westerners in Manila's seedy sex tourist trade in hopes of snagging a wealthy patron, or joining the New People's Army.

The rendezvous between the queer black hybrid Joey Sands and the beauty queen–cum–guerrilla fighter Daisy Avila, alluded to in chapter 4, might be radically positioned against the dictatorship's ideological myth-making that constructed Ferdinand and Imelda Marcos as the undisputed, preordained leaders of the nation. Chapter 1 considered how tropes of the family have been utilized to figure the Philippine nation, but the Marcoses sought to literalize this figuration. The title of an early anti-Marcos critique written by a political exile in the United States, *The Conjugal Dictatorship of Ferdinand and Imelda Marcos* (1976), signals not only the "gendering of power and politics in postwar Philippines," as Mina Roces points out, but also the heterosexual, matrimonial underpinnings of the regime's authoritarianism.[11] Roces notes that Imelda's "role in diplomacy; her new political appointments [including governor of Metro Manila in 1975]; [and] her projects in infrastructure, culture, tourism, civic work, health, human settlements, education, and business" (49) enabled her to exercise a formidable form of unofficial power via "kinship politics," the deployment of "political power for the benefit of the kinship group" (2).

These forms of power were underwritten by gendered iconography that, in turn, sought to dictate and naturalize the terms of the people's relation to the state. Vicente L. Rafael has examined how "Ferdinand and Imelda imaged themselves . . . as the father and mother of an extended Filipino family" by depicting themselves in commissioned art and biographies as Malakas and Maganda, the "legendary Primordial Filipinos."[12] Such depictions "fed the wish for a kind of depoliticized community, one that would make the hierarchy between the leaders and followers seem thoroughly benign" (130). Rolando Tolentino has further explored the embodiment of state power in the First Couple: "The presidential body as the model to emulate" differentiates that model from "national bodies" while producing an identification with its idealized version.[13] Similarly, "Imelda's body and sexuality [serve] as the model for Filipinas' development of their own bodies and sexualities" (69). While this double process of differentiation and idealization "institutionalizes" material inequalities, it also renders sexuality as a politicized terrain: "For the First Couple, sexuality was mobilized to socialize the people to the rudiments of citizenry needed for national development. For the people, sexuality became a form of subversion that bogs down the First Couple's project of nation-building" (74).

Whereas Rafael turns to the youth and student movements of the 1960s and Tolentino considers the (gay and straight) sex worker films of director Lino Brocka during the 1980s as activist and cultural challenges to martial law, I explore the diasporic literary texts of Realuyo, Linmark, and Alumit in order to show how they not only evoke queer socialities that lie outside the realms of national identification and patronage but also force us to consider the impact of U.S. imperialism and immigration on queer practices, desires, and relationships. Reading this work diasporically—situated between and speaking to both nations—is thus crucial if we are to account for the complexities that inhere in both sites and avoid oversimplified ascriptions of sexual prohibition or liberation onto either country.

In his provocative essay "Gay Writing vs. National Literature," J. Neil C. Garcia argues that "the 'Filipino Nation' . . . is really a Tagalog, colonial, bourgeois, Catholic, lowland, macho—and if I may add, heterosexist—arrogation" and concludes: "Gayness, as a specific form of what has precisely been a suppressed and neglected sexuality, can only be outside a 'nation' whose internal and implied content militates most violently against and is obsessively annihilative of it."[14] While Garcia gives the categorical expulsion of gayness from the national imaginary density and specificity within the Philippine context, I argue that queer diasporic Filipino literature does not pursue a politics of national inclusion—precisely because the "nation" is always ambiguous. In destabilizing which/whose nation functions as the locus of queer annihilation, cathexis, or ambivalence, this chapter considers the flipside of Garcia's contention, namely, that the nation is an inadequate analytical framework for reading diasporic Filipino "gay writing." By elucidating the diasporic poetics of queer martial law literature, I suggest that this body of work not only reveals the nation's punitive suppressions of nonnormative sexualities and genders but also bespeaks an abiding ambivalence toward nationalist projects, refusing to be subsumed wholly by the nation's coercive mechanisms of belonging, but not standing immune to its seductive techniques either. What I emphasize, therefore, are alternative scenes of intimacy, solidarity, or affective bonding that are not tethered to the nation, that dwell at the interstices and edges of the novels' social worlds.

## Between the Patriarch and the *Bakla*

Unlike the expansive metropolis evoked in Hagedorn's *Dogeaters*, the Manila delineated in Bino Realuyo's *The Umbrella Country* concentrates on an individual impoverished neighborhood where the first-person, pubescent narrator Gringo (Gregorito) and his family live. Enveloped by the pervasive and paranoiac forces of martial law, the social world of Gringo's childhood is tense and claustrophobic, disciplined by a culture of surveillance: "Ears, eyes, mouths, always awake, alert, watching everything, anything. Listening."[15] It is in this enclosed space under dictatorial rule—a strict curfew marking its temporal boundaries—that the novel probes the emergence of queer desires and masculinities as well as the crushing patriarchal attempts to thwart and redirect them toward normative ends. The brothers' sexual coming-of-age (Gringo is ten when the novel begins, his brother Pipo is eleven; about two years pass before they depart to join their father in Woodside, Queens, "Nuyork") is freighted with shame. In the authoritarian Manila of Realuyo's novel, visual surveillance combines with violent socialization as a technology for producing subjects acquiescent to the law of Marcos and of masculinity. Not surprisingly, then, the protogay protagonists Gringo and Pipo are able to act upon their sexual inclinations only outside the sanctioned limits of the neighborhood and of curfew.

The enforcement of normative masculinity is overt and brutal, ranging from the taunts and bullying perpetrated on the younger boys by Big Boy Jun and his cohort, to the severe beatings inflicted on Pipo, whose penchant for cross-dressing incenses his father. Three-time winner of the children's "Miss Unibers" contests, Pipo early on in the novel gets caught in his room working with his beauty pageant paraphernalia and is flogged by Daddy Groovie: "The long *yantok* was slicing the air. . . . There was the need to hurt Pipo. Whip him with his long, smooth, rounded bamboo stick that he had kept for us before we were even born. A dialogue with his first-born son, he called it. I could hear him cursing. *Puta ka.* [You whore.] *Lalaki ka ba o ano?* Huh? Huh? Are you a man?" (45). The following chapter, "Hallowed Be Thy Name," represents Daddy Groovie reinforcing his corporeal "dialogue" with monologic mandates geared toward shaping Pipo into *"the way men are!"* (51), revealing in the meantime the unnaturalness of gender identity. The chapter interpolates the father's commands ordering Pipo to *"straighten"* his posture, *"not wiggle [his] behind"* (51), and *"[look] at girls straight in the eye"* (55), while threatening him with eternal damnation (*"boys who think they're girls, they burn them in hell"* [58]) and calling upon his own father's hallowed name and blood to secure and transmit masculine continuity: *"all that Papa taught me, now you have it, you carry my blood"* (60).

The most horrific scene lies at the novel's center when Daddy Groovie thrashes Mommy and Pipo after returning from the embassy having failed the medical exam that would have granted him a visa to the United States. Daddy Groovie's fury and the broader valorization of masculinity are partly effects of the economic fallout of martial law. Indeed, the general thrust of the novel is to explain the "dysfunction" of Gringo's family—why Daddy Groovie is a jobless, San Miguel–guz-zling, wife and child beater, and why Mommy does little to intervene in her husband's cruel treatment of the boys. At certain points, the novel links Daddy Groovie's unemployment, drunkenness, and explosive be-havior: "He babbled about losing his construction job again, about rich people who always stepped on poor workers like him. About Martial Law. 'If not for *putang-inang* Martial-martial this and Martial-martial that, I wouldn't lose my job!'" he yells, then finds an excuse to whip Pipo again (61). If punishing those in the domestic space becomes one way for Daddy Groovie to reassert his patriarchal authority, then the desire to escape to "D'merica" signals his other means of compensating for un-employment (188). When Daddy Groovie receives the application forms from the embassy, Gringo narrates, "I knew he was somewhere else, in the States, working at his new job, the job he had been proudly talking about for years while he condemned his inability to maintain a construc-tion job, blaming it on Martial Law, on the president, on curfew because nobody could work at night anymore" (20).

At the familial level, Mommy's cousin Ninang Rola had disclosed to Gringo why Daddy Groovie had screamed "*MALAS. MALAS*" at Pipo and Mommy when the medical results detected a kidney stone in his x-rays (158). "You can't even be a real boy, you're bad luck," Daddy Groovie seethes at Pipo as he brandishes the *yantok* (156). Gringo learns from his godmother that Pipo is the bastard son of de-virginating date-rape and that Estrella (Mommy) had originally wanted to abort the fetus but was convinced otherwise by her cousin. When Estrella and Germano (Daddy Groovie) get married, neither of the couple's families attends the wedding, and Germano's cuts him off financially, leaving the two eco-nomically stranded and emotionally estranged from one another.[16] Thus saddled with an unresponsive, stricken wife and a queer son (the fam-ily members are unaware of Gringo's same-sex desires) and financially strapped, Daddy Groovie places his hopes in emigrating to the United States—an ambition that he eventually fulfills with the sponsorship of his sister Dolores.

But before the brothers follow him there, Pipo is brutalized a sec-ond time. The following chapter describes the aftermath of Pipo being raped by Boy Manicure. Through the open doorway, Gringo sees the effeminate *parlorista* standing naked feeding his fish and singing "glee-fully" the song "*Fly, fly the butterfly*"; Pipo exits, his body trembling: "His behind was bleeding, blood slowly dripping down his thighs" (183).

Wordlessly, Gringo covers Pipo with one of Boy Spit's newspapers and hurries him home. Though hardly sympathetic to the transgendered *bakla*, the "woman trapped in a body of a man that all fathers warned their sons not to become" (59), the novel also shows how little sympathy the vigilant neighbors exhibit toward Boy Manicure. In the penultimate chapter, he is found dead with his hands cut off. The more Gringo hears of the gossip swirling around the police questioning—the protestations of tolerance (246) and the sentiments of divine punishment for Boy Manicure's depravity (241)—the more he realizes that "nobody liked him. . . . Not any one of them," as he tells another budding queer boy, Sergio Putita (254).

What do these queer kids have to contend with, then? Fathers who aim to beat the effeminacy out of their sons; rough, older boys who "walked with that same macho strut, as if their balls were hanging too low, too heavy" (53); a local *bakla* who seduces minors (he nearly lures Gringo into his home as well [171]); and a self-righteous Catholic neighborhood with lidless eyes and loose lips. Even before Pipo is raped, Gringo thinks to himself, "I never wanted to act like Big Boy Jun. Never wanted to be macho like him. Never wanted to hurt anybody. But I didn't want to be like Boy Manicure either" (59). The only way to elude the watchful eyes of the neighborhood, the novel implies, is to slip out at night, past curfew, past the point where the houses end, where the old railroad track lies hidden beneath the grass, beyond all of which lies the cave.

Having watched from his upstairs window Boy Spit peddle newspapers on their street for months, Gringo finally works up the courage to "follow him" and "talk to him" (213). Boy Spit, nearly as quiet and diffident as Gringo, brings the younger boy to his shanty in the slums where "there was no curfew" (226), where "we break all rules" (230), and where the proud shack-owner relaxes: "I really like you," he says to Gringo. "You're funny" (229). Boy Spit then leads Gringo to the cave (formed from tall arching grass), where the moon lights the following view:

> There was a circle joined together by arms. It was hard to recognize faces but after a while, I could tell they were all boys, older than me but not by much. Their backs were bare. Shadows followed the ribbed contours of their bodies. Their belts unbuckled. Pants almost down. They were circling this one boy in the middle who was absorbing all the attention around him. I couldn't see him very well.

They were all the same height, it was hard to see each individual face. Cautiously they started to spread apart in twos, threes. The boy in the middle remained with whoever stayed with him. (232–233)

If not for the "giggles," the "lips [that] were meeting lips," and the "hands joining" described on the next page (234), one might get the impression that the central figure, Pipo, is once again being exploited, forced to kneel in the middle of the circle (jerk) and absorb the boys' *attention*. Though such an inference is possible and could explain why Gringo "nervously took Boy Spit's hands and wrapped them" with his own once he identifies his brother, it would fail to account for the pleasurable sensations that course through *Gringo's* body as he watches the boys, who "all seemed to know how to move parts of their bodies, although they looked young" (234). "I felt warmth inside me," Gringo narrates, "I wanted to keep it in there though there was another feeling I couldn't understand. Fear, perhaps, but not of being caught by police cars patrolling the streets" (233). Whatever the source of that fear (from the shame of seeing his erotic inclinations reflected in the boys' sexual acts; from the uncertainty of Boy Spit's feelings toward him), Gringo allows the pleasure to override those fears. When the boys "[come] together again, holding him [Pipo] tightly," Gringo tells us, "the sensation I felt was unfamiliar and I wanted to feel it more" (233, 234). While the representation of Pipo kneeling in the center of the circle, presumably performing fellatio, is hardly utopian—reading more as a desperate attempt to experience human contact apart from Daddy Groovie's *yantok* and Boy Manicure's ripping intercourse than a manifestation of liberated desire—this fleeting episode nonetheless carves out a space in which Pipo can express his sexuality and Gringo can experience a moment of sexual self-recognition.[17]

Although two chapters remain in the text, I would argue that "Curfew," rather than the final departure scene, constitutes the novel's climax in order to preempt the temptation to map the emigration story directly onto the "coming out" story. It would be a mistake to read the brothers' coming-of-age stories as solely ones of escape from the "backward" attitudes and practices of intolerant patriarchy or transgenderism and toward the alleged modern freedom of the United States. Before the boys depart for Woodside, the novel tenders its most touching scene when Boy Spit, hair combed and shoe-shod, arrives at Gringo's house to say good-bye. Though the two boys have not interacted since the cave, their mutual affection becomes evident at this moment of imminent separation. Gringo invites Boy Spit up to his room and pulls him away from the window where he had watched Boy Spit sell newspapers: "Holding him made me feel as if my hands belonged somewhere close to him, where I could touch him whenever I wished, where I could smell him all the time" (283). For parting gifts, Gringo gives Boy Spit a box of calendars ("for him to know that we had known each other once—the year, the month, the days" [283]) and a bundle of umbrellas to place over the roof of his shanty when it rains (284). Gringo's attempt at a deflating joke, "It doesn't rain in the States," is to no avail, and the two boys embrace, their tears mingling, their "skin touching," as Boy Spit "tenderly" kisses Gringo and Gringo's body openly "accept[s] him" (284).

However sentimental this wet good-bye kiss, it is significant that it takes place *before* the boys leave for the United States, in Gringo's own house, which had been the site of discipline and terror—and silence, for when Gringo feels "the heaviness of everything inside slowly drifting down to my toes" (284), he is alluding to the fact that it is his responsibility to "hold the secrets" of the family—of date-rape, marriage-rape, unwanted children, forced marriage, child and wife abuse—and "keep everything inside" (195). The chapter in which Ninang Rola divulges his parents' past is framed with the warning, "*Certain things are better kept than said, Gringo*" (112). When she proceeds to tell the sordid tale, Ninang Rola extracts a vow of silence from Gringo. Growing up in a family where no one speaks his or her pain aloud, where words are substituted with gestures (Mommy sewing at her Singer machine; Pipo picking flecks of chipped paint off the wall after being whipped by Daddy Groovie), Gringo narrates, "I had learned to speak without saying a word, too" (107).

Although there is no retrospective scene of writing that would definitively locate the narrator's past-tense voice in either space (possibly the United States) or time (perhaps as an adult), one might still ask whether the novel is engaged in a politics of voice. Are we to understand that Gringo *breaks the silence* of family secrets by articulating them—if not within the novel's diegetic world to other characters then within the medium of print to its readers? If so, then we are returned to the poetics and politics of diasporic address. Though published by Ballantine in New York, *The Umbrella Country* does not merely speak to a mainstream U.S. audience. In "A Conversation with Bino Realuyo" appended to the end of the book, the author asserts, "Writing is my dialogue with the Philippines" (n.p.). As with the other writers studied in this book, such diasporic dialogue is fraught with ambivalence, its political implications laden with risk.[18]

Clearly, the novel is critical of the violence committed against queer boys and men and against women, and of the ways that martial law gives impetus and shape to that violence. In this sense, it confirms Garcia's notion that gayness and the Philippine nation are radically incompatible. As the under-the-radar encounters between Pipo and the circle boys and between Gringo and Boy Spit underscore, however, the novel does not call for a more inclusive vision of the "nation," since it is precisely the nation under martial law that gives rise to masculinist violence in the first place.

On the other hand, in "States of Being," Realuyo interrogates the supposition that the boys will be better off in Woodside (Queens) than in Manila. In this chapter, Gringo weaves a second-person voice with third-person description as a way of responding to his father's aerograms sent from Woodside. While Gringo's side of the "dialogue" is at times pointedly critical of his father's enthusiasm for the United States, what is intriguing is Gringo's invention of a phantom interlocutor whom he names "States." Gringo describes him as "the body of an imagined brother" who was "born in Daddy Groovie's mouth," wielding "an enormous power over Pipo and me," and bearing "the face of the future *that might not be there*" (194, my emphasis). Although Gringo had "said" to Daddy Groovie that "I want to go where you are, anywhere but here," the father's unalloyed desire for "D'merica" is much more mixed, threaded with uncertainty and dread, on the son's side (187). Addressing States, Gringo asks, "What is it really like there, where you come from?" (194). When States asks why he wants to know, Gringo rephrases the question, "I don't know. Curious. I just wonder . . . is there a place for someone . . . like me there?" (195, original ellipses). Though he admits that he "didn't know what [he] meant" by "like me" (195), Gringo's question gestures toward the idea that his emerging sexual identity complicates the promise of immigration in a way that Daddy Groovie's ambition to escape poverty does not. Gringo's intuition that there might *not* be a place for him in the United States (due to his race, class, sexuality, and their combinations) prevents us from viewing the United States, even in idealized figural form, as the space where he can live and love free from persecution.

## Before the Gay-Straight Alliance

If *Rolling the R's* (1995) is any indication, the United States is precisely not a space of unfettered queer flourishing. Like *The Umbrella Country*, Linmark's first book takes up issues of queer youth sexuality, transgender performance, and patriarchal and peer homophobia and sets them during the late 1970s. As a dynamic, multigeneric text made up of first-, second-, and third-person narration in pidgin and Standard English, poetry, letters, gossip, dreams, book reports, class assignments, mock prayers, and remixed song lyrics, it also resembles *Dogeaters* in its formal exuberance and nonlinearity as well as its play with U.S. popular culture. Although Kalihi in Honolulu, Hawai'i, is not Queens (indeed, Hawai'i's colonial status is more similar to the neocolonial Philippines than New York City), I position *Rolling the R's* as an indirect response to Gringo's question ("What is it really like there, where you come from?") as a way to examine the social context in which Linmark's evocation of queer kid culture is, by turns, performed and prohibited. And while the book's connection to martial law is less immediate than in the other novels, I discuss it here to highlight an unusual queer bond: the relationship between a closeted, protogay, haole-desiring, immigrant, Filipino boy (Vicente De Los Reyes) and a straight, exiled, intellectual, protopolitical activist, Filipino boy (Florante Sanchez).

This example acquires significance when read next to the queer practices the kids enact and the homophobic proscriptions they endure. *Rolling the R's* portrays the playfully serious ways in which the multiethnic fifth-graders' identifications with and desires for 1970s pop icons are often routed through queer vectors, an operation akin to José Esteban Muñoz's notion of "disidentification," "a remaking and rewriting of a dominant script" that "neither opts to assimilate within such a structure nor strictly opposes it"; rather, disidentification describes a critical and creative practice that "works on and against dominant ideology."[19] The flamboyant Edgar Ramirez, for instance, says on the first page that he "had sex with Scott Baio, Leif Garrett, [and] Matt Dillon" in his dream.[20] While watching *Making Love* in a movie theater, Vicente imagines himself and the man he sits next to "in front of a fireplace with Zack and Bart. The four of them wrapped in each other's arms, watching the ritual of flames" (17). Following the premiere of *Charlie's Angels*, the valedictorian of Farrington High, Orlando Domingo, decides to curl his hair, dress, and wear makeup like Farrah Fawcett—a practice of transgendering that the principal and football coaches can do little about given the "impeccable" school record of the "Filipino faggot whose only desire is to be Farrah from Farrington" (25). The book's alliterative levity notwithstanding, such cross-gender play and the boys' queer sexual activities have serious consequences, evidenced by the older jocks' ruthless teasing and harassment of Edgar (christened by the school nurse as "Queen of Ice Pack and Curad" [6]). As Edgar sits enthralled by the *Happy Days* episode "where Chachi kisses Joanie for the first time," his father grumbles with disgust and warns his son: "Do you want your classmates to start calling you a fag? A mahu?" (4). The following page reveals that the "wanna-be" basketball players already do so:

> "Eh, you guys, check out that Fag, Edgar."
> "What, Mahu, what you starin' at?"
> "No act, Panty, before I give you one good slap."
> "What, Bakla, you like beef right now?"
> "C'mon, Homo."
> "Right here, Sissy."
> "Edga's ooone faaag. He like suck one diiick." (5)

Framed by objectifications, the middle lines direct their interpellative power at Edgar himself, threatening the queer's returned gaze ("what you starin' at?") with physical violence and sexual taunts. In effect, the cultural particularities of the names (Hawaiian "Mahu," Filipino "Bakla") hardly matter since they all belong "to an entire family of comparable terms whose performative force devalues and shames their queer and sissy receiver."[21]

Muñoz writes that "queers are people who have failed to turn around to the 'Hey, you there!' interpellating call of heteronormativity."[22] Edgar's initial response to the interpellations of homophobic abjection is to "turn into the Queen of Mouth and Sizes," calling the boys' bluff by transforming the enticement-as-taunt ("you like beef right now") into a size contest: "I know mine's bigger than yours. C'mon, pull down your pants. What, scared? . . . C'mon, no need be shame" (5). Edgar's challenge seeks to reverse the shame imputed to gay oral sex and reinflect it to reveal the precariousness of heterosexual masculinity ("*prove* how big and strong you really are" [5, my emphasis]). Near the end of the chapter, though, Edgar recalls "all the names people call me. Faggot.

Mahu. Queen. Bakla. Queer. Cocksucker. Dicklover," indicating that his strategy of reversal does not erase the pain and ugliness of homophobic naming/shaming: "Even though most of the names are who I am and what I do, they say 'em with so much hate, like I ugly or somethin'. But I not ugly. I might be mean, but that's cuz I need for be strong when they tryin' for put me down and make like I the one ugly cuz I not like them" (10). Gone here is the flaming flare that erupts from the "Queen of Mouth and Sizes," replaced by a subdued meditation on the performative power and effects of naming.

Despite this homophobic milieu, Edgar's queer desires and sexual activities manage to thrive—though not with the "hapa-babe" who occupies his deepest fantasies (9). In another instance of calling out the heteronormativity of pop culture conventions (the song dedication), "Invisible Edgar" writes to Top 40 host Casey Kasem to convey his desire for the hapa-boy and criticizes Kasem for not reading his letter on air: "How many times I sent you letters already? I so hungry for this boy, Casey. And even if I one boy when you get to my name, how come, Casey, how come you no pick my letter for the week?" (124). Unrecognized by both Kasem and the object of his desire, Edgar finds himself distanced from heterocentric romance and at a loss for words: "How many times I tried to write like Susie Polish Shutz, her words so true to my heart?" (124).

Even more telling is the opening line of Edgar's letter: "You know, I one virgin when come for findin' the right words for explain that what I do and how I feel are not the same" (124). While he might feel hungry for the hapa-babe and would "rather do the splits for [Mr. Campos's] young son" (7), his actual acts of "mutual mastication, hand-to-hand resuscitation" take place during his "*Afterschool Special*" trysts with the married custodian Mr. Campos (1). Playing on the hetero-oriented pedagogy of afternoon television and the extravagant camp practice of diva nomenclature, Edgar goes on to narrate, "After school, I turn into the Queen of Wide World of Sports, I stay in the utility room playin' Rejuvenation Queen for Mr. Campos, the custodian of the century. He say I make him young again. I tell him he make me feel so mature" (7). Their sexcapades are depicted in more graphic detail in the later chapter "Secret," where Linmark anaphorically describes from Edgar's and Mr. Campos's alternating viewpoints their "secret" sex—a secret that Edgar divulges to Vicente and which Vicente observes through the keyhole of the janitor's room (126):

Edgar thinks it's a secret when Mr. Campos buries his face between Edgar's legs because only Mr. Campos can feel his own heart beating louder and louder as Edgar raises his feet higher and higher. Edgar thinks it's a secret because only he can feel his feet stiffening, his small toes curling. Edgar thinks it's a secret Mr. Campos can never tell because it is forever buried in his mouth, alive and young. . . . Mr. Campos thinks it's a secret when, not being able to hold it in, he shoots all over Edgar and groans. He thinks it's a secret despite the loud groans because, though the walls hear him, the walls don't have mouths. He does not know that, though the walls don't have mouths, the door has eyes. (126, 127)

These scenes of adult-kid gay sex are not framed according to "the thesis of child-loving as exploitation, or intergenerational sex as trauma,"[23] nor does Vicente's voyeurism lead to public exposure or punishment. Edgar's willingness to play "Rejuvenation Queen" with Mr. Campos not only compensates for his inability to bag Mr. Campos's son or the hapa-babe but also contrasts with the anxiety Vicente experiences during his sexual encounter. Two chapters after "Secret," Vicente has his only first-person narrative and directs his voice at (an apparently absent) Edgar. Recounting the experience he endures when Edgar pimps him out to the teenager Roberto for $20, Vicente says, "I thought I was going to die in there [in the tool shed], Edgar. . . . I was scared, Edgar, but he said, You scared of me? No need be scared of me. I not goin' hurt you. I only like touch Filipino birdie" (139). Forced to touch Roberto, Vicente is sickened and blames Edgar: "It should've been you in there. Yes, Edgar, you" (139).

Vicente's precarious sexuality stems not only from the unpleasant experience with Roberto or the homophobia at their school, but also from patriarchal interdiction. Paralleling the violence that attends transgendered performance in *The Umbrella Country*, *Rolling the R's* features a scene in the "Encore" chapter in which Vicente sings Donna Summers's "Enough Is Enough" (aka "No More Tears"). He overcomes his stage fright and "lets loose his choirboy voice"—only to have his father pull up in the driveway, his "face heating up like a volcano about to erupt" (39, 40): "With eyes still closed and imagination wide open, Vicente sings to his father. 'I can't go on no longer because enough is enough is enough is I gotta listen close to my heart'" (40). As bitterly ironic as the lyrics might seem when Vicente "sings to his father" (torqued from their original context of a woman jettisoning her no-good man, toward a protogay son asserting his heartfelt identity before his homophobic father), there is little to laugh at when "Mr. De Los Reyes climbs up on the wall and grips his son's neck, wrenching it until Vicente snaps free of his imagination" then "pushes him off the wall" and drags his son away (40).

While Vicente's reluctance to pursue openly and ardently his queer desires in light of these hazardous experiences is certainly understandable, what is less obvious is that Edgar's politics of self-affirmation (he not only asserts his queerness but also scolds the snobby Nelson for claiming an "American" not "Filipino" identity based on his class status [67–68]) serves as the very basis by which he ends up tormenting Vicente. In a late chapter called "The Casting," presented in drama form and serving as a kind of encore to the "Encore" chapter, Loata, Katrina, and Vicente tire of Edgar's bossiness and refuse to play the *Charlie's Angels* characters assigned to them. During the ensuing argument, Edgar accuses Vicente of being a "two-faced closet-case" (131) and, even worse, of cruising the rich, arrogant, white boy: "I see you lookin at Stephen Bean in class, liar. I watch the way you pretend for drop your pencil when all you really after is one quick glance at his dick" (135). Vicente retorts by exposing Edgar's "secret" of having sex with "men old enough to be my great-great-grandfather's grandfather" (134). Both boys deny the charges when Loata and Katrina ask for confirmation.

This moment of discord—Vicente categorically declares "I'm not like you" when Edgar asserts "you just one 'nother fag like me" (134)—complicates the notion that "while the disparate ethnic affiliations of the immigrant adolescents who populate Linmark's novella threaten to divide further their tenuous loyalties, it is precisely sexuality—an obsessive queer sexuality that permeates *Rolling the R's* from beginning to end—that binds them together as a social group with a common sense of purpose and esprit de corps."[24] In "The Casting," it is exactly the obsession over queer sexuality that produces conflict. When the insults escalate into Vicente punching Edgar in the nose and Edgar boiling into a fury, Florante steps in and leads Vicente away; Loata and Katrina follow them, and Edgar screams in their wake, "You guys just wait, assholes, especially you, you fuckin' faggot. You just wait" (137). This is the last time the kids are shown together. Two chapters hence, Edgar resumes his rampage against the others, complaining about getting "the same freakin' gifts this Christmas" when he had thoughtfully selected presents for each of them (140). His rant ends by echoing the threat that closes "The Casting": "Wait til next Christmas" (142).

In the midst of these unsavory, cross-age sexual liaisons, peer insults, patriarchal punishments, and dissolving group bonds, the one relationship that strengthens is that between Vicente and Florante. It is no accident that Florante is the one who intervenes on Vicente's behalf during the fight with Edgar. If not along lines of a common queer sexuality, what brings Vicente and Florante together? Though the book's historiographic impulse engages most energetically with popular culture, it does include one chapter titled "Portraits" that references martial law. Florante invites Vicente to his house, introduces him to Lolo Tasio, and discloses that all the members of his family (except his mother, his grandfather, and himself) were killed in the Philippines: "a speeding jeep chased them off the edge of the road and soldiers started shooting at them. . . . After we buried them, we left the country." Florante explains, "Some people didn't like what my grandparents and parents were writing about" (61). Within the book's freewheeling play with U.S. pop icons, the Sanchez family reminds us of the political persecution and extrajudicial killings rampant during martial law, and the exilic flights they provoked.

Implicitly, what draws Vicente to Florante's story is the sight and memory of corporeal suffering. When Florante's grandfather exits the room, Vicente "sees the geography of scars and welts imprinted on Lolo Tasio's back, reminding him of the men who, during Holy Week, hid their faces, tore their skin open, and dotted the road with their blood" (62). His Aunt Fely had explained that self-flagellation represents a means of "asking for God's forgiveness" because the men "are not faithful to their wives" (62). However, the third-person narrator asserts that "though their heads were covered in T-shirts, everyone in the provincial town, especially the women, knew that they were the bodyguards of the Mayor" (62). What links the scarified "geography" inscribed on Lolo Tasio for his antiauthoritarian writings with Holy Week self-flagellation? Are we to assume that the penitents take advantage of the townswomen due to their status as bodyguards? Or is it that the bodyguards torture political dissidents and thus execute a similar form of punishment on themselves?

It is possible that Vicente connects the Marcos regime's repressive dictatorship with the patriarchal punishment he receives from his father. The posters "bleeding with bikini-clad martyrs, stone-headed presidents, and serial killers" gesture in this direction (62). The reference is to the image of "a cartoon of Mount Rushmore bearing the faces of George Washington, Thomas Jefferson, Ferdinand Marcos, and Charles

Manson. Above their heads, in capital letters, is the phrase ALL IN THE FAMILY" (59). These father figures appear to signal patriarchal authority gone awry. In this sense, the two boys occupy parallel subordinate positions: Vicente vis-à-vis his father's homophobic disciplining of gender-sexual dissidence, and Florante vis-à-vis the Philippine state's "disappearing" of political dissidents.

For his part, Florante seems to sympathize with Vicente's plight as a result of his family's political activism, a social awareness he inherits from his mother and grandfather, "who came from and brought forth a generation of writers" (58). The book's poet, intellectual, and historian, Florante alludes to "the Fall of Bataan" (5); listens to *kundimans* (Tagalog ballads), not disco (8); and refers to the classroom where he, Vicente, and Mai-Lan (the three immigrants) get English pronunciation lessons from Ms. Takara as "the asphixiating room. It reminds him of the colonial history of the Philippines" (49). Whereas queerness is no guarantor of political progressivism in *Dogeaters* or *The Umbrella Country* (much less in *Rolling the R's*), Linmark implies that the opposite can be true: that one who embraces an antiauthoritarian politics can forge an empathetic alliance with a questioning, queer outcast—can, in fact, claim him as "my best friend" (56).[25]

The performative acts within the novel—Edgar brazenly desiring teen boy idols, Orling transgendering into "Farrah Flip," Vicente crooning Donna Summer, Katrina rewriting Judy Blume's *Forever* as part book report and part love column (145–149)—embody the kids' appropriations and queerings of U.S. popular culture. But Linmark's multiply voiced text also enacts performative articulations in relation to its readers, mirroring the kids' disidentifications at the level of cultural production. *Rolling the R's* not only exposes and refunctions the heterocentric workings of (mostly white) popular culture but also addresses multiple characters and audiences through the proliferation of second-person narrative voices.

Though the effects of this technique are multivalent, when the voice is addressed to a particular character or type, we readers are interpellated into that position, whether as a closet case ("Skin, Or Edgar's Advice to Closet Cases"), as an abused wife ("What Manong Rocky Tells Manang Pearly About Carmen, Rosario, and Milagros"), as a pimp ("Mama's Boy"), as cheapskates ("Heart"), as dream-filled kids ("Chain Letter Translated from Saint Malas"), as a lecherous peeping-tom ("You Don't Have to Wait"), as a lovelorn coward ("You Lovely Faggot You"), as a

cheated-on wife ("F for Book Report"), and as a litany of Filipino stereotypes ("They Like You Because You Eat Dog"). The profuse use of the
second-person shifts the politics of representation away from the burden of portraying "social diversity" and toward an implication of readers themselves within the book's humorous, abrasive improvisations.
Denied the luxury of aesthetic distance, we are hailed into the world
of Kalihi, replete with homophobia, misogyny, sexploitation, and racism, as well as queer performances, fantasies, and desires. In a sense, the
initiation of the reader into this social world mirrors yet again the kids'
relation to popular culture, and our responses to those literary interpellations are undoubtedly ambivalent and "disidentificatory" but nonetheless inescapable.

## Bearing Trauma

If Florante Sanchez represents the well-adjusted, astute immigrant boy—
despite (and because of) the killing of more than half his family during
martial law—then Bong Bong Luwad, the protagonist of Noël Alumit's
*Letters to Montgomery Clift*, embodies the opposite. Though he eventually
becomes politically aware when he reaches adolescence, Bong starts out as
a naive, eight-year-old child who is shipped off to Los Angeles to live with
his Auntie Yuna after witnessing martial law thugs beat his parents and
drag away his father in his hometown of Baguio City. Bong's father, Emil,
like Florante's family, "wrote for a newspaper" that "told secrets" about the
regime, such as "killing people and stealing from everyone."[26]
     Rather than thrive in the United States as his mother had hoped,
Bong compulsively returns in traumatic fashion to these constitutive
scenes of loss and rupture. Alumit intertwines this political story of
martial law with Bong's queer coming-of-age from eight to thirty. After
Auntie Yuna unexpectedly disappears, Bong is bounced around the foster care system; ends up with the well-off Filipino family the Arangans
and their daughter, Amada; discovers that they have made their money
through one of Marcos's off-shore money-laundering schemes; learns
of his father's torture and death through an ex-detainee, Mrs. Billaruz;
harbors plans to return to the Philippines to locate his mother; suffers
a psychological breakdown; develops a relationship with the Japanese
American screenwriter Logan; and finally tracks down and reunites with
his mother in Baguio City.

As plot-driven as the novel is, its most intriguing feature is its formal conceit. Bong starts writing letters to Montgomery Clift on December 4, 1976, ten years after Clift's death. He gets the idea from Auntie Yuna, who tells the unwanted boy, "Praying is not enough. . . . Better to put it on paper. Especially in America" (4). Though she instructs her nephew to write only to "saints or dead relatives" (4), Bong secretly writes his letters to Monty after seeing *The Search* (1948), a movie about a soldier who "finds and cares for a small boy whose mother was taken away by bad people" and who "guards the boy till his mama comes" (4–5).

Deprived of his parents, sent to live in a foreign country with a physically abusive alcoholic aunt, abandoned again when she goes "to the liquor store and never [comes] back" (41; we later learn she has been deported), and separated from his classmate Robert Bulanan and his older Filipino American neighbor J, Bong suffers a series of painful losses within the span of four short years. That he copes by writing letters to a dead Hollywood movie star instead of saying prayers to "strange" dead Filipino relatives not only speaks to the irrepressible impulsions of supplication ("I prayed and prayed and prayed") but also to the available array of addressees (13). This enunciative context implies that Bong's situation is unintelligible to, or irreparable by, any living listener in his vicinity. All that J can offer, after Bong tells of his past, is: "Wow" (25). In their cultivation of a fiercely desperate form of intimacy and in their faithful longing for recognition, Bong's letters to Monty operate as a kind of "third" mode of address that is directed neither at a mainstream America nor at a martial law–controlled Philippines but at a dead white film icon.

Though Clift as addressee initially seems arbitrary, the deceased actor takes on increasing dimensions of significance as the novel progresses. Bong not only writes to Clift, he also begins to see him, ghostly and briefly at first, then gradually as a more durable figure. Clift's substitution for Bong's lost mother (indicated by Bong's reading of *The Search*) resonates with Diana Fuss's theory of identification. "Compensating for loss," she writes, is "a profoundly defamiliarizing affair, installing surrogate others to fill the void where we imagine the love-object to have been. . . . Identification, in other words, invokes phantoms. . . . To be open to an identification is to be open to a death encounter, open to the very possibility of communing with the dead."[27] Whereas the Freudian view involves identification with the lost-object itself, I want to hold on here to the notion of surrogacy. Though separated from his mother for decades without news of her existence, Bong refuses to believe that she is dead. His "communing with the dead" takes place not with his mother but with Clift, who functions as a sort of "detour" that does not so much define Bong's "self" as keep it from disintegrating.[28]

Bong's insertion of himself into *The Search* is but one of many moments where he interprets Clift movies in terms of his own life, appropriating their storylines and characters in ways analogous to *Rolling the R's*, and reframing them to comprehend a self that the original films could scarcely have imagined, much less sought to represent. At times, Bong directly identifies with Clift's character on screen, as with his reading of *The Misfits* (1961) (65–66), or analogizes his experience with the Clift character, as when he likens Prewitt's decision to "go AWOL" in *From Here to Eternity* (1953) to his own desire "to go away, disappear" and enter a "fuzzy world" where everything "become[s] a little more bearable" (74). At other times, he views the films through the lens of his parents' experiences of being beaten (*From Here to Eternity* [74]) and imprisoned (*Suddenly, Last Summer* [1959] [94]). At still other moments, Bong uses film narratives to frame his erotic relationship with Clift. When he goes "fuzzy" after learning that the Arangans made their fortune by helping out the Marcoses,[29] he sees Monty in the library: "I could tell from the way he looked at me that he loved me. He loved me the way he loved Elizabeth Taylor in *Suddenly[,] Last Summer*. She was going through a hellish time, locked up in some insane asylum. He was there for her" (91).

The overlaps between vision and film, eroticism and therapy, run throughout Bong's relationship with Monty. The actor's ghostly form is less a haunting than a home, a source of solace in the face of dislocation, distress, and loss (39, 60, 127, 136). But Monty's role as diaphanous maternal surrogate expands to include embodied queer lover as Bong gets older. When the fifteen-year-old Bong peruses Clift biographies and learns that the actor "was attracted to men," Bong's queer sexuality also gets thematized (84).[30] His "relief" in this knowledge extends to himself when Amada assures him, "It's OK if you don't like Anne or any other girl, Bob. I don't care. I really don't" (85).[31] (The "coming out" scene with Amada's parents is just as uneventful [202].) Bong's sexual emergence is further facilitated through contact with Monty "himself." During his second year at the University of Southern California, Bong transforms his first sexual partner into Monty:

And with the moon bright like a silver dollar, I thought of Monty, Montgomery Clift. He entered my head, my mind, pouring out of me, through my eyes, nose, and mouth until he was standing in front of me.

He was the one I was kissing in that parking lot, not Loser Frat Boy. It was him. (151)

As though Monty had been internalized, the dead star cascades out of Bong's orifices and supersedes Loser Frat Boy's material body. Playing on the convention of the newly queer boy pursuing sexploration with multiple partners, Alumit writes: "I couldn't just kiss him once. I had to kiss him again. . . . I found him in a dark bar, where other men look for men of their dreams. . . . I found him in West Hollywood" (152). Ironically, Bong's "promiscuous" phase is actually monogamous: each of his sexual partners is technically Monty. Bong is so devoted to the movie star that he feels "dirty" and "unfaithful" when he first kisses Logan and does not "summon" his apparitional lover (194). During their second kiss, Bong takes Monty's nonappearance as a "sign" that he "wanted me to kiss Logan" (194, 195).

The novel presents Bong's relation to Monty not as a hallucinatory symptom of his psychological problems but as an integral component of his survival strategies (the other major part being his relationship with Amada). Whereas Bong's literary historical namesake in Hagedorn's story "The Blossoming of Bongbong" experiences a series of "visions and revelations" that signal his queer, eccentric "madness,"[32] Alumit's protagonist interacts with Monty as a means of holding madness in abeyance. The novel thematizes this point by contrasting the American Dr. Butterworth (aka "Brainwasher"), who diagnoses Bong as psychotic and delusional, with Dr. Chapman, "a divine woman" originally from Bombay (179) who interprets his self-injuries as effects of childhood "abandonment" and abuse and does not "mock" his relationship with Monty, telling Bong that she asks her deceased mother for "advice" when she "visits" her (180). Unlike Dr. Butterworth's construal of communicating with "ghosts" as pathological, Dr. Chapman treats it as neither culturally essentialist nor extraordinary.

What truly haunts Bong throughout the latter half of the novel are the stories that Mrs. Billaruz tells him of his father's torture and execution, and the uncertainty of his mother's whereabouts. In this respect, Bong's therapeutic and erotic relationship with Monty operates in counterpoint to his self-punishing identification with his parents' traumatic experiences. Bong starts bruising himself immediately after Mrs. Billaruz tells him over the phone that "they did things to" Bong's father, Emil (115). Recalling that he last saw his parents with "bruises," Bong takes to slamming his body into doors, walls, and furniture, linking the "bloom[s]" on his flesh to the "garden of purple daffodils" on his mother's body (117). Whatever solace Monty may offer, Bong asserts that bruising himself "was the right thing to do. Hurting myself seemed appropriate. There was comfort in pain, incredible comfort" (118). Bong's self-injuries grow more severe after he visits Mrs. Billaruz in Hawai'i and learns of his father's torture (154). Far from providing a sense of "closure," the knowledge that Bong had been seeking about his father only produces further trauma.

Bong's survivor's guilt and self-punishment eventually land him in a psychiatric facility after he and Amada argue over Bong's refusal to visit her parents:

> "Your parents don't know shit about pain," I said. "My father was beaten until he was black and blue. That's pain. They hit him like this." I punched myself; I took my fist and hit my chest. "They hit him again!" I smacked my face. I felt warm liquid drip out of my nose, landing on my shirt, leaving a clean red spot there. "They hit him again and again, for hours and hours." I clawed at my arms, digging my nails into my skin, smacking myself, punching myself, grabbing my hair, falling onto the floor kicking away furniture, slamming against the ground. . . . "They knew he was a writer, so they hit him on the hands. They stomped on his fingers. They did it over and over again. Until his joints were gone. They broke his hands! That's what Mrs. Billaruz told me. They broke his hands so he couldn't write anymore. His hands looked like old twisted branches. Then they tortured him again." I threw Amada off of me and slammed my knuckles against the floor, slamming them until they were red, until my hands were weak and the skin was broken. (163–164)

The layers of traumatic "repetition compulsion"[33] are excruciatingly multiplied: Mrs. Billaruz rehearses the story of witnessing Emil's torture; her words insinuate themselves into Bong's dreams and waking hours; he reinscribes the pain onto his own body; and he rearticulates the story to Amada, simultaneously reenacting the corporeal punishment endured by his father.

Bong's self-mutilation continues even after he is hospitalized, bed restraints and Prozac notwithstanding. Finally able to cry over his father, Bong squeezes a light bulb until it shatters, comparing the pain to his father's electrocution: "Electricity bolted through me, like scalding water surging through my veins. I jerked, and jumped. . . . I thought of my dad. I wondered if this is what it felt like." Bong makes explicit the identification with his father's pain: "And I cried. Because at that moment I was my father. . . . It seemed the electricity chased me away, chased all the feeling from my body, . . . making me hollow" (175). Rather than reconstitute a self through the encounters with his lost father in dream and memory, Bong's identification leads to an internal hollowing out.

Ultimately, Bong locates the source of his self-injury in precisely the act that was meant to keep him from harm: his mother's decision to send him to the United States. Released from the hospital and now in the Philippines searching for his mother, Bong reflects:

> I bruised and scarred myself, hating the fact that I was in America, while my parents suffered in the Philippines. I hated that I was healthy, my skin unblemished, knowing, feeling my parents were being hurt, mutilated. I got away. God damn it, I got away. . . . Amada said I had to correct a mistake. Hurting myself was my way of correcting things that went awry. My life in the U.S. was a mistake. I was supposed to have the same fate as my father or mother: imprisonment, torture. Instead I got away, I was saved. I had the wealth of America on my back, and it felt like an enormous burden. (221, 222)

This is an extraordinary commentary on the dynamics of diasporic identification. In this self-flagellating logic, "America" is neither a desirable place where one seeks refuge from dictatorial violence (as his mother had imagined) nor an undesirable place where racist, classist, and homophobic exclusions contradict its mythic idealization as the promised land. Rather, America's very accommodation of the immigrant-refugee becomes a "burden," a weight lifted only by rejecting its welcome and wealth through self-mutilation. America, for Bong, is a "mistake," an irrevocable wrong turn away from what he considers his prescribed fate. His bruises and disfigurements inscribe onto his body an experience that he feels ought to have been his, allowing him to participate in a history of suffering from which he has been unduly ripped. On the other hand, the Philippines is not the place of nostalgic longing where the refugee returns to suture his wounds, but where those wounds are ripped open once more, a recollected site of "imprisonment, torture"—not a lost Eden, but a hell to be relived, regained.

To be sure, the novel ends happily with Bong reuniting with his mother in Baguio City, after the obligatory cold trails, serendipitous encounters, and temporary deferrals. Though the unlikely reunion might seem "formulaic,"[34] what is interesting, again, is how the letters function. Until the moment when Bong returns to the Philippines, the novel frames each chapter with letters to Clift. These are not a "clumsy expository device" that previews what is to come, as one reviewer complained,[35] but rather dialectically interact with the narrative proper to produce a temporally multilayered novel whose audiences are concomitantly multiplied (Monty, the reader, and Mama).

Bong ceases writing letters when he boards the plane headed for the Philippines: "There are no more letters. There is just now. There is just me" (211). This decision harks back to the opening chapter in which Alumit troubles the linear dating of the letters by calling attention to the folded temporality, as it were, of the novel:

> Once the sun strikes this side of earth, Logan will take me to the airport and I'll fly away . . . back to the beginning. Some think time is a straight line that only continues forward. I don't believe that. I think the line of time can be bent backward, so far back, it'll break. And when it does, everything I know will fall apart. I'm going back to see who I was. I'm going to visit Yesterday, hoping to discover what went horribly wrong.
>
> I look at my letters. And by doing so, I've bent the line of time backward. I see who I was: my words written in a child's scribble. Some of my letters are stained, warped spots where moisture used to be. Moisture that was my tears. (2)

Bong returns to the scene of traumatic rending ("My mother attached me to this world. She was my connection—then all of a sudden, that connection was severed" [221]) not with the optimistic prospect that the tear can be mended but with the ominous prediction that everything "will fall apart." What rescues this utter collapse is the material record-keeping of epistolarity (warps, tears, and all), its capacity to bend "time backward." Once Bong's desired addressee is found alive, the letters become the vehicle through which the hitherto lost past is resurrected, serving as a personal archive of memories, visions, and experiences, and enabling the sundered relationship between mother and son to be restored.

When Mama says to Bong, "Tell me, child. Tell me all about your life" (234), Bong "blushe[s]" (235). Although he interprets this embarrassed flush as an indication of what cannot be told to a parent ("I certainly couldn't tell her about my sexual activities" [235]), it also signals a more profound embarrassment at having failed to live the better, safer, pain-free life he was supposed to live in the United States. Bong thus turns to his letters to tell his life, while "fill[ing] in the parts in between" with his own narration: "I pulled out my letters to Montgomery Clift. She read the first one and I said, 'I didn't start seeing Montgomery Clift immediately. I didn't start to depend on him or adore him or desire him or touch him until later . . .'" (235, original ellipses). Bong's story to his mother repeats the bimodal narrative structure of the novel, literally recapitulating the novel's opening. While this recursion to the beginning might imply that we should read the narrative proper as Bong's oral supplement to the written letters, that possibility breaks down by the second page: "If I find Mama . . . when I find her—no, I can only say 'if'" (2). This inconsistency (what is contingent on page 2 becomes actual on page 235) suggests yet another enactment of repetition—but this time a repetition with a serious difference, for if Bong's letters are articulable precisely because they identify an addressee who is disposed to receive and recognize them ("Thank God, I have you. No matter what, you're always willing to listen," he writes to Monty [118]) and intelligible because they propose another recipient in the hoped-for future who will understand the son's constancy and fidelity ("If I find my mother, I'll give them to her. . . . She will read them and I'll explain the parts in between" [2]), the *written* narrative proper can count on no such guarantee of recognition, intelligibility, or understanding from its readers. At the end of the novel, then, Mama becomes the "ideal" reader, listener, respondent:

> She apologized about Auntie Yuna. I told her that wasn't necessary. She shook her head when she read about the foster homes. . . . She bit her lip, tears ran down her cheeks when I told her about how I hurt myself. She held my hand when I talked about my motorcycle accident, my hospitalization.
>
> I was worried when she read about Logan and the other men in my life.

"Logan sounds like a good person," she said.

"He makes me happy," I said, implying that I loved him, needed him. I waited for her to respond.

"Maybe I can meet him someday." She looked at me. With that look, she let me know it was okay; it didn't matter that I preferred men. I was relieved. (235)

Mama's emotional responses, spoken comments, and physical gestures perform the work of recognition that the novel beseeches from its readers: sympathy without judgment for Bong's suffering, acceptance of his gay sexuality.

Mama's capacity to model the reception of Bong's letters and narration is predicated on her own positionality. The restoration between son and mother is not a one-way return to an imaginary origin (the mother, the motherland, the birthplace) but a dialogue with both the homeland's (231) and the mother's intervening years. Reciprocating Mama's willingness to listen, Bong says, "Tell me about you" (236). Her story reveals why she can accept Bong's story before she has even heard it: "'After all I've been through,' she said, 'there is nothing you can tell me that would shock me'" (235). It turns out that Mama hid in Manila while searching for Emil; was branded a subversive, interrogated about her knowledge of Communists, forced to lie naked with a block of ice on her body, transferred to another detention center where she joined other women detainees; belatedly learned of Emil's execution; and experienced "terrible things" in prison (238).

The aftermath of Mama's imprisonment strikingly mirrors Bong's story. Initially imagining that Bong's life in America is for the best, she encounters Yuna a year later and "went crazy": "I could not believe she didn't know where you were. She didn't seem to care. I was put in a hospital, because I almost killed her" (239). Mama's descent into madness parallels Bong's; both attribute their "craziness" to not knowing how the other is faring: "My own child somewhere in the States, all by himself. The thought made me sick" (239). Coincidentally, movies save them both. While convalescing in a hospital, Mama watches *Blood Prom at Hell High*, a film in which Bong had performed as an extra in high school: "This was a sign you were okay. I knew you were leading a life that I could never give you" (240). The dark humor lies not only in the fact that *Blood Prom* is a horror flick "about a bunch of kids who get massacred" (84) but also in Mama's fantasy that Bong is living a "healthy" and "happy" life (240). The reciprocal sharing of stories that closes the narrative proper of *Letters to Montgomery Clift* serves to clarify such misconstruals, even as it posits mutual understanding based on shared suffering. When Mama breaks down at the point where she cannot describe the "terrible things [they do] to women," Bong holds her and narrates, "That was what I was looking for. Someone to give herself to me. Someone for me to give myself to" (238).

Analyzing "the profound link between the death of the loved one and the ongoing life of the survivor," Cathy Caruth writes in her influential book on trauma, "it is the inextricability of the story of one's life from the story of a death, an impossible and necessary double telling, that constitutes their historical witness."[36] In the case of Bong and Mama, both physically survive, and the "double telling" that historical witnessing demands turns out to be the necessary—but not exactly impossible—story of two *lives*. Bong's and Mama's mutual storytelling at the diegetic level is repeated at the level of the book's relation to its readers. If we think of this doubleness (of stories, of audiences) in a diasporic context, we witness another instance of multivalent modes of address: Mama's revelation of her brutal treatment transmits a pedagogical narrative of political dissidence under martial law to U.S. readers (with Bong acting as our proxy), while Bong's letters and storytelling to Mama convey in the opposite direction his painful experiences growing up under a profound sense of loss, shattering any illusions that the United States epitomizes the locus of forgetting, of "starting over." And it is the epistolary archive of the letters to Montgomery Clift that enables such diasporic transmissions and receptions to take place.

## Growing Up Queer?

*Letters to Montgomery Clift* closes with an "Epilogue" in the form of a letter. Ostensibly wrapping up the story lines, it also concludes with a parting address. Bong sees Clift in the film *Indiscretion of an American Wife* (1953) and characteristically applies the impossible on-screen love affair to his own relationship with Monty: "I wept at the end of the movie. I wept for us. I love you, Monty. I want the very best for you, too" (244). Wishing good fortune for Clift's afterlife on screen and in biographies, these closing words also intimate a less certain future than the letter-as-summary implies. Bong's return to the Philippines had spelled the end of his epistolary practice—and, apparently, of Monty's visitations: "I haven't had the need to write," he starts out. "Then again, I haven't see you in a while either" (243). But now that Mama has been found, Bong has not completely given up writing letters to Monty, nor is this last missive exactly a farewell: he does not say, for example, "I *will always* love you."

This ending complicates the neatness of the novel's narrative closures: exile and return, loss and recuperation, the construction of an "alternative" family (mother, son, boyfriend). Indeed, the novel's *gay* story comes off as rather matter-of-fact compared to the traumatic upheavals of the martial law story: the "coming out" scenes with Amada, the Arangans, and Mama are about as unspectacular as they come, and Bong's relationship with Logan is also conventional (or politically correct), not merely in being long term but also "sticky" (Asian-Asian). But the lingering expression of love for Monty—the ghostly figure in whom Bong had invested so much affective energy during moments of acute distress—troubles this developmental trajectory. Refusing to relinquish his first friend and lover, even after Monty's roles as surrogate mother and erotic partner have been filled by others, Bong maintains his queer melancholic attachment as a kind of reminder of the losses he has suffered and the painful identifications with trauma he has experienced, and as a sort of anticipatory safeguard against future catastrophe.

That *Letters to Montgomery Clift* does not render coming out as an internally tormenting or family-rending affair, or thematize the politics of interracial versus intraracial eroticism,[37] might bespeak a sort of coming-of-age of the queer diasporic Filipino novel itself. By sequencing *The Umbrella Country*, *Rolling the R's*, and *Letters to Montgomery Clift* in this order, my discussion brings to the fore the politics of queer diasporic reading, forcing us to think of diaspora as simultaneously a spatial and temporal frame, one that maps childhood to adulthood not only onto the narrative of migration from homeland to new land but also onto the story of presumed racial and sexual naïveté to political maturity. Whereas the epigraph to *Rolling the R's* is from J. M. Barrie's *Peter Pan*, for instance, Alumit's dedication is "to those who have Disappeared." From fantasy land to Amnesty International? Put differently, since these texts feature children or youths and are set about a generation before they were published, they implicitly pose the question: what will queer Filipinos *become*?

Steven Bruhm and Natasha Hurley define the figure of the queer child as "that which doesn't quite conform to the wished-for way that children are supposed to be in terms of gender and sexual roles. In other circumstances, it is also the child who displays interest in sex generally, in same-sex attachments, or in cross-generational attachments."[38] While the desirous and sexually active youth in these novels fit this description, they also do not "conform" to their expected "race" roles either. Though a homophobic viewpoint might retroactively "rationalize" those wayward acts and attachments "as a series of mistakes or misplaced desires" that can be dissolved into heteronormative oblivion (that is, adulthood) (xiv), a homophilic perspective might conversely read them as phases en route to a racially and postcolonially homonormative adulthood. That is, are we to read the transgendered practices that Pipo and the gang perform in the Miss Unibers contest, the pop singing and playacting that Edgar and the gang perform to the tune of 1970s disco and the glow of serial television, and even Joey's desire for a sugar daddy or cougar in *Dogeaters* as phases of *political* immaturity to be outgrown by a more adult politicized consciousness? Read together, do these texts reinforce developmental narratives of sexual, geographical, and political progress: queer child to gay adult, Filipino dictatorship and patriarchal homophobia to American freedom and tolerance, desire for whiteness to desire for likeness?

These reflections resonate with debates around the politics of sexual categorization in current Filipino queer studies. Contesting the view of gay globalization as the Western imposition of sexual epistemology (the binary logic of male/female, heterosexual/homosexual), political strategy (coming out, public visibility, human rights discourse), and capitalist consumption (bar culture, clothing, style, tourism), scholars such as Neil Garcia, Michael Tan, Martin F. Manalansan, and Bobby Benedicto have explored the (in)congruities between Western concepts of "gay" (which encompasses same-sex attraction, identity, behavior, and, in some cases, subcultures) and Philippine notions of "*bakla*" (which can connote effeminacy, cross-dressing, hermaphroditism, working-class positionality, and "real" man sexual object choice).[39] At stake is not merely cultural accuracy but political interpretation and possibility, particularly around the temporality of these concepts (modern gay versus traditional, vestigial remnants of *kabaklaan*).

While the novels explored here are not deeply interested in distinguishing between "Western" and "non-Western" forms of dissident sexuality, I am nonetheless calling attention to their doubled historicity

(1970s/1990s) in order to ask not how they challenge the ascendancy of the gay white male as the primary subject of gay fiction and politics (of course they do) but whether they point toward an emergent normative gay male *of color* in the United States. In this respect, it is necessary to emphasize that the narrative conclusions to these queer characters—Joey Sands in *Dogeaters*, Gringo and Pipo in *The Umbrella Country*, Bong and Montgomery Clift in *Letters to Montgomery Clift*—are left open-ended, while the possibility of maintaining queer sociality in *Rolling the R's* is similarly uncertain, mainly because the fifth-graders do not grow up within the text. As the book's epigraph suggests: "and thus it will go on, so long as children are gay and innocent and heartless."

Linmark's gay kids, of course, are neither innocent (of sexual knowledge, of gender transitivity, of their phobic repercussions), entirely heartless, nor caught in the cyclical time of *Peter Pan*. In his reading of *Rolling the R's*, Victor Bascara offers a way to theorize the "historical gap" between their present and our present, calling attention to the temporal politics at the book's core: "These children re-present to us the conditions of the moment of emergence for new subjectivities when and where newness and subjecthood were differently valorized. The children become prophets of queer postcoloniality under U.S. imperialism."[40] Does the text nostalgically seek to retrieve a historical moment when the utopian energies of "new subjectivities" ("queers of color before such an idea was codified" [118]) were still redolent with hope? Or do the kids figure a future (our present) in which the critical potentialities of "queer" have been compromised by the nationalist logics of postcolonial and imperial normalization and co-opted by the "contradictions of multiculturalism and globalization" (121), dulling those energies into bland rhetorics of cultural diversity and ruthlessly commodified insignia of gayness?

By leaving their conclusions inconclusive, by not showing their protagonists reaching adulthood, and by playing with a variety of formal techniques and conventions, these texts refuse being used as ethnographic "evidence" for sexual, racial, and cultural diversity. If these kids are "prophets of queer postcoloniality under U.S. imperialism," then their predictions remain enigmatic, promising neither a normalized nationalism, a co-opted postcoloniality, nor a disciplined gay normativity. Their outrageous desires, improvisations on popular culture, critiques of masculinist authoritarianism, and heartlessness and tenderness toward each other—these remain (non)utopian strategies to recall and refashion in reimagining queer Filipino futures.[41]

# 6

# The Transpacific Tactics of Contemporary
# Filipino American Literature

IN HER RECENT novel *One Tribe* (2006), M. Evelina Galang expands on the remapping of Filipinos in the United States begun in her earlier collection of short stories *Her Wild American Self* (1996). Bringing us forward from the period of Philippine martial law and U.S. popular culture evoked in the work of Jessica Hagedorn, Bino Realuyo, R. Zamora Linmark, and Noël Alumit, Galang's novel focuses on a Filipino American community in Virginia in the 1990s. The protagonist, Isabel Manalo, moves from a Chicago suburb to Virginia Beach to accept a position at a public school that enrolls a significant population of Filipino American students. It soon becomes evident that the administration and the first-generation Filipino parents have called on Isabel not merely to teach art classes but to assist with the "at-risk" Filipina Americans whose too-cool-for-school attitude, black vernacular appropriations, and gang-related violence are cause for parental anxiety. Throughout the narrative, Isabel's Filipina identity is repeatedly called into question by *las dalagas* (young Filipino women) and by Ferdi Mamaril, a cultural nationalist who embodies a more manic version of Jessica Hagedorn's Carabao Kid in *The Gangster of Love* (1996).

For my purposes here, the novel is striking not only because it underscores the tension between the cultural unity implied in the title (*One Tribe*) and the manifold differences (regional, generational, linguistic, gender, sexual) that are prominently presented in this community, but because it raises the question between reading and identity. At two points, one of the high school girls, Lourdes, argues that the latter is unrelated to the former. "Just cuz you read lots of books about the Philippines doesn't make you Filipino," Lourdes tells her teacher/mentor. "I didn't want you to think that cuz you knew something about our history that it meant you was one of us."[1] Although Lourdes's telescoping conflation of "Philippines," "Filipino," "our history," and "one of us" would

seem to provide Isabel an opportunity to push back against the girl's rea-
soning, she does not. In fact, when Lourdes repeats this challenge later
on, Isabel agrees. "Ain't no matter how many books you read," Lourdes
says. "Nothing's going teach you how to be Pinay. You either is or you
isn't."

> "Those books don't teach you how to be Filipino," she [Isabel] told
> them [las dalagas]. "They talk about our history, our past."
> "They don't help you be Pinay," Lourdes said. "I know that."
> "No." (208)

Isabel's concession is odd since the novel itself not only *proposes* that
the teaching and learning of Philippine and Filipino American history
is crucial to the self-identification of the teenagers and youngsters she
instructs but also *enacts* this pedagogy by including Filipino myths and
history within its pages.

Lourdes's contention notwithstanding, this chapter delves into the
fraught separations and overlaps between the politics of reading and the
politics of identity, between knowledge production and consumption,
and between literature and history. As I explore below, the ethnographic
scholarship produced about second-generation Filipino Americans in
the 1990s shows that at least some of them believe the exact opposite
of Lourdes—that reading is a necessary, if not sufficient, component
in the construction of cultural identity. Juxtaposing next to this social
science scholarship several contemporary literary texts written by "1.5"
or second-generation Filipino Americans—Galang's *Her Wild American Self*, Brian Ascalon Roley's novel *American Son* (2001), Patrick Rosal's poetry collections *Uprock Headspin Scramble and Dive* (2003) and
*My American Kundiman* (2007), and Barbara Jane Reyes's poetry book
*Poeta en San Francisco* (2005)—my discussion seeks to historicize the
discourse of Filipino "invisibility" as a *contemporary*, post-1965 phenomenon. Whereas Lourdes disputes the link between reading and identity
on the basis of something like authentic insiderism, I suggest that the
literature troubles that link by forcing us to account for the differential
politics of gender and sexuality.

Insofar as the discourse of "invisibility" is predicated on nonrecog-
nition or misrecognition of Filipino specificity, the literary texts considered here offer two salient responses to this plight: a (re)turn to
the "homeland" to forge a *Filipino* American identity and culture (that

echoes some of the Flips' efforts of the 1970s), and a turn toward cross-culturality (that resembles Hagedorn's poetics). In the first instance, Galang's *Her Wild American Self* and Roley's novel *American Son* raise issues of racial misrecognition and (non)assimilation but problematize the recovery of homeland practices by portraying the ways that this transpacific act is mediated and hindered by differing values ascribed to gender and sexuality. In the second instance, Rosal's and Reyes's poetry books enact a cross-cultural poetics that traverses racial and national lines in both their formal articulations and social representations and thereby open up the category of "community" to renewed scrutiny.

My focus on these texts extends the queer diasporic framework to analyze literature that, on the surface, seems more concerned with the "domestic" than the "diasporic," and does not thematize nonnormative desires. By discussing this work here, I not only demonstrate how the politics of gender and sexuality are integral to U.S. assimilation/marginalization and to diasporic imaginings and modes of address but also reflect critically on the notion that literature can act as the antidote to the affliction of "invisibility." As I argue, queer diasporic reading enables us to perceive, account for, and possibly even embrace the literary and political practices of "un-oneing."

## "Invisibility," Misrecognition, and the Politics of Knowledge Production

Although the discourse of Filipino "invisibility" encompasses a range of phenomena—including the underrepresentation of Filipinos in mainstream U.S. popular culture, the misrecognition of Filipinos due to the absence of a specific "racial discourse," and the lack of recognition accorded to Filipino literature in the United States[2]—I focus here on the relation between cultural identity and the politics of knowledge production. The ethnographic work conducted in the 1990s is replete with statements made by Filipino American college students claiming the scarcity of information about Filipinos in educational contexts, simultaneously revealing an "intense hunger . . . to know more about Filipino American history, art, and expressive culture," as Sarita Echavez See puts it.[3]

One respondent in Yen Le Espiritu's *Filipino American Lives* (1995), for example, states: "I want to learn more about Filipino culture, but I don't know how to go about it. I wish they would teach that kind of stuff in school because it would make things a lot easier. But if you want to learn about the Filipino culture, you have to go do your own research on your own time." "In school," she adds, "they don't really teach us about the Philippines."[4] A student in Leny Mendoza Strobel's *Coming Full Circle: The Process of Decolonization among Post-1965 Filipino Americans* (2001) reiterates this notion: "I wasn't sure where to get the resources for learning about history, Filipino and Filipino American. I was steered away from learning this history in the classroom. . . . When I do research, there's not too much literature on it. . . . So it's a matter of finding resources."[5] Faced with this curricular lacuna, another student places his hopes on a return visit to the Philippines and intergenerational storytelling: "Knowledge of Filipino history is hard to come by. I would like to start talking to my family, my grandmother especially, to ask about my own family history. I am taking a trip home to the Philippines for Christmas in 1996 and I look forward to my grandmother's stories. . . . Meanwhile, I am still searching for a good Filipino history book."[6]

According to these testimonies, the educational system in the United States during the 1990s failed to provide Filipino American students even a passing understanding of "their" history and culture, while the immigrant parents, who might have filled this gap, refrained from passing on such knowledge, presumably for the sake of upward mobility.[7] One frequently cited effect of this lack of knowledge is a sense of shame. As Strobel writes, "The participants agree that their confusion, ignorance, sense of inferiority comes from the lack of knowledge about Philippine and Filipino American history."[8] In *Building Diaspora: Filipino Cultural Community Formation on the Internet* (2005), Emily Noelle Ignacio quotes a post that conveys a similar sentiment: "I am trying my damnedest to get back to my roots and learn more about my parent's [sic] culture. Similar to other US Born Filipinos/Filipinas I've met, my parents never taught me Tagalog . . . for fear that I would have an accent and that other kids would make fun of me at school. They also neglected to teach me . . . about the culture or history of the Philippines, so now, at age 23, I feel very whitewashed and sad."[9] While the participants often proceed to explain how they have acquired cultural knowledge through extracurricular endeavors, the monographs themselves also seek to remedy this deficit. "I want the book to be a source of information for the younger generations of Filipino Americans," writes Espiritu in the preface to *Filipino American*

*Lives*, those "who probably will learn little about that part of their history in U.S. schools."[10]

Two contexts help to clarify these statements. The first has to do with the history of Filipino migration to the United States. The relaxing of strict immigration laws that limited Filipino entry between 1934 and 1965 has led to an enormous increase in Filipino immigration over the past several decades. One could speculate that the laments are coming from the children of post-1965 immigrants—at times, they indicate as much (not being taught a Philippine language at home; their parents being their only link to the Philippines). Furthermore, although the continental coasts, Hawai'i, and certain metropolitan areas elsewhere remain the places with the densest concentrations of Filipinos, the arrival of professionals through the occupational preferences determined by the Department of Labor has made it possible for Filipinos to live in unexpected locations. Whether racialized in relation to other people of color in urban centers or questioned about their "race" in small towns scattered throughout the United States, Filipinos face not only the query that Asian Americans love to hate—"Where are you from?"—but even more fundamentally: "What are you?"

The other context that makes the student comments more than just idiosyncratic complaints is the institutionalization (and consequent neutralization) of that which was supposed to counter this lack: multiculturalism. Although ostensibly intended to recover occluded histories and celebrate cultural diversity, the dark underside to multiculturalism's normalization is that racially marked others are *expected* to "represent" the culture that their bodies signify and to produce knowledge of that culture *for others* at a moment's notice. To not know is to be open to charges of being a "coconut" or "banana," a cultural traitor, a sell-out. As one of Strobel's participants reflects: "Throughout my life, I have had experiences that have made me feel like I have no respect or pride for my culture or my heritage. That upsets me because I have always been proud of who I am and have never once wanted to be someone else. But now I realize that I really don't know why I am proud; I don't know what being Filipino is all about. I want to be able to say that I am Filipino American and know what that means."[11] In the odd conjunction of brute racism and liberal multiculturalism, the question "what are you?" posed to those who have no common frames of intelligibility to appeal to, takes on renewed, tortured significance. Indeed, at this intersection, multiculturalism becomes synonymous with racism, as both presume "race" as the core of and explanation for one's identity.

To begin to answer the students' challenges—without unduly dismissing them, or uncritically accepting their premises—we must speak honestly about the history and scholarship they seem so intent on accessing. First, the refrain bewailing "the scarcity of materials" and "the dearth of scholarship" in Filipino studies is simply untrue.[12] The ample bibliographies appended to the very monographs that record these complaints belie such allegations. Although unavailable to the students in the early 1990s, the proliferation of scholarship since then further renders untenable the claim that "there is nothing out there."[13] This body of work, moreover, inevitably complicates and confounds the desires expressed by the interlocutors. As valuable and necessary as it is, increasing Filipino knowledge production will not resolve these issues because of the way those issues are framed. One has to wonder, what conception of "culture" and "history" is being appealed to?[14]

As noted in the introduction, the excavation of Filipino history reveals the radical instability of the category "Filipino," in part due to the practice of cross-racialization. This process is traceable in the United States throughout the twentieth century. A prewar *pensionado* named Angel Martinez, for instance, recalls that when he "applied for board and room in a good home, the lady of the house looked him over very carefully and then excused herself for a moment. She promptly returned with an address" for a "Chinese Club." Two other *pensionados* report being denied housing in New York because they were mistaken for Chinese, Japanese, or "Pagan."[15] These perceptual inaccuracies demonstrate how Filipinos, who were considered wards of the colonial state and were studying in the imperial country by virtue of protracted "tutelage," were nevertheless racially unintelligible. Taking place within the "domestic" space of the United States, the *pensionados'* denial of housing redoubles their status as "foreign in a domestic sense."

Such misrecognitions are equally rampant in the contemporary period. In *Home Bound*, Espiritu cites several interviewees who remember being taunted as Chinese, Japanese, Mexican, African American, and Vietnamese.[16] Reinforcing the point that racial discourses of both oppression and resistance are built on negativity, one interlocutor states, "In my high school, they didn't know how to discriminate against me. They called me like Kung Fu. They called me Tojo because of World War II, and they called me VC because of the Vietnam War" (193). These racist misnomers not only reveal a broad ignorance about the existence of Filipinos but also disable the self-assertive project of inversion—which sometimes gives rise to cross-color racisms perpetrated by Filipinos themselves (187).

Elizabeth Pisares has engaged directly with these issues by focusing on the "racial ambiguity" of 1990s pop singer Jocelyn Enriquez, who was "accused of passing herself off first as Latina, then as black to attract listeners who would not accept someone identified as Asian American performing Latin freestyle, house, or R&B."[17] Pisares diagnoses both the accusations and misperceptions of Enriquez's racial identity as effects of Filipino "invisibility," but goes on to challenge what she calls the "neo-colonial explanation" by arguing that we need "to reconsider the neo-colonial subjects' experience of the culture of U.S. imperialism within national boundaries" (188). She thus sketches a historical narrative from the prewar period in which "Filipinos were not 'invisible'" (184) to the postwar period in which Filipinos were racially "lumped" together in the "Asian American" category—a process that resubordinated Filipino Americans due to "the disparity of representation, material resources, and cultural capital" intrinsic to "Asian American cultural nationalism" (189). These conditions lead Pisares to claim that "for racial discourse-deprived Filipino Americans, a language that allows them to understand themselves as racially constituted subjects as do other people of color is yet emergent" (188).

Several scholars have noted how Filipino American students frequently turn to Philippine history to construct a "language" for self-understanding. One of Espiritu's interviewees states that, in trying to "[learn] about myself," "I started checking out the Filipino history books in the library, not Filipino American, but Filipino, the history of the Philippines."[18] The combination of U.S. racism, liberal multiculturalism, and the absence of a Filipino American "racial discourse" provokes this practice of "symbolic transnationalism," as Espiritu calls it, this "desire to be more 'authentically' tied to the 'original' culture."[19] But is Philippine history any more reliable than Filipino American history? Can it fulfill the kinds of epistemic and identificatory desires voiced by the interlocutors? Neferti Xina M. Tadiar points out that "postcolonial nations can never take their 'history' for granted" and reflects on "the vigorous and violent contestations over 'history' that have taken place in the Philippines as a consequence of the continuing crisis of the nation. 'History' is deeply contested at every moment of its expression down to the very assertion of the 'facts.'"[20] Tadiar's reminder that Philippine history is itself a site of struggle troubles the notion that a fixed, unified past can be seized and consumed to consolidate a national or ethnic identity. This caveat notwithstanding, the "indigenization" or "decolonization" movement that took hold among some Filipino scholars, students, and health care workers on the West Coast during the 1990s represents one collective effort to formalize the transpacific endeavor. As described by S. Lily Mendoza in *Between the Homeland and the Diaspora: The Politics of Theorizing Filipino and Filipino American Identities* (2002), this academic undertaking sought to excavate and deploy epistemic frameworks derived from "Filipino" (or precolonial) worldviews, linguistic etymologies, and modes of relationality. The indigenization project began in the Philippines in the early 1970s and aimed "to deconstruct centuries of colonial Eurowestern epistemological legac[ies]" by uncovering "indigenous ways of knowing and being."[21] Interdisciplinary in approach, it was designed to overhaul the methodologies and conclusions in such fields as anthropology, linguistics, history, and psychology.

Mendoza further explains that one "strand" of this movement, *Sikolohiyang Pilipino* (Filipino psychology), was transported and disseminated to the "Filipino American scholarly community" in northern California in the early 1990s by University of the Philippines professor Virgilio Enriquez (12). This discourse "resonated" among Filipino Americans, writes Mendoza, because it "radically contrasted with . . . assimilationist readings of Filipino culture and 'personality'" (12), provided "a language by which many Filipino American student groups could now articulate their new-found sense of connection to a (forgotten) nativeland" (12), and served "as a basis for communal identification and solidarity" (140). The "indigenization" movement thus answers several problems at once. It locates what Wendy Brown terms "a site of blame" in the centuries of Spanish and U.S. colonialism and imperialism,[22] uses that history to assert "Filipino" difference from other Asian Americans,[23] explains Filipino faults through the concept of "colonial mentality,"[24] and provides a means of constructing "a strong sense of Filipino identity" by engaging in the "recovery of indigenous knowledge [and] cultural values" that "were repressed and submerged under colonization."[25]

It is perhaps unsurprising that the college students of the 1990s do not say much about literature.[26] The heterogeneous literary scene and the discrepant literary history delineated in the preceding chapters would seem to militate against the construction of cultural identity via literature. The following sections, then, explore how selected literary texts reframe the issues of racial "invisibility" and misrecognition by centering the significance of gender and sexuality, while also proffering alternative ways of dealing with these conundrums.

## Between the Homeland and the Heartland

Galang's and Roley's texts as well as the decolonization movement pivot on their respective orientations toward the homeland. But whereas the students and scholars whom Mendoza describes find there the sources and traces of indigenous knowledge that can be recovered to counter the uprootings caused by Spanish and U.S. colonialisms, Galang and Roley represent the Philippines as a symbol and site of discipline by weaving structures of transnational address—articulated through issues of gender and sexuality—into the very fabric of their texts. My analysis thus elucidates how these transpacific articulations sunder any simple act of (re)connection with the homeland.

While Mendoza's book negotiates between "the poststructuralism-indigenization debate" and defends the latter position from accusations of "essentialism" (13) by contesting the former's "formulaic invocation regardless of historical, cultural, and contextual specificities" (2), Galang's stories reinflect the homeward-looking discourse through gender difference. Framed by second-person narratives, *Her Wild American Self* foregrounds racial conflation and misrecognition as specifically gendered processes. The opening piece, *"The Look-Alike Women,"* plays on the perception that all Asian women look and act the same. Addressing the implicitly marked Filipina, the narrator states: "Because there seem to be no lines, no walls, between the Japanese, Vietnamese, Koreans, Chinese and the Filipina, even you have come to believe you are no different than the rest."[27] This sort of "racial lumping" is echoed in the two closing pieces. In the aptly named story "Filming Sausage," the aptly named director Dick sexually harasses his Filipina American assistant Elena and takes to calling her "Asia" (172). In the final piece, *"Mix Like Stir Fry,"* shameless strangers in "the big city" ask the addressed "you," "'Are you Japanese? Speak Chinese? Come from Vietnam?'" (183).

Although a story such as "Our Fathers" turns to the homeland to assert Filipina difference in the face of racial misrecognition and to construct continuity out of migrational displacement, other stories demonstrate how the connections between the two locales—through chain migration, intergenerational storytelling, letter writing between ocean-riven relatives—are filtered through racial, gender, and class differences. Set in Peoria, Illinois, the story "Talk to Me, Milagros" allegorizes these diasporic mediations and blockages. The title's directive refers to eleven-year-old Nelda's attempts to draw her newly arrived cousin, the silent Milagros, into conversation. Though Milagros's mother asserts that "she is like you, Nelda" (32), the story elaborates precisely on the ways they are not alike. Refusing to open up to Nelda, Milagros reserves her acts of expression for the letters she writes nightly to her "pen pal" in the Philippines. Nelda admits, "I was jealous of the way she poured words onto the letters she wrote, of how she hoarded the ones from the Philippines as though she were all alone in America" (38).

Confounded by Milagros's silence, Nelda at one point gets "annoyed" when her cousin voices no opinion about the tween idol David Cassidy: "'Why won't you speak? Why won't you ever answer me?' . . . 'Say something. Tell me to shut up. You're in America now, you know: we speak English here. What's the matter with you?'" (41). Milagros does not react until Nelda sends her precious letters sailing across the room. As they quarrel, Nelda resumes her nativist rhetoric: "'What do you know about Americans,' I asked. 'You're the stupid one. You can't even talk English. . . . Go back to the Philippines. Go back to where you belong!'" (42). The story implies that Nelda's resentment is fueled by the "attention" that the immigrant adults lavish on Milagros for fulfilling her "traditional" gender roles (42). When her mother explains that "because life's harder back there, girls learn early how to do housework" (44), Nelda begins to understand why "Milagros was always so serious. . . . She was too busy working" (44). Nelda's recognition of gendered life "back there" is mirrored by Milagros witnessing a racist encounter with the white kids over here (44). A bully teases Nelda for stuffing her bra, while the other kids mock her "nerdy little Chinky glasses" and her "nerdy little Chinky face" (46). Milagros eventually intervenes, throws a stone at the children, and tells them to "leave Nelda alone" (46). As the two walk away from the confrontation, Nelda narrates, "I looked at her and for the first time, I felt I understood" (47).

Despite these scenes of mutual understanding, the story offers no facile bridging of the U.S.-born and the recent immigrant. Commenting on the processes of downward mobility and disillusionment common to the Filipino immigrant experience as Uncle Victor descends from respected lawyer in the Philippines to disrespected busboy in Peoria, the story closes with the once-optimistic man breaking down, his shattered idealism transmuted into "an occasional moan . . . cracking his head against the wall, again and again and again" (48–49). As her mother comforts Uncle Victor in the bedroom, Milagros pushes Nelda out the door: "'Don't worry, Nelda,' she said. 'Never mind.' Then she closed the door and I stood there and stared at the knots" (49–50). Much as Milagros's silence renders her opaque to Nelda's entreaties, so, too, does her act of shutting out Nelda from the family's turmoil and consolation. Filtered through Nelda's perspective, the story itself denies us access to Milagros's consciousness, paralleling the way that Uncle Victor's howl—unleashing humiliation, regret, and rage—remains inarticulate.

Whereas "Talk to Me, Milagros" shows the limits of reciprocity between the heartland and the homeland, the title story "Her Wild American Self" dramatizes even more starkly the gendered meanings attached to either location. Reminiscent of the opening chapter "No Name Woman" in Maxine Hong Kingston's *The Woman Warrior* (1976),[28] the story adopts the motif of cross-generational storytelling whereby Aunt Augustina serves as a "warning" of what might become of "a hardheaded Americana" like the young narrator (67). In the embedded story, the generational conflict is transnationally mapped onto competing versions of femininity. When Augustina stops attending mass, for instance, her father "threaten[s] to send her to the Philippines for lessons in obedience" (68). When she skips school one day, her mother similarly scolds her: "'Do you want your father to send you to the Philippines? Maybe that would teach you how to behave. . . . If you think the rules are strict here, wait till you have to live there'" (135).

These threats find their counterpart in the racism Augustina encounters at the all-girls Catholic school to which she is transferred to "tame her" (68). Snubbed by the other girls for bringing rice and fish to lunch, Augustina experiences a moment of distorted racial self-recognition and isolation: "Augustina looked down the row of milk-white faces, faces so pure and fresh. . . . She had never noticed how brown her skin was until then. She would never have a single girlfriend among them" (69). At another point, a nun singles her out in class and says, "Thanks be to God, Augustina, the Church risked life and limb to save your people, civilize them. Thank God, there were the Spanish and later the Americans" (71). Caught between her parents' efforts to "tame" her and the imperialist racisms she experiences at Catholic school, Augustina turns to her cousin Gabriel for solace.

When the two fall in love, however, Augustina's sexual desire raises again the specter of the disciplinary homeland. Despite her father's warning about Emmy Nolando, who had gotten pregnant out of wedlock and been ostracized from the Filipino American community, Augustina and Gabriel eventually "[slip] across borders they had never crossed till now" (77). In the closing frame of the story, the narrator tells us that her aunt Augustina was sent to the Philippines either to "have a baby" or "to discipline her wild American self" (81). Although the story concludes with an elderly Augustina passing down a cherished necklace to her niece, thereby constructing an alternative female lineage, the narrator herself does not so much question as reinforce the bifurcated meanings of gender and sexuality conferred on the Philippines and America. In both the opening and closing frames, she refers to her family being "stuck somewhere on the Philippine Islands" (67) and wielding the story of Augustina as a cautionary tale: "You're next. Watch out" (81).

Like "Her Wild American Self," stories such as "Figures," "Contravida," and "Miss Teenage Sampaguita" dramatize the familial pressures imposed on Filipina Americans to succeed academically, to embody the chaste "national" beauty without becoming "a sexy little tropical flower" (145), to secure a prestigious and lucrative job, to get married, and to have children only in wedlock. In this regard, Galang's stories largely support Espiritu's point that "Filipino immigrants claim moral distinctiveness for their community by representing 'Americans' as morally flawed, themselves as family-oriented model minorities, and their wives and daughters as paragons of morality."[29] But Galang is careful to show how these disciplinary measures are themselves shaped by the historical legacies of World War II (especially the violence and impoverishment experienced under Japanese occupation) and by the stratifying effects of immigration and racialization, while also emphasizing how the protagonists actively negotiate and resist these normalizing tactics, in part by taking up various artistic and expressive practices,[30] even if those do not pursue a specifically Filipina aesthetic.

Most intriguing about the collection is Galang's use of the second-person narrative voice as a vehicle for articulating the diasporic continuities and discontinuities between "Filipina" and "Filipina American." Whereas the opening piece, *The Look-Alike Women*, raises the problem of racial conflation, the piece that follows "Her Wild American

Self," titled *"Lectures on How You Never Lived Back Home,"* demonstrates that fashioning a Filipina American identity by looking "back home" is fraught with ambivalence as it picks up on Augustina's morality tale and transforms the niece's "I" into a "you." It as if Galang invents a phantom voice that is neither the disciplining conscience of the homeland nor the back-talking insolence of the wild American self to represent the conundrums of the "American-born-Filipina" (86). Illuminating the conflicted positionality of what this empathetic and exhortatory voice calls the "hyphen in American-born" (86), the narrator describes how "you" grew up in "Bucktown, Wicker Park, Ravenswood, Illinois," how "you are not white, and still you are not one of them—the foreigners," how "to the kids at school, you were no different from the other Oriental girl, the one who spoke English with a chopped-up accent," while "to your aunts and uncles you were turning into a *bratty Americana*" (85).

Located neither in the place "your parents call 'back home'" (85) nor in a space with a well-established Filipino American community free from everyday racisms,[31] the "you" is both represented and addressed, insistently reminded that her parents' attitudes toward gender and sexuality are themselves informed by history. Though "Her Wild American Self" implies a developmental model of gender and sexual ideology that correlates "backward" ideas about femininity with being stuck "back there" on the islands, *"Lectures on How You Never Lived Back Home"* complicates that linearity by recalling "your" relative privileges in the United States: you "have never had to obey a curfew because of war. . . . You've never been without heat, without food, without parents" (84). Even while offering an image of transnational connection—"you have always had one foot planted in the Midwest, one foot floating on the islands" (86)—the text declines from embracing "this ideal called 'your people'" without ambivalence (86). As we will see, who "your people" might—or could—be lies at the heart of Roley's, Rosal's, and Reyes's texts as well.

## Wayward on the West Coast

Like Galang's stories, Roley's *American Son* reveals the ways that Filipino Americans are caught and constituted between the multiple forces of U.S. racism, social respectability and upward mobility, and diasporic discipline. Set in California in 1993, the novel is divided into three sections, each of which is framed by a letter from Uncle Betino, who lives in the upscale subdivision of Forbes Park, Metro Manila, to his immigrant sister Ika, who lives in "the poor end of Santa Monica," in Los Angeles.[32] The novel seems less concerned with identifying Filipino distinctiveness than with evoking an array of *effects* of that "lack" of cultural identity. As Roley explains in the headnote that prefaces the "Epilogue" to *American Son* in the anthology *Growing Up Filipino* (2003; not included in the novel), the fifteen-year-old narrator Gabe and his older brother Tomas, "two Hapa (biracial) Filipino American brothers," experience "identity crises, wishing to be at turns White or Mexican; my notion followed from the idea that being invisible, they felt compelled to look elsewhere for a way of presenting themselves to other Americans, and also that their mother was colonialized, ashamed of being Filipina." Echoing the sentiments about Filipino "invisibility," Roley notes, "Few Americans know that the Philippines used to be a U.S. colony; I was never taught about our common history in high school."[33]

Rather than historiographically recovering that past, *American Son* traces a story of "failed" assimilation. From a normative viewpoint, the Sullivan family's "dysfunction" is everywhere on display: Tomas's cross-racial identification with a violent Mexican gangster masculinity, his training and selling of attack dogs, and his theft and reselling of stolen commodities; Gabe's falling grades and his half-hearted willingness to follow his brother's path; and their mother Ika's racial "shame" and inability to control her kids. Roley's spare narrative technique and his studious avoidance of interiority call for an analytical framework that can account for the psychic and material bases informing the characters' situations. Racial melancholia provides one avenue for doing so. As David L. Eng and Shinhee Han write, "In the United States today, assimilation into mainstream culture for people of color still means adopting a set of dominant norms and ideals—whiteness, heterosexuality, middle-class family values—often foreclosed to them. The loss of these norms—the reiterated loss of whiteness as an ideal, for example—establishes one melancholic framework for delineating assimilation and racialization processes in the United States precisely as a series of failed and unresolved integrations."[34] The pressures toward assimilation *and* cultural retention, as the discussion above shows, are particularly vexing for Filipino Americans, and the Sullivans are no exception. As Robert Diaz points out, though, for peoples who have been subjected to U.S. colonial rule, "compulsory 'whiteness' is felt not only in migratory and assimilationary movements," that is, within the space of the territorial United

States, but also "occurs under the complicit ways American colonialism and its aftermaths are felt by individuals outside of the nation's border (in countries like the Philippines)."[35]

Diaz's expansion of racial melancholia helps to keep the imperial and diasporic frame of *American Son* from disappearing, for the Sullivans' desire for and distance from compulsory assimilation is inextricably embedded within a history of empire. In the novel's backstory, the brothers' white American abandoning father, a military serviceman once stationed in the Philippines, embodies neocolonialist racism via sexism. When he returns briefly to Santa Monica from a stint in Germany, he gets drunk, hassles and hits Gabe, and says that "he only married her [their mother] because he wanted someone meek and obedient" and that he came back not to reconstitute the family but "to sleep with her" (24). Troping on the stereotype of the docile Filipina, Roley registers the racial complicity between military and sexual forms of imperialism.

While the novel hints that Ika married her husband and left the Philippines due to the family's "*austerity and dependency,*" as Uncle Betino surmises (135), her "colonialized" view of the Philippines makes a return impossible. During their last trip to the Philippines, she "complained about the heat," the smell, the insects, the unsanitariness of the food and the markets, and the endless gossiping (32). When Tomas says that "you should be used to it" because "you grew up here," his mother answers, "I've lived in the States longer than the Philippines. . . . I'm American now" (33). Ika's "American" existence, however, has not improved her circumstances. The abandonment of her white husband, "her self-conscious[ness] about her accent" (29), her sixty-hour-per-week job at a department store, her "second job looking after an invalid Jewish lady in the Hollywood Hills" (160), and her "rusty Tercel" provoking anxiety about carpooling (188)—all of these point to Ika's "failed" efforts at integrating into U.S. society.

Ika's ex-husband's sister, Aunt Jessica, alludes to how Ika's respective perceptions of the Philippines and the United States are shaped by "American colonialism and its aftermaths" when explaining to Gabe why his mother wants him to attend the resonantly named private school Westward. By this point, Gabe has sold off the family's pet dog Buster, stolen Tomas's car and run away to northern California, broken into houses with Tomas as "penance" for his earlier theft, and nearly been knifed by Eddy Ho when pilfering drugs from his car. Though Aunt Jessica knows little of Gabe's exploits, she still seeks to guilt her nephew into good behavior and better grades by recurring to the familiar narrative of maternal sacrifice: "Look. Gabe. Your mother had hopes when she came to this country. In America you can become successful. That's what she was taught by those nuns the American Catholics sent over. My Aunt Jessica frowns, then seems to check herself and takes a breath. But it's too late for her, Gabe" (166). "She came to this country in the first place, Gabe," Aunt Jessica continues, "because she had dreams that her kids could have a better life than that caste-driven slum you come from" (167). Aunt Jessica's speech illustrates that the "theme of first-generation sacrifice," as Eng and Han suggest, becomes "a compensatory gesture that attaches itself to the parents' losses and failures" and then gets "retroactively projected onto the second generation" as a forfeiture that can never be repaid or "recuperated" (354). Denigrating the Philippines' class conditions, Aunt Jessica's deployment of their mother's sacrifice and "hopes" as rhetorical weapons also overrides her hesitancies regarding the imperial pedagogy constituting Ika's idealized image of America, even as it demonstrates the transnational reach of compulsory assimilation.

The novel further portrays how certain immigrants in the United States intensify the investment in "middle-class family values." At a gathering at Tita Dina's house, Ika's "cousin Tai Pei starts talking about her son who works in Silicon Valley, how he bought a new Mercedes and plans on building a guest cottage behind his house for her to live in in her old age. Somehow the conversation gets on to all their children, the colleges they go to, and their jobs. . . . Earlier Tomas had come in wearing a sleeveless undershirt that showed off his tattoos and got food from the kitchen and ate in a corner without smiling at anyone. I could tell from his bloodshot eyes that he was stoned" (192–193). Ika's embarrassment turns into anger when Tomas, while high, later shows his young cousin Veronica his Colt. "How could you do this to me?" Ika yells, when word gets back to her. "How humiliating. . . . I can't believe you would do this to me" (196). Ika's reaction of making Tomas's bad behavior reflect directly on herself may accord with the Filipino concept of *hiya* (shame), but this scene more importantly indicates the punitive power of the model minority. The story of Tai Pei's "successful" son buttresses "discourses of American exceptionalism and democratic myths of liberty, individualism, and inclusion" by forgetting any prior history of U.S. imperialism or racial exclusion,[36] while also fulfilling the filial duty to care for his mother "in her old age"—both of which Tomas and Gabe patently fail to live up to.

Though Tomas does not pursue upward mobility through conventional means, he does break into homes and steal household items and jewelry "to elevate his mother's status," as Eleanor Ty notes.[37] Whereas Ika's response to her melancholic attachment to compulsory assimilation is to introject that ideal as shame and project it onto her sons, Tomas rejects that course entirely. Indeed, his anger toward the way his mother is mistreated by Uncle Betino (23–24) and U.S. society at large—and particularly by the wealthy Hollywood producer who demands $800 to repair the dent in her Land Cruiser caused by Ika's accident (175–178, 197–200)—partly motivates his cross-racial passing and "delinquency."

Tomas's refusal of "compulsory 'whiteness'" is literal and ideological. He at first passes as a white surfer at Saint Dominic's but then starts "hanging out with Mexicans, who are tougher" (30). Diaz's retooling of racial melancholia to account for cross-racial routings of identification is useful here. Rereading the "bathroom scene" in Kingston's *The Woman Warrior*, Diaz notes that the narrator torturing the Chinese girl, violently disidentifying with the abject traits she seeks to expel from her own "hypochondriacal" body, is framed by her appropriation of a "tough," "Mexican" and "Negro" positionality. This framing "irrevocably obscures the speaker's desire for 'whiteness'" and operates instead through "an idealization of other racial minorities and their apparent 'toughness.'"[38] Tomas's assumption of a Mexican gangster masculinity and perpetration of anti-Asian violence function in a similar fashion: "If anyone tried calling him an Asian he beat them up, and he started taunting these Korean kids who could barely speak English. . . . Finally, Tomas got kicked out of school for smashing a Japanese boy's car window with a tire iron" (30).

It is noteworthy that the novel does not offer detailed scenes of Tomas's gangster life, represent his gang as an alternative collectivity to the family, or have Tomas join a Filipino gang.[39] And while it is possible to read his adoption of the accoutrements of Mexican gang culture as a desire to "reconfigur[e] his body from the feminized Oriental into the more macho Chicano Latino body,"[40] Filipino masculinity cannot be easily conflated with the stereotype of Asian emasculation. Tomas's rejection of whiteness *and* Filipino-ness stems from his melancholic losses of both and are vengefully exacted against his white father's imperialist racism, sexism, and abandonment, and his mother's racial and gendered humiliation.

The contrasting effects of Gabe's racial melancholia (his falling away from American success and his mother's sacrificial injunction) become apparent in Part 2 of the novel. After Tomas beats his younger brother for "disrespecting" him in front of the celebrity to whom they sell their dog, Johan (53–54), Gabe steals Tomas's car, sells their beloved Buster, and heads north into "another California" (59). When the car breaks down, the tow truck man Stone enters as a kind of surrogate father figure. But to secure the man's regard, Gabe acquiesces to and augments Stone's anti-immigrant and racist remarks, amplifying Tomas's anti-Asianism to malign Mexicans as well. The novel implies that Stone's racism derives from getting shot and losing his daughter to racially inflected violence when they used to live in Los Angeles. Stone calls Los Angeles a "fucking shithole" (83) and thinks Venice is overrun by a "bunch of fucking Mexicans" (84). "But it isn't near as bad as San Pedro," he goes on. "Cambodians, Vietnamese, Laotians."

> I say nothing.
> Am I right? he says.
> Sure.
> All those mute Asians won't even learn to speak English.
> My pulse beats in my neck and my temples and my fingertips. My eyes avoid the rearview mirror as a hot itchiness grows in my underarms and I want to take off my sweater. He must be blind. Maybe it's because of my clothes and the way I now cut my hair. (84)

Stone's demand for racist confirmation ("Am I wrong?" "Am I right?" [84]) forces Gabe's assent, despite his discomfort and disbelief. Whereas Asian conflation in *Her Wild American Self* compels an exploration of Filipina specificity, hapa misrecognition coerces Gabe to pass as not nonwhite. He proceeds to demean the Mexicans and Cambodians in his neighborhood (86) and later tells Stone, who mistakes white Aunt Jessica for Gabe's mother, that his dark-skinned mother is the family's "maid" when Stone surreptitiously calls her to retrieve her son (116).

But before this act of maternal (and "racial") betrayal takes place, the novel portrays a peculiar scene of sexual misrecognition. Gabe begins to suspect the man's "fatherly concern" (86) when Stone insists on buying him lunch, then brings him to a hotel but will not let him pay for the room. The hotel owner "regards him [Stone] suspiciously," Stone describes Gabe as his "nephew," and Gabe demands to know why he paid. Stone replies, "Come on, buddy, don't look at me like that. What the hell do you think this is about?" (111). In response, Gabe "blush[es] and look[s] down" (112). When he finds out that his mother paid for the room and that Stone will be meeting her shortly, Gabe narrates, "as if to make matters worse, I begin to feel embarrassed about the things I thought about him and that he knows I thought them" (114).

The novel does not thematize this strange oscillation from paternal compassion to potential cross-age, same-sex seduction, but the first-person, present-tense narration leads the reader, as much as Gabe, to query Stone's intentions. Previously in the tow truck, Stone had "open[ed] his top shirt button, barely able to restrain himself," to produce a gold pendant with his daughter's photo, and then "unbutton[ed] his shirt further" to show Gabe "a quarter-sized red scar on his chest": "and suddenly he takes my hand in his sweaty palm and leads my finger to it. I have to force myself not to jerk away, this is so surprising. His black chest hair feels thick against my fingertip, the skin warm. A pulse beats, though I do not know whether it is his or mine" (86, 87). Later, when Stone brings Gabe to the hotel, Gabe narrates, "it occurs to me that he knows this place well and probably planned to bring me here all along" (109).

My point is neither to determine nor discount whether Stone wants to seduce Gabe, or whether Gabe wishes he had tried, but rather to suggest that Gabe's performance of his mixed-race ambiguity generates the specter of gender and sexual ambiguity. At the start of the novel proper, Roley plays with stock characterization to distinguish the two brothers: "Tomas is the son who helps pay the mortgage by selling attack dogs to rich people and celebrities. . . . I am the son who is quiet and no trouble, and I help our mother with chores around the house" (15). Although the definite articles imply that the novel will complexify their identities, Gabe's quietness, diffidence, sensitivity, and help with domestic chores remain relatively constant and differentiate him from Tomas's version of masculinity. Though the novel does not impute effeminacy as such to Gabe, his fear of being racially "outed" by Stone—"Suddenly I notice my reflection in the mirrored glass and it appears so obviously Asian I almost stop in my tracks. My eyes look narrow, and my hair straight and coarse and black. He must be blind. I have slender Asian hips, and my cheekbones are too high" (90)—is simultaneously bound up with the possibility of being (mis)read as queer. (Are those the slender hips of an Asian or of an effeminate, possibly gay, possibly seducible, boy?) While Gabe can cover his racial hybridity by reinforcing Stone's racism, he cannot, in this instance, analogously recur to homophobia to deflect the potential reading of his body and demeanor as queer.

Whatever Gabe's "sexuality" might be (he is portrayed with neither girlfriends, boyfriends, nor any friends), this context can also illuminate his final violent act inflicted on Ben Feinstein, a boy "only a few years younger" than himself (176). Though we might view it as the outcome of Ika's ineffectuality (and Aunt Jessica's—Gabe is denied acceptance into Westward), as an attempt to emulate his older brother, and as revenge for Mrs. Feinstein's harassment of their mother, Gabe's shoving Ben's face into the car window, indenting his cheek with his trusty ice pick, and swinging a tire iron against his legs (212–215) not only perform a fervent disidentification with Ben à la Kingston's narrator vis-à-vis the Chinese girl and Tomas vis-à-vis the Asian FOBs but also endeavor to erase his questionable masculinity. During the beat down, Gabe narrates, "He is actually afraid of me. Maybe he worries that he gave the impression that he does not think of me as being tough like my brother. . . . A couple of times in the past I have been with a small group of people when someone said a few smart-aleck things about me and Ben laughed even though I was older" (214–215). The language does not specify whether the "smart-aleck things" said about Gabe were racial, sexual, or class-oriented. Whatever their valence, Gabe's violence ensures that his "tough" masculinity renders Ben "respectful, his head bowed" (215).

The scene's framing further supports interpreting Gabe's violence as a compensatory gesture of compromised masculinity. In the car ride to the Feinsteins, Tomas recalls that Gabe used to cry in restaurants, throw tantrums before school, and "always" get beat up when he was younger (207). Tomas additionally attests that their mother would be "embarrassed" at family parties "because someone would find you hiding in some closet, or you'd have walked off down the street and some uncle would have to go looking for you. . . . She was afraid some bully would've gotten to you" (207). Though hiding in a closet may not directly figure Gabe's (homo)sexuality, Tomas's story primes his brother to renounce that earlier self, in part by thrashing Ben.

If neither Aunt Jessica's cajoling guilt trip nor Tai Pei's shameless display of her model minority son can halt Tomas's and Gabe's downward spiral, then the novel suggests that perhaps diasporic discipline can mold them into proper—if not exactly "Filipino," then certainly not "American"—subjects. In her lecture, Aunt Jessica had tried to impress upon Gabe his mother's concern by employing a metaphor of transnational mediation, declaiming that Uncle Betino "can hear on a phone from five thousand miles away on a bad connection that your mother is in pain and lonely and disappointed and scared. Behind a curtain of expensive static" (167–168).

That "bad connection" metaphorizes the diasporic distance—the misunderstandings and misrecognitions—that separates the Sullivans in Santa Monica from the Laurels in Forbes Park. Uncle Betino's letters to his sister repeatedly try to convince Ika to send her sons to live with him in Manila, at one level, by disabusing Ika of her "fetish . . . for being an American" and contesting her negative opinion of the Philippines (134), and, at another, by blaming Tomas's and Gabe's deterioration on the deplorable social conditions of Los Angeles. In the first letter, he writes: "I find it particularly puzzling that a Filipino boy such as Tomas should choose to spend his time with poor Mexican children when there certainly must be nice American and Asian children of successful people in Los Angeles" (12). Defending a "virtu[ous]" Philippines (134), Uncle Betino constructs a homeland superior to Los Angeles' racial and class stratifications, while invoking the model minority Asian as the antithesis of the "poor Mexican" in the process.

Uncle Betino's tactic links familial name and religious instruction to disparage a morally derelict American culture. Lamenting his sister's departure from Manila, he asserts in the opening letter, "Here Tomas would have known what it means to be a Laurel, its responsibilities and expectations" (11). He then urges his sister to enroll Tomas into a "stricter" Catholic school "if that is possible in a place like California" (12). In the second letter, he contrasts the "true Catholic school, one with discipline and supervision" in Manila with "those permissive ones which you will find in America" (57).

Uncle Betino's epistolary mode of diasporic discipline further turns on issues of gender and sexuality. While Diane L. Wolf has argued in her sociological study that second-generation "Filipinas seem to be under greater parental controls over their movements, bodies, and sexualities than their brothers,"[41] American Son demonstrates that boys are also subject to gendered surveillance. In the third letter, Uncle Betino transforms the boys' fraught American biraciality into a Filipino asset that connects heteronormative masculinity with proper comportment and cultural education: "With their mestizo looks they would have been very successful with the girls, no doubt, which perhaps can give quiet boys confidence that will leave them with a serenity allowing greater application to their studies. It is a shame you will not send your boys to live with me in Manila. I could teach them the values of education, work, discipline, and respect for their elders and Asian and Spanish heritage" (133–134).

Since the novel does not represent sex as a sign of the boys' "delinquency," Uncle Betino's supposition that his nephews' "successful" heterosexuality will lead to better study habits is almost laughable. Indeed, the transnational dimension of these exhortatory epistles—Uncle Betino's distance from the Sullivans' experiential lives (save for a couple of visits to Los Angeles [133])—renders dubious his confidence in presuming to know "how to deal with me and Tomas," as Gabe says (22). Uncle Betino admits being puzzled about "why Tomas could have turned out this way," why his sister is "impossible to understand," and why her "sons are equally difficult to figure out" (136), but his ignorance does not deter him from proclaiming what he deems best for the boys. Meanwhile, the Sullivans remain stubbornly indecipherable, coming across fuzzy and indistinct through "a curtain of expensive static."

Galang's and Roley's imagining of the Philippines as, in part, the site of disciplining wild American selves, so to speak, complicates the notion that Filipino American "transnationalism"—the turn to the homeland—is necessarily a felicitous act of resistance against U.S. racism and invisibilization. The diasporic valences of *Her Wild American Self* and *American Son*, furthermore, are striking insofar as these putatively "American" texts stage voices that speak *from*, rather than *to*, the Philippines, literalizing the specters of the homeland that Filipino American youth are haunted by, the burdens they shoulder due to the immigrant generation's "sacrifices." As Galang's phantom-voiced "lectures on how you never lived back home" and Uncle Betino's letters make amply audible, the weight of those expectations are anything but immaterial, not only forcing Filipino Americans to navigate the hazardous terrains of assimilation and marginalization but also troubling any unmediated, salutary relationship to the homeland.

## (Un)Common Denominators on the East Coast

Roley's decision to have Tomas take on another ethnic persona is not unheard of. As "Flip" writer Sam Tagatac says in the 1970s, "I would complete a short story and discover that the character was either Mexican or Spanish, almost any other ethnic group but Filipino. There was just nothing Filipino to identify with at that time, I thought then."⁴² In his contribution to the anthology *Pinoy Poetics* (2004), poet Joel B. Tan analogously writes that "because this project is probably among the first to define Pilipino American Poetics," he found it "necessary to borrow from the poetry and poetics of other marginalized literary traditions: Native American, Chicano, African American, Feminist, and Queer." He proceeds to put a more positive spin on the paucity of available models to draw on: "But perhaps being Pilipino in America also means absorbing and performing other cultures in lieu of not having a culture that is definably/recognizably Pilipino American."⁴³

The reachings across racialized cultures need not necessarily take place in appropriative or compensatory ways, as I tried to show in chapter 4, and as Patrick Rosal's poetry books *Uprock Headspin Scramble and Dive* and *My American Kundiman*, which employ hip-hop as the basis of their poetics, further demonstrate. Rosal's essay in *Pinoy Poetics*, "A Pinoy Needle in a B-Boy Groove," describes his encounters and experiments with dancing and deejaying during the 1970s and 1980s and notes that "hip hop's strongest influence" on his poetry "came from making the music itself. . . . It excited me to think of hip hop as something to speak to and about, something to listen to and to learn from."⁴⁴ Similar to the way that Hagedorn confronts the question of appropriating black music in *The Gangster of Love*, Rosal places his poetry in a dialogic relationship with hip-hop, theorizing its influence not simply as a resource to be borrowed but as an expressive practice "to speak to" and "listen to" as much as represent and enact.

The opening poem of *Uprock*, "B-Boy Infinitives," re-creates the "teenage summers in the early eighties" (268) that Rosal evokes in the essay by linking the infinitive "to be" to the "B-boy" (break-boy) experience:

To be To B-boy To be boys for the ten days
an 8–foot gash of cardboard lasts
after we dragged it
seven blocks then slapped it
on the cracked blacktop To spin
on our hands and backs To bruise
elbows wrists and hips To Bronx-Twist
Jersey version beside the mid-day traffic
To swipe To pop To lock freeze and

drop dimes on the hot pavement—
even if the girls stopped watching
and the street lamps lit buzzed all
night we danced like that
and no one called us home[45]

The poem constructs a youthful homosociality in which break dancing persists beyond the need to impress "the girls" and exists in counterpoint to the domestic "home."

Interestingly, the majority of the poems in both books do not so much represent hip-hop culture as draw on its aesthetic elements as a formal model. As Rosal vividly describes break dancing in the essay: "The movement is like the music. Everything is in the transitions, quick cuts from one thing to another without losing the beat, the busy layers, the leaps, its crescendos, decrescendos and sudden a cappella" (272). The enjambments in "B-Boy Infinitives" ("To spin / on our hands and backs To bruise / elbows wrists and hips") denote one minor instance of the ways such cuts make their way into Rosal's poems. "Uncommon Denominators," cited in the essay and included in *Uprock*, performs this poetics of "transitions," what Rosal refers to as "the designed collisions of things that should never come together" (271). Playing with mathematical vocabulary to show the impossibility of quantifying the manifold relations and "collisions" he sets into motion, Rosal writes in the second stanza:

So I subtract the moon
and the smell of incense on Good Friday
trying to connect Planck's Constant
to the quantum moment between
a candlelit flick and the back of your neck (276)

The figuration of "designed collisions" may be extended to describe not only the construction of Rosal's poems but also the cross-culturality that animates his poetics, a way of theorizing the "uncommon-ness," the unusualness, of the "denominator" hip-hop. In this light, the title of the essay "A Pinoy Needle in a B-Boy Groove" acquires additional resonance, as it likens the Pinoy poet to the record player's stylus, the point that senses the vibrations in the "groove" of the record (that is, the music, the culture) and, in turn, transmits those movements along electric currents, turning vinyl into verse, plastic into poetry. This is not about laying claim to the racial "origins" of hip-hop but about listening to the grooves, the tracks, that have been laid down and inventing something new out of that close listening and participation.

Thinking of this metaphor in social terms helps us read *Uprock*'s epigraph from Langston Hughes's "Laughers":

> Dream-singers,
> Story-tellers,
> Dancers,
> Loud laughers in the hands of Fate—

For those familiar with Hughes's poem, it is impossible not to hear the cutoff subject of the sentence: "My people."[46] The epigraph and the book as a whole not only gesture toward including Filipinos within hip-hop culture but more ambitiously of claiming African Americans (Hughes's original subject) as "my people." The dash points to and leaves lingering this possibility; it does not automatically presume that a shared cultural practice like hip-hop can act as the "common denominator" bridging racial differences. The unenunciated but ghostly audible subject thus acts as a kind of multiplied mode of address, speaking not just about but to (at least) Filipinos and African Americans. Rather than perform a specifically "Pinoy poetics," then, Rosal enacts a dialogic, cross-cultural practice, formally working off the transitions central to break dancing and deejaying, while colliding them with an array of genres and modes (elegy, litany, prayer, rant).

Rosal's second book, *My American Kundiman*, mixes hip-hop techniques with the structure of address and the politicized erotics of the Filipino love ballad. In his "A Note on the Kundiman" that prefaces the book, Rosal explains that the "kundiman is a traditional Filipino song of unrequited love," and he rehearses the interpretation of the music, discussed in chapter 4, as love song and political desire during the revolution against Spain "and into the American occupation": "The kundiman was a coded desire, a manifest longing in song, a beloved poetic subversion composed and sung in a time when overt expressions of love for the Philippines were looked down upon, if not completely prohibited by the nation's occupiers." Seeking "to honor that tradition of kundiman," Rosal positions his poems as "love songs for America."[47] Whereas Hagedorn's "Kundiman" at the end of *Dogeaters* addresses the "motherland" with a combination of rage and longing, Rosal seems to reverse that orientation and use the form as a vehicle to address "America." The collection, however, does not "euphorically [sing] the praises of the American way"[48] or court its solicitous regard. The "America" evoked in *My American Kundiman* is a complex social landscape constructed around brutal and tender multiracial homosocialities, cross-racial heterosexual eroticisms, and anticolored racisms juxtaposed against nonnostalgic memories of the poet's father, mother, grandmother, uncles, nephew, and niece.

The "ambiguous identity" that Rosal in the preface attributes to the "occupied homeland" caught "in the midst of violent erasure, fragmentation, and upheaval" (xi) might also apply to the objects of address, as the poems simultaneously claim and disclaim both America and the Philippines.[49] Such a multivalent mode of address can be inferred from the poem-epigraph that frames Part 1, Spanish poet Luis Cernuda's "Contigo." Like the Hughes lines that open *Uprock*, the first two stanzas of "Contigo" raise the question of "my people" but through the lyric address:

¿Mi tierra?
Mi tierra eres tú

¿Mi gente?
Mi gente eres tú

As though linguistically reminding us of the Spanish colonial legacy in the Philippines as well as of a Spanish tradition of antifascist resistance and exile, the epigraph inquires into and lays claim to a land/country and a people that remain ethnically and nationally unspecified. Thus, the "you" of "Contigo" stays open as the poems traverse across various addressees, restlessly seeking a place and people with whom the poet can speak and live.

The unsentimental *kundiman* poems in the second section enact and depict these erotic attachments. "Kundiman in which a B-Boy Contemplates How Rome (Like Many Fallen Cities) Was Not Built in a Day," for instance, opens:

but you ruin me
—in other words—

in just one You rouse
my blunder-struck

tongue stall
my systolic

boom-bap heart
to a knee-deep

drone . . . (31)

Playing on the rise and fall of Rome motif while alluding to the kind of self-shattering ecstatically articulated by a Donne or Hopkins (or Villa for that matter), the speaker continues:

. . . Wreck me
to travertine

tufa and brick
Demolish me

a metropolis Burn me
down the Babylon

for which my whole
body
            breaks (31)

Given the poems' engagements with hip-hop, one might hear the body's final "breaking" as not only a wreckage but also a rousing, from "blunder struck / tongue stall" to "boom-bap" poetics. In this sense, the poem weaves the keening eroticism of the *kundiman* (its posture of self-subordination before the beloved) with the kinetic energy of hip-hop, the latter not so much coming in to rescue ruin as counterpointing "—in other words—" destruction with dance, brokenness with "breaking."

At the close of her essay, Elizabeth Pisares seeks to describe "the shape of a Filipino American racial discourse" by turning to turntablism, which flourished among Filipino American DJs during the 1990s in San Francisco and Los Angeles.[50] Echoing Rosal's focus on "the break," Pisares writes: "The products themselves, however, are not a music identified as Filipino American—the condition of perceptual absence forecloses their racial categorization. Rather, it is the reconstructive process—to select samples from disparate sources, to decompose them through any of the hundreds of turntable techniques, and to resequence the discrete elements—that offers a model of Filipino American representation" (193). Despite the possibility of "mixing" as "the prototype of Filipino American culture," Pisares suggests that "as mediums of Filipino American representation they are hardly complete or ideal. The abstract character of music that otherwise lends itself to the creativity of those listening from outside racial discourse impedes the ability of Filipino Americans to confront their invisibility via the turntable" (193–194). In other words, because the music is aural and not visual, and because those outside of this cultural milieu hear it as African American (or at least as not "Filipino"), turntablism can only remain a formal practice whose capacity to challenge "invisibility" is perforce limited.

Leaving aside the question of whether mixing is a prototypical Filipino American expressive practice, Rosal's "cross-genre" use of hip-hop in his poetry may offer a way out of this form/representation binary by interrogating not only the rigidity and possessiveness of racially coded art forms but also the very premise of distinctiveness—that whatever one might call "Pinoy poetics" (the title of the anthology where his essay appears) must be unique and above all *racially visible*. Rather, Rosal's poetry poses "my people" ("¿Mi gente?") as a question with no pregiven answers, and as a potentiality with no foregone conclusions, an intimation of collectivities that come into being in serendipitous ways and that cohere around cultural practices rather than racial identities.

## Feminist Anti-imperialism and Epistolary Eroticism across the Pacific

My final example builds off of Rosal's cross-culturality but inflects the diasporic in another register. Written in English, Spanish, Tagalog, the precolonial script baybayin, and a phonetic "translation" of canonical poems, Barbara Jane Reyes's *Poeta en San Francisco* (2005) is a remarkably complex and elusive book-length poem that explores the possibilities of cross-cultural connections through a feminist critique of imperialism. Echoing Federico García Lorca's *Poeta en Nueva York* (1940), Reyes's book alludes to a wide range of literary and cultural texts to map the discordant social geography of San Francisco, and to contest the gendered racial conflations produced by military and cultural imperialism. Improvising on William Carlos Williams's line in "To Elsie"—"The pure

products of America go crazy"—one part in the first section, "orient,"
reads:

> en esta ciudad, where homeless 'nam vets
> wave old glory and pots for spare change;
> she grows weary of the daily routine:
>
> fuckinjapgobacktochina!
> allthemfuckingooknamessoundthesame!
>
> and especially:
> iwasstationedatsubicbay.
>
> aquí, en las calles de esta ciudad,
> they pray their tropical dreams will come
> true again: blow jobs under a sticky table.
> cheaper than a pint of watered down beer.
> they want to touch her. on their greasy lips,
>
> maganda ka mahal kita magkano ka[51]

Registering the ironic contradictions embedded in the insults, these lines
reference the interchangeability of Asian women much like Galang's "*The
Look-Alike Women*," while also particularizing the U.S. military presence
in the Philippines (Subic Bay) and war in Vietnam ("'nam vets"). Indeed,
the Tagalog address (you're beautiful[,] I love you[,] how much do you
cost), presumably spoken by the war veteran to the poem's female subject, identifies her as Filipina.

   The two parts that close "orient" ironize the specific allure of the
Filipina. "[Why choose pilipinas?]" and "[why choose pilipinas, remix]"
conflate geographic with gendered imperialism, playing off the coincidence between "pilipinas" as the name for the Philippines and for Filipino women. The first version initially answers the question by telling
the "dear ally" of the islands' geopolitical value: "the pilipinas are the finest group of islands in the world, its strategic position unexcelled by that
of any global positioning" (37). The second stanza takes a jab at Douglas MacArthur ("he who promises to return, repeatedly returns, ankle-
deep in his reflection pool"), while the third stanza acerbically shows the
sexualization of military operations geared toward the "containment of

communism": "the pilipinas play key logistical roles supporting service fulcrums of american indochina penetration. fleets and stations deploy venereal disease; deflowered local catholics satiate battalions, all vietnam bound. in short, the pilipinas are custom tailored to fit your diverse needs" (37).

The "remix" of the poem personalizes the deplorable sexual effects of imperial war by turning "pilipinas" into women for sale: "now will that be cash or charge?" the poem cuttingly concludes. Brokering between the Filipino woman and the male buyer, the speaker trots out the woman's selling points—her "beauty, grace, charm," and "loyalty"—and describes her as "family-oriented by essence, resourceful, devoted." Assuring the customer of their shared language ("english is the true official language of the pilipinas") and religion ("they believe in the one true god you do") and hence the Filipina's ability to "assimilate quickly," the speaker repeats the refrain from the previous poem: "in short, the pilipinas are custom tailored to fit your diverse needs" (38). The phrase "custom tailored" thus takes on wry overtones, implying that Spanish and U.S. colonialisms, as well as mail-order-bride discourses that the speaker rehearses, constitute the linguistic, religious, and gender conditions that fashion "pilipinas" (as country and women) to fit your needs.

While in other parts of the book Reyes pursues a broader feminist critique of orientalist and imperialist attitudes in the domains of modernist poetry, knowledge production, and urban tourism, I focus here on a series of poetic letters woven throughout the book that address a very different "you" than the male imperialist. Identified only by the salutation "dear love," this other recipient is deeply ambiguous, conjured out of the speaker's hesitant will in the "[prologue]":

> if I crave the secret corners of your city on another continent, in another time, in series of circular coils extending outward, then it is only because I continue to harbor the swirls of galaxies in the musculature and viscera of my body. You will appear because I have mouthed your name in half-wish, reluctant to bring myself to you. You will appear for me, because you always do, with earthen skin outside the possibility of human causation. (11)

*Poeta* implies that this addressee inhabiting "another continent, in another time" is a Vietnamese person who has endured the ravages of the Vietnam/American War. As noted above, Reyes links the Philippines and Vietnam through U.S. imperial incursion and through the veteran's racist conflations. She also develops these connections through allusions to Francis Ford Coppola's film *Apocalypse Now* (1979) and the documentary of the making of the film, *Hearts of Darkness: A Filmmaker's Apocalypse* (1991). Coppola's Vietnam War movie was filmed in the Philippines during, and with the aid of, Ferdinand Marcos's dictatorship.

> dear love,
>
> remember the bamboo tiger cages in those goddamn movies. and napalm, sinister rain, deathly tangerine vapor veiling the islands, for simulation's nothing like the real thing. the real thing. the real thing. military choppers of film script, steel demon birds, called away to quell real life dictatorship's farthest outposts of rebellion. who among us could've told the difference? (23)

The repetition of "the real thing" ironizes the making of a Vietnam War film in the Philippines, but it also references the helicopters that Coppola had rented from the Philippine military and that were called away to fight in the "real life dictatorship's" counterinsurgency battles against nearby Communist and Muslim forces while the filmmaker was trying to shoot an air-strike scene. Reyes makes the connection explicit in "[zoetrope]" (the production company that Coppola formed with George Lucas): "military vehicles rented from martial law dictator he conspires with indelicate savage" (90). One of many moments when the text's lack of punctuation creates ambiguity, the compression here implies not only that Coppola "conspires" with Marcos to suppress resistant forces (with indelicate savagery), but also that Marcos and Coppola are themselves indelicate savages.

Reyes alludes to the film, as well as Joseph Conrad's *Heart of Darkness* (1899), which the screenwriters used as the script's archetype (36), at other moments in the text. Metaphorizing the military chopper as an "angel of blades," she gestures at one point to the famous helicopter strike on the coastal village with Wagner's *The Ride of the Valkyries* blaring in the sky: "heaven is infected wound attack formation sun rising missile dance skimming the skin of ocean" (53). At another point, Reyes references the film's Do Long Bridge sequence in which the lieutenant says farewell to the protagonist Willard by shouting, "You're in the asshole of the world, Captain": "she blows bridges disney electric light show in the asshole of the world. liberators rebuild and she blows them up again" (55). Reyes even quotes from The Clash's "Charlie Don't Surf" (derived from Lieutenant Colonel Kilgore's brash line in the film) that sounds "from the streetcorner's beat up boombox" (33), again showing how "simulations" of the Vietnam/American War insinuate their way into the public streets of San Francisco.

Even as the allusions serve as sites of critique, they also provide the medium through which Reyes's epistolary address travels. The "letter" in which the speaker first refers to *Apocalypse Now* closes:

> they have mistaken my home for a hollywood set of your home. even my language was a stand-in for yours. your country is not a war. my country is no longer mine. this i wished to tell you, because i was thinking of coming home to you.
>
>     yours. (23)

The interchangeability of Asian women in other parts of the book becomes here a geopolitical and linguistic substitutability. The surprise, of course, lies in the last sentence, for if "your country" that is not a war is Vietnam, and "my country" that is "no longer mine" is the Philippines, then where is "home" in the phrase "coming home to you"? It is as if the demystifications articulated in and the intimacy forged through the letters—an intimacy redoubled (or ironized, given the ease of exchangeability in the poem) in the unsigned valediction "yours"—create a "home" that is irreducible to a single material place.

What is particularly striking about the intermittent epistolary sequence is that this intimacy ultimately dissolves. In the second section, "dis.orient," the speaker writes:

> dear love, when you speak of war and memory, bulletsong. what do i know of war? dead butterflies fall out of my mouth when you speak of suffering, how you tire of it.
>
> dear love, you are not my love. you're an emblem, and sometimes a trophy. and sometimes a trope. this street is not yours and the sooner i dissociate you from here the sooner will my war obsession end. (52)

Brought from Vietnam to "this street" in San Francisco through the war veteran, the war film, and The Clash, "you" have become an "emblem" of unalleviated victimization, on the one hand, and unmitigated hate, on the other. The simulated connection produced through film unravels due to their experiential differences ("what do i know of war?"), while the speaker's "love" begins to dissipate as she fears that "you" have been appropriated as a "trope" into the realm of poetry in order to feed her "war obsession."

Their "dissociation" becomes more pronounced in the third section, "re.orient," as the speaker further questions an affection based on shared imperial histories:

> dear love,
>
> today i am through with your surface acts of contrition, i am through witnessing your mimicry of prescribed other, your fervor for the part, your self-damnation for your fervor. . . . once, even up until yesterday, my compassion for you, the tenderness of our peripheral geographies, seduced me. i wanted so much this kinship for which you feign indifference. . . . i swore i loved you once. but now i have grown w(e)ary. dear love, i too am culpable, perhaps i am even uncivil, but i can no longer honor you. (83)

The ethical predicament is that while the speaker seeks "kinship" and even "love" with "you" derived from their "peripheral geographies," she also finds dubious the reduction of "you" to war victim and the ease with which she is "seduced" by their "prescribed" parts as others.

The poem does not resolve this conundrum but turns instead to a metaphor of self-immolation to connote the incendiary fury produced by these irreconcilable demands:

> in this home that is not our home, we have mutually exiled each other. i walk down your street in the rain, and i do not call you. i walk in the opposite direction of where i know to find you. that we do not speak is louder than bombs.
>
> there are times that missing you is a matter of procedure. now is not one of those times. there are times when missing you hurts. so it comes to this, vying for geography. there is a prayer stuck in my throat. douse me in gasoline, my love, and strike a match. let's see this prayer ignite to high heaven. (92)

Here, the speaker abandons the intersubjective dialogue that had previously sustained them and opts for an inarticulable prayer in the form of embodied fire. This apocalyptic burning resonates with Reyes's earlier rewriting of Mark Twain's 1905 anti-imperialist satire "The War Prayer," which she corrosively renames "[the victory prayer]" (24), and perhaps as well with the monks who torched themselves in opposition to President Diem's Catholic repression of Buddhism in South Vietnam during the early 1960s.

The series of letters in *Poeta en San Francisco* offers an especially stunning take on the poetics and politics of diasporic address. While the addresses to the male military and sexual imperialist operate through a recognizable satire, the speaker's epistolary connection with "you" is more complex, rife with ambivalence. The latter's anti-imperialism is a secondary effect of the letter-writer's attempt to construct a bond across different temporal and geographical locations. That is, the poet does not merely record a history of *Filipino* resistance to U.S. military and sexual aggression, summoning her diasporic counterpart in the Philippines (in the way that Carlos Bulosan does in his poem "Letter to Taruc," as noted in chapter 3). Rather, she *orients* (and dis-orients and re-orients) her mode of address to a locale and a recipient that lie beyond both the United States and the Philippines, calling on and into being a Vietnamese interlocutor whose experiences of war and consequent migration to the imperial metropole ("this home that is not our home") partly mirror her own. Even as she invokes these common histories as the ground on which to communicate, she questions its grounding on war, suffering, and peripheralization.

Most arresting is that the eroticism signaled in the address ("dear love") is expressed for an addressee whose gender and name remain unspecified: "tell me your name," the speaker requests early on, but is given no answer (13). The "you" that emerges through the very act of lyric apostrophe materializes "with earthen skin outside the possibility of human causation"—but not outside the realm of poetic invention. The palimpsestic historical contingencies—the parallel imperialist wars (the Philippine-American War was retroactively described as "the first Vietnam" in the early 1970s)[52] and the ironies of a maniacal filmmaker's decision to use "my home for a hollywood set of your home"—bring the two together, and send them on their separate ways. Though not cast in the language of sexual desire, the epistolary address is nonetheless an expression of love, initially motivated by identification and persisting, strangely enough, by mutual exile and mutual loss.

In its enactment of queer diasporic reading, this book is as much invested in the politics of reading as the Filipino Americans cited above. Two final points, then, about the problem of "invisibility" as it pertains to the cultivation of reading. First, although Filipino Americans, especially those who grew up in the 1970s and 1980s, often lament that they were not taught a Philippine language and thereby feel cut off from the homeland, the very forces that militated against that learning (U.S. imperialism and the ideology of assimilation) also produced a century's worth of writing in English *in the Philippines*. This is one of the great ironies of empire and migration to the metropole. And while indigenists and nationalists might hold that anglophone writing is inauthentic, distanced from Philippine realities, and/or tainted by the Western epistemologies and worldviews that suffuse the language, my point is that not knowing a Philippine language does not automatically make the Philippines inaccessible. (I am not, of course, arguing for monolingualism or devaluing the significance of vernacular traditions.)

In a set of letters written by J. Neil C. Garcia in the Philippines to Bino Realuyo in the United States, noted in the previous chapter, Garcia refers to Realuyo's "much-awaited book, *The Umbrella Country*" and remarks on the politics of publishing: "The deplorable fact that very few Filipino American works see the light of day is never lost to us back home. We always eagerly await the newest title of our own countrymen, anywhere in the world they may be."[53] Garcia's letter reveals the extremely uneven terrain of diasporic Filipino literary production and reception. Whereas anglophone Philippine readers may "eagerly await" and avidly read Filipino American literature, the reverse seems less the case. To be sure, the realities of publishing and distribution, as well as the ongoing legacies of U.S. colonialism (the valuation and importation of "stateside" commodities), inform this unevenness. And yet how many of us in the United States, outside the small circle of Filipino literati, know when a new book of anglophone Philippine literature comes out, or even who the contemporary writers are?

The implications of this observation extend beyond the immediate concerns of Filipino Americans, which brings me to the second point. I suggested in the introduction that postcolonial literary studies in the U.S. academy has mostly bypassed the Philippines because the United

States did not produce a robust body of "serious" literature about its colonial involvement in the islands. This, too, is no excuse for the occlusion of Philippine literature in English in U.S. empire studies. As Eric Gamalinda wryly understates it, "Philippine literature hasn't been of much interest to Americans, perhaps because of the rather imbalanced relationship between America and the Philippines: American history, culture, and politics hold a special place in the Filipino soul, but the average American knows nothing about this obscure ex-colony in the Pacific."[54]

When we do analyze anglophone Filipino literature in the United States, however, we must remain self-aware of our reading practices. Though identity politics will likely persist as an organizing framework, I have been arguing that the authentication and legitimation of cultural identity serves, at best, as a starting point, but cannot be the endpoint of the discussion. The texts on which I have focused (and I have only scratched the surface of this literary archive) teach us otherwise, force us to come to terms with a body of work that spins away from any normative center. Read in this light, then, Filipino literature does not so much fortify cultural identity as unsettle it, opening it up to "the , labor , of , un-oneing"—in effect, *queering* it. And it is this practice of reading as queering subjectivity, a practice of queer reading that reads—revolution, no less—queerly, that I take up in the final pages.

# Epilogue

NARRATIVE ENDINGS ABOUT the subordinated and the subjugated are notoriously difficult to achieve. To the extent that the text, from its present vantage point, represents the oppressive conditions by which the represented come to be oppressed, it necessarily registers the *ongoing* nature of hierarchy and stratification. Since this unhappy state of affairs constitutes the preconditions of the text's critical impulse, easily discernible resolutions of assimilationism, withdrawal, or radical transformation can read as abject, evasive, impossibly contrived, or otherwise dissatisfying—hence, why so many endings are, for lack of a more forceful word, ambiguous.

The literature explored in this book reveals in particular the ways that gender, sexuality, and eroticism mediate narrative conclusions: Maximo Kalaw's recourse to reproductive futurity in *The Filipino Rebel* (ca. 1930), José Garcia Villa's queer seriality and self-genesis in his autobiographical stories (1933), Carlos Bulosan's critique of procreative heterosexuality in *The Cry and the Dedication* (ca. 1953), Jessica Hagedorn's affective ambivalence in the "Kundiman" coda to *Dogeaters* (1990), Gringo's uncertainty about migration in Bino Realuyo's *The Umbrella Country* (1998), Katrina's book report–cum–love column in R. Zamora Linmark's *Rolling the R's* (1995), the epistolary "Epilogue" to Noël Alumit's *Letters to Montgomery Clift* (2002), the addressee's "anomalous" Filipina American position in M. Evelina Galang's *Her Wild American Self* (1996),[1] and the persistence of masculine violence in Brian Ascalon Roley's *American Son* (2001).

What is true for literary narratives holds true for literary histories: the monograph's convention of the "conclusion"—summing up what has come before and opening up what lies ahead—may come off as suspiciously tidy, unduly pessimistic, or unconscionably optimistic. With these caveats in mind, this epilogue attempts to fulfill its generic obligations without contravening one of the book's main theses: that the present scene of diasporic Filipino literature is irreducibly heteroge-neous yet remains largely underread.

By framing Filipino literature in the United States within a transna-tional context and reading it through a queer diasporic framework, *Be-yond the Nation* has examined how gender and sexuality are constitutive of U.S. imperialism, Filipino racialization, Philippine nationalism, and the (im)possibilities of assimilation. In their focus on the literary as an expressive and political practice, the chapters have elucidated the ways that Filipino writers utilize multiple forms of address to pursue a variety of initiatives: to criticize U.S. policies that defer independence, while at-tempting to reconstruct "a new nationalism" through reproductive het-erosexual romance (Kalaw); to challenge the artistic and social norms of colonial modernization and migration, while seeking to invent an ex-perimental, metaphysical, "queer" anglophone Filipino literature (Villa); to contest the racially and sexually "degrading" marginalizations of the interwar U.S. polity, while endeavoring to reconnect with and reconfig-ure radical struggles in the Philippines (Bulosan); to cultivate dissident social positions and hybrid musical practices, while lamenting and long-ing for the "defiled" motherland (Hagedorn); to interrogate the homo-phobic violence of martial law patriarchy, while positing queer modes of intimacy and identification (Realuyo, Linmark, Alumit); and to question processes of racial conflation and gendered assimilation, while (ambiva-lently) exploring transpacific and cross-cultural connections (Galang, Roley, Rosal, Reyes).

By emphasizing the diasporic complexity and the gender-sexual politics of these literary performances, I have also sought to compli-cate a reading practice that views texts as mere repositories of cultural information that one consumes and "becomes (more) Filipino" in the process. Though current "Filipino American critique" has already trou-bled the logic that seamlessly links in/visibility, knowledge, and identity, I hope my critique in chapter 6 is not misconstrued as condescending or unsympathetic to those positions. (I, too, was a second-generation col-lege student during the 1990s—and far less conscious about the politics of race, ethnicity, and imperialism than those whose voices are recorded in the scholarship.) Indeed, the research on this project started out with premises and proclivities similar to those students', and it was frequently frustrating to be confronted by what Oscar V. Campomanes describes as the "complexity, diversity, and scope" of diasporic Filipino litera-ture's "nomadic texts and expressions"[2]—a wealth of wanderings that repeatedly foiled attempts to locate this body of work within the literary-historical narratives that I presumed would fall into place.

Accounting for this abiding heterogeneity entails emphasizing how diasporic Filipino literature not only reveals its internal differences but also its outward connections to other(s') traditions and practices. I would argue that the literature's centrifugal drive, its corelessness, its refusal to posit a *center* that needs to be celebrated or interrogated, is something to be cultivated rather than contained. While the history of Filipino imperial interpellation as a racially comparative and gendered-sexualized process might precipitate critiques of misrecognition and the desire for *recognition*, the queer diasporic literary history delineated in this book suggests that racial uncertainty and instability ought more productively to serve as the point of departure for a comparative queer diasporic studies that renders such cross-racial and cross-cultural practices and their intermediations by gender, sexuality, class, and location constitutive of critical knowledge production.

Such a reframing of Filipinos studies' relationship to ethnic, empire, queer, and diaspora studies is certainly an epistemic and political imperative at our present historical juncture of entrenched borders, revitalized racisms, global economic recessions, and ongoing "antiterrorist" tactics and military interventions. Rather than track the recent scholarship that has moved in these comparative directions, I elaborate on the critique of centripetal centralization and extrapolate a notion of unfinished "queer" subjectivity by turning, perhaps counterintuitively, to Gina Apostol's *The Revolution According to Raymundo Mata* (2009), a wondrous novel published in the Philippines that metafictionally reconstructs what historians like Reynaldo Ileto and Vicente Rafael have identified as *the* foundational event that produced Philippine nationalism: the revolution against Spain (1896–1898).[3] As the counterpart to the previous chapter's focus on "domestic" Filipino American literature, this brief meditation on *The Revolution According to Raymundo Mata* not only underscores the need for U.S. readers to engage more concertedly with Philippine literature in English but also illuminates the claim that national historiography is a deeply vexed and conflictive practice that resists homogenization. Resil B. Mojares notes that the "centering idea of a 'national history,' 'national literature,' or 'nation' is a claim against the reality of many unaggregated, dispersed, and competing versions of community." *The Revolution According to Raymundo Mata* calls attention to what "is rendered peripheral, subordinate, or invisible" in "the formation of a national discourse"[4]—not so much to expand that discourse to include more and more peripherals, but to dissolve it from within.

Tracing the eponymous narrator-protagonist's story from his childhood in Kawit, Cavite, in the 1870s, to his experiences as a student and Katipunan member in Manila, and to his imprisonment by the Americans in 1902, the novel resonates with many of the themes explored in this study: the politics of linguistic multiplicity, address, and audience; the critique of U.S. imperialism; the relation between sexuality/desire and nationalist affect; and the need to cast an "'awry' lens" at the pieties of the past.[5] Most important to this epilogue is the text's profession that endings do not end: "Like a novel revolution is never finished" (220). *The Revolution According to Raymundo Mata* suggests that this unendingness arises not merely because the "unfinished revolution" of 1896, as it is known,[6] propels further political transformation and narrative production, but, perhaps most startlingly, because "the act of reading [is] the single, most volatile revolutionary act" (123). So long as we continue to read—and read "awry"—the revolutionary past, implies the novel, will escape being frozen into historical fact and remain open to future renewal. In fact, re-visioning and revaluing what can be regarded *as* "revolutionary," in the wake of official co-optations and ideological dogma, *depends* on reading awry, on what I am calling reading queerly.

To dare such a claim about the political power of reading, the novel recalls the importance of the literate arts in the Philippines during the late nineteenth century. As one of the manuscript's "editors" Estrella Espejo notes, "*A distinctive quality of this war* [with Spain] *was its reliance on reading—literacy was the charming obsession of many a revolutionary. . . . The Philippines may be the only country whose war of independence began with a novel (and a first novel at that)—Rizal's* Noli Me Tangere" (24, 25). Apostol re-creates within the narrative the "*naïve wonder*" engendered by "*the arrival of the* Noli": "*how a united solitude of reading created the doomed idealism of a nation*" (123). Evoking the affective fervor created by the *Noli*'s rapid, furtive circulation among the "*reading classes*" of Manila (123), Raymundo the memoirist appropriates an image from Rizal's novel itself to figure its effect on him as a reader: "It was a bolt— a thunder bolt. . . . It changed my life and the world was new when I was done" (120, 121). This jolting is not so much a shock of self-recognition as a reperception of the world anew. Raymundo goes on to narrate how the "solitude of reading" gave way to heated discussions with others. While his "first reading, a bit juvenile" obsessed over the "romance"

(122) between Maria Clara and Crisostomo Ibarra, he "rushes into other debates" (123) over the novel's depiction of Christianity and the relation between art and politics. To his friend Agapito's ideological interpretation, Raymundo responds: "You can't pulverize a novel to that base reduction. It's not only about correcting society. What about the jokes, the ironical asides, the living grotesques of his human comedy?" (125).

Such a reading practice open to humorous and grotesque "asides" is, of course, what Apostol's novel calls for. Despite its focus on the touchstone period that birthed a nation, *The Revolution According to Raymundo Mata* continually unravels that moment's pious solemnity and centralizing gravity by comically reimagining the revolution from the viewpoint of an irreverent, minor figure, while rewriting it through a highly mediated manuscript whose dubious physical status, multilingual musings, and intertextual allusions spawn "a paratextual prolixity" (30) of multiple introductions (six, in fact), outtakes (three), and internal footnotes written by the nationalist historian Estrella Espejo, who is in the Philippines recovering from a mysterious illness; the "Midwestern mongrel" (9) and psychoanalyst Dr. Diwata, who seems to be roaming the world while commenting via e-mail on the manuscript; and the translator Mimi C. Magsalin (a pseudonym), who is a Ph.D. student in comparative literature at Cornell.[7] Add to this paratextuality and mediation the speculations based on the unauthorized "pirate copies" (30) that have already circulated prior to this version's publication, and one begins to appreciate Neferti Xina M. Tadiar's point, noted in chapter 6, that Philippine "'History' is deeply contested at every moment of its expression down to the very assertion of the 'facts'. Hence numerous controversies over the authenticity of documents, over the dates and places of specific events—not only over the interpretation of historical records and events but of their very existence—plague the writing of Philippine history."[8]

Lacing crisis with comedy through a tonal mix of sympathy and satire, Apostol takes as her point of departure a reference in Pio Valenzuela's memoir to Raymundo Mata, a "blind man" brought along as a decoy by the Katipunan mission that visited the exiled José Rizal in Dapitan on the southern island of Mindanao. Apostol's choice to view the revolution through the fading eyes of a man suffering from *"nightblindness,"* as the novel describes it (67), constitutes one part of that "'awry' lens" that she brings to bear on history. Ironically, Raymundo's poor eyesight qualifies him for the "bit part" (203) that he plays in the unfolding historical drama (that is, so the Spanish guards do not suspect that Valenzuela's trip is to consult with Rizal about the necessity and timing of the revolt). Rather than simply recenter the minor, Apostol exploits the paradox inherent in simultaneously evoking and eroding "the revolution according to Raymundo Mata." Whereas other (actual) memoirs stage themselves, to cite Dr. Diwata, as *"duelling texts, in which each side imagines only his single stubborn version is true"* (75), Raymundo's version not only presents a multiplicity of voices, languages, and codes but also a view from what Mimi the translator describes as the "eccenter" (6). Perhaps most damning (and thereby empowering) of all is the diagnosis pronounced by Rizal the ophthalmologist: "You have a dark, empty area in the center of your vision, the hero explained" (213). Though initially despondent, Raymundo reflects: "I had this odd satisfying feeling of knowing with certainty that nothing will be of help. Truth, I guess, is always a relief" (213). What kind of truth—about the nation's most significant historical events, no less—emerges from a man whose central vision is dark and empty, who is both positioned as, and perceives only, the periphery? An eccentric history, a queer story.

Space does not allow a detailed examination of the novel's eccentric characterizations of the revolution through an eccentric character— from the tributes to lesser-known historical figures (168–169, 171, 241), including the *katipuneras* (113–114) and Raymundo Mata himself (177, 198); to the protagonist's missed opportunity with Rizal in Manila (134), his dashed expectations when he finally meets his hero in Dapitan (185–188), and his deflated and dim recollection of his Katipunan initiation (144–147); to the bawdy scenes of childhood defecation with Emilio Aguinaldo (38–39), of a boyhood game involving *"swiveling one's crotch to crack someone's 'eggs'"* (84), of adolescent masturbation (66–68), and of Raymundo's sexual trysts with rather "improper" women themselves (88, 129–130, 181, 231–248). At one point, Estrella queries whether it is wise to *"foist on our young readers this unexpurgated view of our heroes,"* and Dr. Diwata responds: *"Oh, Estrella, must we be so prim? Were our heroes immaculate conceptions? Did they not have eyes? Did they not have hands, senses, passions, organs?"* (88).

Although *"various esteemed colleagues note he might be gay"* (71), as Dr. Diwata tells us, Raymundo's sexcapades refuse fixed identifications. When his childhood companion from Kawit visits him in Manila, he "felt this weird love at the sight of Kapitan Miong Aguinaldo. No, I was not drunk. And no, I am no invert, bless their ravaged souls, as a number of girls in the melancholy hovels of Calle Iris will tell you" (140). Such

protestations of heterosexuality and confessions of prostitutional pro-
miscuity are less indicative of homosexual panic or masculinist bravado
than of Raymundo's compromised status as revolutionary hero. (That
his peculiar sexuality is not derived from homophobia becomes apparent when he cheerfully remarks of his drama teacher Father Melchior at
Ateneo: "Everyone said he was an 'invert,' but a jolly good one he was,
whatever an invert was" [97].)

In direct opposition to Maximo Kalaw's suturing of heterosexual
romance to nationalist feeling in *The Filipino Rebel*, Apostol separates
eroticism and patriotism in several episodes, portraying Raymundo the
"sexual deviant" diverging from his proper nationalist role (79). During his Katipunan initiation, Raymundo's "thoughts of all things flew
back to the serving girl Orang of Ermita, my erstwhile skeletal love, and
I wondered, with an ache akin to that of rapists, to which forlorn fool
she was now showing her skinny chest?" (148). When he espies Rizal's
mournful mistress, Josephine Bracken, on the boat to Dapitan, he similarly narrates: "On that ship I didn't think for a moment about my blood
compact with the Supremo as long as the lady looked my way with some
glimmer of recognition that at least I was human" (175). And toward
the end of the novel, when the war breaks out and Raymundo is supposed to meet up with Bonifacio, he stammeringly admits that he followed the leper lechera Leonor "because—because—I guess I preferred
to get lost. I didn't think so then, because I was busy spilling it, but it
makes more sense to spend seed than blood, and I'm not much of the
hero type. . . . Really. I'd rather fuck a leper than go to war. That's just
common sense. I know, I know—the Spaniards were our enemies. But
the thing is, I'm just not a killer. I'm not even much of a rapist, as critical
Leonor later smirked. Really, I'm just a reader" (244).

By his own admission, to put it mildly, Raymundo is an unlikely can-
didate for nationalist hero. But his off-color humor and off-center be-
latedness—"History keeps laving my behind, I thought mournfully—I
mean, history keeps leaving me behind, as once more I waddled off to
wash my country's sorrows off my sorry bum" (135–136)—become the
basis, as it were, of his revolutionary role as a reader. Though he considers
himself "a stinking paragon of slime: stealer, klepto, ravisher" (232), it is
precisely his faults that facilitate his bid as a revolutionary. Raymundo's
twin passions—sex and reading ("I don't know what it is about me that
I contain nothing but semen and words" [239])—metaphorically come
together when, after receiving his diagnosis as irreversibly nightblind, he

steals into Rizal's kiosk and "rapes" (in archaic and modern senses) his unfinished third novel:

> Papers. My livid eyes reverted to the sheaves of paper, a film of dirt already settled into a close reading of its fine lines. . . . My first violation, was not intentional—I was only swatting a fly. And my second touch, an awkward sampling, as of a brief, hesitant pinch, was only because, as you well note, one day objects may appear in the wrong shape or size and I will experience the loss of correct colors— though, who knows, peripheral vision will remain. Oh all right, I did: with index and thumb, I held up a dog ear of a page. I didn't lick it, I admired it, holding it up close to my ruined eyes the better to ravage a phrase. Then I read on, and on and on. I took page after page in my criminal hands. I perturbed and caressed and, sheaf after sheaf, word for word, I devoured. I penetrated and entered and sated my lust. There. Are you satisfied? I violated the pristine state of the hero's third novel. Not only that: I kidnapped it. (215–216)

Raymundo carries on with this rapacious language when he returns to Manila with the stolen manuscript, saying that he "was in a state of arousal" while ensconced "in the passion of [his] labors with the secret novel" (222).

To the extent that *The Revolution According to Raymundo Mata* links reading with revolution and (figuratively) with "rape," it also makes reading the precondition of "resurrection." In the novel's account, Rizal stopped working on his third novel when Josephine Bracken gave birth to their stillborn son. With Leonor's help, Raymundo realizes that Josephine, whom he had seen just before pilfering the manuscript, was mourning over her lost son: "The hut was the burial grave: there where he has abandoned his aborted novel, her still child lay" (249). In her "Afterword," Estrella notes that Rizal, according to the (actual) biographer Austin Craig, lit the kiosk on fire before he was taken from Dapitan to Barcelona (then subsequently to Manila, where he was charged with sedition and executed), and she makes explicit the connection between the two abortions ("the other strangled child"): "And in his Orphic angst, not taking a backward look, he [Rizal] understood he was burning not only the child of his loins—in burning the book, so burned his spirit." In doing so, Estrella also transforms Raymundo's "rape" into "resurrection": "Fortunately for the history of Filipinos, that book, unknown to

Rizal, was already absent from its tomb. . . . And so it is that the Philippines owes to the perfidy of that nightblind thief Raymundo Mata the preservation of what one might call a limb of its patrimony—or maybe some other organ: a distorted lens, a partial eye" (270)—an "awry" look at revolutionary history.

Within the universe of Apostol's novel, Raymundo not only saves Rizal's unfinished novel from Orphic ash but actually incorporates (part of) it into his own memoir. Here, the already equivocal status of the manuscript is called further into question. In her "Editor's Preface," the historian Estrella writes that the publisher Trino Trono presented her with an "assortment of unpaginated notes and mismatched sheaves packed in a ratty biscuit tin and stuffed in a tattered medical bag" (2). The translator Mimi similarly remarks that the "original papers are not pristine; some sections have been lost forever" (4) and that the "original sheaves are a bunch of papers in multifarious guises—some handwritten, some typed, some in fine script, some practically illegible, some in green ink, some in that crust of sepia drool, with a kind of spiderweb-splatter of time's ink draining from the grainy scrawl" (6). And she comments throughout her footnotes on the hazards of translation, "beset almost in each sentence by a question of literary provenance, obscure native diction, and Raymundo Mata's frighteningly schizoid tendencies" (7), and by a multitude of languages, including "an ancient Indo-Malayan script," Arabic, Waray, Cebuano, Chabacano, and a Tagalog "irreversibly contaminated by the Spanish"—"a kind of grand Babel of the Filipino soul," as she puts it (4). "The challenge," she summarizes, "was to translate the rich ordinariness of Raymundo's multiple tongues into singular, common English" (3). But as the proliferating paratextuality signals, the processes of narrative reconstruction and linguistic homogenization are doomed at best to partial success.

The fifth and final section of the narrative proper, "Aftermass," is named after Rizal's (actual) incomplete novel *Makamisa*.[9] It closes with the provincial bookworm Ysagani turning away from the spoiled wealthy Cecilia and cranking out pages on his beloved printing press, the first of which repeats the beginning of Raymundo's memoir. While some "critics," like Estrella, see this circularity as evidence that Rizal's third novel has indeed been resurrected (Raymundo's memoir represents in part or in whole the heretofore lost novel), others view it as a "horrible sacrilege" in which Raymundo shamelessly "dares to enlace his own words—interpolate his vile witticisms—with Jose Rizal's" (275). Dr. Diwata, however, calls on Mimi C. Magsalin to produce the original manuscript—in effect, pronouncing the "translation" a forgery:[10]

> The translator's hoax—yes, I use the word boldly, Mimi C., wherever you are—only stokes the fires of a cruel illusion:
> *That a nation so conceived, from the existential exigencies of a young man's first novel, will find redemption in the phoenix of his last words.*
> And so her enterprise preserves the country's painful paradox: it is full of writers who believe a text will save it, even when they know barely anyone will read it. (Perhaps this explains her effrontery.) (277)

All of this is, again, self-reflexive commentary on the fictional status and tempered hope of *The Revolution According to Raymundo Mata*. What strikes me most about Apostol's novel, besides its dizzying metafictionality, marvelous inventiveness, and impious humor, is its remarkable theorization of the connections among writing, redemption, and reading. Reaching back to that moment when Rizal's *Noli Me Tangere* helped to "conceive" a nation, Apostol borrows from Rizal's third novel to evoke the first-time wonder imbuing such passionate reading: "*Everytime he* [Ysagani] *began printing, the product seemed unutterably strange. . . . He couldn't help reading it as if it were the first time*" (266). Rather than mechanical replication, Ysagani's printing press produces something that reads as new, echoing one of Dr. Diwata's prefatory aphorisms: "What is a book? It's in flux. What is a man? An unfinished tome. And what's the state of the postcolonial country founded on the image of another's desire? Undone" (29).

Must that which is "in flux," "undone," and "unfinished"—whether a book, a person, a nation, or a revolution—finally come to stasis and completion? In her analysis of the "unfinished practices of anti-imperialist revolutionary struggle" during the 1970s and 1980s, Tadiar writes, "Counterposed against the finished forms of sovereign subjectivity carried by notions of consciousness, belief, and individual will, 'unfinished' maintains a sense of the indefinite limits to dynamic cultural praxis, a sense that extends the political struggle to the arena of experiential forms and conveys the surplus of being and activity produced out of the project of radical transformation."[11] Apostol's novel, I have been emphasizing, similarly undoes "sovereign subjectivity" by investing in Raymundo's literary and libidinal experiential forms and surplus activities.

To be sure, the novel does not mince words when attributing the un-finished revolution of 1896 to U.S. imperialism. According to the text's conceit, Raymundo wrote and collated his memoir while imprisoned in Bilibid jail, locked up "with my friend Benigno laid out like a cross on a watered floor, somewhere in this maze of torture chambers that we share, here in the American hell" (244). And Estrella emphatically lays the blame for the nation's abortion squarely with "*the treachery of their* [the revolutionaries'] *American 'friends'*" (67), vociferating against the "racist American GIs in the Philippine-American War" (234) for their use of waterboarding, while lamenting the forlorn Raymundo "drown-ing in his excrement and being lapped by dogs in the G.I. prisons of Bili-bid, damn damn damn damn them" (240). In her mind, "G.I. benevo-lence occupied us with terror" (259).

While this critique of U.S. imperialism provides one important link to readers in the United States,[12] the novel also reaches toward a broader audience through its thematic clustering of reading, revolution, and resurrection. As Dr. Diwata announces, "*The Revolution According to Raymundo Mata* is seductive because it implies resurrection, which is a desire that unites all humans, even those who are not Filipinos" (275). In her acknowledgments that conclude the book, Gina Apostol herself echoes this notion:

> This novel in many ways is about recovery. The recovery of a text, a body; the recovery of a hero, a history; the recovery of a country, a past. . . . The power of Rizal, and the power of our history, is that these genii are inexhaustible: we must be glad for the patently "unfinished" and infuriating history that we have—in this way, it seems Filipinos must represent the complexity of everyone's incomplete and indeter-minate selves, and our endless, surprising resurrections. (293)

And, I would add, our contingent relations.

The boldness of Apostol's closing universalist gesture depends on a view of reading and recovery as resurrection and renewal, not as self-rec-ognition and national pedagogy but as coming "undone"—not the rei-fication of identity but its "un-oneing." If Filipinos represent and exem-plify those selves that remain "incomplete and indeterminate," then they are open not only to further transformation but also to connecting with those other selves. By calling this openness to alterity and difference—of being drawn to the *"unutterably strange"*—a queer diasporic reading practice, I am describing not just a mode of critique that discloses the heteronormative logics that govern the production of racial and cultural difference, justify the imposition of colonial rule, found patriarchal nationalisms, or pave the road to smooth assimilation, but a practice of connectivity, of seeking out relationalities that form beyond the strictures of normative social boundaries. Theorizing reading in this manner enables us to reconceptualize identity as unfixed, permeable, and mutually interdependent on others. To argue as much is not to empty out our specific subjectivities but to allow ourselves to be taken over and waylaid by what Tadiar calls in another context our "passionate attachments" to places and peoples to whom we might not rightfully belong but long for anyway.[13]

Reflecting on his nightblindness, Raymundo Mata narrates: "I have a dark, empty area in the center of my vision but an acute sense of sound. No, it's not that. I don't know if I can call it sound, or even sense—how do I put it? It was not my body that had the ability to hear. It was the world that revealed itself to me" (238). What worlds are revealed when we darken the *center* of our vision? Posed as an elaboration of queer reading as queer relationality, this question postures as a reflexive challenge to reconsider the very practice and poetics of knowledge production: the ways that the form and substance of our critical arguments are informed as much by the peripheral objects and decentered subjects under investigation as by those diverse, shape-shifting, and unknowable audiences we want to reach and address, all the more sought after and appealed to for being inconstant and unpredictable.

# Acknowledgments

THIS PROJECT WAS written under the sign of loss, a loss that opened up a sorrow so deep, so boundless, that I nearly quit before I'd begun. That I didn't abandon it—when two months after I submitted a dissertation prospectus my mother unexpectedly died, when half the reason I had decided to pursue research on a history and literature that I had hitherto known next to nothing about, when half my link to a foreign-familiar home halfway around the world suddenly vanished from the face of the earth—that I pressed on with a gnawing reluctance and a perverse indulgence in the profound insignificance of the work before me compared to the immeasurable life that I had once thought to understand and pay respect to through this intellectual journey: this persistence is due to the many people who kept me moving along.

First thanks must go to Brent Edwards. His extraordinary intellect has been an abiding source of inspiration. Marianne DeKoven and Shuang Shen served as insightful and supportive readers, as did Vicente Rafael, who read the dissertation blind and offered words of encouragement and advice. My friends at Rutgers University—Rick Lee, James Mulholland, and Hillary Chute—helped see this project through its initial phase, and I will always be grateful for their enthusiasm, intelligence, and humor.

At Ohio State University (OSU) and in Columbus, I thank Frederick Aldama, Chad Allen, Roland Coloma, Steve Fink, Valerie Lee, Debra Moddelmog, Maurice Stevens, and Judy Wu for reading and commenting on chapter drafts; Koritha Mitchell and Alan Farmer for sharing with me the tribulations of being junior faculty; Judy Wu, Pranav Jani, Binaya Subedi, and Lynn Itagaki for keeping alive Asian American studies at OSU; Rebecca Wanzo and Jared Gardner for reading early drafts of the manuscript and helping me get through fourth-year review; and Jim Phelan for his expert advice during the book proposal process. A special note of gratitude to Debra Moddelmog, my ally, advocate, and dear friend: I couldn't have gotten this far without you. To my many,

many colleagues at OSU who have gone out of their way to make sure, through gestures both big and small, that I'm still breathing: thank you.

I have been fortunate to participate in numerous intellectual communities located inside and outside of OSU. Through the Committee on Institutional Cooperation (CIC) Asian American Studies formation, Jigna Desai, Susan Koshy, and Josephine Lee generously read and offered incisive suggestions on the manuscript at a critical juncture in its development. Parts of the book were first presented at various conferences and collectives, and I am grateful to the following organizers and forums for the opportunities to share my work and receive feedback: Ann Fabian and the American Studies Symposium at Rutgers; Vicente Rafael and the ethnic studies contingent at the University of Washington, Seattle; Judy Wu, Debra Moddelmog, and the Asian American Studies Research Series at OSU; Leslie Alexander, Maurice Stevens, and the Ethnic Studies Research Working Group at OSU; Lauren Rabinovitz, Kent Ono, Grace Wang, and the Center for Ethnic Studies and the Arts at the University of Iowa; Martin Manalansan, Augusto Espiritu, and the Philippine Palimpsests conference at the University of Illinois, Urbana-Champaign; Bernardita Churchill, Belinda Aquino, Karen Barrios, Oscar Campomanes, and the International Conference on Philippine Studies in Quezon City; James Kim, Daniel Kim, and the Future Asian Americas Symposium at Fordham University; and Sony Bolton, Cynthia Marasigan, Josephine Sirineo, the Philippine Study Group Student Association, and The State of Filipino Studies and Its Diaspora symposium at the University of Michigan.

I also thank the Association for Asian American Studies, the American Studies Association, the Modern Language Association, and the American Literature Association at whose national conferences portions of this book found audiences and I found an astonishing array of exciting, smart, fun scholars to listen to, learn from, and forge friendships with—the fleeting no less meaningful than the lasting: Kimberly Alidio, Nerissa Balce, Rick Baldoz, Christine Balance, Victor Bascara, Jody Blanco, Rick Bonus, Lucy Burns, Denise Cruz, Deirdre de la Cruz, Robert Diaz, Kale Fajardo, Neil Garcia, Theo Gonzalves, Anna Guevarra, Leslieann Hobayan, Allan Isaac, Elaine Kim, Paul Lai, Viet Le, Karen Leong, Anita Mannur, Linda Maram, Victor Mendoza, Hoang Nguyen, Viet Nguyen, Rhacel Parreñas, Chandan Reddy, Eric Reyes, Dylan Rodriguez, Robyn Rodriguez, Patrick Rosal, Cathy Schlund-Vials, Sarita See, Felicisima Serafica, Nayan Shah, Celine Shimizu, Stephen Sohn,

Jeffrey Santa Ana, Marie-Therese Sulit, Neferti Tadiar, Chris Vials, and Clod Yambao. Without the hard work and critical interventions pursued by these and numerous other Filipino and Asian American studies scholars, this book would not have been intellectually possible.

Special thanks to Gina Apostol for the gift of her novel, to Eliseo Art Silva for the gift of his art, and to all of the writers—those I discuss in this book and the many more I could not—for their imagination, creativity, and inspiration.

In addition to the intellectual vitality and emotional sustenance provided by these people and spaces, a University and Bevier Dissertation Fellowship from Rutgers University enabled me to complete my Ph.D. in the nick of time; a Bordin-Gillette Researcher Travel Fellowship facilitated my research at the Bentley Historical Library; and an OSU Arts & Humanities grant helped support this book's publication. Thanks to the librarians and circulation staff at Rutgers' Alexander Library, OSU's Thompson Library, the Bentley Historical Library, the University of Washington–Seattle's Special Collections, the University of the Philippines–Diliman's University Library, and Ateneo de Manila University's Rizal Library. This project would not have a life in print without the belief and editorial expertise of Eric Zinner, the encouragement of José Esteban Muñoz and Ann Pellegrini, and the excellent editorial assistance of Ciara McLaughlin at New York University Press. My thanks as well to Tim Roberts and the American Literatures Initiative for backing and publicizing this book, to the two anonymous readers for their helpful suggestions in making this a stronger book, and to Robert Burchfield for his careful copyeditor's eye.

I couldn't have gotten along without the solace and support of loved ones outside of academia. To my many friends and relatives in Wisconsin, New York, Columbus, and around the world—you know who you are: a hearty and heartfelt thanks. My deepest gratitude goes to my father, brother, sister-in-law, and nephews, whose love has remained unwavering. Thanks to the Haberstroh family for welcoming me into their homes and lives. And to Richard Haberstroh, my love and life, for your wit and humor, generosity and practicality, patience and intelligence—and for breaking out into song at the most unexpected times and breaking me into smile: words do not go there.

This book is dedicated to my mother, Minerva Nicolas Ponce, who was, quite simply, the most successful incarnation of being human that I've known.

# Notes

## Notes to the Introduction

1. Leny Mendoza Strobel, "'Born-Again Filipino': Filipino American Identity and Asian Panethnicity," in *Postcolonial Theory and the United States: Race, Ethnicity, and Literature*, ed. Amritjit Singh and Peter Schmidt (1996; repr., Jackson: University Press of Mississippi, 2000), 355.

2. Exceptions include E. San Juan Jr., *The Philippine Temptation: Dialectics of Philippines-U.S. Literary Relations* (Philadelphia: Temple University Press, 1996); and Augusto Fauni Espiritu, *Five Faces of Exile: The Nation and Filipino American Intellectuals* (Stanford, Calif.: Stanford University Press, 2005).

3. Linda Hutcheon, "Rethinking the National Model," in *Rethinking Literary History*, ed. Linda Hutcheon and Mario J. Valdés (Oxford: Oxford University Press, 2002), 13.

4. As Gémino H. Abad reminds us, "It is significant that our first published poem in English, Ponciano Reyes' 'The Flood,' should have appeared in the first issue (April 1905) of *The Filipino Students' Magazine* (pp. 14–15), the 'official organ of the Filipino Students in America.'" Gémino H. Abad, *Our Scene So Fair: Filipino Poetry in English, 1905–1955* (Quezon City: University of the Philippines Press, 2008), 50. For a fine racial-sexual analysis of the *Filipino Students' Magazine*, see Victor Román Mendoza, "Little Brown Students and the Homoerotics of 'White Love,'" *Genre* 39 (2006): 65–83.

5. Stephen Greenblatt, "Racial Memory and Literary History," *PMLA* 116, no. 1 (2001): 60.

6. Sarita Echavez See, *The Decolonized Eye: Filipino American Art and Performance* (Minneapolis: University of Minnesota Press, 2009), xxx.

7. José Garcia Villa, *Volume Two* (New York: New Directions, 1949), 18.

8. King-Kok Cheung, "Re-viewing Asian American Literary Studies," in *An Interethnic Companion to Asian American Literature*, ed. King-Kok Cheung (Cambridge: Cambridge University Press, 1997), 19.

9. Eileen Tabios, "Performance Poetry: Casting Forth a Book and a Poet," *Asian Pacific American Journal* 6, no. 2 (1997): 203n8.

10. Oscar Peñaranda, Serafin Syquia, and Sam Tagatac, "An Introduction to Filipino-American Literature," in *Aiiieeeee! An Anthology of Asian-American Writers*, ed. Frank Chin, Jeffery Paul Chan, Lawson Fusao Inada, and Shawn Hsu Wong (1974; repr., Garden City, N.Y.: Anchor Press, 1975), 37.

11. King-Kok Cheung and Stan Yogi, eds., *Asian American Literature: An Annotated Bibliography* (New York: Modern Language Association of America, 1988), does contain a section on "Filipino American Literature" (111–135). Though now outdated, the list interestingly cites (without explanation) a fair amount of work published in the Philippines. Other selected bibliographies can be found in N. V. M. Gonzalez and Oscar V. Campomanes, "Filipino American Literature," in Cheung, *Interethnic Companion*, 112–120; Nick Carbó, ed., *Pinoy Poetics: A Collection of Autobiographical and Critical Essays on Filipino and Filipino American Poetics* (San Francisco: Meritage Press, 2004), 385–394; and Alfred Yuson, "Filipino Diasporic Literature," in *Philippine English: Linguistic and Literary Perspectives*, ed. Maria Lourdes S. Bautista and Kingsley Bolton (Hong Kong: Hong Kong University Press, 2008), 337–355. To be sure, Filipino literature in the United States before the 1970s is rather sparse. My focus on Kalaw, Villa, and Bulosan is due as much to the theoretical reasons outlined below as to the fact that they are among the handful of pre-1970s writers who produced substantial bodies of work (N. V. M. Gonzalez and Bienvenido Santos would be the other obvious choices). I should add that pre-1970s literature by Filipino women in the United States is even more scarce. Books include Felicidad Ocampo, *The Lonesome Cabin* (Boston: Meador, 1931); Felicidad Ocampo, *The Brown Maiden* (Boston: Meador, 1932); and Yay Panlilio, *The Crucible: An Autobiography by Colonel Yay, Filipina American Guerrilla*, ed. Denise Cruz (1950; repr., New Brunswick, N.J.: Rutgers University Press, 2010). My thanks to Denise Cruz for recovering these hitherto obscured texts.

12. "Philippine literature in English" is the customary term used for anglophone literature produced in the Philippines. While "Filipino American" conventionally denotes literature produced by Filipinos in the United States, I use "diasporic Filipino literature" for reasons explained in this introduction.

13. Chin et al., preface, *Aiiieeeee!* ix. It is not surprising that the follow-up anthology, *The Big Aiiieeeee! An Anthology of Chinese American and Japanese American Literature*, ed. Frank Chin, Jeffery Paul Chan, Lawson Fusao Inada, and Shawn Hsu Wong (New York: Meridian, 1991), excludes Filipino American literature altogether.

14. San Juan, *Philippine Temptation*, 89.

15. Oscar V. Campomanes, "Filipinos in the United States and Their Literature of Exile," in *Reading the Literatures of Asian America*, ed. Shirley Geok-lin Lim and Amy Ling (Philadelphia: Temple University Press, 1992), 50.

16. Kandice Chuh, *Imagine Otherwise: On Asian Americanist Critique* (Durham, N.C.: Duke University Press, 2003), 32. Other studies that foreground U.S. colonialism include E. San Juan Jr., "In Search of Filipino Writing: Reclaiming Whose 'America'?" in *The Ethnic Canon: Histories, Institutions, and Interventions*, ed. David Palumbo-Liu (Minneapolis: University of Minnesota Press, 1995), 213–240; Nerissa Balce-Cortes and Jean Vengua Gier, "Filipino

American Literature," in *New Immigrant Literatures in the United States*, ed. Alpana Sharma Knippling (Westport, Conn.: Greenwood Press, 1996), 67–89; Gonzalez and Campomanes, "Filipino American Literature," 62–124; Angela Noelle Williams, "Border Crossings: Filipino American Literature in the United States," in *Beyond the Borders: American Literature and Post-colonial Theory*, ed. Deborah L. Madsen (London: Pluto, 2003), 122–134; and Rocío G. Davis, "Introduction: Have Come, Are Here: Reading Filipino/a American Literature," *MELUS* 29, no. 1 (2004): 5–18.

17. See Lisa Lowe, *Immigrant Acts: On Asian American Cultural Politics* (Durham, N.C.: Duke University Press, 1996), 67.

18. Balce-Cortes and Vengua Gier, "Filipino American Literature," 69.

19. See, among others, Daniel B. Schirmer, *Republic or Empire: American Resistance to the Philippine War* (Cambridge, Mass.: Schenkman Publishing, 1972); and E. Berkeley Tompkins, *Anti-Imperialism in the United States: The Great Debate, 1890–1920* (Philadelphia: University of Pennsylvania Press, 1970).

20. See Dylan Rodriguez, *Suspended Apocalypse: White Supremacy, Genocide, and the Filipino Condition* (Minneapolis: University of Minnesota Press, 2010).

21. Stuart Creighton Miller, *"Benevolent Assimilation": The American Conquest of the Philippines, 1899–1903* (New Haven, Conn.: Yale University Press, 1982), 253, 266.

22. U.S. Census Bureau, "Selected Population Profile in the United States, Population Group: Filipino alone," http://tinyurl.com/3o9xs68 (accessed February 21, 2009).

23. Yen Le Espiritu, *Home Bound: Filipino American Lives Across Cultures, Communities, and Countries* (Berkeley: University of California Press, 2003), 25. The scholarship on Filipino migration to the United States is vast. See, among others, Rick Baldoz, *The Third Asiatic Invasion: Empire and Migration in Filipino America, 1898–1946* (New York: New York University Press, 2011); Rick Bonus, *Locating Filipino Americans: Ethnicity and the Cultural Politics of Space* (Philadelphia: Temple University Press, 2000), 31–56; Fred Cordova, *Filipinos: Forgotten Asian Americans* (n.p.: Demonstration Project for Asian Americans, 1983); Dorothy Fujita-Rony, *American Workers, Colonial Power: Philippine Seattle and the Transpacific West, 1919–1941* (Berkeley: University of California Press, 2002); and Ronald Takaki, *Strangers from a Different Shore: A History of Asian Americans*, rev. ed. (Boston: Little, Brown, 1998), 315–354.

24. Campomanes, "Filipinos in the United States," 50, 53.

25. Ibid., 53.

26. On colonial visualities, see Abe Ignacio, Enrique de la Cruz, Jorge Emmanuel, and Helen Toribio, eds., *The Forbidden Book: The Philippine-American War in Political Cartoons* (San Francisco: T'Boli, 2004); Angel Velasco Shaw and Luis H. Francia, eds., *Vestiges of War: The Philippine-American War and*

*the Aftermath of an Imperial Dream 1899–1999* (New York: New York University Press, 2002); Gary Y. Okihiro, "Colonial Vision, Racial Visibility: Racializations in Puerto Rico and the Philippines during the Initial Period of U.S. Colonization," in *Racial Transformations: Latinos and Asians Remaking the United States*, ed. Nicholas De Genova (Durham, N.C.: Duke University Press, 2006), 23–39; and Benito M. Vergara, *Displaying Filipinos: Photography and Colonialism in Early 20th Century Philippines* (Quezon City: University of the Philippines Press, 1995). On Filipinos as human exhibits, Jose D. Fermin, *1904 World's Fair: The Filipino Experience* (West Conshohocken, Pa.: Infinity, 2004), includes a fairly extensive bibliography of this well-documented event. See also Hannah M. Tavares, "The Racial Subjection of Filipinos in the Early Twentieth Century," in *The History of Discrimination in U.S. Education: Marginality, Agency, and Power*, ed. Eileen H. Tamura (New York: Palgrave Macmillan, 2008), 17–40; and the essays in "World's Fair 1904," special issue of *Philippine Studies* 52, no. 4 (2004).

27. Quoted in Gonzalez and Campomanes, "Filipino American Literature," 106n21.

28. Miller, *"Benevolent Assimilation,"* 275.

29. Jaime L. An Lim, *Literature and Politics: The Colonial Experience in Nine Philippine Novels* (Quezon City: New Day, 1993), xiv.

30. John Marx, "Postcolonial Literature and the Western Literary Canon," in *The Cambridge Companion to Postcolonial Literary Studies*, ed. Neil Lazarus (Cambridge: Cambridge University Press, 2004), 83.

31. Elaine H. Kim, *Asian American Literature: An Introduction to the Writings and Their Social Context* (Philadelphia: Temple University Press, 1982), 45. See also Larry Lawcock, "'Islands of Despair': The Filipino in American Literature (1841–1941)," *Communication* 9, no. 1 (1980): 152–165.

32. K. Anthony Appiah offers a stylized rendition of this process of negativity and inversion by focusing on the "life-scripts" of black identity, gay identity, and "proper ways of being black and gay" ("Identity, Authenticity, Survival: Multicultural Societies and Social Reproduction," in *Multiculturalism: Examining the Politics of Recognition*, ed. Amy Gutmann [Princeton, N.J.: Princeton University Press, 1994], 162). Closer to this book's archive, Elaine Kim's groundbreaking literary history, *Asian American Literature*, devotes its first chapter to "images of Asians in Anglo-American literature" (3–22) before examining the writings produced by Asian Americans themselves.

33. Allan Punzalan Isaac, *American Tropics: Articulating Filipino America* (Minneapolis: University of Minnesota Press, 2006), 7; Espiritu, *Home Bound*, 47.

34. Quoted in Isaac, *American Tropics*, 25. For similar accounts of the ways that imperial legalism created such contradictory and impossible designations

as "foreign to the United States in a domestic sense," see Amy Kaplan, *The Anarchy of Empire in the Making of U.S. Culture* (Cambridge, Mass.: Harvard University Press, 2002), 1–22; and See, *Decolonized Eye*, xi–xxxiv.

35. E. San Juan Jr., *From Exile to Diaspora: Versions of the Filipino Experience in the United States* (Boulder, Colo.: Westview Press, 1998), 61.

36. Kristin L. Hoganson, *Fighting for American Manhood: How Gender Politics Provoked the Spanish-American and Philippine-American Wars* (New Haven, Conn.: Yale University Press, 1998), 134, 137. See also Espiritu, *Home Bound*, 52.

37. Nerissa S. Balce, "Filipino Bodies, Lynching, and the Language of Empire," in *Positively No Filipinos Allowed: Building Communities and Discourse*, ed. Antonio T. Tiongson Jr., Edgardo V. Gutierrez, and Ricardo V. Gutierrez (Philadelphia: Temple University Press, 2006), 44, 56–58. See also Willard B. Gatewood Jr., *Black Americans and the White Man's Burden, 1898–1903* (Urbana: University of Illinois Press, 1975). Miller quotes one Kansas veteran speaking to a reporter while awaiting deployment: "The country won't be pacified until the niggers are killed off like the Indians"—a succinct statement of derision that combines the antiblack slur with the genocidal treatment of American Indians (*"Benevolent Assimilation,"* 179).

38. Paul A. Kramer, *The Blood of Government: Race, Empire, the United States, and the Philippines* (Chapel Hill: University of North Carolina Press, 2006), 159–227.

39. Vicente L. Rafael, *White Love and Other Events in Filipino History* (Durham, N.C.: Duke University Press, 2000), 6–7. See also Benedict Anderson, *The Spectre of Comparisons: Nationalism, Southeast Asia, and the World* (London: Verso, 1998), 246.

40. Isaac, *American Tropics*, 25.

41. Oscar V. Campomanes, "The New Empire's Forgetful and Forgotten Citizens: Unrepresentability and Unassimilability in Filipino-American Postcolonialities," *Hitting Critical Mass: A Journal of Asian American Cultural Criticism* 2, no. 2 (1995): 150.

42. San Juan, *From Exile to Diaspora*, 65.

43. See, *Decolonized Eye*, 149–150n1.

44. On the difference between nation and language, see Martin F. Manalansan IV, *Global Divas: Filipino Gay Men in the Diaspora* (Durham, N.C.: Duke University Press, 2003), 193n1. On linguistic phonetics in the Philippines, see Antonio J. A. Pido, "Macro-Micro Dimensions of Pilipino Immigration to the United States," in *Filipino Americans: Transformation and Identity*, ed. Maria P. P. Root (Thousand Oaks, Calif.: Sage, 1997), 37n1. On pronunciation and class stratification, see Sucheng Chan, *Asian Americans: An Interpretive History* (Boston: Twayne, 1991), xvi.

45. I use "Philippine" when referring to things related specifically to the

Philippines, and "Filipino" in all other contexts. Although I tend to avoid "Filipino American," especially during the colonial period, I do use it in contemporary contexts where its usage is commonplace.

46. To add (perversely) insult to injury, the epithet that supposedly did originate in the Philippine-American War—"gugu" or "googoo"—was transformed over the course of other wars in Asia and overseas military interventions until it became most recognizable as "gook" during and after the Vietnam/American War. See, among others, Dave Roediger, "Gook: The Short History of an Americanism," *Monthly Review* 42, no. 10 (1992): 50–54.

47. For a critique of these ideas, see S. Lily Mendoza, *Between the Homeland and the Diaspora: The Politics of Theorizing Filipino and Filipino American Identities, a Second Look at the Poststructuralism-Indigenization Debates* (New York: Routledge, 2002), 9–10.

48. Chuh, *Imagine Otherwise*, 56.

49. Nick Joaquin, *Culture and History* (1988; repr., Pasig City: Anvil, 2004), 397. On origins and national historiography, I am thinking of Reynaldo C. Ileto, "Outlines of a Nonlinear Emplotment of Philippine History," in *The Politics of Culture in the Shadow of Capital*, ed. Lisa Lowe and David Lloyd (1988; repr., Durham, N.C.: Duke University Press, 1997), 98–131. On reclaiming Filipino identity in the United States, I have in mind the Pilipino Cultural Nights performed on California campuses from the early 1980s forward. See Theodore S. Gonzalves, *The Day the Dancers Stayed: Performing in the Filipino/American Diaspora* (Philadelphia: Temple University Press, 2010); Barbara S. Gaerlan, "In the Court of the Sultan: Orientalism, Nationalism, and Modernity in Philippine and Filipino American Dance," *Journal of Asian American Studies* 2, no. 3 (1999): 251–287; and chapter 6 of this book.

50. Joaquin, *Culture and History*, 351–367; Gonzalez and Campomanes, "Filipino American Literature," 84.

51. Dolores S. Feria, ed., *The Sound of Falling Light* (Quezon City: University of the Philippines Press, 1960), 70–71.

52. For the former position, see Strobel, "'Born-Again Filipino'"; Leny Mendoza Strobel, *Coming Full Circle: The Process of Decolonization among Post-1965 Filipino Americans* (Quezon City: Giraffe Books, 2001); and Linda A. Revilla, "Filipino American Identity: Transcending the Crisis," in Root, *Filipino Americans*, 95–111. Mendoza's *Between the Homeland and the Diaspora* seeks to negotiate between the two positions, as her title indicates. For elaborations of "Filipino American critique," see Lisa Lowe's foreword and Tiongson's introduction to Tiongson, Gutierrez, and Gutierrez, *Positively No Filipinos Allowed*, vii–ix, 1–14; and Chuh, *Imagine Otherwise*, 56. I return to the yearning for cultural identity on the part of contemporary Filipino Americans in chapter 6.

53. See, for instance, Root, introduction to *Filipino Americans*, xi.

54. Babette Deutsch, "Have Come: A Good Poet," review of *Have Come, Am Here*, by José Garcia Villa, *New Republic*, October 19, 1942, 512.

55. Tabios, "Performance Poetry," 203n8.

56. Nathaniel Mackey, *Discrepant Engagement: Dissonance, Cross-Culturality, and Experimental Writing* (Tuscaloosa: University of Alabama Press), 262–263.

57. José Garcia Villa, "The Rise of the Short Story in the Philippines" (1940), in *The Critical Villa: Essays in Literary Criticism by José Garcia Villa*, ed. Jonathan Chua (Quezon City: Ateneo de Manila University Press, 2002), 283.

58. Renato Constantino, "The Miseducation of the Filipino," in *The Philippines Reader: A History of Colonialism, Neocolonialism, Dictatorship, and Resistance*, ed. Daniel B. Schirmer and Stephen Rosskamm Shalom (1966; repr., Boston: South End Press, 1987), 47. For a more recent critique of "imperial amnesia," see T. Ruanni F. Tupas, "History, Language Planners, and Strategies of Forgetting: The Problem of Consciousness in the Philippines," *Language Problems & Language Planning* 27, no. 1 (2003): 1–25.

59. See Andrew B. Gonzalez, *Language and Nationalism: The Philippine Experience Thus Far* (Quezon City: Ateneo de Manila University Press, 1987), 28; and Anderson, *Spectre of Comparisons*, 255.

60. Edna Zapanta Manlapaz, *Filipino Women Writers in English, Their Story: 1905–2002* (Quezon City: Ateneo de Manila University Press, 2003), 15.

61. Edilberto N. Alegre and Doreen G. Fernandez, eds., *The Writer and His Milieu: An Oral History of First Generation Writers in English* (Manila: De La Salle University Press, 1984), 204.

62. Ibid., 157, 161.

63. Resil B. Mojares, *Origins and Rise of the Filipino Novel: A Generic Study of the Novel until 1940* (1983; repr., Quezon City: University of the Philippines Press, 1998), 342. For a dramatic midcentury rendering of the decline of Spanish, see Nick Joaquin's elegiac play *A Portrait of the Artist as Filipino* (1952), collected in *Prose and Poems* (Manila: Bookmark, 1991), 273–475.

64. Benedict Anderson, "Colonial Language Policies in Indonesia and the Philippines: A Contrast in Intended Aims and Unintended Outcomes," in *Text and Nation: Cross-Disciplinary Essays on Cultural and National Identities*, ed. Laura García-Moreno and Peter C. Pfeiffer (Columbia, S.C.: Camden House, 1996), 9. See also Anderson, *Spectre of Comparisons*, 233.

65. See Manlapaz, *Filipino Women Writers*, 18, 35–36; and Yuson, "Filipino Diasporic Literature," 342.

66. Resil B. Mojares, *Waiting for Mariang Makiling: Essays in Philippine Cultural History* (Quezon City: Ateneo de Manila University Press, 2002), 304.

67. See Anderson, "Colonial Language Policies," 18.

68. On the literary curriculum taught during the U.S. colonial period, see, for example, Isabel Pefianco Martin, "The Literature Filipino Students *Do Not*

Read," in *English in Southeast Asia: Varieties, Literacies and Literatures*, ed. David Prescott (Newcastle: Cambridge Scholars, 2007), 290–315.

69. See Gonzalez, *Language and Nationalism*. On linguistic hierarchies present during the revolution, see Filomeno V. Aguilar Jr., "A Failure of Imagination? The Nation in Narratives of the 1896 Philippine Revolution," *Pilipinas* 31 (1998): 31–45.

70. On these points, see, among others, Paulino Lim Jr., "Finding Your Voice: The Bilingual Writer's Dilemma," in *Journey of 100 Years: Reflections on the Centennial of Philippine Independence*, ed. Cecilia Manguerra Brainard and Edmundo F. Litton (Santa Monica, Calif.: Philippine American Women Writers and Artists, 1999), 217–238; and Alberto S. Florentino, "What Price Filipino Writing in English?" *English Today: The International Review of the English Language* 6 (April 1986): 36–38.

71. These material, ideological, and literary issues are explored in Bautista and Bolton, *Philippine English*, an excellent compilation of essays on the politics of English. On reconceptualizing Philippine English, see also Gémino Abad, "Filipino Poetry in English: A Native Clearing," *World Englishes* 23, no. 1 (2004): 169–181; Isagani Cruz, *The Alfredo E. Litiatco Lectures of Isagani R. Cruz*, ed. David Jonathan Y. Bayot (Manila: De La Salle University Press, 1996), 129–141, 155–165; and R. Kwan Laurel, "Pinoy English: Language, Imagination, and Philippine Literature," *Philippine Studies* 53, no. 4 (2005): 532–562.

72. See Manlapaz, *Filipino Women Writers*, 7–10; Yuson, "Filipino Diasporic Literature," 337–355.

73. Rocío G. Davis, "On the Edge: Paradigms of the Filipino and Filipino American *Bildungsroman*," introduction to *Growing Up Filipino: Stories for Young Adults*, ed. Cecilia Manguerra Brainard (Santa Monica, Calif.: Philippine American Literary House, 2003), x.

74. See S. E. Solberg, "An Introduction to Filipino-American Literature," in *Aiiieeeee!: An Anthology of Asian-American Writers*, ed. Frank Chin, Jeffery Paul Chan, Lawson Fusao Inada, and Shawn Hsu Wong (Washington, D.C.: Howard University Press, 1983), l; Nick Carbó, "Returning a Borrowed Tongue," introduction to *Returning a Borrowed Tongue: An Anthology of Filipino and Filipino American Poetry*, ed. Nick Carbó (Minneapolis: Coffee House Press, 1995), viii; and Nick Carbó, "The Other Half of the Sky," introduction to *Babaylan: An Anthology of Filipina and Filipina American Writers*, ed. Nick Carbó and Eileen Tabios (San Francisco: Aunt Lute Books, 2000), xi.

75. Campomanes, "Filipinos in the United States," 55.

76. San Juan, *Philippine Temptation*, 174.

77. Blanche D'Alpuget, "Philippine Dream Feast," review of *Dogeaters*, by Jessica Hagedorn, *New York Times Book Review*, March 25, 1990, 1. For

a similar critique of the review, see Gladys Nubla, "The Politics of Relation: Creole Languages in *Dogeaters* and *Rolling the R's*," *MELUS* 29, no. 1 (2004): 199–218.

78. Somini Sengupta, "At Lunch With: Jessica Hagedorn; Cultivating the Art of the Melange," *New York Times*, December 4, 1996.

79. Vicente L. Rafael, *The Promise of the Foreign: Nationalism and the Technics of Translation in the Spanish Philippines* (Durham, N.C.: Duke University Press, 2005), 163.

80. Brent Hayes Edwards, *The Practice of Diaspora: Literature, Translation, and the Rise of Black Internationalism* (Cambridge, Mass.: Harvard University Press, 2003), 13.

81. I am thinking, for example, of the "motto, '*Pilipino Kahit Saan, Kahit Kailan*' ('Once a Filipino always a Filipino, anywhere, anytime')" that served as "the theme of the first *Sikolohiyang Pilipino* conference in the U.S. held at UC Berkeley in 1992" (Mendoza, *Between the Homeland*, 128). See also Strobel, "'Born-Again Filipino,'" 360.

82. Benito M. Vergara Jr., *Pinoy Capital: The Filipino Nation in Daly City* (Philadelphia: Temple University Press, 2009), 4.

83. Stuart Hall, "Race, Articulation, and Societies Structured in Dominance," in *Black British Cultural Studies: A Reader*, ed. Houston A. Baker Jr., Manthia Diawara, and Ruth H. Lindeborg (1980; repr., Chicago: University of Chicago Press, 1996), 16–60.

84. Stuart Hall with Lawrence Grossberg, "On Postmodernism and Articulation: An Interview with Stuart Hall," in *Stuart Hall: Critical Dialogues in Cultural Studies*, ed. David Morley and Kuan-Hsing Chen (London: Routledge, 1996), 141–142.

85. Edwards, *Practice of Diaspora*, 12.

86. See Isaac, *American Tropics*; and See, *Decolonized Eye*, xv–xviii.

87. The social science scholarship on the gendered dimensions of Filipino international labor migration is immense. Important works include Nicole Constable, *Maid to Order in Hong Kong: Stories of Filipina Workers* (Ithaca, N.Y.: Cornell University Press, 1997); Kale Bantigue Fajardo, "Transportation: Translating Filipino and Filipino American Tomboy Masculinities through Global Migration and Seafaring," *GLQ: A Journal of Lesbian and Gay Studies* 14, nos. 2–3 (2008): 403–424; Anna Romina Guevarra, *Marketing Dreams, Manufacturing Heroes: The Transnational Labor Brokering of Filipino Workers* (New Brunswick, N.J.: Rutgers University Press, 2010); Jane Margold, "Narratives of Masculinity and Transnational Migration: Filipino Workers in the Middle East," in *Bewitching Women, Pious Men: Gender and Body Politics in Southeast Asia*, ed. Aihwa Ong and Michael G. Peletz (Berkeley: University of California Press, 1995), 274–298; Steven C. McKay, "Filipino Sea Men: Constructing Masculinities in an Ethnic Labour Niche,"

*Journal of Ethnic and Migration Studies* 33, no. 4 (2007): 617–633; Rhacel Salazar Parreñas, *Servants of Globalization: Women, Migration and Domestic Work* (Stanford, Calif.: Stanford University Press, 2001); Rhacel Salazar Parreñas, *Children of Global Migration* (Stanford, Calif.: Stanford University Press, 2005); Robyn Magalit Rodriguez, *Migrants for Export: How the Philippine State Brokers Labor to the World* (Minneapolis: University of Minnesota Press, 2010); and James A. Tyner, *Made in the Philippines: Gendered Discourses and the Making of Migrants* (London: RoutledgeCurzon, 2004).

88. See Neferti Xina M. Tadiar, *Fantasy-Production: Sexual Economies and Other Philippine Consequences for the New World Order* (Hong Kong: Hong Kong University Press, 2003), 37–75.

89. See Martin Joseph Ponce, "Framing the Filipino Diaspora: Gender, Sexuality, and the Politics of Criticism," *Philippine Studies* 56, no. 1 (2008): 86–87, 92–94.

90. See Parreñas, *Servants of Globalization*; and Amit Kama, "Labor Migrants' Self-empowerment via Participation in a Diasporic Magazine: Filipinos at *Manila-Tel Aviv*," *Asian Journal of Communication* 18, no. 3 (2008): 223–238.

91. See, for example, the special issue on OFWs of the online journal *Our Own Voice* (March 2002), http://www.oovrag.com/laptop/editor2002-1.shtml.

92. Elynia S. Mabanglo, *Invitation of the Imperialist: Poems* (Quezon City: University of the Philippines Press, 1998), 3–5.

93. Tadiar, *Fantasy-Production*, 138. For additional commentary, see Marie-Therese C. Sulit, "Through Our Pinay Writings: Narrating Trauma, Embodying Recovery," in *Pinay Power: Peminist Critical Theory: Theorizing the Filipina/ American Experience*, ed. Melinda L. de Jesús (New York: Routledge, 2005), 355–361; and Neferti X. M. Tadiar, *Things Fall Away: Philippine Historical Experience and the Makings of Globalization* (Durham, N.C.: Duke University Press, 2009), 103–140.

94. Luisa A. Igloria, ed., *Not Home, But Here: Writing from the Filipino Diaspora* (Manila: Anvil, 2003), is comprised of essays by writers who reside in Australia, France, Germany, and the Netherlands, in addition to the Philippines and the United States. Yuson, "Filipino Diasporic Literature," also cites a number of writers living in various parts of the world (347).

95. On the relation between forms of address and the constitution of publics, see Michael Warner, *Publics and Counterpublics* (New York: Zone Books, 2005).

96. See Dennis Altman, "Global Gaze/Global Gays," *GLQ: A Journal of Lesbian and Gay Studies* 3, no. 4 (1997): 417–436; Anne-Marie Fortier, "Queer Diaspora," in *Handbook of Lesbian and Gay Studies*, ed. Diane Richardson and Steven Seidman (London: Sage, 2002), 183–197; Cindy Patton and Benigno Sánchez-Eppler, eds., *Queer Diasporas* (Durham, N.C.: Duke University Press,

2000); and Simon Watney, "AIDS and the Politics of Queer Diaspora," in *Negotiating Lesbian and Gay Subjects*, ed. Monica Dorenkamp and Richard Henke (New York: Routledge, 1995), 53–70.

97. Alan Sinfield, *Cultural Politics—Queer Reading*, 2nd ed. (New York: Routledge, 2005), 53.

98. Chuh, *Imagine Otherwise*, 35.

99. See, *Decolonized Eye*, 117 (my emphasis).

100. M. Jacqui Alexander, *Pedagogies of Crossing: Meditations on Feminism, Sexual Politics, Memory, and the Sacred* (Durham, N.C.: Duke University Press, 2005); David L. Eng, *The Feeling of Kinship: Queer Liberalism and the Racialization of Intimacy* (Durham, N.C.: Duke University Press, 2010); Gayatri Gopinath, *Impossible Desires: Queer Diasporas and South Asian Public Cultures* (Durham, N.C.: Duke University Press, 2005); Manalansan, *Global Divas*; Jasbir K. Puar, *Terrorist Assemblages: Homonationalism in Queer Times* (Durham, N.C.: Duke University Press, 2007). See also Arnaldo Cruz-Malavé and Martin F. Manalansan, eds., *Queer Globalizations: Citizenship and the Afterlife of Colonialism* (New York: New York University Press, 2002); David L. Eng, Judith Halberstam, and José Esteban Muñoz, eds., *What's Queer about Queer Studies Now?* special issue of *Social Text* 23, nos. 3–4 (2005); Inderpal Grewal and Caren Kaplan, "Global Identities: Theorizing Transnational Studies of Sexuality," *GLQ: A Journal of Lesbian and Gay Studies* 7, no. 4 (2001): 663–679; JeeYeun Lee, "Toward a Queer Korean American Diasporic History," in *Q & A: Queer in Asian America*, ed. David L. Eng and Alice Y. Hom (Philadelphia: Temple University Press, 1998), 184–209; and Eithne Luibhéid and Lionel Cantú Jr., eds., *Queer Migrations: Sexuality, U.S. Citizenship, and Border Crossings* (Minneapolis: University of Minnesota Press, 2005).

101. "queer, adj., and v.," *OED Online* (September 2009), Oxford University Press, http://dictionary.oed.com (accessed May 23, 2010).

102. Judith Butler, *Bodies That Matter: On the Discursive Limits of "Sex"* (New York: Routledge, 1993), 228 (my emphasis).

103. For examples of literary periodization, see Abad, "Filipino Poetry in English"; Campomanes, "Filipinos in the United States," 55–57; Carbó, "Returning a Borrowed Tongue," vii–viii.

## Notes to Chapter 1

1. Pio Pedrosa, introduction to *The Filipino Rebel: A Romance of American Occupation in the Philippines*, by Maximo Manguiat Kalaw, reissue (Manila: Filipiana Book Guild, 1964), xiii.

2. Denise Cruz, "Transpacific Femininities: Unmapping the Narratives of Philippine–United States Contact" (Ph.D. diss., University of California, Los Angeles, 2007), notes that the original publication date of *The Filipino Rebel* is

uncertain, with some scholars putting it at 1927, others in 1931 (162n2). The 1964 reissue appears to be the only version currently available. Cruz's dissertation contains one of the few recent analyses of *The Filipino Rebel*, and my reading necessarily builds off of her incisive feminist reading.

3. Nerissa S. Balce, "The Filipina's Breast: Savagery, Docility, and the Erotics of the American Empire," *Social Text* 87, vol. 24, no. 2 (2006): 92.

4. Maximo Manguiat Kalaw, *The Filipino Rebel: A Romance of American Occupation in the Philippines* (Manila: Filipiana Book Guild, 1964), 62. The Jones Law, or the Philippine Autonomy Act of 1916, represented the first official promise of Philippine independence by the U.S. government once a "stable government" was established. The Tydings-McDuffie Act, or the Philippine Independence Act of 1934, provided for independence after a ten-year transition known as the Commonwealth period.

5. On the politics of gender, sexuality, and early nationalism, see, among others, Cruz, "Transpacific Femininities"; Caroline S. Hau, *On the Subject of the Nation: Filipino Writings from the Margins, 1981–2004* (Quezon City: Ateneo de Manila University Press, 2004), 147–188; Elizabeth Mary Holt, *Colonizing Filipinas: Nineteenth-Century Representations of the Philippines in Western Historiography* (Quezon City: Ateneo de Manila University Press, 2002); Raquel A. G. Reyes, *Love, Passion and Patriotism: Sexuality and the Philippine Propaganda Movement, 1882–1892* (Singapore: NUS Press, and Seattle: University of Washington Press, 2008); and Mina Roces, "Reflections on Gender and Kinship in the Philippine Revolution, 1896–1898," in *The Philippine Revolution of 1896: Ordinary Lives in Extraordinary Times*, ed. Florentino Rodao and Felice Noelle Rodriguez (Quezon City: Ateneo de Manila University Press, 2001), 31–48.

6. That his first two books—*The Case for the Filipinos* (1916) and *Self-Government in the Philippines* (1919)—were published in the United States supports this point. *Ang bagong Katipunan* roughly translates as "the new society." "*Katipunan*" can mean "association" or "gathering," but it is impossible not to hear the echoes of the name of the secret society (Katipunan) that was formed in the early 1890s by Andres Bonifacio and that spearheaded the revolt against Spain. Kalaw's novel does not make any explicit references to the Katipunan, and indeed the newness of its nationalism resides precisely in its politically normative character. On the Katipunan, see Teodoro A. Agoncillo, *The Revolt of the Masses: The Story of Bonifacio and the Katipunan* (Quezon City: University of Philippines Press, 1956); and Reynaldo C. Ileto, *Pasyon and Revolution: Popular Movements in the Philippines, 1840–1910* (Quezon City: Ateneo de Manila University Press, 1979), 74–113.

7. See Ileto, *Pasyon and Revolution*; Reynaldo C. Ileto, *Filipinos and Their Revolution: Event, Discourse, and Historiography* (Quezon City: Ateneo de Manila University Press, 1998), 165–176; Rafael, *White Love*, 19–51, 204–227; and See, *Decolonized Eye*, 3–37.

8. Maria Teresa Martinez-Sicat, *Imagining the Nation in Four Philippine Novels* (Quezon City: University of the Philippines Press, 1994), 39.

9. Quoted in Ignacio et al., *Forbidden Book*, 19.

10. Rudyard Kipling, "The White Man's Burden," *McClure's Magazine* 12, no. 4 (February 1899): 290–291.

11. See Jim Zwick, *Confronting Imperialism: Essays on Mark Twain and the Anti-Imperialist League* (West Conshohocken, Pa.: Infinity, 2007), 1–43.

12. Miller, *"Benevolent Assimilation,"* 46.

13. Apolinario Mabini, "A Filipino Appeal to the People of the United States," *North American Review* 170 (January 1900): 58–59.

14. Mark Twain, "To the Person Sitting in Darkness," *North American Review* 531 (February 1901): 165, 169.

15. A copy of the Benevolent Assimilation Proclamation appears in Hazel M. McFerson, ed., *Mixed Blessing: The Impact of the American Colonial Experience on Politics and Society in the Philippines* (Westport, Conn.: Greenwood Press, 2002), 267–268.

16. See, among others, Maria Serena I. Diokno, "'Benevolent Assimilation' and Filipino Responses," in McFerson, *Mixed Blessing*, 75–88; and Julian Go and Anne L. Foster, eds., *The American Colonial State in the Philippines: Global Perspectives* (Durham, N.C.: Duke University Press, 2003).

17. Kramer, *Blood of Government*, 110.

18. Scholarship on colonial education in the Philippines includes Kimberly Alidio, "'When I Get Home, I Want to Forget': Memory and Amnesia in the Occupied Philippines, 1901–1904," *Social Text* no. 59 (1999): 105–122; Alexander A. Calata, "The Role of Education in Americanizing Filipinos," in McFerson, *Mixed Blessing*, 89–97; Roland Sintos Coloma, "Disidentifying Nationalism: Camilo Osias and Filipino Education in the Early Twentieth Century," in *Revolution and Pedagogy*, ed. E. Thomas Ewing (New York: Palgrave MacMillan, 2005), 19–38; Douglas Foley, "Colonialism and Schooling in the Philippines from 1898 to 1970," in *Education and Colonialism*, ed. Philip G. Altbach and Gail P. Kelly (New York: Longman, 1978), 69–95; and Mary Racelis and Judy Celine Ick, eds., *Bearers of Benevolence: The Thomasites and Public Education in the Philippines* (Pasig City: Anvil, 2001).

19. On the rebound effect of U.S. imperialism into domestic national discourse, see Kaplan, *Anarchy of Empire*.

20. On racist anti-imperialism, see Miller, *"Benevolent Assimilation,"* 122–128; and Kramer, *Blood of Government*, 117–119.

21. See Warwick Anderson, *Colonial Pathologies: American Tropical Medicine, Race, and Hygiene in the Philippines* (Durham, N.C.: Duke University Press, 2006); Ileto, *Pasyon and Revolution*; and David R. Sturtevant, *Popular Uprisings in the Philippines: 1840–1940* (Ithaca, N.Y.: Cornell University Press, 1976).

22. See Robert L. Beisner, *Twelve Against Empire: The Anti-Imperialists, 1898–1900* (New York: McGraw-Hill, 1968); Roger J. Bresnahan, *In Time of Hesitation: American Anti-Imperialists and the Philippine-American War* (Quezon City: New Day, 1981); Gerald E. Markowitz, ed., *American Anti-Imperialism 1895–1901* (New York: Garland, 1976); Erin L. Murphy, "Women's Anti-Imperialism, 'The White Man's Burden,' and the Philippine-American War: Theorizing Masculinist Ambivalence in Protest," *Gender & Society* 23, no. 2 (2009): 244–270; Tompkins, *Anti-Imperialism in the United States*; and Zwick, *Confronting Imperialism*.

23. Galicano Apacible, *To the American People* (1900). Jim Zwick notes that the pamphlet was originally published in Spanish and English without publisher or location, and was reprinted in the *Public* on July 28, 1900 (Jim Zwick, ed., *Anti-Imperialism in the United States, 1898–1935*, http://www.historyillustrated.com/ai [accessed July 23, 2007]). The late Zwick hosted this Web site and archived many uncollected texts from this period, but he eventually took it down due to others' copyright infringements.

24. Zwick, *Confronting Imperialism*, 36.

25. Bernardita Reyes Churchill, *The Philippine Independence Missions to the United States, 1919–1934* (Manila: National Historical Institute, 1983). For a useful analysis that juxtaposes "compadre colonial politics" with "popular radicalism," see Ileto, *Filipinos and Their Revolution*, 135–163.

26. Kramer, *Blood of Government*, 392–431.

27. On Kalaw's biography, see Manuel Quezon, introduction to *The Case for the Filipinos*, by Maximo M. Kalaw (New York: Century, 1916); and Cruz, "Transpacific Femininities," 171–172. Kalaw submitted "The Development of Philippine Politics (1872–1920): An Account of the Part Played by the Filipino Leaders and Parties in the Political Development of the Philippines" as his Ph.D. dissertation to the University of Michigan in 1925. Published in Washington, D.C., the *Filipino People* ran for four years (1912–1916) and included English and Spanish texts by Quezon, other Filipino intellectuals, and U.S. commentators. Quezon declared that the "journal is devoted solely to the interests of the Filipino people, whose name it bears; and to the fair and truthful exposition of the relations between the Philippines and the United States; with a view to hastening the ultimate establishment of Philippine independence upon a self-governing basis; by the aid and with the recognition of the United States" (*Filipino People* 1, no. 1 [1912]: 12). Kalaw published several articles in its pages.

28. Maximo M. Kalaw, *Self-Government in the Philippines* (New York: Century, 1919), 14.

29. Maximo M. Kalaw, "Ideals of the Philippines," *Annals of the American Academy of Political and Social Science* 122 (November 1925): 20. Among other preferential privileges, the Platt Amendment gave the U.S. government the

right to intervene in Cuban affairs under the guise of preserving Cuban independence and protecting "life, property, and individual liberty," as Article III states.

30. Maximo M. Kalaw, "The Filipinos' Side," *Nation*, December 5, 1923, 629.

31. Maximo M. Kalaw, "Why the Filipinos Expect Independence," *Foreign Affairs* 10, no. 2 (1932): 310.

32. General Leonard Wood and ex-governor General W. Cameron Forbes were sent by President Harding to gather information about the Philippines' state of affairs in 1921. Their controversial report argued against granting Philippine independence.

33. Maximo M. Kalaw, "International Aspects of Philippine Independence: A Filipino View," *Pacific Affairs* 6, no. 1 (1933): 17–18.

34. Kalaw, "Why the Filipinos Expect Independence," 304.

35. Kalaw, *Case for the Filipinos*, xi, xii.

36. The Clarke Amendment, which was defeated, would have set a more definite timetable for independence: not fewer than two years and not more than four years from when the bill became law. As passed, the Jones Law left unspecified the time frame for independence.

37. Kalaw, *Self-Government in the Philippines*, viii.

38. Kalaw, *Case for the Filipinos*, xiv.

39. Anderson, *Spectre of Comparisons*, 58–74.

40. Andrew Parker, Mary Russo, Doris Sommer, and Patricia Yaeger, introduction to *Nationalisms and Sexualities*, ed. Andrew Parker, Mary Russo, Doris Sommer, and Patricia Yaeger (New York: Routledge, 1992), 1.

41. See Andrew Hebard, "Romantic Sovereignty: Popular Romances and the American Imperial State in the Philippines," *American Quarterly* 57, no. 3 (2005): 805–830; Hoganson, *Fighting for American Manhood*; and Kaplan, *Anarchy of Empire*, 92–120.

42. Vicente L. Rafael, "Parricides, Bastards and Counterrevolution: Reflections on the Philippine Centennial," in Shaw and Francia, *Vestiges of War*, 365–366.

43. See, for example, Norma Alarcón, Caren Kaplan, and Minoo Moallem, eds., *Between Woman and Nation: Nationalisms, Transnational Feminisms, and the State* (Durham, N.C.: Duke University Press, 1999); Anne McClintock, *Imperial Leather: Race, Gender and Sexuality in the Colonial Contest* (New York: Routledge, 1995); and Parker et al., *Nationalisms and Sexualities*.

44. See Fujita-Rony, *American Workers*, 44–46.

45. See Cordova, *Filipinos*, 147–153. Angeles Monrayo, *Tomorrow's Memories: A Diary, 1924–1928*, ed. Rizaline R. Raymundo (Honolulu: University of Hawai'i Press, 2003), offers a personal account of a young Filipino woman in

Hawai'i and California during this period, and also appends informative essays by Jonathan Okamura and Dawn Bohulano Mabalon.

46. See Jim Zwick, foreword to *The Story of the Lopez Family*, ed. Canning Eyot (1904; repr., Manila: Platypus, 2001).

47. See Mina Roces, "Is the Suffragist an American Colonial Construct? Defining 'the Filipino Woman' in Colonial Philippines," in *Women's Suffrage in Asia: Gender, Nationalism, and Democracy*, ed. Louise Edwards and Mina Roces (London: RoutledgeCurzon, 2004), 24–58.

48. Clemencia Lopez, "Women of the Philippines," *Woman's Journal* (June 7, 1902): 184.

49. See Roces, "Is the Suffragist?"; and Denise Cruz's forthcoming book on "transpacific femininities." On U.S. suffragists' complex relation to U.S. imperialism and Philippine independence, see Allison L. Sneider, *Suffragists in an Imperial Age: U.S. Expansion and the Woman Question, 1870–1929* (Oxford: Oxford University Press, 2008), 117–136.

50. Lee Edelman, *No Future: Queer Theory and the Death Drive* (Durham, N.C.: Duke University Press, 2004), 11.

51. Maximo M. Kalaw, "The New Philippine Government," *American Political Science Review* 13, no. 3 (August 1919): 416, 417.

52. Mina Roces, *Women, Power, and Kinship Politics: Female Power in Post-War Philippines* (Westport, Conn.: Praeger, 1998).

53. Kalaw, "New Philippine Government," 416.

54. Kramer, *Blood of Government*, 18.

55. See Ileto, *Pasyon and Revolution*, 190.

56. Parreñas, *Children of Global Migration*, 36.

### Notes to Chapter 2

Parts of chapter 2 were previously published in Martin Joseph Ponce, "José Garcia Villa's Modernism and the Politics of Queer Diasporic Reading," *GLQ: A Journal of Lesbian and Gay Studies* 17, no. 4 (2011): 575–602.

1. "José Garcia Villa—Hero of the U.P.," *Philippines Free Press*, June 29, 1929.

2. *José Garcia Villa: A Bio-Bibliography* (Quezon City: The Library, University of the Philippines, 1973), Appendix "B."

3. Ibid., n.p. [last page].

4. "Why Villa's Story Received Grand Prize," *Philippines Free Press*, December 14, 1929, quoted in Chua, *Critical Villa*, 49n. My analysis is deeply indebted to the meticulous research Jonathan Chua makes available in this anthology. Further citations from Villa's critical essays refer to this text and are cited as *CV*.

5. Edilberto N. Alegre and Doreen G. Fernandez, eds., *The Writer and His Milieu: An Oral History of First Generation Writers in English* (Manila: De La Salle University Press, 1984), 299.

6. José Garcia Villa, "Mir-i-nisa," *Philippines Free Press*, August 24, 1929; reprinted in José Garcia Villa, *Mir-i-nisa* (Manila: Alberto S. Florentino, 1966).

7. O. Sevilla, "Song XIV: Testament" of "Man-Songs," *Philippines Herald Magazine*, June 2, 1929, 10; reprinted in *José Garcia Villa: A Bio-Bibliography*, Exhibit "A," 3; and in José Garcia Villa, *Many Voices: Selected Poems* (Manila: Philippine Book Guild, 1939), 191.

8. José Garcia Villa, *Have Come, Am Here* (New York: Viking, 1942); Villa, *Volume Two*; José Garcia Villa, *Selected Poems and New* (New York: McDowell, Obolensky, 1958). He had published two earlier collections in the Philippines: *Many Voices* (1939) and *Poems by Doveglion* (Manila: Philippine Writers' League, 1941).

9. San Juan, *Philippine Temptation*, 173.

10. Eric Keenaghan, *Queering Cold War Poetry: Ethics of Vulnerability in Cuba and the United States* (Columbus: Ohio State University Press, 2009), 9–30.

11. Gémino H. Abad, "One Hundred Years of Filipino Poetry," *World Literature Today* 74, no. 2 (2000): 328.

12. I expand on this point with respect to Villa's fiction in Ponce, "José Garcia Villa's Modernism and the Politics of Queer Diasporic Reading."

13. Chua, introduction to *Critical Villa*, 1–31, offers a useful overview of Villa's reception in the Philippines. Timothy Yu, "Asian/American Modernisms: José Garcia Villa's Transnational Poetics," in Carbó, *Pinoy Poetics*, 343–367, focuses on Villa's reception in the United States. Espiritu, *Five Faces of Exile*, 236–238n19, includes a wealth of reviews and criticism in both the Philippines and the United States.

14. San Juan, *Philippine Temptation*, 171. Three anthologies of Villa's work have been published fairly recently: Chua, *Critical Villa*; John Edwin Cowen, ed., *Doveglion: Collected Poems* (New York: Penguin, 2008); and Eileen Tabios, ed., *The Anchored Angel: Selected Writings by José Garcia Villa* (New York: Kaya Press, 1999).

15. J. Neil C. Garcia, *Philippine Gay Culture: Binabae to Bakla, Silahis to MSM* (Hong Kong: Hong Kong University Press, with the University of the Philippines Press, 2009), 30.

16. J. Neil C. Garcia, *Closet Queeries* (Pasig City: Anvil, 1997), 133, 134. For innuendos implying Villa's "gayness," see Jessica Hagedorn, foreword to Tabios, *Anchored Angel*, xiii; and Nick Carbó, "Gossip Gossip Gossip: José Garcia Villa as New York Literary Celebrity," in Tabios, *Anchored Angel*, 224.

17. San Juan, *Philippine Temptation*, 185.

18. See Maximo Ramos and Florentino B. Valeros, eds., *Philippine Harvest: An Anthology of Filipino Writing in English*, rev. ed. (Quezon City: Phoenix, 1964), 9; Peñaranda, Syquia, and Tagatac, "Introduction to Filipino-American Literature," 41–42; Quijano de Manila [Nick Joaquin], "Viva Villa!" in

*Doveglion and Other Cameos* (Manila: National Book Store, 1977), 189–190; Yu, "Asian/American Modernisms," 345; and Espiritu, *Five Faces*, 79–82. Chua (*Critical Villa*, 48–49n) and Espiritu make clear that Villa was suspended, not expelled, from the University of the Philippines.

19. "José Garcia Villa—Hero of the U.P.," 33.

20. Chua, introduction to *Critical Villa*, 23.

21. O. Sevilla, "Man-Songs," *Philippines Herald Magazine*, May 26, 1929, 7; Mona Vita [Loreto Paras], "Songs of Serenity," *Philippines Herald Magazine*, May 19, 1929, 10.

22. O. Sevilla, "Man-Songs," *Philippines Herald Magazine*, June 9, 1929, 10. On Paras's and Latorena's pseudonyms, see Chua, *Critical Villa*, 48n; and Edna Zapanta Manlapaz, *Our Literary Matriarchs 1925–1953: Angela Manalang Gloria, Paz M. Latorena, Loreto Paras Sulit, and Paz Marquez Benitez* (Quezon City: Ateneo de Manila University Press, 1996), 26.

23. Vita [Paras], "Songs of Serenity," 10.

24. O. Sevilla, "Song I" of "Man-Songs," *Philippines Herald Magazine*, May 26, 1929, 7.

25. Vicente Rafael pointed out to me that the pseudonym could also be read aurally as a rescripting of the Tagalog "O, si Villa!" (Oh, it's Villa!) (correspondence, June 12, 2005). Manlapaz re-creates a scene in which critic and writer Fred Mañgahas reads aloud, presumably to a group of University of the Philippines students, a letter from Villa describing his "first snow" in the United States. Afterward, "Cheers and catcalls. Chuckling to herself, Loreto [Paras] remembered one of the pen names Villa had coined for himself. O. Sevilla. *O si Villa, nga naman. Iba talaga*" (Oh, that's truly Villa alright. Really unique) (Manlapaz, *Our Literary Matriarchs*, 42).

26. O. Sevilla, "Song XI: Song to Artists" of "Man-Songs," *Philippines Herald Magazine*, June 9, 1929, 10; reprinted in *José Garcia Villa: A Bio-Bibliography*, Exhibit "A," 1–2.

27. O. Sevilla, "Song VIII: Song of the Waiting Lover" of "Man-Songs," *Philippines Herald Magazine*, June 2, 1929, 10; reprinted in Villa, *Many Voices*, 187; and in José Garcia Villa, *Appassionata: Poems in Praise of Love* (New York: King and Cowen, 1979), 4.

28. O. Sevilla, "Song IX: Song of Ripeness" of "Man-Songs," *Philippines Herald Magazine*, June 9, 1929, 10; reprinted in *José Garcia Villa: A Bio-Bibliography*, Exhibit "A," 1; and as "The Coconut Poem," in Villa, *Selected Poems and New*, 209.

29. Nick Joaquin reports that Villa, age fifty-two, said of "Man-Songs": "They were very manly, very juicy. My juices had started running and had begun to express themselves. I have ever since believed in juices, and I don't mean fruit juices" ("Viva Villa!" 190). Given the gender ambiguity of the poems, the

ways in which "Man-Songs" is "manly" nevertheless leave open the potential for *fruit* juices.

30. O. Sevilla, "Song X: Song of a Swift Nude" of "Man-Songs," *Philippines Herald Magazine*, June 2, 1929, 10; reprinted in *José Garcia Villa: A Bio-Bibliography*, Exhibit "A," 1; in *Lion and Crown* 1, no. 2 (1933): 26; and in Villa, *Appassionata*, 37.

31. O. Sevilla, "Song XIV: Testament" of "Man-Songs," *Philippines Herald Magazine*, June 2, 1929, 10; reprinted in *José Garcia Villa: A Bio-Bibliography*, Exhibit "A," 3; and in Villa, *Many Voices*, 191.

32. See, for example, "Villa's Story No Hit," *Philippines Free Press*, May 13, 1933; and Marcelo D. Gracia Concepcion, "Literary Eccentricities and Others," *Philippines Herald Magazine*, July 19, 1933, 8, both of which refer to the story "She Asked Him to Come" (1933). A photographic reprint of it appears in Alegre and Fernandez, *Writer and His Milieu*, 288. The four-paragraph narrative anticipates Villa's "comma poems" by inserting a multitude of periods that cut up the phrases into varying intervals. Repetitiously using a small pool of words, it also resonates with erotic connotations. It begins: "She asked him. To come. She asked. Him. To Come." It ends: "She. Should not. Have asked. Him. To come. He did. Not. Come."

33. Virginia Woolf, "Modern Fiction" (1919/1925), in *The English Modernist Reader, 1910–1930*, ed. Peter Faulkner (Iowa City: University of Iowa Press, 1986), 110.

34. In justifying his representations "of the body and its passions" (304), Villa also makes passing references to Anatole France, Emile Zola, Guy de Maupassant, art critic Henry McBride, and Whitman's *Leaves of Grass*. But he names Sherwood Anderson as his greatest influence (303). The title of the last poem, "Testament," and "Man-Songs" more generally seem to be modeled after Anderson's *A New Testament* (New York: Boni and Liveright, 1927), which itself includes a prose poem titled "Testament."

35. Leonard Casper, *New Writing from the Philippines: A Critique and Anthology* (Syracuse, N.Y.: Syracuse University Press, 1966), 105.

36. San Juan, *Philippine Temptation*, 192.

37. Joseph M. Conte, *Unending Design: The Forms of Postmodern Poetry* (Ithaca, N.Y.: Cornell University Press, 1991), 22.

38. Judith Halberstam, *In a Queer Time and Place: Transgender Bodies, Subcultural Lives* (New York: New York University Press, 2005), 1.

39. Villa first printed "Untitled Story" in the inaugural issue of the mimeographed magazine he edited while at the University of New Mexico, *Clay* 1 (1931): 17–26. "White Interlude" and "Walk at Midnight: A Farewell" appeared in the following issue, *Clay* 2 (1931–1932): 25–31, 49–52.

40. See, for example, Blair Niles, *Strange Brother* (New York: Liveright, 1931); Wallace Thurman, *Infants of the Spring* (1932; repr., London: X Press,

2003); and Richard Meeker [Forman Brown], *Better Angel* (1933; repr., Boston: Alyson, 1987). One comparable intertext from this period might be Richard Bruce Nugent's story, "Smoke, Lilies and Jade," *Fire!!* (1926): 33–39, for its formal innovation (the copious use of ellipses), its reflections on the role of the artist, its stagings of male-female and male-male eroticism, and its relative lack of racial thematization.

41. Review of *Footnote to Youth: Tales of the Philippines and Others*, by José Garcia Villa, *New Republic*, November 22, 1933, 56.

42. T. M. Pearce, review of *Footnote to Youth: Tales of the Philippines and Others*, by José Garcia Villa, *New Mexico Quarterly* 3, no. 4 (1933): 261; "Philippine Stories," review of *Footnote to Youth: Tales of the Philippines and Others*, by José Garcia Villa, *New York Times Book Review*, October 8, 1933, 7. On narrative rhythm, Villa writes: "Genuine substance is achieved only when a pulse beats through the correlated facts, however tender or brutal its rhythm may be" (*CV* 93).

43. None of the other autobiographical stories has received this isolated treatment. First published in *Clay* in 1931, "Untitled Story" also appeared that year in Manila in *Graphic* (September 9, 1931) and in Vienna in *Story* 1, no. 4 (1931): 45–53, and was reprinted in the United States in Edward J. O'Brien, ed., *Best American Short Stories of 1932* (New York: Dodd, Mead, 1932), 253–263. Since then, it has been anthologized in Leopoldo Y. Yabes, ed., *Philippine Short Stories 1925–1940* (Quezon City: University of the Philippines Press, 1975), 172–180; Jessica Hagedorn, ed., *Charlie Chan Is Dead: An Anthology of Contemporary Asian American Fiction* (New York: Penguin, 1993), 462–475; and Tabios, *Anchored Angel*, 106–116.

44. None of the publications of "Untitled Story" inserts punctuation between the two clauses "I was very angry I became a poet," as if the two were inseparable. At the end of the story, the narrator relinquishes this anger against the father and instead links "love" with "poetry." The imagery of the phallic "purple flower" that the narrator makes love to with his "long fingers" and that his father rejects more specifically connects *homo*erotics with art in opposition to materialism, thereby implicating the patriarch's incapacity for appreciating metaphor with his refusal to recognize his son's homoeroticism.

45. San Juan, *Philippine Temptation*, 192.

46. On this point, see Denise Cruz, "José Garcia Villa's Collection of 'Others': Irreconcilabilities of a Queer Transpacific Modernism," *Modern Fiction Studies* 55, no. 1 (2009): 29–30.

47. On Asian-white gay relationships, see, most recently, Kenneth Chan, "Rice Sticking Together: Cultural Nationalist Logic and the Cinematic Representations of Gay Asian-Caucasian Relationships and Desire," *Discourse* 28, no. 2 (2008): 178–196.

48. Espiritu speculates in passing that "Greenwich Village represented

sexual freedom for Villa, the space upon which to discover and explore his homosexuality, alongside numerous 'queer' American writers and artists who had likewise found refuge there," but he does not offer any evidence to support this claim (*Five Faces*, 180).

49. Horace Gregory, review of *Footnote to Youth*, by José Garcia Villa, *New York Herald Tribune Books*, October 1, 1933, 15.

50. Quoted in James G. Wingo, "Looking Back on the Year of Hare-Splitting," *Philippines Free Press*, January 6, 1934.

51. Carlos Quirino, "Insurgent Villa: Modernist, Idealist," *Graphic*, October 26, 1932, 49.

52. Edward J. O'Brien, introduction to *Footnote to Youth*, by José Garcia Villa (New York: Charles Scribner's Sons, 1933), 5.

53. Amador Daguio, "Don't Follow Villa," *Graphic*, January 30, 1936, 16.

54. Salvador P. Lopez, "The Poetry of José Garcia Villa," in *Literature and Society: Essays on Life and Letters* (Manila: Philippine Book Guild, 1940), 141, 142. Further citations from Lopez's essays refer to this text.

55. On the reverberations of the Wilde trials, and the connections among decadence, aestheticism, and male homosexuality, see Ed Cohen, *Talk on the Wilde Side: Toward a Genealogy of a Discourse on Male Sexualities* (New York: Routledge, 1993); and Alan Sinfield, *The Wilde Century: Effeminacy, Oscar Wilde, and the Queer Movement* (New York: Columbia University Press, 1994).

56. Manuel X. Burgos Jr., "The Poet's Songs," *Philippines Herald Magazine*, June 30, 1929, 5. Burgos also parodies Villa's dedications to "Mona Vita" and "Mina Lys" by addressing his retort "To José Garcia Villa, alias O. Sevilla."

57. Lopez, *Literature and Society*, 159.

58. See Chua, introduction to *Critical Villa*, 12–14; and Yu, "Asian/American Modernisms," 365.

59. Stanley J. Kunitz, "Villa, José Garcia," in *Twentieth Century Authors First Supplement*, ed. Stanley J. Kunitz (New York: H. W. Wilson, 1955), 1036.

60. José Garcia Villa, "Guggenheim Fellowship: Plan for Work," in Tabios, *Anchored Angel*, 132.

61. See Louise Bogan, review of *Have Come, Am Here*, by José Garcia Villa, *New Yorker*, October 31, 1942, 80–81; Babette Deutsch, "Have Come: A Good Poet," review of *Have Come, Am Here*, by José Garcia Villa, *New Republic*, October 19, 1942, 512; Richard Eberhardt, "The, World, Of, the, Spirit," review of *Volume Two*, by José Garcia Villa, *New York Times Book Review*, December 4, 1949, 57; Cornelio Faigao, "The Element of Religion in the Poetry of José Garcia Villa" (master's thesis, University of San Carlos, Cebu City, Philippines, 1951); and Angel R. Hidalgo, "Approach to God," *Literary Apprentice* 12, no. 15 (1948–1949): 72–76.

62. José Garcia Villa, "7," in *Volume Two*, 20.

63. Faigao, "Element of Religion," 81–82.

64. On this point, see San Juan's use of Adorno's essay "Lyric Poetry and Society" (1974) to read Villa's "abstract" poems as social critique. San Juan, *Philippine Temptation*, 204–206.

65. José Garcia Villa, "3," in *Volume Two*, 15.

66. José Garcia Villa, "A Note on the Commas," in *Volume Two*, 5.

67. José Garcia Villa, "4," in *Volume Two*, 17.

68. Yu, "Asian/American Modernisms," 348.

69. Bienvenido Lumbera and Cynthia Nograles-Lumbera, *Philippine Literature: A History and Anthology* (Manila: National Book Store, 1982), 95.

70. José Garcia Villa, ed., *A Doveglion Book of Philippine Poetry* (Manila: Katha, 1962); José Garcia Villa, ed., *A Doveglion Book of Philippine Poetry in English: 1910 to 1962* (Manila: A. S. Florentino, 1965); José Garcia Villa, ed., *The New Doveglion Book of Philippine Poetry* (Manila: Caliraya Foundation on Consciousness and the Environment, 1975); José Garcia Villa, ed., *The New Doveglion Book of Philippine Poetry* (Manila: Anvil, 1993).

71. See Lucila Hosillos, "Escapee to Universality (Portrait of a Filipino Poet as Escapee to the Non-existent Kingdom of Universalism)," *Diliman Review* 18 (October 1970): 329–340.

72. On this point, see, for example, Jonathan Chua, "In His Own Words: An Interview with Francisco Arcellana on José Garcia Villa," *Kritika Kultura* 2 (2002): 111.

73. José Garcia Villa, „A Composition,„ *Literary Apprentice* (1953): 59–61; reprinted in Tabios, *Anchored Angel*, 134. Further citations refer to the latter.

74. Manalansan, *Global Divas*, 5.

75. Luis H. Francia, introduction to Cowen, *Doveglion*, xxxiv.

76. José Garcia Villa, "162: The Anchored Angel," in *Selected Poems and New*, 152.

77. Leopoldo Yabes, "Sizing Up Villa," *Graphic*, May 25, 1933, 61.

78. Feria, *Sound of Falling Light*, 73.

### Notes to Chapter 3

1. Carlos Bulosan, *The Cry and the Dedication*, ed. E. San Juan Jr. (Philadelphia: Temple University Press, 1995).

2. E. San Juan Jr., introduction to *The Cry and the Dedication*, by Carlos Bulosan, xxi.

3. The standard account of the movement is Benedict J. Kerkvliet, *The Huk Rebellion: A Study of Peasant Revolt in the Philippines* (Berkeley: University of California Press, 1977). On the role of U.S. counterinsurgency in the Philippines during this period, see Michael McClintock, *Instruments of Statecraft: U.S. Guerrilla Warfare, Counterinsurgency, and Counterterrorism, 1940–1990* (New York: Pantheon, 1992), 82–126.

4. San Juan, introduction to *The Cry and the Dedication*, xxxvn7.

5. It is unclear whether Bulosan meant to end the narrative here. At three points in the book, San Juan signals that "the text breaks off here," so obviously the manuscript was not entirely completed.

6. Other texts on World War II in the Philippines published in the United States during this period include Stevan Javellana, *Without Seeing the Dawn* (Boston: Little, Brown, 1947); and Panlilio, *Crucible*. A huge thanks to Denise Cruz for retrieving Panlilio's memoir from its "fall into obscurity" (xxv).

7. Tim Libretti and Jeffrey Arellano Cabusao follow San Juan's reference to Amilcar Cabral's phrase "return to the source" (introduction to *The Cry and the Dedication*, xiii). See Tim Libretti "First and Third Worlds in U.S. Literature: Rethinking Carlos Bulosan," *MELUS* 23, no. 4 (1998): 147, 151; and Jeffrey Arellano Cabusao, "Returns and Resistant Rearticulations: Asian American Studies, Carlos Bulosan, and Our Long Memory" (master's thesis, University of California, Los Angeles, 2001), 42.

8. San Juan, introduction to *Cry and the Dedication*, xxix.

9. In his introduction to *The Cry and the Dedication*, San Juan opines that "the actual model for this novel is Luis Taruc's *Born of the People*" (xxxivn2), but he does not pursue the connection further. Bulosan undoubtedly knew of *Born of the People* since his signature graces an undated letter distributed by the Committee to Sponsor Luis Taruc's Autobiography (Box 3, Folder 4, Carlos Bulosan papers, Special Collections, University of Washington Libraries, Seattle). *Born of the People* (New York: International Publishers, 1953) has long been out of print but remains an extraordinary postwar document that narrates Taruc's peasant and political life from his birth in 1913 in a Pampanga barrio, to his growing radicalization during the 1930s, his formation of the Huks, his disillusionment with governmental politics following the war, and his reorganization of the Huks as an anti-imperialist movement. Similar to Bulosan's *America Is in the Heart*, Taruc's life story is embedded within a wider context of radical social history. As he writes in the conclusion: "Looking back through these pages I find that there is less of me here than there is of the movement itself. And that is as it should be. The people's movement is made up of many, many lives, and all the struggles of which I have spoken are but a part of the life of our people as a whole. In a most important respect this book is not an autobiography; it is a chapter in the biography of the Filipino people" (278).

10. On Bulosan's reemergence within Asian American studies in the 1970s, see chapter 4. On the relation between *America Is in the Heart* and Philippine literature in English, see Martin Joseph Ponce, "On Becoming Socially Articulate: Transnational Bulosan," *Journal of Asian American Studies* 8, no. 1 (2005): 49–80.

11. Carlos Bulosan, "Autobiographical Sketch," in E. San Juan Jr., ed., *On*

*Becoming Filipino: Selected Writings of Carlos Bulosan* (Philadelphia: Temple University Press, 1995), 216.

12. For a quite different approach to *America* as a literacy narrative, see Morris Young, *Minor Re/Visions: Asian American Literacy Narratives as a Rhetoric of Citizenship* (Carbondale: Southern Illinois University Press, 2004), 78–96.

13. On this point, see Petronilo Bn. Daroy, "Carlos Bulosan: The Politics of Literature," *St. Louis Quarterly* 6, no. 2 (1968): 193–206.

14. For a critique of the "collective representation" thesis, see Ponce, "On Becoming Socially Articulate," 52–56.

15. Isaac, *American Tropics*, 133.

16. Carlos Bulosan, *America Is in the Heart: A Personal History* (1946; repr., Seattle: University of Washington Press, 1973), 152.

17. On this point, see Rachel Lee, *The Americas of Asian American Literature: Gendered Fictions of Nation and Transnation* (Princeton, N.J.: Princeton University Press, 1999), 17–43.

18. Melinda Luisa María de Jesús, "Rereading History/Rewriting Desire: Reclaiming Queerness in Carlos Bulosan's *America Is in the Heart* and Bienvenido Santos' *Scent of Apples*," *Journal of Asian American Studies* 5, no. 2 (2002): 104.

19. Quoted in Takaki, *Strangers from a Different Shore*, 328.

20. See de Jesús, "Rereading History/Rewriting Desire," 103; and Chuh, *Imagine Otherwise*, 40–41.

21. Roderick A. Ferguson, *Aberrations in Black: Toward a Queer of Color Critique* (Minneapolis: University of Minnesota Press, 2003), 15, quoting Lowe, *Immigrant Acts*, 23.

22. Lee, *Americas of Asian American Literature*, 17. For discussions of a "feminized America" in Bulosan's work, see Kim, *Asian American Literature*, 52–53; Sheng-Mei Ma, *Immigrant Subjectivities in Asian American and Asian Diasporic Literatures* (Albany: State University of New York Press, 1998), 78–90; and Viet Thanh Nguyen, *Race and Resistance: Literature and Politics in Asian America* (New York: Oxford University Press, 2002), 87–106.

23. For a fictional rendering of this issue, see Carlos Bulosan, "As Long as the Grass Shall Grow," in San Juan, *On Becoming Filipino*, 77–84.

24. On this point, see Patricia Chu, *Assimilating Asians: Gendered Strategies of Authorship in Asian America* (Durham, N.C.: Duke University Press, 2000), 48–49.

25. The reference is to Clara Weatherwax and her novel *Marching! Marching!* (New York: John Day, 1935; repr., Detroit: Omnigraphics, 1990). The book won the *New Masses* contest for a novel on an American proletarian theme. Michael Denning notes this allusion in *The Cultural Front: The*

*Laboring of American Culture in the Twentieth Century* (London: Verso, 1996), 519n33.

26. See Ponce, "On Becoming Socially Articulate," 49–80.

27. As Bulosan writes in a letter dated August 20, 1946, to Philippine intellectual Leopoldo Yabes: "I would like to visit the Islands. I have several books in mind that I would like to write, all about the Philippine peasant; but I feel that I need first-hand information before attempting the project" (Feria, *Sound of Falling Light*, 34).

28. The connection between Bulosan/Allos and Dante can be inferred through the publications of their first poetry books. Both *The Cry and the Dedication* (194–195) and *America Is in the Heart* (320–321) document this scene. The references are to Carlos Bulosan, *Letter from America* (Prairie City, Ill.: J. A. Decker, 1942).

29. See Ponce, "On Becoming Socially Articulate," 64–68.

30. Jeffrey Arellano Cabusao, "Some Notes for Reconsidering Carlos Bulosan's Third World Literary Radicalism," *Our Own Voice* (March 2006), http://www.ourownvoice.com/essays/essay2006a-2.shtml.

31. See Bulosan, *Cry*, 56, 130; Taruc, *Born*, 38, 249–250.

32. See Bulosan, *Cry*, 99; Taruc, *Born*, 154–157. While the events in Taruc's book take place during the war, Bulosan's novel is set after the war (ca. 1948–1950). Bulosan worries less about chronology and more about ideological consciousness-raising.

33. See Bulosan, *Cry*, 160; Taruc, *Born*, 227. The United States made Philippine World War II damage claims contingent on the passing of the Bell Trade Act of 1946. While tying the Philippine economy directly to the U.S. economy through trade agreements and pegging the peso to the dollar, the bill also contained the controversial "Parity" provision, which allowed U.S. investors the same rights as Filipino citizens to develop the Philippines' natural resources and operate public utilities. Accommodating this provision required a constitutional amendment approved by a majority of the legislature, hence why Roxas refused to seat the seven representatives likely to oppose the measure.

34. Carlos Bulosan, ed., *Chorus for America: Six Philippine Poets* (Los Angeles: Wagon and Star, 1942), xi.

35. Perhaps the most forceful critique in his nonfiction lies in Carlos Bulosan, "Terrorism Rides the Philippines," in *Selected Writings of Carlos Bulosan*, ed. E. San Juan Jr., special issue of *Amerasia Journal* 6, no. 1 (1979): 139–142. The text was published in the *1952 Yearbook, International Longshoremen's and Warehousemen's Union, Local 37*, which Bulosan edited during this period (27), and can be found in Box 3, Folder 11, Carlos Bulosan papers. A photograph of Taruc appears with the article.

36. Libretti, "First and Third Worlds," 140.

37. Bulosan, "Autobiographical Sketch," 216.

38. Carlos Bulosan, "How My Stories Were Written," in San Juan, *On Becoming Filipino*, 109–114. It seems that the essay was not published when it was originally written. Implicitly referring to the essay "I Am Not a Laughing Man," which appeared in *The Writer* in 1946, "How My Stories Were Written" must have been composed in the late 1940s or early 1950s, that is, contemporaneous with *The Cry and the Dedication*.

39. Libretti, "First and Third Worlds," 139.

40. On the "blood compact" ritual used by the Katipunan, see Rafael, *Promise of the Foreign*, 168–182.

41. Carlos Bulosan, "Letter to Taruc," Box 6, Folder 12, Carlos Bulosan papers.

42. Luis V. Teodoro Jr., "Notes on *The Power of the People*: Towards Coming to Terms with Philippine Exile Literature," *Mithi* 1 (1985): 10.

43. See Lucy Mae San Pablo Burns, "'Splendid Dancing': Filipino 'Exceptionalism' in Taxi Dancehalls," *Dance Research Journal* 40, no. 2 (2008): 23–40; Linda España-Maram, *Creating Masculinity in Los Angeles's Little Manila: Working-Class Filipinos and Popular Culture, 1920s–1950s* (New York: Columbia University Press, 2006), 105–133; Mae M. Ngai, *Impossible Subjects: Illegal Aliens and the Making of Modern America* (Princeton, N.J.: Princeton University Press, 2004), 109–116; Rhacel Salazar Parreñas, "'White Trash' Meets the 'Little Brown Monkeys': The Taxi Dance Hall as a Site of Interracial and Gender Alliances between White Working Class Women and Filipino Immigrant Men in the 1920s and 30s," *Amerasia Journal* 24, no. 2 (1998): 115–134; and Ruby C. Tapia, "'Just Ten Years Removed from a Bolo and a Breech-cloth': The Sexualization of the Filipino 'Menace,'" in Tiongson, Gutierrez, and Gutierrez, *Positively No Filipinos Allowed*, 61–70.

44. Nguyen, *Race and Resistance*, 82.

45. Vina A. Lanzona, *Amazons of the Huk Rebellion: Gender, Sex, and Revolution in the Philippines* (Madison: University of Wisconsin Press, 2009), 7.

46. Lanzona also notes that the Huks did not acknowledge "homosexual relationships . . . in either official or unofficial histories of the Huk rebellion" (*Amazons*, 187). On the Huks and sexuality, see also Jeff Goodwin, "The Libidinal Constitution of a High-Risk Social Movement: Affectual Ties and Solidarity in the Huk Rebellion, 1946 to 1954," *American Sociological Review* 62, no. 1 (1997): 53–69.

47. See, for example, Michael Warner, *The Trouble with Normal: Sex, Politics, and the Ethics of Queer Life* (New York: Free Press, 1999).

48. Caroline S. Hau, *Necessary Fictions: Philippine Literature and the Nation, 1946–1980* (Quezon City: Ateneo de Manila University Press, 2000), 240.

49. Carlos Bulosan, "Epilogue: Unknown Soldier," in *The Voice of Bataan* (New York: Coward-McCann, 1943), 28.

50. Lanzona, *Amazons*, 231.

51. To put this amount into perspective, Benedict Kerkvliet writes: "United States assistance to the Philippines in fiscal years 1951 through 1956 totaled $500 million—$383 million of economic assistance and $117 million of military assistance. This supplemented the $700 million the United States had delivered from 1946 through 1950 to assist Filipinos to rebuild after World War II and to help finance government armed forces. American aid provided roughly half of the funds designated for agrarian projects in the government's 'psych war' against the Huk rebellion between 1951 and 1955" (*Huk Rebellion*, 244). Clearly, Felix's aid does not compare to the massive financial assistance provided by the U.S. government's counterinsurgency efforts.

52. Patricio N. Abinales, *Love, Sex, and the Filipino Communist* (Manila: Anvil, 2004); Ninotchka Rosca, *State of War* (New York: Simon and Schuster, 1988); Jessica Hagedorn, *Dogeaters* (New York: Penguin, 1990). In 2005, the New People's Army (the armed wing of the Communist Party) famously officiated the first gay male marriage in the Philippines.

53. Feria, *Sound of Falling Light*, 57.

54. Carlos Bulosan, "I Am Not a Laughing Man" (1946), in San Juan, *On Becoming Filipino*, 138–142.

55. See also, Feria, *Sound of Falling Light*, 10, 12.

56. Ibid., 51–52.

57. Ibid., 40.

58. Ibid., 46.

59. Leopoldo Y. Yabes, "Prefatory Note," in Yabes, *Philippine Short Stories*, viii. The "war novel" alluded to is Stevan Javellana's *Without Seeing the Dawn*.

60. Feria, *Sound of Falling Light*, 40.

61. Ibid., 45.

62. See Ponce, "On Becoming Socially Articulate," 63–64. On Bulosan's mixed reception in the Philippines, see Espiritu, *Five Faces of Exile*, 220–222n5. One posthumous negative assessment of Bulosan's work can be found in Edilberto K. Tiempo, "Carlos Bulosan Demystified: The Problem of Artistic Insensibility," *Solidarity* 130 (1991): 33–43.

### Notes to Chapter 4

1. Sengupta, "At Lunch With: Jessica Hagedorn."

2. Jessica Hagedorn, "Music for Gangsters and (Other) Chameleons," in *Stars Don't Stand Still in the Sky: Music and Myth*, ed. Karen Kelly and Evelyn McDonnell (New York: New York University Press, 1999), 254.

3. Jessica Hagedorn, *The Gangster of Love* (Boston: Houghton Mifflin, 1996), 16.

4. On Hagedorn's relation to black music and poetics, see Eileen Tabios,

"Jessica Hagedorn Sings: Listen to 'PICTURE THIS,'" in *Black Lightning: Poetry-in-Progress* (New York: Asian American Writers' Workshop, 1998): "I was groping in the dark, and I guess my voice as a writer coming up in the 1970s was influenced and inspired by the Black vernacular. Back then, that particular music was most comfortable to me" (274).

5. Kenneth Rexroth, ed., *Four Young Women: Poems* (New York: McGraw-Hill, 1973); reprinted in Jessica Hagedorn, *Danger and Beauty* (New York: Penguin, 1993), 1–19.

6. Jessica Hagedorn, *Dangerous Music* (San Francisco: Momo's Press, 1975); reprinted in Hagedorn, *Danger and Beauty*, 22–77.

7. Jessica Hagedorn, *Pet Food and Tropical Apparitions* (San Francisco: Momo's Press, 1981); reprinted in Hagedorn, *Danger and Beauty*, 79–170.

8. Hagedorn, "Music for Gangsters," 253.

9. On her "multicultural identity," see Jessica Hagedorn, "The Exile Within/ The Question of Identity," in *The State of Asian America: Activism and Resistance in the 1990's,* ed. Karin Aguilar-San Juan (Boston: South End Press, 1994), 180.

10. Hagedorn, *Gangster of Love*, 201.

11. For a fine analysis of some of these West Coast writers, see Jean Vengua Gier, "'. . . to have come from someplace': *October Light, America Is In the Heart*, and 'Flip' Writing After the Third World Strikes," *Hitting Critical Mass: A Journal of Asian American Cultural Criticism* 2, no. 2 (1995): 1–33.

12. Jessica Hagedorn, "Solea," "Souvenirs," "Justifiable Homicide," in *Liwanag: Literary and Graphic Expressions by Filipinos in America*, ed. Liwanag Collective (San Francisco: Liwanag Publishing, 1975), 47–51.

13. Originally published in 1946, Bulosan's *America Is in the Heart* was reprinted by the University of Washington Press in 1973. Excerpts from the text also appeared in Chin et al., *Aiiieeeee!* 57–65; and Emma Gee, ed., *Counterpoint: Perspectives on Asian America* (Los Angeles: Asian American Studies Center, 1976), 365–371, 485–488. It was during this period as well that E. San Juan Jr. edited the *Selected Writings of Carlos Bulosan* special issue of *Amerasia Journal*.

14. Hagedorn, *Danger and Beauty*, ix.

15. Emily Porcincula Lawsin, "Jessica Hagedorn," in *Words Matter: Conversations with Asian American Writers*, ed. King-Kok Cheung (Honolulu: University of Hawai'i Press, with UCLA Asian American Studies Center, 2000), 30.

16. See Jessica Hagedorn, "Chiquita Banana," "Canto de Nada/ Para ti, M'wandishi," "Smokey's Gettin' Old," in *Third World Women* (San Francisco: Third World Communications, 1972), 118–125; "Natural Death," "Poem for the Art Ensemble of Chicago," "Solea," in *Time to Greez! Incantations from the Third World*, ed. Janice Mirikitani et al. (San Francisco: Glide/Third World

Communications, 1975), 28–32; "Bump City," *Yardbird Reader* 4 (1975): 90–93.

17. Hagedorn, *Danger and Beauty*, xi.

18. See Laurie Carlos, Jessica Hagedorn, and Robbie McCauley, *Teenytown*, in *Out from Under: Texts by Women Performance Artists*, ed. Lenora Champagne (New York: Theatre Communications Group, 1990), 91–117.

19. Hagedorn, *Danger and Beauty*, ix.

20. Hagedorn, "Music for Gangsters," 254.

21. Sengupta, "At Lunch With: Jessica Hagedorn."

22. The phrase "stay crazy under pressure" is taken from "Easter Sunday," the poem that immediately follows "The Blossoming of Bongbong" in *Dangerous Music* (Hagedorn, *Danger and Beauty*, 57).

23. Jessica Hagedorn, "The Blossoming of Bongbong," in *Dangerous Music*, n.p.; reprinted in Hagedorn, *Danger and Beauty*, 40. Further citations refer to the latter text.

24. The guru Ra might allude to the keyboardist, composer, and bandleader Sun Ra (1914–1993) and/or to tenor saxophonist, flutist, multi-instrumentalist, and bandleader Rahsaan Roland Kirk (1936–1977), who was known for his circular breathing technique.

25. James C. Hall, *Mercy, Mercy Me: African American Culture and the American Sixties* (Oxford: Oxford University Press, 2001), 114.

26. Lewis Porter, *John Coltrane: His Life and Music* (Ann Arbor: University of Michigan Press, 1998), 267.

27. Leroi Jones [Amiri Imamu Baraka], *Black Music* (1968; repr., New York: Da Capo, 1998), 193.

28. Hall, *Mercy, Mercy Me*, 142.

29. Ibid., 114.

30. De Sayles R. Grey, "John Coltrane and the 'Avant-Garde' Movement in Jazz History" (Ph.D. diss., University of Pittsburgh, 1986), 54.

31. Madhav Chari, "Pundit Coltrane Shows the Way," *Journal of Asian American Studies* 4, no. 3 (2001): 268, 278–279.

32. Kimberly W. Benston, *Performing Blackness: Enactments of African-American Modernism* (London: Routledge, 2000), 146.

33. See, among others, Hazel V. Carby, *Race Men* (Cambridge, Mass.: Harvard University Press, 1998); Herman Gray, "Black Masculinity and Visual Culture," *Callaloo* 18, no. 2 (1995): 401–405; and Sherrie Tucker, "Big Ears: Listening for Gender in Jazz Studies," *Current Musicology* 71–73 (2001/2002): 375–408.

34. Jessica Hagedorn, "Tenement Lover: no palm trees / in new york city," in *Between Worlds: Contemporary Asian-American Plays*, ed. Misha Berson (New York: Theatre Communications Group, 1990), 78.

35. For an approach that emphasizes the novel's engagement with racial

hybridity and affect in the context of global capitalism, see Jeffrey Santa Ana, "Feeling Ancestral: The Emotions of Mixed Race and Memory in Asian American Cultural Productions," *positions: east asia cultures critique* 16, no. 2 (2008): 457–482.

36. See Kevin Fellezs, "Silenced but Not Silent: Asian Americans and Jazz," in *Alien Encounters: Popular Culture in Asian America*, ed. Mimi Thi Nguyen and Thuy Nguyen Tu (Durham, N.C.: Duke University Press, 2007), 69–108; Oliver Wang, "Rapping and Repping Asian: Race, Authenticity, and the Asian American MC," in Nguyen and Tu, *Alien Encounters*, 35–68; and Deborah Wong, *Speak It Louder: Asian Americans Making Music* (New York: Routledge, 2004), 161–193.

37. Vijay Prashad, *Everybody Was Kung Fu Fighting: Afro-Asian Connections and the Myth of Cultural Purity* (Boston: Beacon Press, 2001).

38. Hagedorn, "Music for Gangsters," 254.

39. Ibid. While the notion that Filipino musicians are consummate mimics is widespread in popular culture, the history of Filipino mimicry more generally extends at least to the U.S. colonial period. See Rafael, *White Love*, 34–35; and Anderson, *Colonial Pathologies*, 180–206.

40. As Paul Gilroy writes, presumably referring to Hendrix's final album, *Band of Gypsys* (1970), "Hendrix would later rationalise his ambivalence towards both blackness and America through the nomadic ideology of the gypsy that appeared in his work as an interestingly perverse accompaniment to the decision to play funkier and more politically engaged music with an all-black band" (*The Black Atlantic: Modernity and Double Consciousness* [Cambridge, Mass.: Harvard University Press, 1993], 94).

41. Harry Shapiro and Caesar Glebbeek, *Jimi Hendrix: Electric Gypsy* (New York: St. Martin's Press, 1990), 312.

42. Jeremy Wells, "Blackness 'Scuzed: Jimi Hendrix's (In)visible Legacy in Heavy Metal," in *Race Consciousness: African-American Studies for the New Century*, ed. Judith Jackson Fossett and Jeffrey A. Tucker (New York: New York University Press, 1997), 56.

43. On Hendrix's "hybridity," see also Steve Waksman, *Instruments of Desire: The Electric Guitar and the Shaping of Musical Experience* (Cambridge, Mass.: Harvard University Press, 1999), 167–205; and Lauren Onkey, "Voodoo Child: Jimi Hendrix and the Politics of Race in the Sixties," in *Imagine Nation: The American Counterculture of the 1960s and '70s*, ed. Peter Braunstein and Michael William Doyle (New York: Routledge, 2002), 189–214.

44. Sengupta, "At Lunch With: Jessica Hagedorn."

45. Hagedorn, "Music for Gangsters," 254.

46. See Paul Gilroy, *Against Race: Imagining Political Culture beyond the Color Line* (Cambridge, Mass.: Harvard University Press, 2000).

47. See Jonathan Mayhew, *Apocryphal Lorca: Translation, Parody, Kitsch*

(Chicago: University of Chicago Press, 2009). For a Filipino poetic take, see Nick Carbó, *Andalusian Dawn* (Cincinnati: Cherry Grove Collections, 2004).

48. Jessica Hagedorn, "Solea," in *Dangerous Music*, n.p.; reprinted in Hagedorn, *Danger and Beauty*, 61. Further citations refer to the latter text.

49. María Frías, "Nights of Flamenco and Blues in Spain: From Sorrow Songs to *Soleá* and Back," in *Blackening Europe: The African American Presence*, ed. Heike Raphael-Hernandez (New York: Routledge, 2004), 141.

50. Ralph Ellison, "Flamenco" (1954), in *The Collected Essays of Ralph Ellison*, ed. John F. Callahan (New York: Modern Library, 1995), 9, 10–11.

51. Langston Hughes, *I Wonder as I Wander* (1956; repr., New York: Hill and Wang, 1993), 333.

52. Sascha Feinstein, "Epistrophies: Poems Celebrating Thelonious Monk and His Music," *African American Review* 31, no. 1 (1996): 56.

53. Harry Smallenburg, "Monk, Bop, and a New Poetics," *Caliban* 4 (1988): 36–37.

54. Hagedorn, "Exile Within," 176.

55. Nathaniel Mackey, "Cante Moro," in *Sound States: Innovative Poetics and Acoustical Technologies*, ed. Adalaide Morris (Chapel Hill: University of North Carolina Press, 1997), 195. Of all of Hagedorn's musically inflected poems, "Solea" is the only one included in the anthology *Moment's Notice: Jazz in Poetry & Prose*, ed. Art Lange and Nathaniel Mackey (Minneapolis: Coffee House Press, 1993), 330–332.

56. See Frías, "Nights of Flamenco," 143; Mackey, "Cante Negro," 195; and Gerhard Steingress, "Flamenco Fusion and New Flamenco as Postmodern Phenomena: An Essay on Creative Ambiguity in Popular Music," in *Songs of the Minotaur: Hybridity and Popular Music in the Era of Globalization*, ed. Gerhard Steingress (Munster: Lit Verlag, 2002), 169–216.

57. Jessica Hagedorn, "Los Gabrieles," in Hagedorn, *Danger and Beauty*, 209, 207.

58. E. San Juan Jr., "Mapping the Boundaries: The Filipino Writer in the U.S.A.," *Journal of Ethnic Studies* 19, no. 1 (1991): 118.

59. The language of "collage" and "montage" to describe *Dogeaters* saturates scholarship on the novel, and film and feminism (and, in a few cases, queer theory) are often linked. See Nerissa Balce-Cortes, "Imagining the Neocolony," *Hitting Critical Mass: A Journal of Asian American Cultural Criticism* 2, no. 2 (1995): 95–120; Juliana Chang, "Masquerade, Hysteria, and Neocolonial Femininity in Jessica Hagedorn's *Dogeaters*," *Contemporary Literature* 44, no. 4 (2003): 637–663; Giovanna Covi, "Jessica Hagedorn's Decolonialization of Subjectivity: Historical Agency beyond Gender and Nation," in *Nationalism and Sexuality: Crises of Identity*, ed. Yiorgos Kalogeras and Domna Pastourmatzi (Thessalonki, Greece: Hellenic Association of American Studies, 1996), 63–80; Maria Teresa de Manuel, "Jessica Hagedorn's *Dogeaters*: A Feminist

Reading," *Likha* 12, no. 2 (1990–1991): 10–32; Jacqueline Doyle, "'A Love Letter to My Motherland': Maternal Discourses in Jessica Hagedorn's *Dogeaters*," *Hitting Critical Mass: A Journal of Asian American Cultural Criticism* 4, no. 2 (1997): 1–25; Isaac, *American Tropics*, 149–177; Lee, *Americas of Asian American Literature*, 73–105; Myra Mendible, "Desiring Images: Representation and Spectacle in *Dogeaters*," *Critique: Studies in Contemporary Fiction* 43, no. 3 (2002): 289–304; Nguyen, *Race and Resistance*, 125–141; and Maria C. Zamora, *Nation, Race & History in Asian American Literature: Re-membering the Body* (New York: Peter Lang, 2008), 83–106. For a brilliant queer reading of Rio, see Victor Mendoza, "A Queer Nomadology of Jessica Hagedorn's *Dogeaters*," *American Literature* 77, no. 4 (2005): 815–845.

60. Lee, *Americas of Asian American Literature*, 87.

61. Hagedorn, *Dogeaters*, 233.

62. Isaac, *American Tropics*, 173.

63. Lee, *Americas of Asian American Literature*, 104.

64. See E. San Juan Jr., "Transforming Identity in Postcolonial Narrative: An Approach to the Novels of Jessica Hagedorn," *Post Identity* 1, no. 2 (1998): 10, 19; Mendible, "Desiring Images," 292; and Nguyen, *Race and Resistance*, 126–127, 139.

65. Kay Bonetti, "An Interview with Jessica Hagedorn," *Missouri Review* 18, no. 1 (1995): 96.

66. Hagedorn, *Danger and Beauty*, xl.

67. José Rizal, *Noli Me Tangere*, trans. María Soledad Lacson-Locsin (Honolulu: University of Hawai'i Press, 1997). Part 2 of *Dogeaters* opens with an epigraph from Rizal's novel (119).

68. For other readings of the maternal addressee, see de Manuel, "Jessica Hagedorn's *Dogeaters*," 29; and Doyle, "'Love Letter,'" 2.

69. Della G. Besa, "Our Signature Love Song," in *Kasaysayan: The Story of the Filipino People: A Timeline of Philippine History*, vol. 10, ed. Henry S. Totanes ([Hong Kong]: Asia Publishing, 1998), 124.

70. Ernesto V. Epistola, *Nicanor Abelardo: The Man and the Artist, a Biography* (Manila: Rex Book Store, 1996), 13.

71. Ibid., 49.

72. Quoted in ibid., 25.

73. Christi-Anne Castro, "Musical Mestizaje in the Pearl of the Orient," in *Musical Cultures of Latin America: Global Effects, Past and Present*, ed. Steven Loza (Los Angeles: Department of Ethnomusicology and Systematic Musicology, 2003), 297.

74. "The Spanish Colonial Tradition in Music," in *CCP Encyclopedia of Philippine Art: The Multimedia CD-ROM Edition* ([Manila]: Cultural Center of the Philippines, 1998), n.p.

75. Arsenio E. Manuel, *Francisco Santiago, Composer and Pianist Virtuoso*

(Quezon City: Valerio Publishing House for the Philippineasian Society, 1997), 21.

76. Epistola, *Nicanor Abelardo*, 111.

77. Ramón Pagayon Santos, *Tunugan: Four Essays on Filipino Music* (Quezon City: University of the Philippines Press, 2005), 16.

78. Ileto, *Pasyon and Revolution*, 105.

79. Ibid.

80. "I do italics instinctively," Hagedorn says in an interview. "Some of them were because they're meant to be in another voice than the poet's. . . . It's a way to suggest another voice" (Tabios, *Black Lightning*, 272).

81. Ileto, *Pasyon and Revolution*, 105.

82. See Manuel, *Francisco Santiago*, 105; and Castro, "Musical Mestizaje," 297.

83. Bonetti, "Interview with Jessica Hagedorn," 96.

84. Mackey, "Cante Moro," 203.

85. Hagedorn describes her poetic process in strikingly similar terms: "I can hear the poem. I actually hear it as I write. I hear voices in my head. When the poem takes control of me or takes over, it's writing itself" (Tabios, *Black Lightning*, 272).

86. Mackey, "Cante Moro," 198.

87. San Juan, "Transforming Identity," 9.

88. Doyle, "'Love Letter,'" 4.

89. Peter O'Leary, "An Interview with Nathaniel Mackey," *Chicago Review* 43, no. 1 (1997): 39.

90. Antonio J. Molina, "The Sentiments of Kundiman," in *Filipino Heritage: The Making of a Nation*, vol. 8 (Manila: Lahing Pilipino Publishing, 1978), 2026.

91. Besa, "Our Signature Love Song," 124; Ramón P. Santos, "Constructing a National Identity through Music," *Bulawan: Journal of Philippine Arts and Culture* 2 (2001): 29.

92. Stuart Hall, "Cultural Identity and Diaspora," in *Identity: Community, Culture, Difference*, ed. Jonathan Rutherford (London: Lawrence & Wishart, 1990), 236.

93. My thanks to Kimberly Alidio, Deirdre de la Cruz, and Sarita See for this exquisite phrase.

94. Kwame Anthony Appiah, "Is the Post- in Postmodernism the Post- in Postcolonial?" *Critical Inquiry* 17, no. 2 (1991): 349, 353.

95. Caroline Hau, "*Dogeaters*, Postmodernism and the 'Worlding' of the Philippines," in *Philippine Postcolonial Studies: Essays on Language and Literature*, ed. Cristina Pantoja Hidalgo and Priscelina Patajo-Legasto (1993; repr., Quezon City: University of the Philippines Press, 2004), 116.

96. Barbara Christian, "The Race for Theory," *Feminist Studies* 14, no. 1

(1988): 73, 71. See also Nancy Hartsock, "Rethinking Modernism: Minority vs. Majority Theories," *Cultural Critique* no. 7 (1987): 187–206.

97. See Ruth Jordana Luna Pison, *Alternative Histories: Martial Law Novels as Counter-Memory* (Quezon City: University of the Philippines Press, 2005), 71–84.

98. Hagedorn, *Gangster of Love*, 58.

### Notes to Chapter 5

1. For a brief survey of contemporary texts, see Patricia Justine Tumang, "Revelations and Revolutions: Queer Filipino Literature," *Lambda Book Report* (June/July 2005): 8–10. The issue also includes "an abbreviated book list" that cites anthologies, fiction, poetry, and nonfiction (14).

2. See, for example, the introductions to Eng and Hom, *Q & A*; and E. Patrick Johnson and Mae G. Henderson, eds., *Black Queer Studies* (Durham, N.C.: Duke University Press, 2005).

3. With the exception of Rio Gonzaga in Hagedorn, *Dogeaters*. See Lee, *Americas of Asian American Literature*, 99–105; and Mendoza, "Queer Nomadology," 815–845.

4. Chea Villanueva, "Girlfriends," in *Jessie's Song and Other Stories* (New York: Richard Kasak, 1995), 177.

5. Chea Villanueva, "The Chinagirls: A Butch and Femme Epistolary," in *Bulletproof Butches* (New York: Hard Candy, 1997), 129–130. See also Nice Rodriguez, "Stone Butch," in *Throw It to the River* (Toronto: Women's Press, 1993), 11–15.

6. On the meanings and politics of these terms as they circulate globally, see Fajardo, "Transportation," 403–424.

7. Jhoanna Lynn B. Cruz, "Writing Lesbian, Lesbian Writing: As a Struggling Lesbian Writer, Where Shall I Find a Literary Mother?" *Bulatlat* 5, no. 4 (2005), http://www.bulatlat.com/news/5-43/5-43-lesbian.htm (accessed August 19, 2009). Cruz has since published *Women Loving: Stories and a Play* (Pasig City: Anvil, 2010). See also Malu Marin, "Stolen Strands: The In and Out Lives of Lesbians in the Philippines," in *Amazon to Zami: Towards a Global Lesbian Feminism*, ed. Monika Reinfelder (London: Cassell, 1996), 30–55.

8. See Madge Bello and Vince Reyes, "Filipino Americans and the Marcos Overthrow: The Transformation of Political Consciousness," *Amerasia Journal* 13, no. 1 (1987): 73–84; Catherine Ceniza Choy, "Towards Trans-Pacific Social Justice: Women and Protest in Filipino American History," *Journal of Asian American Studies* 8, no. 3 (2005): 293–307; Barbara S. Gaerlan, "The Movement in the United States to Oppose Martial Law in the Philippines, 1972–1991: An Overview," *Pilipinas* 33 (1999): 75–98; Helen C. Toribio, "We Are Revolution: A Reflective History of the Union of

Democratic Filipinos (KDP)," *Amerasia Journal* 24, no. 2 (1998): 155–177; and Vergara, *Pinoy Capital*, 109–133. Trinity A. Ordona, "Asian Lesbians in San Francisco: Struggles to Create a Safe Space, 1970s–1980s," in *Asian/Pacific Islander American Women: A Historical Anthology*, ed. Shirley Hune and Gail M. Nomura (New York: New York University Press, 2003), 319–334, briefly discusses lesbians in the KDP. Gil Mangaoang, "From the 1970s to the 1990s: Perspective of a Gay Filipino American Activist," in *Asian American Sexualities*, ed. Russell Leong (New York: Routledge, 1996), 101–111, reflects on the author's difficulties reconciling his political activism with his sexuality.

9. On the rise of sex work in the Philippines, see Rene E. Ofreneo and Rosalinda Pineda Ofreneo, "Prostitution in the Philippines," in *The Sex Sector: The Economic and Social Bases of Prostitution in Southeast Asia*, ed. Lin Lean Lim (Geneva: International Labour Office, 1998), 100–129. On the political economy of martial law and international labor migration, see Parreñas, *Children of Global Migration*, 15–18; and Rodriguez, *Migrants for Export*, 9–14.

10. See Mendoza, "Queer Nomadology," 817.

11. Roces, *Women, Power, and Kinship Politics*, 1; Primitivo Mijares, *The Conjugal Dictatorship of Ferdinand and Imelda Marcos* (San Francisco: Union Square, 1976).

12. Rafael, *White Love*, 122.

13. Rolando Tolentino, "National Bodies and Sexualities," *Philippine Studies* 48, no. 1 (2000): 54, 57.

14. J. Neil C. Garcia, *Slip/pages: Essays in Philippine Gay Criticism (1991–1996)* (Manila: De La Salle University Press, 1998), 52.

15. Bino A. Realuyo, *The Umbrella Country* (New York: Ballantine, 1999), 5.

16. It is possible that Estrella is queer. Ninang Rola's explanation of her cousin's reluctance to date Germano is framed by this commentary: "*Stonewomen, that's what we called them in my time. They never got married, never had a need for men, for the love of men. Yes, that's what she was, a woman of stone*" (121). Toward the end of the novel, Gringo overhears a conversation between the two women in which Mommy reveals, "Whenever he touched me, my pores tightened, my throat clogged. I ended up gasping for air. Every time he touched me, my insides got all intertwined, as if my heart was going to burst out of my chest" (267). In effect, sex is rape for the married couple. As Gringo recalls to himself, "I could hear Mommy asking Daddy Groovie to stop, *stop, stop, I don't want any more*. That was how I was brought into the world. The same way Pipo was" (268). Whether Mommy is repulsed by Daddy Groovie because of what he did to her in the past and/or because she "*never had a need for men*" in general is unclear. Certainly, the novel never shows Estrella pursuing women or men.

17. For a less optimistic reading of the "circle scene," see Eleanor Ty, *The*

*Politics of the Visible in Asian North American Narratives* (Toronto: University of Toronto Press, 2004), 181–182.

18. Interestingly, Neil Garcia has published several letters he wrote to Realuyo (he does not print Realuyo's side of the correspondence) (J. Neil C. Garcia, "Notes from 'Umbrella Country': Letters to Bino Realuyo," in *Performing the Self: Occasional Prose* [Quezon City: University of the Philippines Press, 2003], 83-92). Garcia's letters remind us that novelistic "dialogues" across national borders have actual recipients and interlocutors. They also participate in what might be construed as a *transnational* politics of recognition that I briefly consider in the following chapter.

19. José Esteban Muñoz, *Disidentifications: Queers of Color and the Performance of Politics* (Minneapolis: University of Minnesota Press, 1999), 23, 11.

20. R. Zamora Linmark, *Rolling the R's* (New York: Kaya Press, 1995), 1.

21. Garcia, *Performing the Self*, 252. For readings of *Rolling the R's* that emphasize its multilingualism, see Joshua L. Miller, "Multilingual Narrative and the Refusal of Translation: Theresa Hak Kyung Cha's *Dictee* and R. Zamora Linmark's *Rolling the R's*," in *How Far Is America from Here?* ed. Theo D'haen, Paul Giles, Djelal Kadir, and Lois Parkinson Zamora (Amsterdam: Rodopi, 2005), 467–480; and Nubla, "Politics of Relation," 199–218.

22. Muñoz, *Disidentifications*, 33.

23. Steven Bruhm and Natasha Hurley, "Curiouser: On the Queerness of Children," introduction to *Curiouser: On the Queerness of Children*, ed. Steven Bruhm and Natasha Hurley (Minneapolis: University of Minnesota Press, 2004), xxv.

24. David L. Eng, *Racial Castration: Managing Masculinity in Asian America* (Durham, N.C.: Duke University Press, 2001), 225.

25. For a quite different reading of Vicente as a sacrificial figure who embodies melancholic loss, see Crystal Parikh, "Blue Hawaii: Asian Hawaiian Cultural Production and Racial Melancholia," *Journal of Asian American Studies* 5, no. 3 (2002): 212.

26. Noël Alumit, *Letters to Montgomery Clift* (San Francisco: MacAdam/Cage, 2002), 21.

27. Diana Fuss, *Identification Papers* (New York: Routledge, 1995), 1.

28. Ibid., 2.

29. As Bello and Reyes point out, "Not a few Filipino (and American) community leaders and publicists were suspected of hitting pay dirt as a result of wheeling and dealing with the Marcos machinery" ("Filipino Americans and the Marcos Overthrow," 79). Alumit alludes to this practice and explains that the Arangans, somewhat unknowingly, accepted a money-laundering proposal in exchange for expedited immigration papers and start-up investment funds for a small business in the United States (*Letters to Montgomery Clift*, 83, 192).

30. For a useful sexual critique of Clift biographies, see Thomas Waugh, *The*

*Fruit Machine: Twenty Years of Writings on Queer Cinema* (Durham, N.C.: Duke University Press, 2000), 93–100.

31. Mrs. Arangan decides to change Bong's name to Bob because, she alleges, it is "more appropriate for your life in the States" (55).

32. Hagedorn, "Blossoming of Bongbong," in Hagedorn, *Danger and Beauty*, 50.

33. Cathy Caruth, *Unclaimed Experience: Trauma, Narrative, and History* (Baltimore: Johns Hopkins University Press, 1996), 61. Caruth further explains, "the survival of trauma is not the fortunate passage beyond a violent event, a passage that is accidentally interrupted by reminders of it, but rather the endless *inherent necessity* of repetition, which ultimately may lead to destruction" (62–63).

34. Alumit reflexively comments on narrative formulas: "Logan once told me he wrote 'formula' screenplays. He wrote movies where the lovers managed to get together in the end, where the good guys always won, and no matter how poor or disheveled a family was, they managed to afford great gifts for the children at Christmas. He believed all that stuff. He believed in formula; it worked. In a formulaic manner, he said, 'I'll stick by you.' Good. And I loved him a little more" (*Letters to Montgomery Clift*, 209).

35. Jeff Zaleski, review of *Letters to Montgomery Clift*, by Noël Alumit, *Publishers Weekly* 249, no. 4 (January 28, 2002): 270.

36. Caruth, *Unclaimed Experience*, 8.

37. The one interracial scene when Bong embarks on his short-lived sexual spree is treated cursorily. A white guy asks him, "What are you? Chinese? Vietnamese?" Bong replies, "Filipino." Paul says, "You were tasty. Gimme your number." Bong gives him made-up numbers (153).

38. Bruhm and Hurley, "Curiouser," x.

39. See Garcia, *Philippine Gay Culture*; Michael Tan, "From Bakla to Gay: Shifting Gender Identities and Sexual Behaviors in the Philippines," in *Conceiving Sexuality: Approaches to Sex Research in a Postmodern World*, ed. John G. Parker and John H. Gagnon (New York: Routledge, 1995); Michael L. Tan, "Survival through Pluralism: Emerging Gay Communities in the Philippines," in *Gay and Lesbian Asia: Culture, Identity, Community*, ed. Gerard Sullivan and Peter A. Jackson (New York: Harrington Park Press, 2001), 117–142; Manalansan, *Global Divas*; Bobby Benedicto, "The Haunting of Gay Manila: Global Space-Time and the Specter of *Kabaklaan*," *GLQ: A Journal of Lesbian and Gay Studies* 14, nos. 2–3 (2008): 317–338; and Bobby Benedicto, "Desiring Sameness: Globalization, Agency, and the Filipino Gay Imaginary," *Journal of Homosexuality* 55, no. 2 (2008): 274–311.

40. Victor Bascara, *Model-Minority Imperialism* (Minneapolis: University of Minnesota Press, 2006), 120.

41. On queerness as a utopian, future-oriented impulse, see José Esteban

Muñoz, *Cruising Utopia: The Then and There of Queer Futurity* (New York: New York University Press, 2009).

### Notes to Chapter 6

1. M. Evelina Galang, *One Tribe* (Kalamazoo: Western Michigan University Press, 2006), 120.

2. On the last aspect, see Nick Carbó, introduction to *Pinoy Poetics*, v–xi.

3. See, *Decolonized Eye*, xxxiii.

4. Yen Le Espiritu, *Filipino American Lives* (Philadelphia: Temple University Press, 1995), 198.

5. Leny Mendoza Strobel, *Coming Full Circle: The Process of Decolonization among Post-1965 Filipino Americans* (Quezon City: Giraffe Books, 2001), 141, 142.

6. Ibid., 169.

7. For a more optimistic reading of "Filipino cultural values" that are "centered on the family" and the children's "future socioeconomic security," see Jonathan Y. Okamura, *Imagining the Filipino American Diaspora: Transnational Relations, Identities, and Communities* (New York: Garland, 1998), 27.

8. Strobel, *Coming Full Circle*, 92.

9. Emily Noelle Ignacio, *Building Diaspora: Filipino Cultural Community Formation on the Internet* (New Brunswick, N.J.: Rutgers University Press, 2005), 41.

10. Espiritu, *Filipino American Lives*, xi.

11. Strobel, *Coming Full Circle*, 135.

12. Espiritu, *Filipino American Lives*, ix; Ignacio, *Building Diaspora*, 49.

13. Espiritu, *Home Bound*, 196.

14. The notion that knowledge is constitutive of identity is not limited to college students. Strobel, for example, writes: "Without this knowledge [about Philippine history and culture], the claim to being Filipino American is mere 'form' without substance" ("'Born-Again Filipino,'" 353). My analysis here is not meant to single out specific individuals. The very pervasiveness of claims to "invisibility" in the expansive sense indicates the trope's prevalence—hence, why I read it as a *discourse* rather than as random, idiosyncratic utterances.

15. Walter W. Marquardt, "Interesting Experiences of Pensionados Related," *Philippines Herald Magazine*, August 14, 1939. For other examples during this period, see Takaki, *Strangers from a Different Shore*, 324–325.

16. Espiritu, *Home Bound*, 186–193.

17. Elizabeth H. Pisares, "Do You Mis(recognize) Me: Filipina Americans in Popular Music and the Problem of Invisibility," in Tiongson, Gutierrez, and Gutierrez, *Positively No Filipinos Allowed*, 174, 173.

18. Espiritu, *Home Bound*, 197. See also, Okamura, *Imagining the Filipino American Diaspora*, 27.

19. Espiritu, *Home Bound*, 11, 196.

20. Tadiar, *Fantasy-Production*, 152, 155.

21. Mendoza, *Between the Homeland and the Diaspora*, 11–12.

22. Wendy Brown, *States of Injury: Power and Freedom in Late Modernity* (Princeton, N.J.: Princeton University Press, 1995), 74.

23. Strobel's essay "'Born-Again Filipino'" is explicitly cast as a critique of "Asian panethnic consciousness" (349).

24. Strobel, *Coming Full Circle*, ix.

25. Ibid., 20.

26. A few recall encountering Carlos Bulosan's autobiographical *America Is in the Heart* (1946). See Strobel, *Coming Full Circle*, 165, 169, 174. For an incisive reading of Pilipino Cultural Nights as partly compensation for lack of formal ethnic education on the part of West Coast Filipino American college students, see Gonzalves, *The Day the Dancers Stayed*.

27. M. Evelina Galang, *Her Wild American Self* (Minneapolis: Coffee House Press, 1996), 12.

28. Maxine Hong Kingston, *The Woman Warrior: Memoirs of a Girlhood among Ghosts* (New York: Vintage, 1976).

29. Espiritu, *Home Bound*, 160.

30. On this point, see Helena Grice, "Artistic Creativity, Form, and Fictional Experimentation in Filipina American Fiction," *MELUS* 29, no. 1 (2004): 181–198.

31. Galang does portray family gatherings and community functions as a way to document Filipino American social life in the Midwest, particularly in "Our Fathers" and "Miss Teenage Sampaguita." She also recalls growing up in the midst of such community activities in the Milwaukee suburb of Brookfield. See "The Struggle for Form: A Conversation between Nick Carbó and M. Evelina Galang," *MELUS* 29, no. 1 (2004): 283–284.

32. Brian Ascalon Roley, *American Son* (New York: W. W. Norton, 2001), 21.

33. Brian Ascalon Roley, "*American Son* Epilogue," in Brainard, *Growing Up Filipino*, 104.

34. David L. Eng and Shinhee Han, "A Dialogue on Racial Melancholia," in *Loss: The Politics of Mourning*, ed. David L. Eng and David Kazanjian (Berkeley: University of California Press, 2003), 344.

35. Robert G. Diaz, "Melancholic Maladies: Paranoid Ethics, Reparative Envy, and Asian American Critique," *Women & Performance* 16, no. 2 (2006): 202.

36. Eng and Han, "Dialogue," 347.

37. Eleanor Ty, "Abjection, Masculinity, and Violence in Brian Roley's *American Son* and Han Ong's *Fixer Chao*," *MELUS* 29, no. 1 (2004): 126.

38. Diaz, "Melancholic Maladies," 206.

39. On the history of Filipino gangs in Los Angeles, see Bangele D. Alsaybar, "Filipino American Youth Gangs, 'Party Culture,' and Ethnic Identity in Los Angeles," in *The Second Generation: Ethnic Identity among Asian Americans*, ed. Pyong Gap Min (Walnut Creek, Calif.: AltaMira Press, 2002), 129–152.

40. Ty, "Abjection, Masculinity, and Violence," 123.

41. Diane L. Wolf, "Family Secrets: Transnational Struggles among Children of Filipino Immigrants," *Sociological Perspectives* 40, no. 3 (1997): 459.

42. Peñaranda, Syquia, and Tagatac, "Introduction to Filipino-American Literature," 49.

43. Joel B. Tan, "Brown Faggot Poet: Notes on Zip File Poetry, Cultural Nomadism, and the Politics of Publishing," in Carbó, *Pinoy Poetics*, 317, 319.

44. Patrick Rosal, "A Pinoy Needle in a B-Boy Groove: Notes on Poetry and Cross-Genre Influence in the Generation of Hip Hop," in Carbó, *Pinoy Poetics*, 268.

45. Patrick Rosal, *Uprock Headspin Scramble and Dive* (New York: Persea Books, 2003), 3–4.

46. Langston Hughes, "Laughers," in *Fine Clothes to the Jew* (New York: Alfred A. Knopf, 1927), 77–78.

47. Patrick Rosal, *My American Kundiman* (New York: Persea Books, 2006), xi.

48. Anne Anlin Cheng, *The Melancholy of Race* (Oxford: Oxford University Press, 2000), 23.

49. In a conversation (November 13, 2008), Rosal mentioned that he felt he needed to choose which direction his poems, as *kundimans*, should face, expressing dissatisfaction with both the necessity to decide and with the choice that ended up in the preface. I am, in turn, suggesting that the poems are oriented in multiple directions.

50. Pisares, "Do You Mis(recognize) Me," 191.

51. Barbara Jane Reyes, *Poeta en San Francisco* (Kaneohe, Hawai'i: Tinfish Press, 2005), 21.

52. Luzviminda Francisco, "The First Vietnam: The U.S.-Philippine War of 1899," *Bulletin of Concerned Asian Scholars* 5 (1973): 2–16.

53. Garcia, "Notes from 'Umbrella Country,'" 91.

54. Eric Gamalinda, "One Hundred Years of Invisibility," *Manoa: A Pacific Journal of International Writing* 9, no. 2 (1997): 41.

**Notes to the Epilogue**

1. Galang, *Her Wild American Self*, 183.

2. Gonzalez and Campomanes, "Filipino American Literature," 75.

3. Ileto, *Filipinos and Their Revolution*, 177–201; Rafael, "Parricides, Bastards and Counterrevolution," 361–375.

4. Mojares, *Waiting for Mariang Makiling*, 307.

5. Gina Apostol, *The Revolution According to Raymundo Mata* (Pasig City: Anvil, 2009), 290.

6. In addition to Ileto, see also Hau, *Necessary Fictions*, 214–242.

7. The copious footnoted annotations written by Estrella, Dr. Diwata, and Mimi are in italics.

8. Tadiar, *Fantasy-Production*, 155.

9. See Ambeth R. Ocampo, *Makamisa: The Search for Rizal's Third Novel*, rev. ed. (Pasig City: Anvil, 2008).

10. In her ironic "Abecedary of the Revolution," Mimi C. Magsalin asserts that "*Plagiarism*" is a "form of flattery" (18), and, under the entry "*Forgers*," writes: "Though forgery is, okay, a felony, aren't such attempts also an extreme form of *cryptomania*, a kind of love for the revolution?" (15), reflexively alluding to Raymundo's theft. Mimi also notes in the entry "*Magsalin*" that the matronymic name of the *Noli*'s hero is also "a pun. It means the infinitive transitive verb 'to translate' as well as 'to transfuse,' as in blood" (17). Dr. Diwata draws attention to Mimi's clever name: "is it possible that the Translator, the pseudonymous Mimic, has had us in the trap of her infernal arts all along, and history is only a blind alley of her imagination?" (278).

11. Tadiar, *Things Fall Away*, 305, 329.

12. In the "*Fil-Am*" entry of her "Abecedary," Mimi jokes: "It is easier for a rich man to go through the eye of a camel than it is for a *Fil-Am* to understand his parents' country" (14–15).

13. Tadiar, *Fantasy-Production*, 265.

# Index

Abad, Gémino H., 59, 237n4, 244n71, 247n103
Abelardo, Nicanor, 145
Abinales, Patricio N., 116
address: articulation and, 21–22; diasporic Filipino literature and, 2, 3, 14, 18–19, 20–21, 25, 222; letters and, 24–25; Mablango and, 25; Philippine nationalism and, 30, 33, 36–38, 55–56; U.S. colonial discourse and, 31–35. *See also* diasporic Filipino literature; modes of address *under individual authors*; queer diasporic reading
Agoncillo, Felipe, 32–33, 40
Aguinaldo, Emilio, 32, 33, 44, 46, 47, 226
*Aiiieeeee!* (Chin, Chan, Inada, Wong), 5–6, 122, 238n13, 264n13
Alegre, Edilberto N., 243n61, 252n5, 255n32
Alexander, M. Jacqui, 26
Alidio, Kimberly, 249n18, 269n93
Alumit, Noël: 3, 153, 156, 184, 222; America as burden, 176; Clift, Montgomery, 172–174, 180–181, 221; coming out, 173, 181; gender, 179–180; homoeroticism in, 173–174; letters, 172, 177–179; *Letters to Montgomery Clift*, 171–181, 183, 221; martial law, 171, 173, 179; modes of address, 172, 178, 180; trauma, 171, 174–177, 180

Anderson, Benedict, 17, 45, 241n39, 243n59, 243n67
Anderson, Warwick, 249n21, 266n39
Anti-Imperialist League, 32, 250n22
Apacible, Galicano, 37–38
Apostol, Gina: 3; metafictional, 225, 229, 230; modes of address, 224, 231; "queer" subjectivity, 223, 230–232; reading, 224–225, 227–228, 230; resurrection, 228, 231; *Revolution According to Raymundo Mata, The*, 223–232; sexuality, 226–227
Appiah, K. Anthony, 150, 240n32
Arguilla, Manuel, 98, 101
articulation, 2, 21–22, 25
assimilation: 2, 222; Alumit and, 176–177; Bulosan and, 97; Galang and, 186, 196, 205; Hagedorn and, 124–125, 128; Kalaw and, 39; Linmark and, 164; Realuyo and, 163; Reyes and, 213; Roley and, 186, 197–198, 199–200, 204–205; Rosal and, 208–209; U.S. colonialism and, 12, 35–36, 218; Villa and, 57, 60–61, 67, 72–73, 85, 97

Balce, Nerissa, 10, 30, 238n16, 239n18, 267n59
Baraka, Amiri (LeRoi Jones), 120, 127
Bascara, Victor, 183
Bautista, Maria Lourdes S., 238n11, 244n71

Bell Trade Act (1946), 102
Bello, Madge, 270n8, 272n29
Benedicto, Bobby, 182
Benevolent Assimilation, 2, 7, 26,
   34–36, 61, 249n16. *See also* colo-
   nialism, U.S.
Benston, Kimberly W., 127
Besa, Della G., 268n69, 269n91
Beveridge, Alfred J., 32
blues, 133, 137–138, 152
Bocobo, Jorge, 58, 65, 77
Bolton, Kingsley, 238n11, 244n71
Bonetti, Kay, 268n65, 269n83
Bonifacio, Andres, 106, 146, 227,
   248n6
Brown, Wendy, 191
Bruhm, Steven, 182, 272n23
Bulosan, Carlos: 3, 120, 222; *America
   Is in the Heart*, 13, 90, 92–99, 100,
   101, 108, 112, 114–115, 117, 120,
   122, 264n13, 275n26; anti-imperialism, 102–104; Asian American
   studies and, 92, 264n13; "Autobiographical Sketch," 92, 106; *Chorus
   for America*, 87, 103; collaboration
   with Yabes, 117–119; *Cry and the
   Dedication, The*, 13, 89–91, 99–
   116, 221; gender politics, 96–97,
   98, 101, 109–115; homoeroticism
   in, 94; "How My Stories Were
   Written," 106; "I Am Not a Laughing Man," 117, 262n38; "Letter
   to Taruc," 106–107, 217; literacy,
   95–99, 107–108; modes of address,
   91, 98–99, 103, 105–107; pastoralism, 98–102, 111; Philippine literature in English and, 19, 92, 98,
   118–119, 259n10, 263n62; "queer,"
   117; radicalism, 91, 98–101, 102–
   105, 109, 110, 114–115; reception
   of, 19, 90–93; sexual politics, 91,
   92–97, 107–116; Taruc and, 91, 98,

102–107, 109; on Villa, 88; *Voice of
   Bataan, The*, 114
Burgos, Manuel, Jr., 76–77
Butler, Judith, 27

Cabusao, Jeffrey Arellano, 102, 259n7
Campomanes, Oscar V., 6, 8, 13, 222,
   238n11, 239n16, 241n41, 244n75,
   247n103
Carbó, Nick, 238n11, 244n74,
   247n103; 253n16, 267n47, 274n2,
   275n31
Caruth, Cathy, 180, 273n33
Casper, Leonard, 87, 255n35
Castro, Christi-Anne, 268n73,
   269n82
Chari, Madhav, 127
Chase, Gilbert, 137
Cheung, King-Kok, 237n8, 238n11
Christian, Barbara, 151, 152
Chua, Jonathan, 243n57, 252n4,
   253n13, 254n18, 254n20, 254n22,
   257n58, 258n72
Chuh, Kandice, 6, 12, 26, 94, 242n52
Churchill, Bernardita, 39
Clarke Amendment (1916), 43, 45
colonialism, U.S.: amnesia of, 7, 8,
   9, 243n58; Apostol and, 231; Benevolent Assimilation and, 34–36;
   Bulosan and, 95, 102–104; debates
   about, 7; education and, 15–16, 18,
   243n68, 249n18; Hagedorn and,
   142, 149, 150; Kalaw and, 39–45,
   52–53; Linmark and, 170; migration and, 8; Philippine-American
   War and, 6–10, 31–39; Reyes and,
   212–213; Roley and, 198; Rosal
   and, 208; U.S. literature and, 9;
   Villa and, 15–16; visualities and,
   239n26; World's Fair (1904) and,
   240n26. *See also under* diasporic
   Filipino literature

Coltrane, John, 124, 126–128, 135, 138

community: Alumit and, 173, 181; Apostol and, 223–224, 231–232; Bulosan and, 92–93, 98, 100, 101, 104, 107, 119; diaspora and, 21, 23, 25; diasporic Filipino literature and, 25; Galang and, 184, 192–193, 196; Hagedorn and, 123, 129, 142, 147, 149–150; Kalaw and, 54; Linmark and, 168; nation and, 2; queer martial law literature and, 157; Realuyo and, 160–161; Reyes and, 186, 215–217; Roley and, 199, 200; Rosal and, 186, 206–207, 208, 209, 211; Villa and, 84–85. *See also* assimilation; nationalism, Philippine

Constantino, Renato, 16

Cordova, Fred, 239n23, 251n45

Cruz, Denise, 51, 238n11, 247n2, 256n46, 259n6

Cruz, Jhoanna Lynn B., 154

cultural nationalism, 2, 3, 122–123

Daguio, Amador, 75

Davis, Miles, 130, 133, 137

Davis, Rocío G., 239n16, 244n73

Deutsch, Babette, 14

diaspora: address and, 14, 21, 25; as analytical frame, 2, 14, 19, 25; as gendered international migration, 22–23, 245n87; letters and, 23, 246n90; literature and, 24, 246n91; queer and, 25–26, 181

diasporic Filipino literature: Asian American literature and, 5–6, 238n13; contemporary flourishing of, 1; diversity of, 1, 3, 191, 222, 223; framing of, 2, 3, 14, 19, 25; lack of scholarship on, 1, 5, 222; literary history and, 2, 223; modes

of address and, 2, 3, 14, 18–19, 20, 25; periodization and, 27–28; Philippine literature in English and, 5–6, 19, 218–219, 223, 238n12; "queerness" of, 2; scarcity of, 5, 28, 238n11; U.S. colonialism and, 2, 6, 7, 238n16. *See also individual authors*

Diaz, Robert, 197–198, 200

Doyle, Jacqueline, 148, 268n59, 268n68

*duende*, 140–141, 148

Edelman, Lee, 54

Edwards, Brent Hayes, 21–22

Ellison, Ralph, 137, 138

Eng, David L., 26, 197, 199, 247n100, 270n2, 272n24

Espiritu, Augusto Fauni, 237n2, 253n13, 254n18, 256n48, 263n62

Espiritu, Yen Le, 10, 186–188, 189–190, 195, 239n23, 241n36

Faigao, Cornelio, 79, 257n61

Fajardo, Kale, 245n87, 270n6

Feinstein, Sascha, 138

Ferguson, Roderick A., 95

Feria, Dolores S., 242n51

Fernandez, Doreen, 243n61, 252n5, 255n32

Filipino American literature. See diasporic Filipino literature

Filipino identity: Asian American and, 6, 190; cross-racial identification and, 134, 190, 197, 200, 205–206; cross-racialization of, 10, 189, 241n37, 242n46; diasporic Filipino literature and, 14, 191–192, 219, 222; heterogeneity of, 6, 12, 28, 152; instability of, 10–13, 21, 26; knowledge and, 184–185, 186–188; misrecognition of, 186,

189–190, 192, 201, 211–212; names for, 11–12, 241n45; Philippine history and, 190–191; *Sikolohiyang Pilipino* (Filipino psychology) and, 191. *See also* identity politics; "invisibility"

Filipino studies: 13–14, 22, 223, 232; Asian American studies and, 6; literature and, 1; U.S. colonialism and, 8

flamenco, 124, 135, 137–138, 140–141, 148

Flips generation, 5, 19, 28, 122, 186

Francia, Luis H., 85, 87, 118, 239n26

Frías, María, 137, 267n56

Fujita-Rony, Dorothy, 239n23, 251n44

Fuss, Diana, 172–173

Gaerlan, Barbara S., 242n49, 270n8

Galang, Evelina M.: 3, 185–186, 222; discipline, 194, 195; gender, 192–194, 195; *Her Wild American Self*, 192–196, 201, 205, 212, 221; Midwest, 196; misrecognition, 186, 192–193; modes of address, 192, 195–196, 205; *One Tribe*, 184–185; racism, 194–195; reading and identity, 184–185; sexuality, 195–196

Gamalinda, Eric, 219

Garcia, J. Neil C., 60, 157, 163, 182, 218, 272n18, 272n21

Gilroy, Paul, 134, 266n40

Gonzalez, Andrew, 18, 243n59

Gonzalez, N. V. M., 5, 238n11

Gonzalves, Theodore S., 242n49, 275n26

Gopinath, Gayatri, 26

Grey, De Sayles, 127

Hagedorn, Jessica: 3, 184, 222;

"Blossoming of Bongbong, The," 124–128, 135, 138, 141, 174; on Bulosan, 122; cross-cultural poetics, 120–121, 123–124, 127, 128–129, 132–135, 137, 263n4; *Danger and Beauty*, 123, 144; *Dogeaters*, 1, 20, 116, 124, 141–151, 155–156, 183, 221, 270n3; Filipino American arts scene, 122–123; Gangster Choir, The, 120, 121, 123; *Gangster of Love, The*, 120–121, 124, 128–135, 150, 152, 184, 206; gender, 128–130, 134–135, 136, 142, 147; homoeroticism in, 125, 128, 153, 155; "Los Gabrieles," 141; mimicry, 131–132; modes of address, 20, 124, 133, 135, 143–147, 150, 151; multicultural, 121, 129; "Music for Gangsters," 121, 123, 129, 132, 133; postmodernism, 131, 141–142, 151; queer politics, 124–126, 128, 147, 155–156; reception of, 20, 122, 144, 150–152, 267n59; "Solea," 124, 135–141, 148; on Villa, 253n16

Halberstam, Judith, 67, 247n100

Hall, James, 127, 128

Hall, Stuart, 21–22, 149

Han, Shinhee, 197, 199

Hau, Caroline, 113, 150–152, 248n5, 277n6

Hendrix, Jimi, 124, 130, 132–135

Hentoff, Nat, 128, 137

Hoganson, Kristin, 10, 251n41

Hughes, Langston, 137–138, 140, 208, 209

Hukbalahap rebellion, 89–90, 102, 105, 110, 115. *See also* Taruc, Luis

Hurley, Natasha, 182, 272n23

Hutcheon, Linda, 2

identity politics, 9–10, 12, 13–14, 185,

219, 240n32, 242n49, 245n81. *See also* Filipino identity; representation, politics of
Ignacio, Emily Noelle, 187, 274n12
Ileto, Reynaldo C., 30, 146–147, 223, 242n49, 248n6, 248n7, 249n21, 250n25, 252n55
immigration. *See* migration
Immigration and Naturalization Act (1965), 8
imperialism, U.S. *See* colonialism, U.S.
"invisibility": 28, 56, 185, 211, 222; knowledge and, 186–189, 190–192; reading and, 218–219; Roley and, 197; U.S. colonialism and, 8–10, 12, 14; U.S. literature and, 9
Isaac, Allan Punzalan, 10, 22, 93, 142, 241n40, 268n59

Japanese occupation, 1, 17, 89, 105, 195
Javellana, Stevan, 5, 259n6, 263n59
Jesús, Melinda Luisa María de, 93, 94
Joaquin, Nick, 9, 12–13, 243n63, 254n18, 254n29
Jones Law (1916), 30, 39–40, 43, 248n4

Kalaw, Maximo M.: 3, 222; biography, 39; *Filipino Rebel, The*, 22, 29–30, 43–55, 60, 114, 221; genre, 29–31; independence writings, 39–44; modes of address, 30–31, 51–52, 55–57; reproductive heterosexuality and nationalism, 22, 30–31, 53–55
Kaplan, Amy, 241n34, 249n19, 251n41
Katipunan: 248n6, 262n40; Apostol and, 224, 225, 226, 227; Bulosan and, 104, 106; Hagedorn and, 146–147; Kalaw and, 30

Keenaghan, Eric, 59
Kerkvliet, Benedict J., 258n3, 263n51
Kim, Elaine H., 9, 240n32, 260n22
Kingston, Maxine Hong, 194, 200, 203
Kipling, Rudyard, 9, 32
Kramer, Paul, 10, 35, 39, 56, 249n20
*kundiman*: Hagedorn and, 120, 124, 141, 143, 144–150; Linmark and, 170; Rosal and, 208–210

language, politics of: 244n69, 244n70, 244n71; Hagedorn and, 20; Japanese occupation and, 17; Linmark and, 272n21; Reyes and, 211–212; Rosal and, 209; U.S. colonialism and, 15–19
Lanzona, Vina A., 110, 115
Lee, Rachel, 142, 260n17, 268n59, 270n3
Libretti, Tim, 105, 107, 259n7
Lim, Jaime An, 9.
Linmark, R. Zamora: 3, 153, 156, 184, 222; friendship, 169–170; gender, 164–165; genre, 164; homoeroticism in, 166–167; homophobia, 164–166; martial law, 169–170; modes of address, 170–171; patriarchy, 167–168, 169–170; popular culture, 164–166, 167–168, 170; *Rolling the R's*, 164–171, 181, 183, 221
Lopez, Clemencia, 51
Lopez, Salvador P., 17, 75–77, 98
Lorca, Federico García, 120, 135, 141, 148, 211
Lowe, Lisa, 6, 242n52

Mabini, Apolinario, 33, 44
Mablango, [Ruth] Elynia S., 24–25
Mackey, Nathaniel, 15, 140–141, 148, 149, 267n56

Manalansan, Martin F., 26, 85, 182, 241n44, 247n100
Manlapaz, Edna Zapanta, 16, 17, 243n65, 244n72, 254n22, 254n25
Manuel, Maria Teresa de, 267n59, 268n68
Marcos, Ferdinand and Imelda, 1, 143, 153, 155–156. *See also* martial law
martial law: Alumit and, 171, 173, 175–176, 179, 180; antimartial law movement and, 154, 270n8; gender and sexual politics of, 153, 154, 155–156; Hagedorn and, 141–143, 151, 155; Linmark and, 169–170; Realuyo and, 157–159, 163; Reyes and, 214
Martinez-Sicat, Maria Teresa, 31
McKinley, William, 7, 33, 34–35, 38, 41. *See also* Benevolent Assimilation
Mendible, Myra, 268n59, 268n64
Mendoza, S. Lily, 191, 192, 242n47, 242n52, 245n81
Mendoza, Victor, 237n4, 268n59, 270n3, 271n10
migration: 188, 239n23; gender and, 50–51; U.S. colonialism and, 8, 10, 36
Miller, Stuart Creighton, 7, 9, 33, 241n37, 249n12, 249n20
Mojares, Resil B., 17–18, 223–224
Molina, Antonio, 145, 269n90
Monk, Thelonious, 124, 135, 136, 138–41, 148
multiculturalism, 11, 183, 188–189
Muñoz, José Esteban, 164, 165, 247n100, 273n41

nationalism, Philippine: 10–11; Apostol and, 223, 226, 227; Bulosan and, 104–105; gender and

sexuality of, 25, 57, 111, 155–157, 248n5; Hagedorn and, 145–147, 155–157; independence missions and, 39; Kalaw and, 30–31, 45–55; language and, 18, 244n71; Villa and, 60, 83–84, 88
New People's Army, 142, 155, 263n52
Nguyen, Viet Thanh, 109, 113, 260n22, 268n59, 268n64
Nubla, Gladys, 245n77, 272n21
Nugent, Richard Bruce, 256n40

Okamura, Jonathan Y., 252n45, 274n7, 275n18

Panlilio, Yay, 238n11, 259n6
Paras, Loreto (Loreto Paras-Sulit), 62, 254n25
Parreñas, Rhacel Salazar, 57, 246n87, 246n90, 262n43, 271n9
*pasyon* (passion), 146–147, 149
Pedrosa, Pio, 29–30
"People Power" revolution, 142–143, 154
Philippine-American War. *See under* colonialism, U.S.
Pisares, Elizabeth H., 190, 210–211
Platt Amendment (1903), 40
postcolonial: 2; Apostol and, 230; Hagedorn and, 131, 144, 149, 150; history and, 190; literary studies and, 9, 28, 218–219; queerness and, 26, 183
postmodernism, 131, 141–142, 150–151
Puar, Jasbir K., 26

queer: 25–27; diaspora and, 2, 25, 26–27, 181, 246n96, 247n100; Filipino culture and, 182; Filipino women's literature and, 153–154; identity and, 219, 223; interracial

desire and, 71, 181; nationalism and, 25, 157; race and, 153
queer diasporic reading: 2–3, 14, 25–28, 218–219, 222, 232; Alumit and, 180; Apostol and, 224; articulation and, 22; Bulosan and, 91, 98–99, 112–113, 115–116; contemporary Filipino American literature and, 186; Galang and, 195–196, 205; Hagedorn and, 121, 124, 144; Kalaw and, 31; Linmark and, 170–171; queer martial law literature and, 156–157, 182–183; Realuyo and, 161, 162–163; Reyes and, 217–218; Roley and, 201–203, 205; Rosal and, 208–209; Villa and, 60, 61, 85, 88. *See also* address
Quezon, Manuel, 39, 43, 51, 250n27

racial melancholia, 197–198, 200–201
Rafael, Vicente: on address, 21; on "Filipino," 11; on Marcosian nationalism, 156; on mimicry, 266n39; on mourning, 30; on revolutionary nationalism, 46–47, 223, 262n40; on Villa, 254n25
Realuyo, Bino: 3, 153, 156, 184, 218, 222; *bakla*, 159–160; gender, 158, 160, 163, 271n16; homoeroticism in, 160–162; martial law, 157–159, 163; modes of address, 162–163; patriarchy, 158–159, 160; *Umbrella Country, The,* 157–163, 181, 183, 221
recognition, politics of: diasporic Filipino literature and, 2, 87, 118, 218–219; Filipino studies and, 13–14, 19, 223; nationalism and, 30–31, 33, 42, 56; Villa and, 79, 82, 83–84. *See also* Filipino identity; identity politics; representation, politics of
representation, politics of: diasporic

Filipino literature and, 14, 20, 28; Hagedorn and, 20; Kalaw and, 39, 42–44; nationalism and, 36–38, 56; U.S. colonialism and, 10; U.S. literature and, 9, 240n31. *See also* address; identity politics
Reyes, Barbara Jane: 3, 185–186, 222; *Apocalypse Now,* 214–215; cross-cultural, 211, 213, 215–217; gender and sexuality, 212–213; modes of address, 213, 215, 217–218; *Hearts of Darkness,* 214; Marcos, 214; *Poeta en San Francisco,* 211–218; Vietnam/American War, 212, 213–214, 217
Reyes, Vince, 270n8, 272n29
Rizal, José, 88, 144, 224–231
Roces, Mina, 51–52, 54–55, 156, 248n5, 252n47
Rodriguez, Dylan, 239n20
Rodriguez, Robyn Magalit, 246n87, 271n9
Roley, Brian Ascalon: 3, 185–186, 192, 222; *American Son,* 196–205, 221; California, 196; cross-racial identification, 197, 200; "delinquency," 200; discipline, 198–200, 203–205; gender, 198, 200, 202–203, 204–205; mixed-race, 197, 200, 202, 204; modes of address, 192, 203–205; racism, 198, 200, 201; sexuality, 201–203, 204–205
Rosal, Patrick: 3, 185–186, 222; cross-cultural poetics, 206, 207–208, 210, 211; gender, 207; hip-hop, 206–207, 208, 210; *kundiman,* 208; modes of address, 208–209; *My American Kundiman,* 208–210; sexuality, 208–210; *Uprock Headspin Scramble and Dive,* 206–208
Rosca, Ninotchka, 116

San Juan, E., Jr.: on Bulosan, 90,
258n2, 259n5, 259n7, 259n9,
264n13; on Filipino studies, 6,
237n2, 238n16; on Hagedorn,
141–142, 148, 268n64; on U.S. colonialism, 12, 241n35; on Villa, 19,
60, 71, 253n9, 255n36, 258n64
Santiago, Francisco, 145
Santos, Bienvenido, 5, 238n11
Santos, Ramón, 146, 269n91
See, Sarita Echavez, 12, 22, 26, 30,
186, 237n6, 241n34, 269n93
Sengupta, Somini, 245n78, 263n1,
265n21, 266n44
Sinfield, Alan, 247n97, 257n55
Strobel, Leny Mendoza, 187, 188,
237n1, 242n52, 245n81, 274n14,
275n23, 275n24, 275n25, 275n26

Tabios, Eileen, 237n9, 243n55
Tadiar, Neferti, 24, 190–191, 225, 230,
232, 246n88, 246n93
Tagatac, Sam, 5, 205–206
Takaki, Ronald, 239n23, 260n19,
274n15
Tan, Joel B., 206
Tan, Michael, 182
Taruc, Luis, 91, 98, 102–107, 109
Teodoro, Luis, Jr., 107, 112
Tolentino, Rolando, 156
Tompkins, E. Berkeley, 239n19,
250n22
Toribio, Helen, 239n26, 270n8
trauma, 14, 175, 180, 246n93
Twain, Mark, 33–34, 217
Ty, Eleanor, 200, 271n17
Tydings-McDuffie Act (1934), 8, 10,
30, 39, 55, 248n4

"un-oneing" (Villa): as analytical
framework, 4, 28, 186; diasporic

Filipino literature and, 5–6; identity and, 219, 231; language and,
14–15; U.S. colonialism and, 7–8,
22; Villa and, 3–4

Vengua Gier, Jean, 238n16, 239n18,
264n11
Vergara, Benito M., 21, 240n26, 271n8
Villa, José Garcia: 3, 91, 120, 222;
aesthetic theory, 65–66, 74–75,
77–78; "Anchored Angel, The,"
86–87; autobiographical stories,
66–73, 221; „Composition, A,„‚
84–85; critical essays, 15–16,
65–66, 74–75, 77–78, 255n34;
editorial work, 61, 82–84, 87, 119,
255n39; experimentalism, 4, 60;
homoeroticism in, 59, 64, 67–70,
71–72, 256n44; interiority and
metaphysicality, 60, 65–67, 74–
75, 77–82, 85; letter of defense,
65–66; "Man-Songs," 58–60,
61–65; "Mir-i-nisa," 58–59; modernism, 58, 59, 82, 87; modes of
address, 72–73, 80–82, 87; queer
poetics, 22, 59–60, 62–65, 66–67,
70–71, 85; race and ethnicity, 4,
60, 71; reception of, 19, 60–61,
73–77, 87–88; religion, 4, 78–79;
serial poetics, 62–63, 66–67, 68,
70, 81; sexuality of, 60, 73–74, 76,
253n16, 254n29; suspended from
University of the Philippines, 58,
85, 253n18; U.S. colonialism and,
60–61; "Villa-Lopez controversy,"
75–77; Volume Two, 3–4, 14,
79–82
Villanueva, Chea, 153–154

Warner, Michael, 246n95, 262n47
Wolf, Diane L., 204

Wood-Forbes mission, 41
Woolf, Virginia, 66, 154
World War II, 1, 17, 41, 103, 189, 195,
    259n6, 261n33, 263n51

Yabes, Leopoldo Y., 87–88, 117–119,
    261n27

Yu, Timothy, 253n13, 254n18,
    257n58, 258n68
Yuson, Alfred, 238n11, 243n65,
    244n72, 246n94

Zwick, Jim, 249n11, 250n22, 250n23,
    250n24, 252n46

# About the Author

MARTIN JOSEPH PONCE is associate professor of English at The Ohio State University.